# BARGAINING FOR DEVELOPMENT:

## A Handbook on Development Agreements, Annexation Agreements, Land Development Conditions, Vested Rights, and the Provision of Public Facilities

Copyright © 2003 Environmental Law Institute
1616 P Street NW, Washington, DC 20036

Published July 2003.

Printed in the United States of America
ISBN 1-58576-061-7

# BARGAINING FOR DEVELOPMENT:

A Handbook on
Development Agreements,
Annexation Agreements,
Land Development Conditions,
Vested Rights,
and the
Provision of Public Facilities

by
David L. Callies
Daniel J. Curtin Jr.
and
Julie A. Tappendorf

ENVIRONMENTAL LAW INSTITUTE
Washington, D.C.

# BARGAINING FOR DEVELOPMENT:
## A Handbook on Development Agreements, Annexation Agreements, Land Development Conditions, Vested Rights, and the Provision of Public Facilities

## Table of Contents

# Authors

**David L. Callies** is the Benjamin A. Kudo Professor of Law at the William S. Richardson School of Law, where he teaches property, land use, and state and local government law. He holds law degrees from the University of Michigan (J.D.) and Nottingham University (LL.M., town planning law) and is a life member of Clare Hall, Cambridge University. A past chair of the Hawaii State Bar Association Section on Real Property and Financial Services and the American Bar Association (ABA) Section on State and Local Government Law, and coeditor of the annual *Land Use and Environmental Law Review*, he is also an elected member of the American Law Institute and of the College of Fellows of the American Institute of Certified Planners. The author of 12 books and over 100 articles on property and land use, his coauthored casebooks on land use and real property are widely used throughout the United States.

**Daniel J. Curtin Jr.** concentrates his practice on local government and land use law representing both private and public sector clients. He is a member of the firm of Bingham McCutchen LLP in the Walnut Creek office.

Mr. Curtin serves as Immediate Past Chair and on the Council, the governing body, of the State and Local Government Law Section of the ABA. He was Past Chair of the Land Development, Planning & Zoning Section of the International Municipal Lawyers Association (formerly NIMLO). He is past Vice Chair of the Executive Committee of the Real Property Law Section of the State Bar of California. Mr. Curtin has also served as President of the City Attorneys' Department of the League of California Cities, as a member of the Board of Directors of the League, and as Regional Vice President of the International Municipal Lawyers Association.

In recognition of his extensive contributions to NIMLO and to the entire municipal law community nationwide, as well as his years of leadership and service to the legal profession, Mr. Curtin was honored with NIMLO's Charles S. Rhyne Award for Lifetime Achievement in Municipal Law. He is the recipient of the American Planning Association's National Distinguished Leadership award for 20 years of writing, teaching, encouraging, and supporting planning ideas. He also was named Honorary Life Member of the California Park and Recreation Society in recognition of his exceptional service to the field of parks and recreation.

Mr. Curtin is the author of numerous publications on California land use and subdivision law, which have been cited frequently by the California Courts, including *Curtin's California Land Use and Planning Law*, published and revised annually by Solano Press, *Subdivision Map Act Manual*, published by Solano Press, and *Subdivision Map Act and the Development Process*, published by California Continuing Education of the Bar, Berkeley, California. He is a frequent lecturer for the University of California Extension and Continuing Education of the Bar and was an adjunct professor for the University of San Francisco Law School teaching land use law.

Mr. Curtin received his A.B. from the University of San Francisco and his J.D. from the University of San Francisco School of Law. He has served as Assistant Secretary of the California State Senate, Counsel to the Assembly Committee on Local Government, Deputy City Attorney of Richmond, and City Attorney of Walnut Creek.

**Julie A. Tappendorf** is an attorney in the Chicago office of Holland & Knight. She practices in the Real Estate, Land Use, and Government Group, with a focus on local government and zoning law. She represents numerous Chicago area local governments and developers advising them on annexation, planning, zoning, development, and general municipal matters. Ms. Tappendorf has authored a number of articles on development agreements and conditions, as well as architectural design controls, and frequently lectures on local government and land use issues, including sunshine laws, ethics, annexation and development agreements, and architectural regulations. Ms. Tappendorf received her J.D. from the University of Hawaii's William S. Richardson School of Law and her B.A. from Illinois State University. She is admitted to the practice of law in the state of Illinois and is a member of the ABA and the Chicago Bar Association.

# Foreword

The purpose of our handbook is twofold: to explore the policy and planning principles behind land development conditions, vested rights, and development/annexation agreements, and to provide guidance for the practicing professional, government, and land development communities in evaluating the need for, and the drafting of, land development statutes, ordinances, and agreements. Our basic premise is twofold as well. First, land development and annexation agreements provide an excellent vehicle for government and landowners to provide in detail for land developments. Second, because of the law pertaining to vested rights and land development conditions, the development community needs more assurances concerning the continued viability of their projects and the government community needs more in the way of public facilities than the common-law grants to either. Vested rights to proceed with a development, including the multistage variety, are not easy for the landowner to come by under the applicable legal principles. Public facilities that are not closely tied to a land development project through nexus and proportionality are similarly difficult for government to legally obtain. A development agreement provides nicely for both.

We are grateful for the assistance of a number of able helpers and supporters throughout the research and writing of this handbook. David Callies would particularly like to thank the Pacific Legal Foundation for the research funds provided over the past two years through the Hawaii Property Law Project, and Heidi Guth, a 2002 graduate of the William S. Richardson School of Law, for her research and editing assistance. Dan Curtin thanks David Petersen, an associate in the Walnut Creek office of Bingham McCutchen LLP, for his contributions and research efforts. Julie Tappendorf is grateful for the valuable research and assistance provided by Jennifer Jackson, a law clerk at Holland & Knight LLC. Finally, we all would like to thank Jinhee Kim and Dominique Tansley, for submitting designs which influenced the production of the present cover, and Eric Damien Kelly, editor of the treatise, *Zoning and Land Use Controls*, which first published chapters on development agreements and vested rights in the 1990s written by David Callies and Julie Tappendorf, and which formed the organizational basis for much of what appears in this handbook on those subjects. Callies and Tappendorf have used this structure in recent writings on development agreements that have appeared in Patricia Salkin (ed.) *Trends in Zoning Law From A to Z*, published by the American Bar Association Press in early 2001, and in an article entitled *Unconstitutional Land Development Conditions and the Development Agreement Solution: Bargaining for Public Facilities After* Nollan *and* Dolan that appeared in 51 CASE W. L. REV. 663 (2001).

# Bargaining for Development:
## A Handbook on Development Agreements, Annexation Agreements, Land Development Conditions, Vested Rights, and the Provision of Public Facilities

## I. Introduction

F ormal agreements between landowners and local government respecting the use of land have increased substantially in number over the past 25 years. Such agreements change the relationship between landowner and government in the land development process from confrontation to some measure of cooperation. While there are several kinds of such agreements (cooperative and housing agreements, for example), only two link vesting land development rights with the dedication and funding of public facilities: the annexation agreement and the development agreement. The principal difference between the two (which is implied in their names) is that the annexation agreement applies to land about to be annexed to a village, town, city, or other general purpose municipal corporation, as opposed to a development agreement where the land subject to the agreement is already a part of the municipal corporation.[1] Otherwise, both the theory and the principal reasons for negotiating such agreements are, with one exception, the same. The landowner generally wishes to guarantee that local government's land use regulations, conditions, and exactions remain fixed during the life of a prospective land development on the subject parcel. The local government, on the other hand, seeks as many concessions and land development conditions as possible beyond what it could reasonably require through subdivision exactions, impact fees, and other conditions under the normal exercise of its regulatory authority or police power.

The principal difference between the two types of agreement is the benefit/burden of annexing the subject property to the local government's territory under an annexation agreement. The landowner generally obtains a variety of services and protections as a part of the local government's territorial jurisdiction but must subject itself to that local government's land use regulations, as well as property and other taxes. The local government obtains additional tax revenues together with a larger tax base for general obligation borrowing but must provide police, fire, and often utility services to its newly annexed territory. Which side is the most advantaged or disadvantaged depends, of course, on the circumstances of the annexation. A new shopping center, for example, may be more attractive to a local government than a sprawling single-family residential project. Both will require a level of municipal services, but the former will, in all likelihood, generate more revenue (particularly if the local government collects a sales or business tax) and require fewer services than the latter.

The purpose of the development agreement, on the other hand, is to vest certain development rights in the landowner/developer in exchange for construction and dedication of public improvements:

> [D]evelopment agreements . . . between a developer and a local government limit the power of that government to apply newly enacted ordinances to ongoing developments. Unless otherwise provided in the agreement, the rules, regulations,

---

1. Except in California, which permits development agreements before annexation (CAL. GOV'T CODE §65865(b)) although it cannot be effective until annexation is complete.

and official policies governing permitted uses, density, design, improvement, and construction are those in effect when the agreement is executed.[2]

As it is legally difficult, if not impossible, for the landowner/developer to obtain enforceable assurances that land use regulations will not change during the life of a major land development project—particularly multiphase development projects extending over many years—and, as there are significant limits to what a local government can exact as a price for permitting land development,[3] both parties, in theory, have adequate reason to negotiate such an agreement. From a contractual perspective, there is adequate consideration flowing to support such a bilateral agreement. This may be particularly important given the frequent use of conditional zoning whereby local government units reclassify property to permit more intense development upon the promise of the developer to limit the number of otherwise permitted uses in the new zone, and to do or provide certain things which are memorialized in one or more unilateral covenants deposited with the local government and recorded. However, such covenants are generally devoid of any mutuality, and local government actions to enforce them have often been unsuccessful.[4] Moreover, the recording of a unilateral covenant by the developer provides little assurance that the local government will maintain the zoning for which the promises contained in the covenants were made. Therefore, a bilateral agreement, particularly one sanctioned by the state through enabling legislation reciting the public purpose behind such agreement, is by far a more legally sound way to proceed.

This book commences with an overview of the major problems faced by government and landowners solved by the development agreement, together with a summary of common land development conditions (exactions, dedications, and impact fees) as well as a discussion of vested rights. The balance of the book is concerned with the problems—common to both types of agreements—of authority (generally statutory) to enter into such agreements, bargaining away the police power, and permissible subject matter of such agree-

---

2. City of W. Hollywood v. Beverly Towers, 52 Cal. 3d 1184, 1191 n.6, 805 P.2d 329, 334 n.6 (1991). The court continued: "The purpose of . . . the development agreement is to allow a developer who needs additional discretionary approvals to complete a long-term development project as approved, regardless of any intervening changes in local regulations." *Id.* at 1194, 805 P.2d at 334-35.

3. *See* Fred P. Bosselman & Nancy Stroud, *Mandatory Tithes: The Legality of Land Development Linkage*, 9 NOVA L.J. 381 (1985) [hereinafter Bosselman & Stroud, *Mandatory Tithes*] (describing legal issues posed by "linkage" programs, by which "local regulations . . . condition the approval of certain types of land development on the developer's agreement to contribute to certain other types of development that further public purposes").

4. *See* Russell v. Palos Verdes Properties, 32 Cal. Rptr. 488, 492-93, 218 Cal. App. 2d 754, 761-62 (1963):

(There is no claim that mutually enforceable restrictions were ever created, nor has there been an attempt to enforce any restrictions as covenants running with the land or any rights arising out of the unilateral declaration of restrictions. . . . [T]he unilateral declaration of restrictions . . . failed to create mutually enforceable restrictions. . . .).

ments. Following a discussion of these fundamental legal issues, the book continues with a discussion of more particular problems, such as comprehensive plan conformity, character of the agreement (administrative or legislative), and binding of other governmental agencies. It ends with a series of model statutes, ordinances, checklists, and agreements in a comprehensive appendix.

## II. Land Development Conditions

### A. Introduction and Background

Land development of any size and substance requires a variety of public facilities to support it. Most common is the need for additional roads, public utilities, parks, and schools. To this list one could logically add police and fire stations and sanitary landfills. The time is long past since government, particularly local government, has borne the principal burden of the costs of these facilities. State and local financial resources have been woefully inadequate at least since the end of massive federal subsidies in the early 1980s. For decades, local government has charged land developers for a part of the cost of such public facilities, at least with respect to those facilities intrinsic to the development, in the form of subdivision dedications and fees. Initially "charged" as the price of drawing and recording the simpler and cheaper subdivision plat in place of the lengthy, tedious, and easily flawed metes and bounds description for land development, these fees and dedications soon became part of the regulatory land use process, exercised by local government under the police power for the health, safety, and welfare of the people, often as a method to control or manage growth.[5]

---

5. ROBERT H. FREILICH, FROM SPRAWL TO SMART GROWTH (1999); JULIAN CONRAD JUERGENSMEYER & THOMAS E. ROBERTS, LAND USE PLANNING AND CONTROL LAW (2d ed. 2002); EXACTIONS, IMPACT FEES, AND DEDICATIONS: SHAPING LAND-USE DEVELOPMENT AND FUNDING INFRASTRUCTURE IN THE *Dolan* ERA (Robert H. Freilich & David W. Bushek eds., 1995); DAVID L. CALLIES ET AL., CASES AND MATERIALS ON LAND USE 148 (West 3d ed. 1999) [hereinafter CALLIES ET AL., CASES AND MATERIALS ON LAND USE]; ROBERT H. FREILICH & MICHAEL M. SHULTZ, NATIONAL MODEL SUBDIVISION REGULATIONS, PLANNING, AND LAW 1-6 (Planners Press 1994); DANIEL R. MANDELKER, LAND USE LAW (4th ed. 1997); Susan P. Schoettle & David G. Richardson, *Nontraditional Uses of the Utility Concept to Fund Public Facilities*, 25 URB. LAW. 519, 519-22 (1993); Frona M. Powell, *Challenging Authority for Municipal Subdivision Exactions: The Ultra Vires Attack*, 39 DEPAUL L. REV. 635, 635-36 (1990); Julian Conrad Juergensmeyer & Robert M. Blake, *Impact Fees: An Answer to Local Government's Capital Funding Dilemma*, 9 FLA. ST. U. L. REV. 415 (1981); Thomas M. Pavelko, *Subdivision Exactions: A Review of Judicial Standards*, 25 J. URB. & CONTEMP. L. 269 (1983); DEVELOPMENT EXACTIONS (James E. Frank & Robert M. Rhodes eds., 1987).

The British also continue to experiment with land development conditions. *See, e.g.*, Tom Cornford, *Planning Gain and the Government's New Proposals on Planning Obligations*, 3 J. PLAN. & ENVTL. L. 796 (2002); David L. Callies & Malcolm Grant, *Paying for Growth and Planning Gain: An Anglo American Comparison of Development Conditions, Impact Fees, and Development Agreements*, 23 URB. LAW. 221 (1991) [hereinafter Callies & Grant, *Paying for Growth and Planning Gain*].

However, by justifying such land development dedications and fees as police power regulations, rather than "voluntary" costs of using the subdivision process, local governments invite judicial scrutiny under the Takings Clause of the Fifth Amendment to the U.S. Constitution, which permits the taking of private property for public use only upon payment of just compensation. While early cases generally upheld such intrinsic dedications and fees, the more recent charges of "impact fees" for the shared construction by several land developments of large and expensive public facilities (such as municipal wastewater treatment plants and sanitary landfills) outside or extrinsic to the development upon which the fee is levied, led knowledgeable courts to scrutinize the connection between these fees and the need generated by the charged development for the particular facility in question.[6] Nevertheless, it is generally agreed that the law applicable to impact fees, exactions, and in lieu fees, as well as to compulsory dedications, is similar, given that they all represent land development conditions levied at some point in the land development process, such as subdivision plat approval, shoreline management permit application, building permit application, occupancy permit application, or utility connection.[7] Therefore, except where the test specifically makes such distinctions, the terms are used here interchangeably.

The major legal issue with respect to fees, dedications, and exactions, is the connection or "nexus" to the land development. Without this connection or "nexus," such land development regulations are generally unconstitutional takings of property without compensation, particularly after the U.S. Supreme Court decisions in *Nollan v. California Coastal Commission*,[8] and *Dolan v. City of Tigard*.[9] Therefore much of this part II is devoted to these cases and their progeny.

Critical as the takings/nexus issue is, there are other legal requirements for attaching conditions to the development of land. Among these are the need for authority to levy such dedications, fees, and other exactions, in the form of enabling legislation and local ordinances, to avoid the charge that they are "ad hoc," and the need to expend the fee, whether "in lieu" of a dedication requirement or an impact fee, within a reasonable period of time after collection. As the history and cases make abundantly clear, such land development conditions are development driven, i.e., to be valid, they must be collected (and exactions and dedications re-

---

6. Ira M. Heyman & Thomas K. Gilhool, *The Constitutionality of Imposing Increased Community Costs on New Suburban Residents Through Subdivision Exactions*, 73 YALE L.J. 1119 (1964); *see also* John D. Johnston Jr., *Constitutionality of Subdivision Exactions: The Quest for a Rationale*, 52 CORNELL L.Q. 871 (1967).

7. Board of County Comm'rs v. Bainbridge, Inc., 929 P.2d 691, 698 (Colo. 1996) (citing DONALD G. HAGMAN & JULIAN CONRAD JUERGENSMEYER, URBAN PLANNING AND LAND DEVELOPMENT CONTROL LAW §9.8 (West 2d ed. 1986)); DEVELOPMENT EXACTIONS, *supra* note 5, at 3-4.

8. 483 U.S. 825, 107 S. Ct. 3141, 97 L. Ed. 2d 677, 17 ELR 20918 (1987).

9. 512 U.S. 374, 114 S. Ct. 2309, 129 L. Ed. 2d 304, 24 ELR 21083 (1994).

quired) for, and only for, public facilities and infrastructure for which land development causes a need.[10] Courts uniformly strike down—usually as an unauthorized tax—land development conditions that are not so connected. Generally, this includes attempts to remedy existing infrastructure deficiencies[11] or to provide for operation and maintenance of facilities.[12] Of course, if payment for a public facility, or its construction or dedication, is in part fulfillment of a landowner's contractual obligations under a development agreement between landowner and local government, then the legal issues and analysis are entirely different and the need for nexus and proportionality, at least as a matter of constitutional law, disappears.[13] Parts III and IV of this book discuss this issue in more detail.

In a few states, local governments have the authority to impose excise taxes that may accomplish the same purpose as an impact fee. The key here is "authorization," almost always through a specific enabling statute. For example, the Colorado Supreme Court determined that a road impact fee levied by Cherry Hills Village was actually a tax, but it went on to hold that it was an excise tax that the city was authorized to impose.[14] In a much later case, the Ohio Supreme Court upheld a local road impact fee after rejecting an appellate court's application of the tax/fee distinction; the Ohio high court found that the distinction was not critical in Ohio.[15] The Pennsylvania Supreme Court has upheld an excise tax imposed on gross receipts of a construction company, holding that it was a valid gross receipts tax and not an unauthorized tax on homebuilding.[16] In contrast, the Washington Supreme Court has struck down a "residential development unit fee" imposed on rental dwelling units, in addition to a business licensing fee imposed on the entire business location. The court found that the fee was an unauthorized property tax and not an excise tax, which would have been allowed under the Washington Constitution.[17] The Massa-

---

10. James C. Nicholas, *Impact Exactions: Economic Theory, Practice, and Incidence*, 50 LAW & CONTEMP. PROBS. 85 (1987); JAMES C. NICHOLAS ET AL., A PRACTIONER'S GUIDE TO DEVELOPMENT IMPACT FEES 37-38 (1991); TAKINGS: LAND DEVELOPMENT CONDITIONS AND REGULATORY TAKINGS AFTER *Dolan* AND *Lucas* (David L. Callies ed., 1996).

11. Rohn v. City of Visalia, 263 Cal. Rptr. 319, 214 Cal. App. 3d 1463 (1989).

12. *But see* Bloom v. City of Fort Collins, 13 Brief Times Rptr. 1548, 784 P.2d 304 (Colo. 1989).

13. Callies & Grant, *Paying for Growth and Planning Gain, supra* note 5, at 239-50.

14. Cherry Hills Farms, Inc. v. City of Cherry Hills, 670 P.2d 779 (Colo. 1983).

15. Home Builders Ass'n of Dayton & the Miami Valley v. City of Beavercreek, 89 Ohio St. 3d 121, 729 N.E.2d 349 (Ohio 2000).

16. School Dist. of Scranton v. Dale & Dale Design & Dev., 559 Pa. 398, 741 A.2d 186 (1999).

17. Harbour Village Apts. v. City of Mukilteo, 139 Wash. 2d 604, 989 P.2d 542 (1999).

chusetts Court of Appeals has also held a school impact fee to be an unauthorized tax.[18]

## B. Nexus, Proportionality, and Takings

### 1. Overview

A land use regulation or action must not be so unduly restrictive that it causes a "taking" of a landowner's property without just compensation. The Fifth Amendment to the Constitution states, in part, "nor shall private property be taken for public use, without just compensation."[19] This section begins by discussing the historical development of the current two-part federal constitutional standard for takings: the nexus requirement set forth in *Nollan*[20] and the "rough proportionality" requirement established by *Dolan*.[21] Next, this section examines attempts to establish that land development conditions constitute a taking under the *Nollan* and *Dolan* tests. Finally, this section reviews the level of detail that has been required by the courts to satisfy the nexus and rough proportionality tests, and summarizes several landmark cases on the issue.

### 2. Federal Constitutional Standard

Determining whether a land use decision amounts to a taking prohibited by the Fifth Amendment to the Constitution has been a difficult task for the courts. The Court itself candidly admitted that it never has been able to develop a "'set formula' to determine when 'justice and fairness' require that economic injuries caused by public action be compensated by the government, rather than remain disproportionately concentrated on a few persons."[22] Instead, the Court has observed that "whether a particular restriction will be rendered invalid by the government's failure to pay for any losses proximately caused by it depends largely 'upon the particular circumstances [in that] case.'"[23] The question of

---

18. Greater Franklin Developers Ass'n v. Town of Franklin, 49 Mass. App. Ct. 500, 730 N.E.2d 900 (2000). Note that in Massachusetts, towns have no authority to impose any sort of tax. *Id.* at 502, 730 N.E.2d at 901-02 (citing Mass. Const. art. 89, §7).

19. *See also* Cal. Const. art. I, §19. For an excellent overview of both federal and California takings law, see Justice Richard M. Mosk's majority opinion in Landgate, Inc. v. California Coastal Comm'n, 17 Cal. 4th 1006, 953 P.2d 1188, 28 ELR 21236 (1998), and in Santa Monica Beach, Ltd. v. Superior Court (Santa Monica Rent Control Bd.), 19 Cal. 4th 952, 968 P.2d 993 (1999). *See also* Garneau v. City of Seattle, 147 F.3d 802 (9th Cir. 1998); Thomas E. Roberts, ed., Taking Sides on Takings Issues: Public and Private Perspectives (ABA Section of State and Local Government Law 2002).

20. 483 U.S. at 825, 107 S. Ct. at 3141, 97 L. Ed. 2d at 677, 17 ELR at 20918.

21. 512 U.S. at 374, 114 S. Ct. at 2309, 129 L. Ed. 2d at 304, 24 ELR at 21083.

22. Penn Cent. Transp. Co. v. City of New York, 438 U.S. 104, 124, 98 S. Ct. 2646, 2659, 57 L. Ed. 2d 631, 648, 8 ELR 20528, 20533 (1978).

23. *Id.*

whether a regulation has gone too far and a taking has occurred has been an ad hoc, factual inquiry with respect to partial takings.[24] In 1997, the California Supreme Court reiterated this point, holding that "the inquiry in any particular case is 'essentially ad hoc.'"[25] Recently, the Court in *Palazzolo v. Rhode Island*[26] and *Tahoe-Sierra Preservation Council, Inc. v. Tahoe Regional Planning Agency*[27] also confirmed the ad hoc approach favored by the Court in *Penn Central Transportation Co. v. City of New York*,[28] noting that the Court had "identified several factors that have particular significance in these essentially ad hoc, factual inquiries."[29] However, when an owner of real property is called upon to sacrifice all economically beneficial uses in the name of the common good, i.e., to leave his property economically idle, there is a categorical or total taking, and different standards apply.[30] In *Agins v. City of Tiburon*,[31] the Court set forth the basic legal test for a taking. Still in use by the Court, the *Agins* test has been applied to takings cases involving both regulations on the use of land and conditions on development.[32]

In the *Agins* dispute, the city of Tiburon adopted ordinances modifying existing zoning ordinances that allowed five units to be built without further land use approval and placed the Agins' property in a more restrictive Residential Planned Development and Open Space Zone. The modified zoning permitted single-family dwellings, accessory buildings, and open space uses. Density restrictions would have permitted the Aginses to build, with city approval, between one and five single-family residences on their five-acre tract. However, the Aginses never sought approval for development of their land under the zoning ordinance, deciding instead to file suit in state court alleging a taking of

---

24. *Id.*

25. Kavanau v. Santa Monica Rent Control Bd., 16 Cal. 4th 761, 774, 941 P.2d 851, 859 (1997) (citing *Penn Cent. Transp. Co.*, 438 U.S. at 124, 98 S. Ct. at 2659, 57 L. Ed. 2d at 648, 8 ELR at 20533).

26. 533 U.S. 606, 121 S. Ct. 2448, 150 L. Ed. 2d 592, 32 ELR 20516 (2001).

27. 535 U.S. 302, 122 S. Ct. 1465, 152 L. Ed. 2d 517, 32 ELR 20627 (2002).

28. 438 U.S. 104, 124, 98 S. Ct. 2646, 2659, 57 L. Ed. 2d 631, 648, 8 ELR 20528, 20533 (1978).

29. *Palazzolo*, 533 U.S. at 633, 121 S. Ct. at 2466, 150 L. Ed. 2d at 617, 32 ELR at 20525.

30. Lucas v. South Carolina Coastal Council, 505 U.S. 1003, 112 S. Ct. 2886, 120 L. Ed. 2d 798, 22 ELR 21104 (1992).

31. 447 U.S. 255, 100 S. Ct. 2138, 65 L. Ed. 2d 106, 10 ELR 20361 (1980).

32. *See* Dolan v. City of Tigard, 512 U.S. 374, 114 S. Ct. 2309, 129 L. Ed. 2d 304, 24 ELR 21083 (1994); *Lucas*, 505 U.S. at 1033, 112 S. Ct. at 2886, 120 L. Ed. 2d at 798, 22 ELR at 21104; Keystone Bituminous Coal Ass'n v. DeBenedictis, 480 U.S. 470, 107 S. Ct. 1232, 94 L. Ed. 2d 472, 17 ELR 20440 (1987); Nollan v. California Coastal Comm'n, 483 U.S. 825, 107 S. Ct. 3141, 97 L. Ed. 2d 677, 17 ELR 20918 (1987). For further comment on the relevance of *Agins*, see Edward J. Sullivan, *Return of the Platonic Guardians:* Nollan *and* Dolan *and the First Prong of* Agins, 34 URB. LAW. 39 (2002).

their property, contending that the city had "completely destroyed the value of [their] property for any purpose or use whatsoever."[33]

Affirming the decision of the California Supreme Court, the Court held that the ordinances did not constitute a taking. The Court stated that the application of a general zoning law to a particular property becomes a taking if the ordinance either (1) "does not substantially advance legitimate state interests" or (2) "denies an owner economically viable use of his land."[34] The *Agins* Court concluded that the city of Tiburon's open space ordinances substantially advanced a legitimate governmental goal, that of discouraging premature and unnecessary conversion of open space land to urban uses, and was a proper exercise of the city's police power to protect its residents from the effects of urbanization.[35] Also, the Court held that although the ordinances limited development, "they neither prevent the best use of [the] land . . . nor extinguished a fundamental attribute of ownership."[36]

In *Keystone Bituminous Coal Ass'n v. DeBenedictis*,[37] the Court acknowledged that the two prongs of the *Agins* test have become integral parts of the takings analysis. However, citing numerous precedents and several other factors important to the takings analysis, the Court gave an additional gloss to the first part of the test. The Court suggested that even among those regulations that "substantially advance" a "legitimate state interest," some governmental interests are more "legitimate" than others; that is, the more defensible the state's interest is in regulating property, the more likely the regulation will be upheld. The Court cited *Pennsylvania Coal Co. v. Mahon*[38] for the proposition that "the nature of the State's interest in the regulation is a critical factor in determining whether a taking has occurred, and thus whether compensation is required."[39]

The Court also noted another important factor:

> [T]he type of taking alleged is also often a critical factor. It is well settled that a "taking may more readily be found when the interference with property can be characterized as a physical invasion by the government [citation omitted] than when interference arises from some public program adjusting the benefits and burdens of economic life to promote the common good."[40]

---

33. *Agins*, 447 U.S. at 258, 100 S. Ct. at 2140, 65 L. Ed. 2d at 110, 10 ELR at 20362.

34. *Id.* at 260, 100 S. Ct. at 2141, 65 L. Ed. 2d at 112, 10 ELR at 20362.

35. *Id.* at 261-62, 100 S. Ct. at 2142, 65 L. Ed. 2d at 112, 10 ELR at 20362.

36. *Id.* at 262, 100 S. Ct. at 2142, 65 L. Ed. 2d at 112, 10 ELR at 20362.

37. 480 U.S. 470, 485, 107 S. Ct. 1232, 1241, 94 L. Ed. 2d 472, 488, 17 ELR 20440, 20443 (1987).

38. 260 U.S. 393, 43 S. Ct. 158, 67 L. Ed. 322 (1922).

39. *Keystone Bituminous Coal Ass'n*, 480 U.S. at 488, 107 S. Ct. at 1243, 94 L. Ed. 2d at 490, 17 ELR at 20444.

40. *Id.* at 488-89 n.18, 107 S. Ct. at 1243 n.18, 94 L. Ed. 2d at 490 n.18, 17 ELR at 20444 n.18 (citing Penn Cent. Transp. Co. v. City of New York, 438 U.S. 104, 124, 98 S. Ct. 2646, 2659, 57 L. Ed. 2d 631, 648, 8 ELR 20528, 20533 (1978)).

## II. LAND DEVELOPMENT CONDITIONS

### 3. *Nollan* and the Nexus Requirement

While much of the recent case law dealing with such conditions and exactions has developed from challenges to the impact fee, the language is applicable to all three. To be enforceable and valid, an impact fee must be levied upon a development to pay for public facilities, the need for which is generated, at least in part, by that development.[41] This is the so-called rational nexus test developed by the courts in Florida and other jurisdictions that have considered such fees and exactions.[42] First proposed in 1964,[43] it became the national standard by the end of the 1970s.[44]

The test essentially has two parts. First, the particular development must generate a need to which the amount of the exaction bears some rough proportionate relationship.[45] Second, the local government must demonstrate that the fees levied will actually be used for the purpose collected.[46]

This test was confirmed and made applicable to all land development conditions by a decision of the Court in 1987. Decided on the last day of the Court's 1987 term, *Nollan*[47] deals ostensibly with beach access. Property owners sought a coastal development permit from the California Coastal Commission to tear down a beach house and build a bigger one. The commission granted the permit only upon condition that the owner give the general public the right to walk across the owner's backyard beach area, an easement over one-third of the lot's total area. The purpose, the commission said, was to preserve visual access

---

41. David L. Callies, *Impact Fees, Exactions, and Paying for Growth in Hawaii*, 11 U. HAW. L. REV. 295 (1989) [hereinafter Callies, *Impact Fees*]; Brian W. Blaesser & Christine M. Kentopp, *Impact Fees: The Second Generation*, WASH. U. J. URB. & CONTEMP. L. REV. 28 (1990); JULIAN CONRAD JUERGENSMEYER, FUNDING INFRASTRUCTURE: PAYING THE COSTS OF GROWTH THROUGH IMPACT FEES AND OTHER LAND REGULATION CHARGES (Lincoln Institute of Land Policy Monograph 85-5, Feb. 1985) [hereinafter JUERGENSMEYER, FUNDING INFRASTRUCTURE]; CALLIES ET AL., CASES AND MATERIALS ON LAND USE, *supra* note 5, at ch. 4.

42. *See, e.g.*, Hernando County v. Budget Inns of Fla., Inc., 15 Fla. L. Weekly 26, 555 So. 2d 1319 (Fla. Dist. Ct. App. 1990); Frisella v. Town of Farmington, 131 N.H. 78, 550 A.2d 102 (1988); Baltica Constr. Co. v. Planning Bd. of Franklin Township, 222 N.J. Super. 428, 537 A.2d 319 (1987); Batch v. Town of Chapel Hill, 326 N.C. 1, 387 S.E.2d 655 (1990); Unlimited v. Kitsap County, 50 Wash. App. 723, 750 P.2d 651 (1988).

43. Ira Michael Heyman & Thomas K. Gilhool, *The Constitutionality of Imposing Increased Community Costs on New Suburban Residents Through Subdivision Exactions*, 73 YALE L.J. 1119 (1964); *see also* Fred P. Bosselman & Nancy Stroud, *Legal Aspects of Development Exactions, in* DEVELOPMENT EXACTIONS, *supra* note 5 [hereinafter Bosselman & Stroud, *Legal Aspects*].

44. *See* Bosselman & Stroud, *Legal Aspects*, *supra* note 43, at 74.

45. *Id.*

46. Bosselman & Stroud, *Mandatory Tithes*, *supra* note 3, at 397-99; *see also* Holmdel Builders Ass'n v. Township of Holmdel, 121 N.J. 550, 583 A.2d 277 (1990).

47. 483 U.S. at 825, 107 S. Ct. at 3141, 97 L. Ed. 2d at 677, 17 ELR at 20918.

to the water, which was impaired by the much bigger beach house. The Court, however, held that, assuming the commission's purpose to overcome the psychological barrier to the beach created by overdevelopment was a valid one, it could not accept that there was any *nexus* between these interests and the public lateral access or easement condition attached to the permit:

> It is quite impossible to understand how a requirement that people already on the public beaches be able to walk across the Nollan's property reduces any obstacles to viewing the beach created by the new house. It is also impossible to understand how it lowers any "psychological barrier" to using the public beaches, or how it helps to remedy any additional congestion on them caused by construction of the Nollan's new house. We therefore find that the Commission's imposition of the permit condition cannot be treated as an exercise of its land use power for any of these purposes.[48]

However, the Court said, it is an altogether different matter if there is an "essential nexus" between the condition and what the landowner proposes to do with the property:

> Thus, if the Commission attached to the permit some condition that would have protected the public's ability to see the beach notwithstanding construction of the new house—for example, a height limitation, a width restriction, or a ban on fences—so long as the Commission could have exercised its police power (as we have assumed it could) to forbid construction of the house altogether, imposition of the condition would also be constitutional. Moreover (and here we come closer to the facts of the present case), the condition would be constitutional even if it consisted of the requirement that the Nollans provide a viewing spot on their property for passersby with whose sighting of the ocean their new house would interfere . . . . The evident constitutional propriety disappears, however, if the condition substituted for the prohibition utterly fails to further the end advanced as the justification for the prohibition . . . . [T]he lack of nexus between the condition and the original purpose of the building restriction converts that purpose to something other than what it was. The purpose then becomes, quite simply, the obtaining of an easement to serve some valid governmental purpose, but without payment of compensation. Whatever may be the outer limits of "legitimate state interests" in the takings and land-use context, this is not one of them.[49]

---

48. *Id.* at 838-39, 107 S. Ct. at 3149, 97 L. Ed. 2d at 690, 17 ELR at 20921. For full discussion, see Callies & Grant, *Paying for Growth and Planning Gain, supra* note 5.

49. 483 U.S. at 836-37, 107 S. Ct. at 3148-49, 97 L. Ed. 2d at 689, 17 ELR at 20921. *See also* Bosselman & Stroud, *Mandatory Tithes, supra* note 3; Callies, *Impact Fees, supra* note 41; Brenda Valla, *Linkage: The Next Stop in Developing Exactions,* 2 GROWTH MGMT. STUD. NEWSL., June 1987, at 4; Jerold S. Kayden & Robert Pollard, *Linkage Ordinances and Traditional Exactions Analysis,* 50 LAW & CONTEMP. PROBS. 127 (1987); Rachelle Alterman, *Evaluating Linkage and Beyond,* 32 WASH. U. J. URB & CONTEMP. L. 3 (1988); CALLIES ET AL., CASES AND MATERIALS ON LAND USE, *supra* note 5. *But see Holmdel Builders Ass'n,* 121 N.J. at 550, 583 A.2d at 277 (upholding impact fees for housing as functional equivalents of mandatory set-asides, which the court had already approved under New Jersey's constitutionally based "fair share" doctrine).

## II. LAND DEVELOPMENT CONDITIONS

Cases decided in state and lower federal courts after *Nollan* make it clear that the nexus test for land development conditions of any variety is now the law of the land.

The importance of the rational nexus requirement in levying impact fees is difficult to overstate. First, most recent cases setting out the rational nexus test requirement are impact fee cases.[50] Second, impact fees are, by definition, charged for regional facilities that only partially benefit each landowner charged a portion of the cost. Third, the public facility will almost certainly be located off-site rather than within the landowner-payer's contemplated development project. Fourth, the landowner will almost always pay cash rather than construct a facility in order to satisfy his or her development condition when it is in the form of an impact fee, since each landowner is paying only a proportionate share of the cost of the facility that their combined land developments make necessary. For example, a solid waste disposal site costing millions of dollars may well be paid through a combination of impact fees charged to several landowners and general tax revenues. Its location will depend only marginally on proximity to the development sites, as long as it is in the general area of the proposed development.

There are several important factors for local governments to consider in levying impact fees:

1. The fees must generally be charged as part of the land *development* process, not the land reclassification or rezoning process. Fees are development-driven, and land reclassification, while it may well be a prelude to development, does not create any need for public facilities whatsoever.
2. Collected fees do not belong in the general fund, or once again the need becomes questionable.
3. The fees cannot be kept by government for years and years, for the same reason stated in number 2 above.[51]

Ignoring the foregoing raises a presumption, as a matter of both law and policy, that the impact fee is nothing more than a revenue-raising device, either for a facility that has nothing to do with the land development upon which the fee is raised, or for undetermined fiscal purposes generally. In either case, the "fee" is then presumed to be a tax. This characterization as a tax is almost always fatal to an impact fee, since most local governments have very little specific authority to tax beyond the property tax and, occasionally, a sales or income tax. Since an im-

---

50. *See* Home Builders & Contractors Ass'n of Palm Beach County v. Board of County Comm'rs of Palm Beach County, 469 U.S. 976, 105 S. Ct. 376, 83 L. Ed. 2d 311 (1984); Hollywood, Inc. v. Broward County, 431 So. 2d 606 (Fla. Dist. Ct. App. 1983); Coulter v. City of Rawlins, 662 P.2d 888 (Wyo. 1983); Contractors & Builders Ass'n of Pinellas County v. City of Dunedin, 444 U.S. 867, 100 S. Ct. 140, 62 L. Ed. 2d 91 (1979).

51. In California, such fees can be charged when land is rezoned to planned unit development (PUD) or planned development (PD) special zones in most jurisdictions, often carrying with it developmental rights. *See* DANIEL J. CURTIN JR. & CECILY T. TALBERT, CURTIN'S CALIFORNIA LAND USE AND PLANNING LAW 61 (Solano Press Books 23d ed. 2003).

pact fee is none of the above, and since all local government taxes must be supported by specific statutory authority, the fee is almost always declared illegal.[52]

### 4. *Dolan* and the Proportionality Requirement

But neither the *Nollan* decision nor its progeny address the second part of the *Agins* takings test; it merely embellished the first part of the test by adding a focus on "nexus." The *Nollan* Court did not discuss the required degree of connection between the exaction imposed and the projected impacts of the proposed development. This issue was left open until the Court's 1994 decision in *Dolan*.[53] In this landmark 5-4 decision, the Court held for the first time that, in making an adjudicative decision, a city must demonstrate a "reasonable relationship" between the conditions imposed on a development permit and the development's impact.[54]

Florence Dolan owned a plumbing business and electrical supply store located in the business district of Tigard, Oregon, along Fanno Creek, which flowed through the southwestern corner of the lot and along its western boundary. Dolan applied to the city for a building permit to further develop the site. Her proposed plans called for nearly doubling the size of the store and paving the 39-space parking lot.

The planning commission granted Dolan's permit application subject to conditions imposed by Tigard's Community Development Code, which contained the city's Comprehensive Plan. To mitigate for increased runoff from her property that would result from her expansion plans, the commission required that Dolan dedicate to the city the portion of her property lying within the 100-year floodplain along Fanno Creek for a public greenway. To mitigate for increased traffic and congestion caused by an increase in visitors to her store, the commission also required that Dolan dedicate an additional 15-foot strip of land adjacent to the floodplain as a public pedestrian/bicycle pathway.

Dolan requested variances and appealed to the Oregon Land Use Board of Appeals (LUBA), a state-created body that serves as an intermediate hearing body for local land use decisions before they reach the court system. Dolan opposed the city's dedication requirements on the grounds that they were not related to the proposed development and therefore constituted a taking. LUBA found a "reasonable relationship" between the proposed development and the requirement to dedicate land along Fanno Creek for a greenway, and also found

---

52. *See, e.g.*, Town of Longboat Key v. Lands End Ltd., 433 So. 2d 574 (Fla. Dist. Ct. App. 1983); Lafferty v. Payson City, 642 P.2d 376 (Utah 1982); Home Builders Ass'n of Cent. Ariz., Inc. v. Riddel, 109 Ariz. 404, 510 P.2d 376 (1973). *See generally* JUERGENSMEYER, FUNDING INFRASTRUCTURE, *supra* note 41; Robert Mason Blake & Julian Conrad Juergensmeyer, *Impact Fees an Answer to Local Governments' Capital Funding Dilemma*, 3 LAND USE & ENVTL. L. REV. 14, 247 (1987).

53. 512 U.S. at 374, 114 S. Ct. at 2309, 129 L. Ed. 2d at 304, 24 ELR at 21083.

54. *Id.* at 390, 114 S. Ct. at 2319, 129 L. Ed. 2d at 319, 24 ELR at 21085.

a reasonable relationship between alleviating the impact of increased traffic from the development and facilitating the pedestrian/bicycle pathway as an alternative means of transportation.

While the Oregon appellate and supreme courts upheld the city's conditions, the Court held that the conditions did not meet the required rough proportionality test. In so doing, the Court established a two-step process for evaluating land development condition takings claims. First, courts must determine whether an "essential nexus" exists between the "legitimate state interest" and the permit condition exacted by the city.[55] Second, after finding that a nexus exists, courts must decide the required degree of connection between the exactions and the projected impact of the proposed development. The Court noted that it was not required to address this question in *Nollan*, because in the earlier case no nexus existed between the condition (dedication of a lateral public easement) and a legitimate governmental interest (diminishing the blockage of the view of the ocean caused by construction of the enlarged house). The Court stated that the absence of a nexus in *Nollan* left the California Coastal Commission in the position of simply trying to obtain an easement "through gimmickry," which converted a valid regulation of land use into an "'out-and-out plan of extortion.'"[56]

In the *Dolan* situation, the Court stated that no such gimmicks were associated with the permit conditions and found that the required nexus did, in fact, exist. However, under the second part of the analysis, the Court had to determine whether the degree or amount of the exactions demanded by the city's permit conditions were sufficiently related to the projected impact of the development proposed. The Court coined the term "rough proportionality" to describe the required relationship between the exactions and the projected impact of the proposed development.[57] The Court then stated "no precise mathematical calculation is required, but the city must make some sort of individualized determination that the required dedication is related both in nature and extent to the impact of the proposed development."[58]

With this premise in mind, the Court reviewed the exactions (the two required dedications, of the public greenway and the pedestrian/bicycle pathway) and found that the city had not met its burden of demonstrating the required relationship. After analyzing the findings upon which the city relied, the Court found that the city had not shown the "required reasonable relationship" between the easements and Dolan's expansion plans.

As to the public greenway, the Court held that the public nature of the required dedication bore no reasonable relationship to the city's ostensible flood control purpose. The Court agreed that keeping the floodplain free from devel-

---

55. *Id.* at 386, 114 S. Ct. at 2317, 129 L. Ed. 2d at 317, 24 ELR at 21085.

56. *Id.* at 387, 114 S. Ct. at 2317, 129 L. Ed. 2d at 318, 24 ELR at 21086.

57. After coining the term "rough proportionality," the Court, in its majority opinion, never used that term again when it applied its decision to the facts; instead it continued to use the words "required reasonable relationship" or "reasonably related." *Id.* at 388, 114 S. Ct. at 2318, 129 L. Ed. 2d at 318, 24 ELR at 21086.

58. *Id.*

opment would likely mitigate the impact of Dolan's expansion plans on flood risks in Fanno Creek, but did not agree that a public greenway, as opposed to a private one, served the interests of flood control. The Court saw no reasonable relationship between requiring Dolan to permit the public to enter onto her property at any time, and the flood control rationale set forth by the city. As to the pedestrian/bicycle path, the Court found that the city had not met its burden to show that the additional number of vehicle and bicycle trips generated by Dolan's development reasonably related to the city's required dedication. The city's vague statement that the dedication "could offset" some of the traffic demand from the expansion was insufficient.

Together, these cases require that to pass constitutional muster, land development conditions imposed by government:

1. Must seek to promote a legitimate state interest;
2. Must be related to the land development project upon which they are being levied by means of a rational or essential nexus; and
3. Must be proportional to the need or problem which the land development project is expected to cause, and the project must accordingly benefit from the condition imposed.

Under the first standard, legitimate state interest, an agency may only require a landowner to dedicate land (or interests in land) or contribute money for public projects and purposes, such as public facilities, and in most jurisdictions, public housing.

Under the second standard, essential nexus, an agency must find a clear connection between the need or problem generated by the proposed development and the land or other exaction or fee required from the landowner/developer. Thus, for example, a residential development will in all probability generate a need for public schools and parks. A shopping center or hotel in all probability will not. Both will generate additional traffic and therefore generate a need for more streets and roads.

Under the third standard, proportionality, a residential development of, say, 300 units may well generate a need for additional classroom space, but almost certainly not a new school or school site. On the other hand, such a residential development of several thousand units would, when constructed, likely generate a need for a new school and school site, depending upon the demographics of the new residents.

## 5. Applicability of *Nollan* and *Dolan* to Land Development Conditions Generally

A number of courts have struck down land development conditions for failure to comply with *Nollan*'s and *Dolan*'s three-part test. An excellent example is the U.S. Court of Appeals for the Eighth Circuit's decision in *Christopher Lake Development Co. v. St. Louis County*,[59] in which the court applied *Dolan* to strike down a county drainage system requirement.[60] The county granted the

---

59. 35 F.3d 1269 (8th Cir. 1994).

60. *Id.* at 1274-75.

owner of 42 acres preliminary development approval for 2 residential communities on the condition that the owner provide a drainage system for an entire watershed. First, the court dealt with the public purpose issue: part one of the *Dolan* test.[61] The court stated that "even assuming the legitimacy of the County's purpose in requiring a drainage system, the application of the Criteria may violate the equal protection clause."[62] Citing *Nollan* for the nexus or second part of the test, the court then opined that although "the County's objective to prevent flooding may be rational, it may not be rational to single out the Partnership to provide the entire drainage system."[63] The court then found such a requirement disproportionate to the drainage problems resulting from the proposed development:

> [F]rom our review of the record, the County has forced the Partnership to bear a burden that should fairly have been allocated throughout the entire watershed area. A strong public desire to improve the public condition will not warrant achieving the desire by a shorter cut than the constitutional way of paying for the change.[64]

As for a remedy, the court said: "We believe that the Partnership is entitled to recoup the portion of its expenditures in excess of its pro rata share and remand to the district court to determine the details and amounts."[65]

An even more egregious case is *Walz v. Town of Smithtown*.[66] There, landowners were denied access to the public water supply when they refused to deed the front 15 feet of their property to Smithtown for road-widening purposes.[67] Finding a total lack of nexus between water service and road widening, the court found that "[a]s landowners, the Walzes surely had a right not to be compelled to convey some of their land in order to obtain utility service."[68]

Lack of proportionality between the exaction and the problem it is meant to solve is the basis for other courts to nullify exactions. In *Steel v. Cape Corp.*,[69] a Maryland appellate court held that the denial of a rezoning application based on the inadequacy of school facilities resulted in an unconstitutional regulatory taking, citing *Dolan* and *Nollan*: "While the provision of public facilities is a legiti-

---

61. *Id.* at 1274.

62. *Id.*

63. *Id.*

64. *Id.* at 1275 (quoting Dolan v. City of Tigard, 512 U.S. 374, 396, 114 S. Ct. 2309, 2323, 129 L. Ed. 2d 304, 313, 24 ELR 21083 (1994)).

65. *Id.* at 1275.

66. 46 F.3d 162, 25 ELR 20770 (2d Cir. 1995).

67. *Id.* at 164-65, 25 ELR at 20771.

68. *Id.* at 169, 25 ELR at 20773 (citing *Dolan*, 512 U.S. at 386-87, 114 S. Ct. at 2317, 129 L. Ed. 2d at 317, 24 ELR at 21085); *see also* Art Piculell Group v. Clackamas County, 142 Or. App. 327, 334, 922 P.2d 1227, 1233 (1996); Nielson v. Merriam, 91 Wash. App. 1049 (1998) (holding that there was no nexus between a county-required easement and any problems created by a proposed subdivision).

69. 111 Md. App. 1, 677 A.2d 634 (1996).

mate concern of the County, the burden of providing adequate schools is disproportionately placed upon Cape Corporation when residential use is denied to them while being granted to its neighbors."[70] Similarly, in *Burton v. Clark County*,[71] a Washington court of appeals held that while a road dedication requirement for a three-lot subdivision met the nexus test, there was no evidence to sustain a finding of rough proportionality.[72] As the court noted in a footnote to the opinion: "[T]he government may not use the permitting process as a vehicle for solving public problems not created or exacerbated by any project."[73]

Substantially further afield is the application of *Dolan* in *Manocherian v. Lenox Hill Hospital*,[74] in which the New York Court of Appeals struck down a rent-stabilization statute in part because it did not advance "a closely and legitimately connected State interest."[75] Citing both the *Dolan* and *Nollan* cases, the court said that:

> The Supreme Court refrained from placing any limitations or distinctions or classifications on the application of the "essential nexus" test. This suggests and supports a uniform, clear, and reasonably definitive standard of review in takings cases. Indeed, Justice [William J.] Brennan, in dissent in *Nollan*, expressly attributed to the majority's holding in *Nollan* an impact *on all regulatory takings cases*, stating that the Court's "exactitude . . . is inconsistent with our standard for reviewing the rationality of a State's exercise of its police power for the welfare of its citizens."[76]

In *Homebuilders Ass'n of Dayton v. City of Beavercreek*,[77] the court held *Dolan* inapplicable because the impact ordinance in this case was legislatively imposed rather than "adjudicative," but nonetheless applied a proportionality and nexus standard to invalidate a road impact fee for:

1. Insufficient "quantification";
2. Unreasonable traffic projections;
3. Arbitrary and capricious application because "buildout" was too far away and there were too many exceptions;
4. Failure to segregate administrative expenses or interest on the funds; and
5. Intent to deposit fee collected in general fund.

---

70. *Id.* at 33-36, 677 A.2d at 650-52.

71. 91 Wash. App. 505, 958 P.2d 343 (1998).

72. *Id.* at 525-26, 958 P.2d at 356-57.

73. *Id.* at 522 n.42, 958 P.2d at 354 n.42.

74. 84 N.Y.2d 385, 643 N.E.2d 479 (1994).

75. *Id.* at 389, 643 N.E.2d at 480.

76. *Id.* at 393-94, 643 N.E.2d at 483 (emphasis added) (alteration in original) (citations omitted) (quoting Nollan v. California Coastal Comm'n, 483 U.S. 825, 842-43, 107 S. Ct. 3141, 3151-52, 97 L. Ed. 2d 677, 692-93 (1987) (Brennan, J., dissenting)).

77. Nos. 97-CA-113, -115, 1998 WL 735931 (Ohio App. 2d 1998).

## II. LAND DEVELOPMENT CONDITIONS

In *Isla Verde International Holdings Inc. v. City of Camas*,[78] the court struck down a 30% open-space dedication requirement on a 52-lot subdivision approval, while upholding a road dedication requirement for emergency vehicles in absence of evidence concerning the cost of the road and its effects on the subject property. In *Reynolds v. Inland Wetlands Commission of the Town of Trumbull*,[79] the court struck down a requirement that the landowner grant a conservation easement over three of his lots as a condition of developing a fourth lot, in part on the ground that such a condition would not pass a "nexus" test. In *Amoco Oil Co. v. Village of Schaumburg*,[80] the court struck down a road widening dedication, holding that the taking of 20% of Amoco's land for roadway widening purposes on the basis of a .4% increase in traffic caused by the proposed development "does not correspond with the slightest notions of rough proportionality." Other examples: *Schultz v. City of Grants Pass*,[81] striking down a road dedication; *Timber Trails Corp. v. Planning & Zoning Commission of the Town of Sherman*,[82] striking down a road dedication; *Property Group, Inc. v. Planning Commission of the Town of Tolland*,[83] striking down a road widening dedication; *Lexington-Fayette Urban County Gov't v. Schneider & Hi Acres Dev. Co.*,[84] striking down bridge dedication requirement; *Cobb v. Snohomish County*,[85] striking down a road improvement fee; *Dellinger v. City of Charlotte*,[86] striking down a road dedication requirement; *Castle Homes & Development v. City of Brier*,[87] striking down a per-lot road impact fee; and *McClure v. City of Springfield*,[88] invalidating a sidewalks and "clipped corners" exaction in the absence of specific findings explaining how these exactions were relevant or proportional to the city's interest in safe streets at the location of the proposed development.

In *St. Johns County v. Northeast Florida Builders Ass'n*,[89] the court held that a fee of $448 per single-family dwelling met the rational nexus test when applied to a 100-unit subdivision, but failed a proportionality standard because it was not clear that the money collected would necessarily benefit those who paid the fee. In *Volusia County v. Aberdeen at Ormond Beach Ltd. Liability Partnership*,[90] the same court held that a school impact fee as applied to a retirement community failed the rational nexus test because the community was sub-

---

78. 99 Wash. App. 127, 990 P.2d 429 (1999).

79. No. 309721, 1996 WL 383363 (Conn. Super. 1996).

80. 277 Ill. App. 3d 926, 661 N.E.2d 380 (1995).

81. 131 Or. App. 220, 884 P.2d 569 (1994).

82. No. 272170, 1992 WL 239100 (Conn. Super. 1992).

83. 226 Conn. 684, 628 A.2d 1277 (1993).

84. 849 S.W.2d 557 (Ky. App. 1992).

85. 64 Wash. App. 451, 829 P.2d 169 (1991).

86. 114 N.C. App. 146, 441 S.E.2d 626 (1994).

87. 76 Wash. App. 95, 882 P.2d 1172 (1994).

88. 175 Or. App. 425, 28 P.3d 1222 (2001).

89. 16 Fla. L. Weekly 264, 583 So. 2d 635 (Fla. 1991).

90. 25 Fla. L. Weekly 390, 760 So. 2d 126 (Fla. 2000).

ject to covenants prohibiting minors from residing there. In *Everett School District No. 2 v. Mastro*,[91] a Washington appeals court upheld a school impact mitigation fee based on the average number of students in 869 apartments in 25 buildings as a condition for the issuance of a building permit for an apartment complex. The court noted with approval that the fee calculation provided for no impact from studio apartments and was based on the exact number of one- and two-bedroom apartments in the complex.

Of course, exactions and dedications may well be proper, assuming they meet nexus and proportionality tests, if they are attached to land development permits of some kind. Thus, for example, California courts have upheld the imposition of development impact fees by local governments and school districts for schools to account for rapid community growth where children were likely to reside.[92] There are also literally dozens of pre-*Nollan/Dolan* cases upholding various impact fees and exactions for roads, sewers, water, and housing where at least the nexus standard later imposed by the Court appears to have been met. For a comprehensive list of such cases, see *City of Annapolis v. Waterman*.[93]

In *Nollan* and *Dolan*, the government conditioned a development permit on the property owner's dedication of land. So long as there is the required nexus and proportionality, courts will broadly construe the governmental interests to be advanced. Indeed, several California cases before the 1994 Court decision in *Dolan* interpreted the *Nollan* requirement—that a regulation "substantially" advance a legitimate governmental interest—as applying only where the regulation involves a physical encroachment.[94] What if a city or other local agency requires payment of an impact fee or imposes some other sort of development condition not requiring the dedication of land? Does the *Nollan/Dolan* nexus test apply?

*Benchmark Land Co. v. City of Battle Ground*[95] adds to the growing consensus that the so-called "heightened security" applicable to dedications also applies to monetary fees and exactions. There, a developer successfully challenged a city condition of subdivision plat approval requiring half-street improvements to a street adjoining, but extrinsic, to the proposed development, based upon the length of the development adjoining the street. The subdivision did not directly access the street subject to the improvements. The court held that such a condi-

---

91. 97 Wash. App. 1013 (1999).

92. *See* Candid Enters., Inc. v. Grossmont Union High Sch. Dist., 39 Cal. 3d 878, 705 P.2d 876 (1985); McLain Western #1 v. San Diego County, 146 Cal. App. 3d 772, 194 Cal. Rptr. 594 (1983).

93. 357 Md. 484, 745 A.2d 1000 (2000) (though the decision itself is badly flawed and demonstrates a misunderstanding of takings and exactions law).

94. *See* Saad v. City of Berkeley, 30 Cal. Rptr. 2d 95, 24 Cal. App. 4th 1206 (1994); City & County of San Francisco v. Golden Gate Heights Invs., 18 Cal. Rptr. 2d 467, 469-70, 14 Cal. App. 4th 1203, 1209 (1993) (and cases cited therein); Blue Jeans Equities W. v. City & County of San Francisco, 4 Cal. Rptr. 2d 114, 117-18, 3 Cal. App. 4th 164, 168-71 (1992).

95. 94 Wash. App. 537, 972 P.2d 944 (1999).

tion met neither the essential nexus test nor the requirement of rough proportionality, and so was an unconstitutional land development condition.

A year later, the Washington Court of Appeals reconsidered the case following the Court's decision in *City of Monterey v. Del Monte Dunes at Monterey, Ltd.*[96] There, the Court said that it had never applied their "heightened scrutiny" in *Nollan/Dolan* beyond a land dedication. Nevertheless, the court found that the *Dolan* rough proportionality test still applied: because the city required the developer to pay for something outside the relevant property that was not impacted by the new development, the condition was invalid.[97] "Surely if the issues for an exaction of money are the same as for an exaction of land, the test must be the same: a showing of 'nexus' and 'proportionality.'"[98]

Using a different and more strict test, a federal court also held that a street improvement fee violated a state constitution because it was not specifically attributable to the new development for which it was charged. In *Chicago Title Insurance Co. v. Village of Bollingbrook,*[99] two developers paid fees, under protest, for timely final plat recordings of their subdivision plats. The court found that Bolingbrook did not meet its burden of showing that the impact fees for the cost of future or recent improvements of existing or proposed streets were specifically attributable to the specific developments. The village followed an equation that failed to consider whether the developments created any more traffic, which made the resultant fees arbitrary. The court found that the village had violated the state constitution by recapturing fees for roads that abutted the development whether or not the developments impacted the road use.[100] In a prior case, the Illinois Supreme Court had found two state enabling statutes and subsequent ordinances to be unconstitutional because they imposed transportation impact fees on new developments that should have been collected as a tax on the communities in general.[101] In that case, the state supreme court required the community to refund all fees that had been collected under the implementing ordinances.

Other courts have also specifically applied *Nollan/Dolan* beyond dedications to monetary exactions. Thus, the U.S. Court of Appeals for the Ninth Cir-

---

96. 526 U.S. 687, 119 S. Ct. 1624, 143 L. Ed. 2d 882, 29 ELR 21133 (1999); Benchmark Land Co. v. City of Battle Ground, 103 Wash. App. 721, 727, 14 P.3d 172, 175 (2000).

97. *Id.*

98. *Id.* For commentary agreeing that the *Del Monte* decision does not foreclose heightened scrutiny to fees and exactions beyond dedication of land, see Bruce W. Bringardner, *Exactions, Impact Fees, and Dedications: National and Texas Law After* Dolan *and* Del Monte Dunes, 32 URB. LAW. 561 (2000).

99. No. 97 C 7055, 1999 WL 65054 (N.D. Ill. Feb. 5, 1999).

100. *Id.* at *29. This case was later overturned because the U.S. Court of Appeals for the Seventh Circuit had found that a district court should not take a position that opines on a state constitutional matter. Chicago Title Insurance Co. v. Village of Bollingbrook, No. 97 C 7055, 1999 WL 259952 (N.D. Ill. Apr. 6, 1999).

101. Northern Ill. Home Builders Ass'n v. County of DuPage, 165 Ill. 2d 25, 649 N.E.2d 384 (1995).

cuit, in *Garneau v. City of Seattle*,[102] specifically applied the doctrine of those cases to other than physical dedications even though it found them inapplicable for other reasons as discussed below.[103] While noting that the case before it was not appropriate for setting out precise rules, nevertheless an Oregon appellate court held in *Clark v. City of Albany*,[104] that "[t]he fact that *Dolan* itself involved conditions that required a dedication of property interests does not mean that it applies only to conditions of that kind."[105]

### 6. Legislative Decisions

While the question of extending *Nollan/Dolan* beyond physical exactions appears to be settled, whether to apply the tests from these cases to "legislative" determinations—as well as the contextual meaning of "legislative"—is not so clear. In its broadest context, as noted by Justice Clarence Thomas in his dissent from a denial of a petition for certiorari in *Parking Ass'n of Georgia, Inc. v. City of Atlanta*,[106] "[t]he lower courts are in conflict over whether Tigard's test for property regulation should be applied in cases where the alleged taking occurs through an act of the legislature."[107] After citing, inter alia, *Trimen Development Co. v. King County*[108] and the *Manocherian* decision, Justice Thomas observed:

> It is not clear why the existence of a taking should turn on the type of governmental entity responsible for the taking. A city council can take property just as well as a planning commission can. Moreover, the general applicability of the ordinance should not be relevant in a takings analysis. . . . The distinction between sweeping legislative takings and particularized administrative takings appears to be a distinction without a constitutional difference.[109]

Recently, however, many courts have ruled to the contrary, and not applied the *Dolan* test to legislative decisions. For example, the California Supreme Court, in *Ehrlich v. City of Culver*,[110] held that if a city bases a development or impact fee on an ordinance or rule of general applicability, the fee will be within the city's police power and will not be subject to the heightened constitutional scrutiny of the *Nollan/Dolan* nexus test. However, if an impact fee is adjudicatively imposed on an individual property owner, it will be subject to heightened scrutiny under the *Nollan/Dolan* test.

---

102. 147 F.3d 802 (9th Cir. 1998).

103. *Id.* at 809-11.

104. 137 Or. App. 293, 904 P.2d 185 (1995).

105. *Id.* at 299, 904 P.2d at 189.

106. 515 U.S. 1116, 115 S. Ct. 2268, 132 L. Ed. 2d 273 (1995).

107. *Id.* at 1117, 115 S. Ct. at 2273, 132 L. Ed. 2d at 274 (Thomas, J., dissenting)

108. 124 Wash. 2d 261, 877 P.2d 187 (Wash. 1994).

109. *Parking Ass'n of Georgia*, 515 U.S. at 1117-18, 115 S. Ct. at 2274-75, 132 L. Ed. 2d at 274.

110. 12 Cal. 4th 854, 911 P.2d 429 (1996).

## II. LAND DEVELOPMENT CONDITIONS

In the early 1970s, Ehrlich acquired a vacant 2.4-acre lot in Culver City. At his request, the city amended its general plan and zoning and adopted a specific plan to provide for the development of a privately operated tennis club and recreational facility. In 1981, in response to financial losses from operating the facility, Ehrlich applied to the city for a change in land use to construct an office building. The application was abandoned when the planning commission recommended against approval on the grounds that the existing club provided a needed commercial recreational facility within the city. In 1988, Ehrlich closed the facility as a result of the continuing financial losses and applied for an amendment to the general plan and the specific plan, and a zoning change, to allow construction of a 30-unit condominium complex valued at $10 million. At that time, the city expressed interest in acquiring the property for operation as a city-owned sports facility. After the city completed a feasibility study, the idea was dropped because the city found it lacked the funds to purchase and operate the club. At the same time, the city council rejected Ehrlich's application based on concerns about the loss of a recreational land use needed by the community. Ehrlich then tore down the existing improvements and donated the recreational equipment to the city.

After denial of his application, Ehrlich filed suit and then entered into discussions with the city to secure the necessary approvals to redevelop the property. After a closed-door meeting, ostensibly to discuss the pending litigation, the city council voted to approve the project conditioned upon the payment of certain monetary exactions, including a $280,000 recreation mitigation fee for the loss of the private tennis facility, payment of $33,200 for art in public places, and a $30,000 in lieu parkland dedication fee. The $280,000 fee was to be used "for partial replacement of the lost recreational facilities" occasioned by the specific plan amendment. The amount of the fee was based upon a city study which showed that the replacement costs for the recreational facilities "lost" as a result of amending the specific plan would be $250,000 to $280,000 for the pool, $135,000 to $150,000 for the paddle tennis courts, and $275,000 to $300,000 for the tennis courts. After formally filing a protest pursuant to Government Code §§66020 and 66021, Ehrlich challenged the $280,000 recreation fee and the in lieu art fee but not the parkland dedication fee.

After the trial court struck down the conditions, the appellate court upheld them.[111] After granting a writ of certiorari, the court then remanded the matter back to the court of appeals to be reexamined in light of its recent decision in *Dolan*. Following the remand, the court of appeals, in an unpublished opinion in 1994, again upheld both fees. The California Supreme Court then granted a petition to consider the important and unsettled question concerning the extent to which *Nollan* and *Dolan* applied to development permits that exact a fee as a condition of issuance, as opposed to the possessory dedication of real property at issue in both *Nollan* and *Dolan*. The justices unanimously upheld the public art fee, and five justices upheld the right of the city to impose a "mitigation fee" based on a "rezoning" application, but rejected the ad hoc recreational fee.

---

111. Ehrlich v. City of Culver, 19 Cal. Rptr. 2d 468, 15 Cal. App. 4th 1737 (1993).

In arriving at its decision, the *Ehrlich* court reviewed the *Nollan/Dolan* decisions and the two-part nexus test. Citing *Nollan*, the *Ehrlich* court expressed concern that adjudicative, ad hoc conditions on development present "an inherent and heightened risk that local government will manipulate the police power to impose conditions unrelated to legitimate regulatory ends, thereby avoiding what would otherwise be an obligation to pay just compensation."[112] The court emphasized the "extortion[ary]" danger of this "form of regulatory 'leveraging.'"[113] In response to this concern, the court drew a distinction between legislatively formulated development fees imposed on a class of property owners and individually imposed conditions.

The court held that in the "relatively narrow class of land use cases" that involve individual "land use 'bargains' between property owners and regulatory bodies . . . where the individual property owner-developer seeks to negotiate approval of a planned development . . . the combined *Nollan/Dolan* test quintessentially applies."[114] In the situations when exactions are imposed pursuant to a general legislative act or rule, cities act within their traditional police powers. The court stated that the discretionary aspect of conditioning an individual approval heightens the risk that the city may manipulate the police power to impose conditions unrelated to legitimate land use regulatory ends. On this point, the court stated:

> It is the imposition of land use conditions in individual cases, authorized by a permit scheme which by its nature allows for both the discretionary deployment of the police power and an enhanced potential for its abuse, that constitutes the *sine qua non* for application of the . . . standard of scrutiny formulated by the court in *Nollan* and *Dolan*.[115]

The court next considered whether the *Nollan/Dolan* test applies to general development fees in addition to dedications. The court noted that the courts in *Blue Jeans Equities West v. City & County of San Francisco*[116] (transit fees) and *Commercial Builders of Northern California v. City of Sacramento*[117] (affordable housing fees) had held that "any heightened scrutiny test contained in *Nollan* is limited to possessory rather than regulatory takings."[118] The *Ehrlich* court distinguished and clarified these cases because they both involved "legislatively formulated development assessments imposed on a broad class of property owners," and therefore did not require heightened scrutiny.[119] The court then rejected the city's argument that the *Nollan/Dolan* test only applies

---

112. *Ehrlich*, 12 Cal. 4th at 869, 911 P.2d at 439.

113. *Id.* at 867, 911 P.2d at 438.

114. *Id.* at 868, 911 P.2d at 438.

115. *Id.* at 869, 911 P.2d at 439.

116. 4 Cal. Rptr. 2d 114, 3 Cal. App. 4th 164.

117. 941 F.2d 872 (9th Cir. 1991).

118. *Id.* at 875 (quoting *Blue Jeans*, 4 Cal. Rptr. 2d at 118, 3 Cal. App. 4th at 171).

119. *Id.* at 876.

to possessory dedications and not to fees. Instead, the court found that the applicability of the *Nollan/Dolan* test to a fee depends on whether the fee is an ad hoc determination or a legislative regulation.[120]

The *Ehrlich* court found the middle ground in the application of the *Nollan/Dolan* test to impact fees. Since that ruling, California courts have enjoyed the luxury of a bright-line rule, shunning the heightened scrutiny of the *Nollan/Dolan* nexus test in the case of legislatively imposed fees, while invalidating individually imposed development fees that do not satisfy the requirements of a nexus and rough proportionality.[121] Nationally, a trend has emerged favoring the *Ehrlich* approach as well. However, some states have held that the test applies to both legislative and adjudicative determinations,[122] while a few

---

120. *Id.* at 906. *See also* Loyola Marymount Univ. v. Los Angeles Unified Sch. Dist., 53 Cal. Rptr. 2d 424, 45 Cal. App. 4th 1256 (1996). It should be noted that despite the California Supreme Court's definitive holding, the Court remains in flux with regard to the applicability of the Fifth Amendment Takings Clause to regulations that affect private property other than real property. In Eastern Enters. v. Apfel, 524 U.S. 498, 118 S. Ct. 2131, 141 L. Ed. 2d 451 (1998), which did not address land use but rather explored the various constitutional challenges that could potentially be applied to allocation of retirement fund liability under the Coal Industry Retiree Health Benefit Act, the plurality took the position that such an allocation was constitutionally invalid under the Fifth Amendment Takings Clause. The dissenters declined to find a taking, instead upholding the law under the Due Process Clause on the grounds that the case involved an ordinary liability to pay money rather than an interest in physical or intellectual property, which have traditionally been the exclusive realm of takings claims. Justice Anthony M. Kennedy, concurring with the plurality, supported invalidation of the Act under the Due Process Clause, stating that the Act does not involve the type of property to which the Fifth Amendment has traditionally applied. However, despite this leaning toward limiting the applicability of the Takings Clause, Justice Kennedy implied that it should not be so limited as to exclude land development conditions. His concern was rather curtailing the reach of the Fifth Amendment so as to ensure it does not apply to "all governmental action." *Id.* at 543, 118 S. Ct. at 2156, 141 L. Ed. 2d at 483-84.

121. *See, e.g., Loyola Marymount,* 53 Cal. Rptr. 2d at 424, 45 Cal. App. 4th at 1256; Breneric Assocs. v. City of Del Mar, 81 Cal. Rptr. 2d 324, 69 Cal. App. 4th 166 (1998) (declining to apply *Nollan/Dolan* based on *Ehrlich's* admonition that such heightened scrutiny is inapplicable to traditional land use regulations that are legislatively imposed); San Remo Hotel Ltd. Partnership v. City & County of San Francisco, 27 Cal. 4th 643, 41 P.3d 87, 32 ELR 20533 (2002) (heightened security test for exactions did not apply to residential hotel conversion fee enacted by general legislation).

122. Benchmark v. City of Battle Ground, 103 Wash. App. 721, 14 P.3d 172 (2000) (holding *Nollan/Dolan* applicable to impact fees but failing to distinguish between legislatively determined and adjudicatively imposed fees); Northern Ill. Home Builders Ass'n v. County of DuPage, 165 Ill. 2d 25, 649 N.E. 2d 384 (1995) (holding that two legislatively imposed impact fees were valid under *Nollan/Dolan*, but that the second, more general fee failed to meet the higher standard of "specifically and uniquely attributable" that the Illinois Supreme Court had articulated in Pioneer Trust Sav. Bank v. Village of Mount Prospect, 22 Ill. 2d 375, 176 N.E.2d 749 (1961)); Trimen Dev. Corp. v. King County, 124 Wash. 2d 261, 887 P.2d 187 (1994) (upholding legislatively imposed parkland development fees under the *Nollan/Dolan* test); Home Builders Ass'n of Dayton & the Miami Valley v. City of

have held that the test does not apply to fees at all.[123] However, other states facing this issue have concurred in the *Ehrlich* court's conclusion that only the ad hoc imposition of development fees is characterized by the level of discretion and potential for extortionate abuse of the police power that requires more than a generalized determination of reasonableness. Following is a brief overview of cases in which states other than California have adopted the *Ehrlich* approach or applied an *Ehrlich*-like approach:

**Home Builders Ass'n of Central Arizona v. City of Scottsdale.**[124] In this case, the Arizona Supreme Court cited *Ehrlich* in declining to apply *Dolan* to a legislatively imposed water resources development fee. In so doing, the court stated: "[T]he California court suggested that the *Dolan* analysis applied to cases of regulatory leveraging that occur when the landowner must bargain for approval of a particular use of its land. The risk of that sort of leveraging does not exist when the exaction is embodied in a generally applicable legislative decision."

**Waters Landing Ltd. Partnership v. Montgomery County.**[125] Preceding *Ehrlich*, the Maryland Court of Appeals concurred in the approach, declining to apply *Dolan* to a development impact fee that was imposed by legislative enactment and not by adjudication.

**Arcadia Development Corp. v. City of Bloomington.**[126] The Minnesota Court of Appeals held *Dolan*'s rough proportionality test inapplicable to a requirement that landowners choosing to cease operation of a mobile home park compensate tenants with a relocation fee. The court stated that because such a fee was a citywide, legislative land use regulation, *Dolan*'s "rough proportionality" test did not apply.

**Henderson Homes v. City of Bothell.**[127] Although declining to cite to *Nollan/Dolan* and preceding *Ehrlich*, the Washington Supreme Court nevertheless declined to uphold development fees "voluntarily" paid by individual landowners as a condition of permit issuance, holding that the local government had failed to make a finding that the fees were reasonably necessary as a direct result of the proposed development.

---

Beavercreek, 89 Ohio St. 3d 121, 729 N.E. 2d 349 (2000) (applying *Nollan/Dolan* to invalidate a legislatively imposed impact fee).

123. McCarthy v. City of Leawood, 257 Kan. 566, 894 P.2d 836 (1995) (holding that a traffic impact fee was subject to the "reasonable relationship" test, and not the heightened scrutiny of *Nollan/Dolan*, because it did not involve the dedication of land).

124. 187 Ariz. 479, 930 P.2d 993 (1997).

125. 337 Md. 15, 650 A.2d 712 (1994).

126. 552 N.W.2d 281 (Minn. Ct. App. 1996).

127. 124 Wash. 2d 240, 877 P.2d 176 (1994).

## II. LAND DEVELOPMENT CONDITIONS

***Krupp v. City of Breckenridge.***[128] The Colorado Supreme Court refused to apply *Nollan/Dolan* to a legislatively imposed mandatory plant investment fee, holding that the case did not fall into the narrow class of exactions, such as that imposed in *Ehrlich*, in which the exactions stem from adjudications particular to the landowner and the parcel, and therefore was not subject to a takings analysis.

***Northern Illinois Home Builders Ass'n v. County of DuPage.***[129] The Illinois Supreme Court upheld a revised transportation fee enabling act requiring that the transportation improvements for which the impact fees are imposed must be "specifically and uniquely attributable to the traffic demands generated by the new development paying the fee."[130] An earlier enabling act that did not contain the "specifically and uniquely attributable"[131] language was constitutionally suspect.

***Rogers Machinery Inc. v. Washington County.***[132] The Oregon Court of Appeals, after reviewing many decisions throughout the United States and relying heavily on *Ehrlich*, and *San Remo*, held that a traffic impact fee imposed on new development by way of a legislative act—an ordinance—imposing such a fee on a range of categories of property was not subject to the *Dolan*'s heightened scrutiny test. In its conclusion, the court said that "we are persuaded by the reasoning of other state courts, representing a nearly unanimous view, that *Dolan*'s heightened scrutiny test does not extend to development fees of that kind."[133]

In *City of Scottsdale*,[134] the Arizona Supreme Court specifically refused to apply any heightened scrutiny to Scottsdale's water resource development fee, deciding that *Nollan/Dolan* was inapplicable to generally legislative fees of this type.[135] The U.S. Court of Appeals for the Fifth Circuit also declined to apply such scrutiny to a challenge to a general zoning ordinance prohibiting trailer coaches on any lot in the city except trailer parks, in *Texas Manufactured Housing Ass'n v. City of Nederland*.[136] These cases are, of course, explainable as turning back attempts to apply *Nollan/Dolan* generally to all takings cases.

---

128. 19 P.3d 687 (Colo. 2001).

129. 165 Ill. 2d 25, 649 N.E.2d 384 (1995).

130. *Id.* at 33, 649 N.E.2d at 389.

131. *Id.* at 35, 649 N.E.2d at 390.

132. 181 Or. App. 369, 45 P.3d 966 (2002).

133. *Id.*

134. 187 Ariz. at 479, 930 P.2d at 993.

135. *Id.* at 485, 930 P.2d at 999-1000; *cf.* GST Tucson Lightwave, Inc. v. City of Tucson, 190 Ariz. 478, 485-86, 949 P.2d 971, 978-79 (Ariz. Ct. App. 1997) (deciding that *Nollan/Dolan* was inapplicable to a "franchise or license issued by a municipality to use public rights-of-way").

136. 101 F.3d 1095, 1105 (5th Cir. 1996).

Other cases are not as easy to explain and more clearly follow the Arizona court in *City of Scottsdale*.[137] In *Arcadia Development Corp.*,[138] a Minnesota court of appeals refused to apply *Nollan/Dolan* to a requirement that "mobile home park owners who close their parks . . . pay relocation costs to park residents," on the ground that as a citywide ordinance, a legitimate government interest test, rather than a rough proportionality test, applied.[139] While not nearly so definite, the Supreme Judicial Court of Maine "assign[ed] weight to the fact that the easement requirement derives from a legislative rule of general applicability and not an ad hoc determination" in *Curtis v. Town of South Thomaston*.[140] It nevertheless did apply a rough proportionality test in determining the fee was a valid exercise of the police power. Moreover, several aforementioned cases applying *Nollan/Dolan* stressed the quasi-judicial nature of the land development condition before them.[141]

On the other hand, some courts share the puzzlement of Justice Thomas as to why the legislative character of the land development condition should affect whether it is an unconstitutional land development condition. Citing Justice Thomas' certiorari petition dissent in *Parking Ass'n of Georgia*, an Illinois appellate court disagreed that a municipality could "skirt its obligation to pay compensation . . . merely by having the Village Board of trustees pass an 'ordinance' rather than having a planning commission issue a permit."[142] Oregon appellate courts have consistently applied *Nollan/Dolan* to legislative and quasi-judicial exactions alike, whether required by a zoning ordinance or not.[143]

---

137. In some jurisdictions, subdivision exactions found in a generally applicable subdivision statute have been held to fall outside *Nollan/Dolan*. *See* Marshall v. Board of County Comm'rs, 912 F. Supp. 1456, 1471-74 (D. Wyo. 1996). The decision in Home Builders Ass'n v. City of Beavercreek, Nos. 94-CV-0012, 94-CV-0062, 1996 WL 812607, at **17-18 (Ohio Ct. C.P. Feb. 12, 1996), cites and follows *City of Scottsdale*, 187 Ariz. at 479, 930 P.2d at 993. *Accord* Harris v. City of Wichita, 862 F. Supp. 287, 294 (D. Kan. 1994) (stating that "*Dolan*'s rough proportionality test does not apply to this case").

138. 552 N.W.2d at 281.

139. *Id.* at 283, 286.

140. 1998 Me. 63, 708 A.2d 657, 660 (1998).

141. *See, e.g.*, Garneau v. City of Seattle, 147 F.3d 802, 811 (9th Cir. 1998); Art Piculell Group v. Clackamas County, 142 Or. App. 327, 332, 922 P.2d 1227, 1231 (1996); Burton v. Clark County, 91 Wash. App. 505, 517, 958 P.2d 343, 351-52 (1998). *Commentary in accord* Edward H. Ziegler, *Development Exactions and Permit Decisions: The Supreme Court's* Nollan, Dolan, *and* Del Monte Dunes *Decisions*, 34 URB. LAW. 155 (2002).

142. Amoco Oil Co. v. Village of Schaumburg, 277 Ill. App. 3d 926, 940-41, 661 N.E.2d 380, 389-90 (1995).

143. *See, e.g.*, State v. Altimus, 137 Or. App. 606, 608, 905 P.2d 258, 259 (Or. Ct. App. 1995); J.C. Reeves Corp. v. Clackamas County, 131 Or. App. 615, 623-24, 887 P.2d 360, 365 (Or. Ct. App. 1994) (holding *Nollan/Dolan* applicable "whether [the condition] is legislatively required or a case-specific formulation"); Schultz v. City of Grants Pass, 131 Or. App. 220, 227, 884 P.2d 569, 572-73 (Or. Ct. App. 1994).

## II. LAND DEVELOPMENT CONDITIONS

7. Level of Detail Required for Showing Nexus and Proportionality

In *Home Builders Ass'n of Northern California v. City of Napa*,[144] plaintiffs claimed that a generally applicable inclusionary housing ordinance, which offered developers a number of alternative modes of compliance and allowed a waiver under certain circumstances, effected a taking under *Nollan* and *Dolan*. The court disagreed, holding that such a generally applicable ordinance did not warrant the heightened standard of review accorded to the type of individualized land use bargain that creates a heightened risk of extortionate use of the police power to exact unconstitutional exactions.

In 1999, the Court in *Del Monte Dunes* made it quite clear that the rough proportionality test of *Dolan* was not applicable to a denial of a development permit.[145] In a major victory for public agencies, the Court in this case unanimously confirmed that it had not expanded the rough proportionality test of *Dolan* beyond the "special context of exactions—land use decisions conditioning approval of development on the dedication of property to public use."[146] The Court stated that the rule applied in *Dolan* considers whether dedications demanded as conditions of development are proportional to the development's anticipated impacts. It was not designed to address, and is not readily applicable to, the much different questions arising where the landowner's challenge was based not on excessive exactions but on denial of development. The Court stated: "We believe, accordingly, that the rough proportionality test of *Dolan* is inapposite to a case such as this one."[147] The *Del Monte Dunes* decision is in line with California court cases, especially *Breneric Associates v. City of Del Mar*,[148] in which the court rejected the argument of amicus that the *Nollan/Dolan* test should be applicable to denial of a design review permit.[149]

In 1991, the *Nollan* test was met successfully in *Long Beach Equities, Inc. v. County of Ventura*,[150] where the court upheld local growth measures as satisfy-

---

Such also is a reasonable implication from the U.S. Court of Appeals for the First Circuit's opinion in City of Portsmouth v. Schlesinger, 57 F.3d 12, 16 (1st Cir. 1995). *Accord* GST Tucson Lightwave, Inc. v. City of Tucson, 190 Ariz. 478, 486, 949 P.2d 971, 979 (Ariz. Ct. App. 1997) "*Dolan* applies to 'a city's adjudicative decision to impose a condition tailored to the particular circumstances of an individual case' but not to 'a generally applicable legislative decision by the city.'" (quoting *City of Scottsdale*, 187 Ariz. at 485, 930 P.2d at 999; Pringle v. City of Wichita, 22 Kan. App. 2d 297, 303, 917 P.2d 1351, 1357 (1996); *Arcadia Dev. Corp.*, 552 N.W.2d at 286).

144. 108 Cal. Rptr. 2d 60, 90 Cal. App. 4th 188 (2001).

145. *Del Monte Dunes*, 526 U.S. at 687, 119 S. Ct. at 1624, 143 L. Ed. 2d at 882, 29 ELR at 21133.

146. *Id.* at 702, 119 S. Ct. at 1635, 143 L. Ed. 2d at 900, 29 ELR at 21135.

147. *Id.* at 703, 119 S. Ct. at 1635, 143 L. Ed. 2d at 900, 29 ELR at 21135.

148. 81 Cal. Rptr. 2d 324, 69 Cal. App. 4th 166.

149. *Id.* at 330, 69 Cal. App. 4th at 175.

150. 282 Cal. Rptr. 877, 231 Cal. App. 3d 1016 (1991).

ing the test for substantial relationship to the public welfare.[151] In that case, the plaintiff alleged that the land use regulations of the county of Ventura and of the city of Simi Valley, on their face and as applied, would so greatly delay development as to render any use of its property economically infeasible.[152]

Long Beach Equities (LBE) in 1984 purchased 250 acres of land in unincorporated territory adjacent to the city and within an "area of interest" of the city, relying, it said, on promised city approval for the building of 1,100 units there. After a substantial investment by LBE in public service facilities, the city first declared a moratorium on land use permits and then in 1988 advised LBE that only about 325 units would be designated to occupy that property. After amending its general plan to designate LBE's property as one unit per 160 acres (OS-160), the county refused to allow LBE to apply to process the project, stating that any such project must occur in the city after annexation. The developer sued both city and county, claiming among other things, that the governmental changes and delays supported a cause of action for inverse condemnation taking.

The appellate court upheld both the county's and city's legislation against LBE's facial attack stating: "Local government legislation is constitutional on its face if it bears 'a substantial relationship to the public welfare . . .' and inflicts no irreparable injury on the landowner."[153] The court reasoned that the county enacted guidelines to promote efficient and effective delivery of community services and to conserve the resources of the county by encouraging urban development to occur within cities. The guidelines emphasized annexation as a means to accomplish these purposes.

The city enacted its growth control ordinance:

> "[T]o protect the unique, hill-surrounded environment; enhance the quality of life; promote public health, safety or welfare and the general well-being of the community...." By limiting the rate, distribution, quality and type of residential development on an annual basis, with periodic reviews of the ongoing situation, City seeks "to improve local air quality, reduce traffic demands . . . and ensure that future demands for such essential services as water, sewers and the like are met . . . ."[154]

The *Long Beach Equities* court held: "Courts have long recognized the legitimacy of such ordinances because such laws are designed to protect the public health."[155]

LBE also argued that the county's and city's actions were designed to thwart LBE's project and that they were contrary to California Government Code provisions which support the development of housing, citing Govern-

---

151. *Id.*

152. The court held that plaintiff's "as-applied" attack on the ordinances was not ripe because Long Beach Equities had not secured a "final determination" as to uses that would be allowed by the city on its property.

153. *Id.* at 885, 231 Cal. App. 3d at 1030 (citing Agins v. City of Tiburon, 447 U.S. 255, 261, 10 ELR 20361, 20362 (1980); Euclid v. Ambler Realty Co., 272 U.S. 365, 397, 100 S. Ct. 2138, 2142, 65 L. Ed. 2d 106, 112 (1926)).

154. *Long Beach Equities*, 282 Cal. Rptr. at 885, 231 Cal. App. 3d at 1030.

155. *Id.*

ment Code §§65580, 65581, and 65583. Although these code sections promote the development of residential housing, the court said there are also countervailing governmental interests in conserving needed open space and preventing urban sprawl.[156]

*C. Cost and Calculation of Fees*

Impact fees are imposed by local governments for a variety of public facilities, including without limitation, roadway improvements, water and sewer facilities, solid waste disposal, parks, schools, libraries, and police and fire stations. These fees are typically imposed as part of the subdivision or development approval process and are common provisions in both development and annexation agreements. According to various studies, these fees can be quite extensive and can add considerably to the cost of the development upon which they are levied.[157] For example, according to one California agency publication, in 1999, California home builders paid fees averaging $24,325 for each single-family home constructed, with fees ranging from $11,176 to a high of $59,703.[158] When impact fees are added to other development costs, such as building permit and zoning and planning application fees, the cost of development above and beyond acquisition and construction costs can be staggering, as shown in the following survey of residential development fees in selected suburban communities in California[159]:

---

156. *See* Cal. Gov't Code §65560 et seq.

157. James C. Nicholas & Dan Davidson, Impact Fees in Hawaii: Implementing the State Law 9 (Land Use Research Foundation of Hawaii 1992).

158. California, Department of Housing & Community Development, Pay to Play: Residential Development Fees in California Cities and Counties 1999, at 103 (2001).

159. *Id.* at 61.

**Table 6: Residential Development Fees in Selected Suburban Communities**

| | Brentwood | Carlsbad | Corona | Fairfield | Fresno | Irvine | LA County | Roseville | Salinas | Tracy |
|---|---|---|---|---|---|---|---|---|---|---|
| 1998 Population | 17,000 | 73,700 | 111,500 | 91,600 | 411,600 | 133,200 | 997,000 | 66,900 | 128,300 | 47,550 |
| 1996-98 Avg. New Residential Permits | 694 | 1,129 | 1,817 | 524 | 1,685 | 1,530 | 3,104 | 2,033 | 673 | 674 |
| Planning & Zoning Fees | $172 | $219 | $304 | $207 | $639 | $788 | $657 | $22 | $420 | $192 |
| Envtl. Documentation Fees | 73 | 41 | 35 | 41 | 0 | 0 | 26 | 6 | 12 | 453 |
| Subdivision and Related | 618 | 935 | 403 | 205 | 1,198 | 1,271 | 241 | 69 | 329 | 704 |
| Other Planning | 280 | 174 | 419 | 185 | 134 | 60 | 2 | 13 | 105 | 945 |
| **TOTAL PLANNING FEES** | **1,143** | **1,369** | **1,161** | **639** | **1,971** | **2,119** | **927** | **110** | **866** | **2,294** |
| Building Permit | $949 | $477 | $588 | $1,492 | $327 | $692 | $1,392 | $1,422 | $2,462 | $1,291 |
| Building Plan Check | 617 | 310 | 590 | 116 | 18 | 143 | 1,252 | 835 | 1,527 | 853 |
| Engineering Fees (Plumbing Mech., Elec.) | 1,335 | 240 | 459 | 260 | 366 | 512 | 1,083 | 0 | 98 | 508 |
| Other Building & Public Work Fees | 676 | 971 | 3,010 | 57 | 488 | 1,110 | 259 | 262 | 857 | 2,320 |
| **TOTAL BUILDING PERMIT AND CHECK FEES** | **3,577** | **1,997** | **4,647** | **1,926** | **1,199** | **2,456** | **3,986** | **2,519** | **4,944** | **4,973** |

Table 6: Residential Development Fees in Selected Suburban Communities (cont.)

| | Brentwood | Carlsbad | Corona | Fairfield | Fresno | Irvine | LA County | Roseville | Salinas | Tracy |
|---|---|---|---|---|---|---|---|---|---|---|
| School Fees | $4,825 | $0 | $4,825 | $4,785 | $4,825 | $4,825 | $4,825 | $7,283 | $4,825 | $4,825 |
| School Mitigation Fees | 5,603 | 783 | 0 | 0 | 0 | 0 | 0 | 3,525 | 0 | 0 |
| Highway, Road, Traffic & Transit | 12,278 | 0 | 11,400 | 2,183 | 716 | 3,831 | 0 | 1,355 | 1,330 | 1,670 |
| Water, Wastewater, Sewer & Drainage Fees | 8,630 | 8,357 | 2,727 | 10,193 | 6,136 | 1,055 | 3,848 | 7,568 | 5,226 | 3,368 |
| Park & Recreation Fees (including Quimby) | 6,456 | 1,755 | 4,311 | 4,230 | 338 | 4,084 | 1,049 | 2,487 | 2,128 | 4,958 |
| Public Safety Fees | 296 | 0 | 248 | 0 | 326 | 0 | 0 | 1,033 | 0 | 0 |
| General-Purpose Capital Facilities Fees | 1,628 | 870 | 493 | 3,356 | 0 | 0 | 0 | 925 | 490 | 1,616 |
| Other Facility & Impact Fees | 1,786 | 30 | 6,185 | 2,480 | 0 | 35 | 535 | 1,730 | 162 | 0 |
| TOTAL CAPITAL IMPROVEMENTS FEES | 41,502 | 11,795 | 30,189 | 27,227 | 12,341 | 13,830 | 10,257 | 25,906 | 14,161 | 16,437 |
| TOTAL FEES | $46,221 | $15,161 | $35,997 | $29,792 | $15,511 | $18,405 | $15,169 | $28,536 | $19,971 | $23,704 |

Typically, local governments adopt ordinances to set the rate or schedule for these fees. Most ordinances adopt one of two methods in calculating impact fees. The first method is a fixed fee based on a unit of development. For example, Palm Beach, Florida's, road impact fee ordinance has established a set fee of $300 per single-family home, $200 per multiple-family home, and $175 per mobile home.[160] The second adopts a variable formula based on the need for the facilities or improvements generated by the new development.[161] Although the fixed fee method is much simpler to adopt and apply, the formula method more accurately reflects the proportionate costs of public facilities attributable to specific types of new development.[162] This is particularly important in light of the *Dolan* decision. Some communities have adopted an alternative method of calculating the appropriate fee. Under this alternative method, the municipality in essence allows the developer to set its own fee by demonstrating that its share is less than the fee set by ordinance through the submission of independent studies and economic data.[163]

An impact fee ordinance should relate the impact fee that is charged to the developer to the needs generated by the new development. Calculation of the fees should be tied to a study, report, or plan based on an analysis of the new development's impact.[164] For example, most water and sewer impact fees are based on the amount of flowage required by a certain type of development, sometimes measured in population equivalents (PEs).

Courts have generally upheld fees based on average flow (for sewer) or usage (for water) or impact (for many other facilities or improvements). For example, the court in *Amherst Builders Ass'n v. City of Amherst*,[165] upheld the city's impact fee schedule that calculated sewage impact fees based on the average sewage flow for various types of structures, as estimated by the U.S. Environmental Protection Agency (EPA). The city responded to charges that the connection fee of $400 was invalid by introducing evidence that the "capital cost" of each connection averaged $1,186. The court found that the sewage impact fee was reasonable and proportionate to the sewage flow anticipated by the new development.[166]

---

160. Home Builders & Contractors Ass'n of Palm Beach County v. Board of County Comm'rs of Palm Beach County, 446 So. 2d 140 (Fla. Dist. Ct. App. 1983).

161. NICHOLAS, ET AL., *supra* note 10, at 37-38.

162. David L. Callies, *Exactions, Impact Fees, and Other Land Development Conditions, in* ZONING AND LAND USE CONTROLS (Eric. D. Kelly ed., 2001).

163. *Home Builders & Contractors Ass'n*, 446 So. 2d at 145.

164. *Id.; see also* F&W Assocs. v. County of Somerset, 276 N.J. Super. 519, 648 A.2d 482 (1994) (upholding traffic impact fee ordinance that was adopted only after a comprehensive study of existing road facilities, current zoning, projected population growth, and existing commercial uses).

165. 61 Ohio St. 2d 345, 346, 402 N.E.2d 1181, 1182 (Ohio 1980).

166. *Id.* at 349, 402 N.E.2d at 1184; *see also* Contractors & Builders Ass'n v. City of Dunedin, 329 So. 2d 314, 318 (Fla. 1976) (upholding water and sewer connection fees that were less than the costs the city would incur in accommodating new uses of its water and sewer systems).

## II. LAND DEVELOPMENT CONDITIONS

With respect to park and school impact fees, the calculation of the fees should ensure that the fee is reasonably proportionate to the cost of providing the additional park or school facilities attributable to the new development.[167] Just what those fees may be used for depends upon the enabling statute or ordinance. Thus, for example, an Illinois court recently interpreted a school impact fee statute so that school impact fees may only be used to acquire land for school sites (and not to fund existing school expenses).[168] An Ohio court struck down park impact fees that were collected and used for the operation and maintenance of existing recreational facilities because the city failed to show the nexus between the proposed development and the use of fees for existing park facilities.[169] In some communities, the local governmental entity adopts an impact fee ordinance to impose park and school fees, then enters into an agreement with the impacted district, i.e., the school or park district, to set out the procedures for collecting and remitting these fees.[170]

Impact fees should also be calculated to address the impact the new development is expected to have on nearby facilities. For example, the Illinois statute authorizing the imposition of road impact fees provides that the fee shall not "exceed the development's proportionate share of road improvements" that are specifically and uniquely attributable to the new development.[171] In applying this standard, DuPage County, Illinois, adopted a road impact fee ordinance[172] that established a standard fee table for residential, commercial, and other types of development based on the cost of road construction and the number of motor

---

167. Wellington River Hollow, Ltd. Liab. Corp. v. King County, 113 Wash. App. 574, 54 P.3d 213 (2002) (upholding school impact fee against challenge that the fees were not reasonably related to the proposed development).

168. Thompson v. Village of Newark, 329 Ill. App. 3d 536, 768 N.E.2d 856 (2002), holding that

> the village's power to pass its impact fee ordinance is found, if at all, in section 11-12-5 of the Illinois Municipal Code. That section governs the ability of a municipality to prepare and implement a comprehensive plan for the municipality's future development. Specifically, the plan may be implemented by ordinances "establishing reasonable requirements governing the location, width, course, and surfacing of public streets and highways, alleys, ways for public service facilities, curbs, gutters, sidewalks, street lights, parks, playgrounds, *school grounds*, size of lots to be used for residential purposes, storm water drainage, water supply and distribution, sanitary sewers, and sewage collection and treatment."

*Id.* at 540, 768 N.E.2d at 858 (emphasis added).

169. Building Indus. Ass'n of Cleveland & Suburban Counties v. City of Westlake, 103 Ohio App. 3d 546, 552, 660 N.E.2d 501, 505 (1995) (holding park impact fee unreasonable as it required only new construction developers to shoulder the burden of funding existing park facilities).

170. *See, e.g.*, VILLAGE OF NORTHBROOK, ILL., SUBDIVISION & DEVELOPMENT CODE §4-101G14.

171. 605 ILL. COMP. STAT. 5/5-904.

172. 605 ILL. COMP. STAT. 5/5-901 et seq. See Appendix III for the full text of the Illinois Statute.

35

vehicle trips generated by different types of land uses.[173] The county calculated the fees using formulas that traced cars as they left particular developments and entered the roads. The court upheld the fee, finding that the county's fees were calculated in such a way to be specifically and uniquely attributable to the impact of the new development. Further studies included the creation of a computer model to determine future travel patterns.

Similarly, a Florida court upheld a road impact fee ordinance intended to pay the cost of road construction necessitated by new development, finding that the formula for calculating the fee was reasonable.[174] Calculation of the applicable road impact fee was based on the costs of road construction and the number of motor vehicle trips generated by various land uses. The ordinance required a $300 fee per unit for single-family homes, $200 per unit for multiple-family developments, and $175 per unit for mobile homes, with other amounts for commercial and other types of development. The court noted that the formula for calculating the fee was flexible and allowed the developer to furnish its own data to demonstrate that its share was less than the ordinance formula amount.

In California, the basis for calculating impact fees is governed by the Mitigation Fee Act, which requires the local government to do all the following:

1. Identify the purpose of the fee.
2. Identify the use to which the fee is to be put. If the use is financing public facilities, the facilities shall be identified. That identification may, but need not, be made by reference to a capital improvement plan as specified in §65403 or §66002, may be made in applicable general or specific plan requirements, or may be made in other public documents that identify the public facilities for which the fee is charged.
3. Determine how there is a reasonable relationship between the need for the public facility and the type of development project on which the fee is imposed.
4. Determine how there is a reasonable relationship between the need for the public facility and the type of development project on which the fee is imposed.[175]

The Mitigation Fee Act requires jurisdictions charging fees to demonstrate that there is a reasonable connection between specific fee amounts and the cost of the public facilities. Such relationships are to be documented in the form of written "nexus studies" and then certified by ordinance or resolution as findings.[176]

---

173. Northern Ill. Home Builders Ass'n v. County of DuPage, 251 Ill. App. 3d 494, 621 N.E.2d 1012 (1993).

174. Home Builders & Contractors Ass'n of Palm Beach County v. Board of County Comm'rs of Palm Beach County, 446 So. 2d 140, 145 (Fla. Dist. Ct. App. 1983).

175. CAL. GOV'T CODE §66001(a). See Appendix I for the full text of the California Statute.

176. CURTIN & TALBERT, *supra* note 51, at 294; *see also* CALIFORNIA, DEPARTMENT OF HOUSING & COMMUNITY DEVELOPMENT, PAY TO PLAY, *supra* at 158, at 49.

## II. LAND DEVELOPMENT CONDITIONS

The Act permits a developer to challenge the imposition of a fee by filing a written protest and filing suit within 180 days.[177]

Impact fee ordinances commonly use charts or graphs to calculate the total applicable impact fees for a proposed development. For example, a typical fixed-fee impact fee calculation is illustrated below:

### Impact Fee Calculation Table

| TYPE OF IMPACT FEE | RESIDENTIAL DWELLING (PER UNIT) |
|---|---|
| Road | $1,567 |
| Park | $1,035 |
| Public Facility | $910 |
| Police | $120 |
| Fire | $217 |
| Library | $130 |
| School | $2,663 |
| Water | $1,225 |
| Sewer | $1,558 |
| **TOTAL** | **$9,425** |

In 1972, the city of Naperville, Illinois, passed an ordinance that has served as a model for communities throughout Illinois in imposing impact fees for schools and parks.[178] The intent of the ordinance was to meet certain demands caused by increasing development in Naperville without raising taxes. The ordinance imposes fees in order to place responsibility on the developers who create the need to pay for services and facilities and is authorized by an enabling statute.[179]

The Naperville Ordinance was specifically enacted to provide for the dedication of park lands and school sites, or for the payment of fees in lieu thereof.[180] The ordinance provided that, as a condition of being granted approval of a subdivision plat or a planned unit development, any developer building within one and one-half miles of the city and seeking to annex to the city had to dedicate land (in amounts to be determined by a formula) to the school district and to the

---

177. Cal. Gov't Code §66000-66025; *see also* Curtin & Talbert, *supra* note 51, at 294-95.

178. Krughoff v. City of Naperville, 68 Ill. 2d 352, 369 N.E.2d 892 (1977).

179. 65 Ill. Comp. Stat. 5/11-12-8.

180. *Krughoff*, 68 Ill. 2d at 352, 369 N.E.2d at 892.

park district for new school sites and parks or donate cash in lieu of land. The Naperville Ordinance was upheld by the Illinois Supreme Court in *Krughoff v. City of Naperville*.[181]

Many Illinois communities have adopted some form of the "Naperville Ordinance" to calculate school and park fees. For example, an Illinois municipality has incorporated into its Subdivision and Development Code various land dedication and in lieu fee requirements as a condition to subdivision approval, as well as annexation to the municipality.[182] The code requires an applicant for subdivision approval to:

> dedicate land for park and recreational purposes and for school sites to serve the immediate and future needs of the residents of the proposed subdivision, or to agree to the payment of a cash contribution in lieu of actual land dedication, or to provide a combination of land and cash contributions, at the option of the Village.[183]

It then calculates the required dedication of land or cash contribution utilizing a density formula based on the estimated population per dwelling unit, as follows[184]:

---

181. 68 Ill. 2d 352, 359, 369 N.E.2d 892, 895 (1977). *See also* 65 ILL. COMP. STAT. 5/11-12-8.

182. VILLAGE OF NORTHBROOK, ILL., SUBDIVISION & DEVELOPMENT CODE §4-101G.

183. *Id.* §4-101G1(a).

184. *Id.* §4-101G2(a).

Table of Estimated Ultimate Population Per Dwelling Unit Children Per Dwelling Unit[185]

| Type of Unit | Pre-School 0-4 Years | Elementary Grades K-5 5-10 Years | Junior High Grades 6-8 11-13 Years | TOTAL Grades K-8 5-13 Years | High School Grades 9-12 14-17 Years | Adults (18-up) | Total Per Unit |
|---|---|---|---|---|---|---|---|
| **Single-Family Detached** | | | | | | | |
| 2 Bedroom | 0.133 | 0.136 | 0.048 | 0.184 | 0.020 | 1.700 | 2.017 |
| 3 Bedroom | 0.292 | 0.369 | 0.173 | 0.542 | 0.184 | 1.881 | 2.899 |
| 4 Bedroom | 0.418 | 0.530 | 0.298 | 0.828 | 0.360 | 2.158 | 3.764 |
| 5 Bedroom | 0.283 | 0.345 | 0.248 | 0.593 | 0.300 | 2.594 | 3.770 |
| **Single-Family Attached** | | | | | | | |
| 1 Bedroom | 0.000 | 0.000 | 0.000 | 0.000 | 0.000 | 1.193 | 1.193 |
| 2 Bedroom | 0.064 | 0.088 | 0.048 | 0.136 | 0.038 | 1.752 | 1.990 |
| 3 Bedroom | 0.212 | 0.234 | 0.058 | 0.292 | 0.059 | 1.829 | 2.392 |
| 4 Bedroom or More | 0.323 | 0.322 | 0.154 | 0.476 | 0.173 | 2.173 | 3.145 |
| **Multiple-Family Dwelling and Community Residence** | | | | | | | |
| Efficiency | 0.000 | 0.000 | 0.000 | 0.000 | 0.000 | 1.294 | 1.294 |
| 1 Bedroom | 0.000 | 0.002 | 0.001 | 0.003 | 0.001 | 1.754 | 1.758 |
| 2 Bedroom | 0.047 | 0.086 | 0.042 | 0.128 | 0.046 | 1.693 | 1.914 |
| 3 Bedroom or More | 0.052 | 0.234 | 0.123 | 0.357 | 0.118 | 2.526 | 3.053 |

**NOTE:** The determination of the number of bedrooms contained in a building shall be made by the Village Manager. Rooms designated by an applicant as den, library, study, sewing room, exercise room, or the like may be designated by the Village Manager as bedrooms if they are suitable for such accommodations.

185. *Id.* fig. 4-1.

The estimated population table is used to calculate the amount of land required for school sites in accordance with a formula set forth in the Subdivision and Development Code. Specifically, the number of children estimated for the proposed subdivision is divided by the maximum number of students to be served in each school classification, which number is then multiplied by the minimum number of acres for each school site for each school classification, as set forth in the code.[186] The municipality calculates any required in lieu fee based on the fair market value of the acres of land in the proposed subdivision.[187] The developer then pays these fees directly to the respective park or school districts pursuant to an agreement between the municipality and the districts.[188]

*D. Planning Consistency*

Regulation of land use in the United States occurs almost exclusively at the local level. Consequently, regulations and procedures vary widely from jurisdiction to jurisdiction, with varying degrees of success. From a national perspective, it is highly unlikely that the U.S. Congress will undertake either land use regulation or an effort to standardize land use processes across the country. Consequently, reforms to deal with common problems will likely continue to develop at the local level.

Interestingly, local jurisdictions are implementing the comprehensive plan as part of their land use planning process. Although specifics vary widely, most jurisdictions with a comprehensive plan view it as the "constitution" for development within that community. Typically all subsequent land use decisions must be "consistent" with the vision for growth and development reflected in the comprehensive plan.[189]

In California, land use regulations and approvals, including approvals of development agreements, must, in most instances, be consistent with the general plan and any applicable specific plans.[190] Under §65860(a) of the California statute, for example, a zoning ordinance is consistent with such plans only if:

- The city has officially adopted such a plan; and
- The various land uses authorized by the zoning ordinance are compatible with the objectives, policies, general land uses, and programs specified in such a plan.[191]

---

186. *Id.* §4-101G4(a)&(b).

187. *Id.* §4-101G5.

188. *Id.* §4-101G14.

189. JUERGENSMEYER & ROBERTS, LAND USE PLANNING AND CONTROL LAW, *supra* note 5, at 33-39; *see generally* JOSEPH DiMENTO, THE CONSISTENCY DOCTRINE AND THE LIMITS OF PLANNING (1980).

190. CAL. GOV'T CODE §§65860(a) and 65867.5(c).

191. CAL. GOV'T CODE §65860.

## II. LAND DEVELOPMENT CONDITIONS

In the *City of Irvine v. Irvine Citizens Against Overdevelopment*[192] case, the California court of appeal held that a land use regulation is consistent with a city's general plan where, considering all of its aspects, the ordinance furthers the objectives and policies of the general plan and does not obstruct their attainment.[193] A city's findings that a land use regulation is consistent with its general plan can be reversed only if it is based on evidence from which no reasonable person could have reached the same conclusion.[194]

The California courts have stated that a land use regulation inconsistent with the general plan at the time of enactment is "void ab initio," meaning it was invalid when passed.[195] If a land use regulation becomes inconsistent with a general plan by reason of an amendment to the plan, or to any element of the plan, the regulation must be amended within a reasonable time so that it is consistent with the amended general plan.[196] Since general plan consistency is required, the absence of a valid general plan, or the failure of any relevant elements thereof to meet statutory criteria, precludes the enactment of zoning ordinances and the like.[197]

All states require that zoning take place "in accordance with" some sort of comprehensive or master plan. In California, this plan is known as the general plan. The states vary, however, in the use of the comprehensive plan as a significant or decisive factor in evaluating land use regulations, although over time there has been slow and incremental increase nationwide in the quasi-constitutional status of the comprehensive plan. Currently, the states fall into three major categories in terms of the role of the comprehensive plan in the land use regulatory process.

The first category probably remains the majority rule—that there is no requirement that local governments prepare a plan that is separate from the zoning regulations. Examples of states falling into this category with recent judicial decisions upholding this "unitary view" are Arkansas,[198] Connecticut,[199] Illinois,[200] and New York.[201]

---

192. 30 Cal. Rptr. 2d 797, 25 Cal. App. 4th 868 (1994).

193. *Id.* at 803, 25 Cal. App. 4th at 879.

194. A Local & Reg'l Monitor (ALARM) v. City of Los Angeles, 20 Cal. Rptr. 2d 228, 239, 16 Cal. App. 4th 630, 648 (1993).

195. Lesher Communications, Inc. v. City of Walnut Creek, 52 Cal. 3d 531, 802 P.2d 317 (1990); *City of Irvine*, 30 Cal. Rptr. 2d at 797, 25 Cal. App. 4th at 868; Building Indus. Ass'n v. City of Oceanside, 33 Cal. Rptr. 2d 137, 27 Cal. App. 4th 744 (1994); DeBottari v. City Council, 217 Cal. Rptr. 790, 171 Cal. App. 3d 1024 (1985).

196. CAL. GOV'T CODE §65860(c).

197. Resource Defense Fund v. County of Santa Cruz, 184 Cal. Rptr. 371, 374, 133 Cal. App. 3d 800, 806 (1982).

198. Rolling Pines Ltd. Partnership v. City of Little Rock, 73 Ark. App. 97, 40 S.W.3d 828 (Ark. Ct. App. 2001).

199. Heithaus v. Planning & Zoning Comm'n, 258 Conn. 205, 779 A.2d 750 (2001).

States in the second category give some significance to the comprehensive plan as a factor in evaluating land use regulations, but do not make it the exclusive factor. The weight to be given to the plan varies from state to state. Examples of states in this category are Missouri,[202] Montana,[203] and New Jersey.[204]

The third category of states are those, like California, which grant the comprehensive plan quasi-constitutional status regulating ordinances and other actions of the local government in implementing the plan. Other states within this category include Florida,[205] Oregon,[206] and Washington.[207]

### E. Land Development Conditions for Specific Facilities

There is little difference in the law pertaining to land development conditions based upon the subject matter of the condition. Whether the exaction or dedication is for a street or road, a school, a park, a library, a police or fire station, a sanitary landfill, or a utility (water and sewer) system, the condition must further a legitimate state purpose, have a rational or essential nexus to the public facility/infrastructure need or other problem which the proposed development will create, and be proportional to the extent of the problem which the development will cause. Nevertheless, courts and communities are more likely to be persuaded of the validity or invalidity of a land development condition if supporting cases are factually as close as possible to that condition. What follows is a summary of case law divided by subject matter, with emphasis on the law of each case, both holding and, where relevant, guiding principles dealing with land development conditions.

### 1. Streets and Roads

One of the most common types of land development conditions required for the approval of subdivision plats and permits is for the purpose of constructing roads and road improvements made necessary by increased traffic that the pro-

200. City of Chicago Heights v. Living Word Outreach Full Gospel Church & Ministries, Inc., 196 Ill. 2d 1, 749 N.E.2d 916 (2001).

201. Yellow Lantern Kampground v. Town of Cortlandville, 279 A.D.2d 6, 716 N.Y.S.2d 786 (2000).

202. Fairview Enters., Inc. v. City of Kansas City, No. WD 58947, 2001 WL 967787 (Mo. Ct. App. Aug. 28, 2001).

203. Greater Yellowstone Coalition v. Board of County Comm'rs of Gallatin County, 305 Mont. 232, 25 P.3d 168 (2001).

204. Medical Ctr. at Princeton v. Township of Princeton Bd. of Adjustment, 343 N.J. Super. 177, 778 A.2d 482 (2001).

205. Buck Lake Alliance v. Board of County Comm'rs, 25 Fla. L. Weekly 1493, 765 So. 2d 124 (Fla. Dist. Ct. App. 2000).

206. Jackson County Citizens' League v. Jackson County, 171 Or. App. 149, 15 P.3d 42 (2001).

207. Ahamann-Yamane, Ltd. Liab. Corp. v. Tabler, 105 Wash. App. 103, 19 P.3d 436 (2001).

## II. LAND DEVELOPMENT CONDITIONS

posed land development is expected to generate. As the following cases demonstrate, these are generally upheld when the fee, exaction, or dedication is designed for additional street and road facilities that closely approximate the additional traffic resulting from the proposed development. Otherwise, the condition is generally regarded as an invalid taking under the general rules of *Nollan/Dolan* and/or a state case clone thereof.

In *Home Builders Ass'n v. Board of County Commissioners of Palm Beach County,*[208] the Florida District Court of Appeals applied the rational nexus test for impact fees established by the Florida Supreme Court in *Contractors & Builders Ass'n v. City of Dunedin,*[209] and followed in *Hollywood, Inc. v. Broward County.*[210] In *Home Builders*, the court upheld an ordinance requiring new land development activity generating road traffic, including residential, commercial, and industrial users, to pay a fair share of the cost of expanding new roads attributable to the new development.[211] The ordinance survived challenges that it lacked statutory authority, was an invalid tax, and did not sufficiently benefit the new development paying the fees.

California also has long upheld the validity of local governments requiring off-site road improvements as a condition of development. In *Ayres v. City Council of Los Angeles,*[212] the California Supreme Court held that a condition imposed on a developer to dedicate land to widen streets outside, but abutting the subdivision, was a valid exercise of the police power:

> In a growing metropolitan area each additional subdivision adds to the traffic burden. It is no defense to the conditions imposed in a subdivision map proceeding that their fulfillment will incidentally also benefit the city as a whole. Nor is it a valid objection to say that the conditions contemplate future as well as more immediate needs.[213]

*Ayres* has influenced the trend of California cases that generally uphold the validity of an exaction, including impact fees, where there is a reasonable relationship to the needs created by the development.[214] This test of reasonableness requires a much looser nexus than the rational nexus test adopted by the Florida courts and the majority of other jurisdictions. While there is clearly a rational nexus between the road fee and the development which generates traffic, the broad "reasonable relationship" test as set out in *Ayres* must be interpreted in connection with *Nollan,*[215] in which the Court struck down a development con-

---

208. 446 So. 2d 140 (Fla. Dist. Ct. App. 1983).

209. 329 So. 2d 314 (Fla. 1976).

210. 431 So. 2d 606 (Fla. Dist. Ct. App. 1983).

211. 446 So. 2d at 141.

212. 34 Cal. 2d 31, 207 P.2d 1 (1949).

213. *Id.* at 41, 207 P.2d at 7.

214. DANIEL J. CURTIN, DEDICATIONS, EXACTIONS, AND IN LIEU FEES: THE INVERSE CONDEMNATION-TAKING ISSUE 9 (1986) (originally presented at County Counsel Association Spring Conference, Santa Cruz, Cal., May 1986).

215. 483 U.S. at 825, 107 S. Ct. at 3141, 97 L. Ed. 2d at 677, 17 ELR at 20918.

dition for lack of an "essential nexus" test, extending broader protection to property rights, as guaranteed by the Constitution's Fifth Amendment. Thus, after *Ehrlich*,[216] in California an adjudicatively imposed fee must not only pass the broad "reasonable relationship" test as set out in *Ayres*, it must also satisfy the essential nexus and rough proportionality tests of *Nollan*[217] and *Dolan*.[218] Also, a challenge to the constitutionality of such a fee must be brought pursuant to the procedures of the California Mitigation Fee Act.[219]

Other cases involving off-site improvements, like *Ayres*, deal with requirements imposed on developers and subdividers as a condition of obtaining plat or site plan approval. *Miller v. City of Port Angeles*[220] involved the imposition of a fee for off-site road improvements and a requirement that the developer widen adjacent roads. The court found authority for the conditions in a state statute empowering local governments to condition subdivision approval upon the adequacy of access to and within the proposed subdivision.[221] The conditions overcame the challenge of being an invalid tax because (1) the need for the improvements arose directly from the new developments as demonstrated by an environmental impact statement (EIS), (2) the developer was not required to pay more than his fair share of the cost, and (3) it contained a refund provision providing that all funds be returned to the developer if not expended at the end of seven years.[222] Regarding "fair share," the court noted that the developers were required to improve only the side of the road that abutted their property and that their contributions to the road improvement fund amounted to only 18% of the projected total.[223]

The New Hampshire Supreme Court adopted the rational nexus test in *Land/Vest Properties v. Town of Plainfield*.[224] The town planning board conditioned subdivision approval on the developer's upgrading, at his own expense, two highways leading to, but located outside, the subdivision. First, the court held that the conditions imposed were a valid exercise of the police power to protect public safety, based on subdivision enabling statutes authorizing improvement of streets as a condition to subdivision plat approval.[225] The court then held that a subdivider can be compelled "only to bear that portion of the cost which bears a rational nexus to the needs created by, and special benefits conferred upon, the subdivision."[226] The court analogized this special benefit to

---

216. 911 P.2d at 429.

217. 483 U.S. at 825, 107 S. Ct. at 3141, 97 L. Ed. 2d at 677, 17 ELR at 20918.

218. 512 U.S. at 374, 114 S. Ct. at 2309, 129 L. Ed. 2d at 304, 24 ELR at 21083.

219. CAL. GOV'T CODE §§66000-66025.

220. 38 Wash. App. 904, 691 P.2d 229 (1984).

221. *Id.* at 909, 691 P.2d at 233.

222. *Id.* at 908-10, 691 P.2d at 234-35.

223. *Id.* at 910-11, 691 P.2d at 234.

224. 117 N.H. 817, 379 A.2d 200 (1977).

225. *Id.* at 820, 379 A.2d at 202.

226. *Id.* at 823, 379 A.2d at 204.

assessments, but disagreed with the "proportionality test" applied by the trial court based on frontage alone. Other factors must be considered, including present road standards, potential traffic increase necessitated by the proposed subdivision, the potential for development of the neighborhood served by these roads, and the number of residences presently fronting on or whose residents normally used these roads.[227] The case was remanded for determination of the appropriate allocation of the cost of improvements.

A Michigan ordinance provided that developers applying to extend private roads must upgrade any nonconforming sections to meet current road standards.[228] When a subdivider applied for building permits on a landlocked parcel, accessible only by a private road from a public highway, he was required to comply with the new road standards, and no variance was available, even though another property owner would also benefit from the road improvement, without having to pay for it. The town relaxed some of the requirements, but still conditioned the building permits on the road's improvement. The developer argued that the regulations unconstitutionally restricted his use of the property. The court found no regulatory taking, however, because plaintiff had not investigated using his property without subdividing it, the safety reasons for upgrading the road made the regulations legitimate state interests, and improving the road to adequately support the new residences was in rough proportion to the increased traffic[229]:

> Although constitutional principles forbid forcing one person to absorb the costs of a public benefit, neither do they require forcing others to shoulder the burdens of one person's aspirations to develop real property.... There is no way to balance perfectly all interested persons' interests and burdens. The scheme to which we give our approval in this instance at least has the virtue of placing the burdens of development on the person initiating the activity. In a situation where rough accommodations cannot be avoided, we are satisfied that the burdens defendant is placing on plaintiff are in "rough proportion" to the public needs to which plaintiff's plans would give rise.[230]

The Washington Court of Appeals has upheld a requirement that a developer build a secondary access road to a proposed development in a remote area subject to wildfire hazards.[231] In *Lampton v. Pinaire*,[232] the Kentucky Court of Appeals held that subdivision regulations requiring on-site and off-site dedication of land for road improvements were not unconstitutional on their face. The court adopted a test of reasonableness, stating its rationale as follows:

---

227. *Id.* at 824, 379 A.2d at 205.

228. Dowerk v. Charter Township of Oxford, No. 204032, 1998 WL 842266 (Mich. App. Dec. 4, 1998).

229. *Id.*

230. *Id.*

231. Isla Verde Int'l Holdings v. City of Camas, 99 Wash. App. 127, 990 P.2d 429 (1999).

232. 610 S.W.2d 915 (Ky. Ct. App. 1981).

The intent of dedication is not to put an unreasonable burden on the landowner, but to permit him to develop his land without putting an unreasonable burden on others. So long as the taking of a portion of the land, whether on the exterior or from the interior, is based on the reasonably anticipated burdens to be caused by the development, the dedication requirements as a condition precedent to plat approval are not an unconstitutional taking of land without just compensation.[233]

The case was remanded to determine whether the dedication in question was reasonable in consideration of any reasonably anticipated future traffic burden that the development of the subdivision would impose on the existing road.[234]

Similarly, in *Bethlehem Evangelical Lutheran Church v. City of Lakewood*,[235] the Colorado Supreme Court upheld conditions imposed on a church for issuance of a building permit to construct a gymnasium. The church was required to improve an abutting street as well as dedicate land for city streets. The court found authority for such conditions in the statutory scheme permitting the assessment of property improvement costs to abutting property, as long as the property is especially benefitted by the improvements over and above the general benefit to the public at large.[236] The court cited *Ayres*[237] for the proposition that such conditions are a reasonable exercise of the police power:

It is the Church which is seeking to obtain the benefits from an enlarged use of its property, and the duty rests upon it to comply with reasonable conditions, conceived in the public interest, to prevent and avoid adverse effects on the vehicular and pedestrian traffic on the streets adjacent to the Church property.[238]

Road exactions can involve complex facts and interesting planning problems. One federal appellate case involved a dispute over a "privacy buffer," reserved by developers of a small 14-lot subdivision at the end of a cul-de-sac.[239] The McKenzies, who were the subdividers, reserved a small "privacy buffer" at the end of the cul-de-sac in the subdivision, precluding its connection to an adjoining subdivision. At one point the city acquired one of the lots for the erection of a water tower but used it for storage and for "dumping" instead. When the McKenzies later decided to resubdivide some of their remaining lots, the city conditioned the resubdivision approval on the McKenzies' granting access across the "privacy buffer" and the city also refused to issue building permits on some of the lots until the McKenzies transferred title to the buffer. Ultimately,

---

233. *Id.* at 919.

234. *Id.*

235. 626 P.2d 668 (Colo. 1981).

236. *Id.* at 672.

237. 34 Cal. 2d at 31, 207 P.2d at 1.

238. *Bethlehem Evangelical Lutheran Church*, 626 P.2d at 673. Whether the Religious Land Use and Institutionalized Persons Act (RLUIPA) applies to such local land use development requirements where the "developer" is a religious institution remains to be seen.

239. McKenzie v. City of White Hall, 112 F.3d 313 (8th Cir. 1997).

the McKenzies gave the city a contingent easement across the buffer, allowing the city to create access across it, if and when there was residential development on the adjacent property. The McKenzies then sued the city under §1983.[240] An appellate court held that the McKenzies' takings claims were not ripe, because they had failed to pursue compensation through Arkansas statutes expressly providing for such relief.[241] Although upholding the trial court in dismissing the takings claim, the court found that equal protection and due process claims were ripe and should have been heard.

The Colorado Supreme Court struck down as unauthorized a requirement imposed on a developer of a planned unit development (PUD) to improve a 4.73-mile off-site access road.[242] As an alternative, the developer could pay a "per living unit fee" to the county to cover the cost of the road construction.[243] After examining various state statutes authorizing county planning, zoning, and subdivision and PUD regulations, the court held that in proper circumstances it is within the county's police power to require a developer to contribute to road improvements as a condition of PUD approval.[244] However, the court found that the county regulations were not specific enough:

> Therefore, notwithstanding the general delegation of authority by the legislature to consider adequacy of access, the obvious concern of the county regulations about this same subject, and the general policy of the county to require new development to pay its own way and share in the cost of upgrading county facilities to the extent that it is fair and equitable, we conclude that the statutes and regulations, taken in combination, do not authorize imposition of the road improvement condition at issue here. This is because they provide insufficient standards and safeguards to ensure that county action in response to a PUD application will be rational and consistent and that judicial review of that action will be available and effective.[245]

When an Oregon landowner submitted a plan for a drive-in fast food restaurant, conditions for approval included street improvements for the adjoining road, drainage, curbs, and sidewalks. The landowner appealed to the

---

240. Section I of the Federal Civil Rights Act of 1871, codified as amended at 42 U.S.C. §1983, provides:

> Every person who, under color of any statute, ordinance, regulation, custom or usage, of any State or Territory of the District of Columbia, subjects, or causes to be subjected, any citizen of the United States or other person within the jurisdiction thereof to the deprivation of any rights, privileges, or immunities secured by the Constitution and laws, shall be liable to the party injured in an action at law, suit in equity, or other proper proceeding for redress.

Id.

241. *McKenzie*, 112 F.3d at 318.

242. Beaver Meadows v. Board of County Comm'rs, 709 P.2d 928 (Colo. 1985).

243. *Id.* at 931.

244. *Id.*; *see* Bethlehem Evangelical Lutheran Church v. City of Lakewood, 626 P.2d 668, 671-74 (Colo. 1981).

245. *Beaver Meadows*, 709 P.2d at 938.

LUBA,[246] stating that the seven conditions were each contrary to *Dolan*. LUBA only agreed that the two conditions requiring the landowner to design street widening improvements beginning 150 feet away from the restaurant and then to pay for those improvements were exactions not meeting the rough proportionality requirement of *Dolan*.[247] Oregon's court of appeals concurred because the city was unable to show that the restaurant would be the sole or main beneficiary of the improvements, and that the project's impacts somehow require the improvements.[248] The appellate court also found that the condition requiring wider sidewalks, which must be on the development plans for the building permit to issue, could violate *Dolan* and remanded the question to LUBA.[249]

*Country Joe, Inc. v. City of Eagan*,[250] involved a "road unit connection charge," clearly intended as a road impact fee made to look as much as possible like well-accepted sewer and water connection fees. Although the district court ruled for the city in a challenge by homebuilders, the court of appeals reversed and the Minnesota high court agreed with the appellate court. A critical defect in the scheme was the failure to use fund accounting to segregate the funds.[251] The court rejected the city's analogy between the fee and sewer and water connection charges. Interestingly, however, the Minnesota high court did not reach the question of whether Eagan, a statutory city (in a state with a home-rule option for municipal governments) had the authority to levy impact fees. It held instead that the Eagan fee did not meet the test of impact fees as set forth in the cases cited by the city, specifically because the city had failed to update the fee since 1979.

Courts strike down road exactions either because the court cannot find a basis or authority for the local government to levy an impact fee or impose an exaction, or because the local government cannot demonstrate any connection or nexus between the fee or exaction and the development upon which the fee or exaction was levied. In *Amoco Oil Co.*,[252] the village conditioned Amoco Oil's

---

246. Oregon established LUBA in 1979, and the statewide board of appeals has the power to review all land use decisions of local governments, state agencies, or special districts. The decisions may be legislative or quasi-judicial, effectively making LUBA a "court of first impression." *See generally* T. Morgan & J. Shonkwiler, *State Wide Land Use Planning in Oregon, With Special Emphasis on Housing Issues*, 11 URB. LAW. 1 (1979); Edward J. Sullivan, *Oregon Blazes a Trail, in* STATE & REGIONAL COMPREHENSIVE PLANNING ch. 3 (Peter A. Buchsbaum & Larry J. Smith eds., 1993); GEMIT KNAPP & ARTHUR NELSON, THE REGULATED LANDSCAPE: LESSONS ON STATE LAND USE PLANNING FROM OREGON (1992).

247. Clark v. City of Albany, 137 Or. App. 293, 298, 904 P.2d 185, 188 (Or. 1995).

248. *Id.* at 299-300, 904 P.2d at 189.

249. *Id.* at 302, 904 P.2d at 191.

250. 560 N.W.2d 681 (Minn. 1997).

251. The court noted that, "the city's Finance Director testified that road unit connection charges collected are commingled with the city's ad valorem tax levy, some special assessment collections, interest earnings' and other miscellaneous revenue sources in the Major Street Fund." *Id.* at 682.

252. 277 Ill. App. 3d at 926, 661 N.E.2d at 380.

special use permit on a dedication of a section of the lot for highway improvement. The court struck down the dedication, holding that the need to widen the road existed notwithstanding the development; therefore no proportionality existed for the village to require a dedication of more than 20% of Amoco's property.

Similarly, the court in *Schultz v. City of Grants Pass*[253] struck down the city's condition that Schultz dedicate a parcel for street widening in exchange for approval of an application to partition the parcel. The court first addressed the extent of the dedication, concluding that the dedication would require the owners to part with 20,000 square feet of their land. The city had determined that with full development of the parcel, 15 to 20 homes could be placed on the parcel, causing considerable impact on transportation on the streets. The court held that the city was required to examine the actual proposed development, here partitioned into two lots, to determine the impact on transportation. Applying *Dolan* to the proposed condition, the court concluded that a slight increase in traffic from the two lots did not justify a 20,000-square-foot dedication, and therefore there was no rough proportionality between the exaction and the impact from the development.

The Washington Supreme Court upheld a county's conditioning of approval of a short plat application on the developer dedicating rights-of-way for road improvements.[254] The Sparks filed four short plat applications with the Douglas County Planning Office. Upon reviewing the plat applications, the planning director noted deficiencies in the right-of-way width and approved the short plat application subject to certain conditions, including dedication of rights-of-way for future street improvements bordering the plats.[255] The Sparks appealed the committee's decision to the planning commission, which affirmed the committee's recommendation and conditions. The county superior court affirmed the committee's and planning commissioner's findings, but the court of appeals reversed, finding that there was no evidence that the Sparks' development would adversely impact the adjacent streets, and concluding that the dedication was an unconstitutional taking. However, the Washington Supreme Court applied the *Dolan* test of essential nexus and rough proportionality to hold first that an essential nexus existed between the required dedication of rights-of-way and the county's legitimate interest in promoting road safety.[256] The court then applied the rough proportionality prong of the *Dolan* test to the required dedication, concluding that the county's findings, records, reports, and studies all reflected that the required degree of proportionality existed between the impact and the condition.[257]

---

253. 131 Or. App. 220, 884 P.2d 569 (1994).

254. Sparks v. Douglas County, 127 Wash. 2d 901, 904 P.2d 738 (1994).

255. *Id.* at 904, 904 P.2d at 740.

256. *Id.* at 914, 904 P.2d at 745.

257. *Id.* at 915, 904 P.2d at 745-46.

*Benchmark Land Co.*[258] adds to the growing consensus that the so-called heightened security applicable to dedications also applies to monetary fees and exactions. There, a developer successfully challenged a city condition of subdivision plat approval requiring half-street improvements to a street adjoining, but extrinsic to the proposed development, based upon the length of the development adjoining the street. The subdivision did not directly access the street subject to the improvements. The court held that such a condition met neither the essential nexus test nor the requirement of rough proportionality, and so was an unconstitutional land development condition.

A year later, the Washington Court of Appeals reconsidered the case following the Court's decision in *Del Monte Dunes.*[259] There, the Court said that it had never applied their "heightened scrutiny" in *Nollan/Dolan* beyond a land dedication. Nevertheless, the court of appeals found that the *Dolan* rough proportionality test still applied: because the city required the developer to pay for something outside the relevant property that was not impacted by the new development, the condition was invalid.[260] "Surely if the issues for an exaction of money are the same as for an exaction of land, the test must be the same: a showing of 'nexus' and 'proportionality.'"[261]

Using a different and more strict test, a federal court also held that a street improvement fee violated a state constitution because it was not specifically attributable to the new development for which it was charged. In *Chicago Title Insurance Co.*,[262] two developers paid fees under protest for timely final plat recordings of their subdivision plats. The court found that Bollingbrook did not meet its burden of showing that the impact fees for the cost of future or recent improvements of existing or proposed streets were significantly attributable to the specific developments. The village used an equation that failed to consider whether the developments created any more traffic, which made the resultant fees arbitrary. The court found that the town had violated the state constitution by recapturing fees for roads that abutted the development whether or not the developments impacted the road use.[263] In a prior case, the Illinois Supreme Court had found two state enabling statutes and subsequent ordinances to be unconstitutional because they imposed transportation impact fees on new developments that should have been collected as a tax on the communities in

---

258. 94 Wash. App. at 537, 972 P.2d at 944.

259. Benchmark Land Co. v. City of Battle Ground, 103 Wash. App. 721, 14 P.3d 172 (2000) (citing *Del Monte Dunes*, 526 U.S. at 687, 119 S. Ct. at 1624, 143 L. Ed. 2d at 882, 29 ELR at 21133).

260. *Id.* at 727.

261. *Id.*

262. 1999 WL 65054 at *1.

263. *Id.* at *29. This case was later overturned because the Seventh Circuit had found that a district court should not take a position that opines a state constitutional matter. Chicago Title Insurance Co. v. Village of Bollingbrook, No. 97 C 7055, 1999 WL 259952 (N.D. Ill. Apr. 6, 1999).

general.[264] In that case, the state supreme court required the community to refund all fees that had been collected under the implementing ordinances.

In Pennsylvania, however, an appellate court found that a township's street-widening impact fee was legal because it did not require contributions in exchange for the approval of subdivision plans. Instead, the ordinance provided an alternate venue for obtaining such approval. In *Soliday v. Haycock Township*,[265] the court found that the ordinance requiring a subdivision or other new development to make any existing street conform to the municipality's standards for right-of-way or to pay into a fund used for street improvement allowed the property owner to compare costs and choose which was preferable.[266] This choice led the court to hold that the fee was reasonable and did not adversely affect the owner, thus upholding the conditions for approval of a subdivision plan.[267]

Again, a Texas appellate court found that the *Dolan* test applied to a development exaction requiring a developer to pay the total cost of, and do all the work of, replacing a two-lane, abutting, asphalt road with a concrete one.[268] Because the road improvements were conditions for plat approval, and because the town had exempted other developers from such conditions, the fee and conditions were made individually, thus triggering the need for a *Dolan* analysis.[269] The court found that the town failed to meet the rough proportionality requirements of the test, even though a nexus existed between the legitimate state interests of safety and durability, and the plat approval condition of better roads.[270] Forcing the developer to demolish a one-year-old road and repave it with concrete at the developer's expense was excessive, given that the town did not show why this particular development required such work. The court then held that the town owed the developer damages equivalent to the amount that the developer overpaid for improvements that would be roughly proportional to the subdivision's impacts on the road.[271]

Where a particular development will have direct impact on an existing road system, however, courts have upheld conditions for studying those impacts or, alternatively, for improving the roads.[272] When a construction company applied to Clark County, Washington, for a conditional use permit (CUP) to build and operate an asphalt plant at its rock quarry, the county hearing examiner re-

---

264. Northern Ill. Home Builders Ass'n v. County of DuPage, 165 Ill. 2d 25, 649 N.E. 2d 384 (Ill. 1995).

265. 785 A.2d 139 (Pa. Commw. Ct. 2001).

266. *Id.* at 17.

267. *Id.* at 19.

268. *See* Town of Flower Mound v. Stafford Estates Ltd. Partnership, 71 S.W.3d 18 (Tex. App. 2d 2002).

269. *Id.* at 30 (citing Ehrlich v. City of Culver City, 911 P.2d 429, 439 (Cal. 1996)).

270. *Id.* at 35.

271. *Id.* at 46.

272. *See* Kiewit Constr. Group, Inc. v. Clark County, 83 Wash. App. 133, 920 P.2d 1207 (1996).

quired an EIS. After the final EIS, the examiner approved the CUP, with conditions, including mitigation of increased truck traffic over a two-lane highway and its access road, which connected with the highway so sharply that trucks could not traverse traffic in both directions. The increased truck traffic also would impact the planned bicycle trail alongside the highway, and the trucks must use the highway to access the state freeway. The county reevaluated an EIS and directed the construction company to either submit a supplemental EIS (SEIS) to address the traffic issues or build new access ramps from the quarry road to the freeway. In *Kiewit Construction Group, Inc. v. Clark County*,[273] the Washington Court of Appeals held that the board had the right to order an SEIS when there is some new information that may indicate a proposal's probable significant adverse environmental impacts. The condition was merely an alternative to preparing an SEIS, and thus not an illegal, unilateral requirement.

Another issue before courts has been whether potential impact fees counteract the need to consider "special benefits" in determining the value of condemned land. For example, Colorado's Public Highway Authority condemned ribbons of land for highway construction through two undeveloped properties, dividing each property into two portions.[274] Landowners argued that if the estimated value of "special benefits" that their property might gain from the highway was subtracted from their compensation package, that would be equivalent to double charging them, because they would also have to pay the Colorado Public Highway Authority an expansion fee based on any new development's proximity to the highway. The Colorado Supreme Court found that the highway fee would be used for maintenance and was based on type of development, traffic generated by the development, and the development's nearness to the highway.[275] Only the latter relates to the "special benefits" of a property's gain from a condemned property's use and the court remanded for subtraction of those "special benefits" from the condemnation compensation.

When a development corporation claimed that a city's conditions for plat approval duplicated previously paid traffic impact fees, the appellate court in *United Development Corp. v. City of Mill Creek*[276] found that the prior agreements had only included three roads, while the total development's increased traffic would impact nine. The court found that although some portions of the project may have been mitigated by earlier agreements, the whole project had not, and the whole project had to respect changes in the city's regulatory framework.[277] The court also found that the city's impact fees were reasonable, with a legitimate public purpose, and roughly proportional to the subdivision's impact.[278]

---

273. 83 Wash. App. 133, 142, 920 P.2d 1207, 1212 (1996).

274. *See, e.g.*, Public Highway Auth. v. 455 Co., 3 P.3d 18 (Colo. 2000).

275. *Id.* at 26.

276. 106 Wash. App. 681, 26 P.3d 943 (2001).

277. *Id.*

278. *Id.* at 698, 26 P.3d at 951-52.

## II. LAND DEVELOPMENT CONDITIONS

Failure to implement statutory authority resulted in invalidation of traffic impact fees levied on the enlargement of a golf course.[279] Although statute allowed for impact fees, the town had not enacted an impact fee ordinance. The town argued that this was irrelevant because the planning board charged the fees, which the New Hampshire Supreme Court had previously held to be within the planning board's authority.[280] The statute relied upon in the previous case, however, had been replaced by the one requiring municipalities to adopt their own ordinances; thus, the impact fee was illegal.[281]

In Washington State, counties have been enabled to write laws requiring counties to make "appropriate provision for the public health, safety, and welfare before approving a subdivision."[282] One board of county commissioners approved a preliminary plat for 21 lots and imposed 6 conditions, including 1 requiring the developer to get right-of-way over someone else's property and then to improve that road.[283] The developer challenged that condition, but a court of appeals found it not to be arbitrary or capricious.[284] Plaintiff's property was between a highway and a 12-foot-wide lane. The board conditioned plaintiff's project on his obtaining rights-of-way across third-party properties between his property and the lane, and then widening the lane to 50 feet—the board's minimum standard required by the amount of traffic coming to the area because of the new project. The appellate court agreed that the lane should be improved to provide adequate access to and by the new development.[285] The court also found that the conditions did not result in an unconstitutional taking because the landowner was not being required to dedicate any of his property to obtain development approval.[286]

Landowners must seek remedies for invalid exactions properly. Thus, in *Sundance Homes, Inc. v. County of DuPage*,[287] builders who had paid road improvement impact fees that were later found to be unconstitutional were barred from recovering those fees by the five-year statute of limitations that had run from the date when they paid the fees. The court compared the payment of the impact fees to the payment of a tax, and applied the state statute of limitations on tax refunds to the impact fees.[288]

---

279. *See* Simonsen v. Town of Derby, 145 N.H. 382, 383, 765 A.2d 1033, 1034 (N.H. 2000).

280. *Id.* at 386, 765 A.2d at 1036; *see* N.E. Brickmaster v. Town of Salem, 133 N.H. 655, 663, 582 A.2d 601, 606 (N.H. 1990) (allowing planning boards to condition site plan approval on off-site road improvement fees).

281. *Simonsen*, 145 N.H. at 387, 765 A.2d at 1036-37.

282. Snider v. Board of County Comm'rs of Walla Walla County, 85 Wash. App. 371, 376, 932 P.2d 704, 707 (1997).

283. *Id.*

284. *Id.*

285. *Id.* at 377, 932 P.2d at 708.

286. *Id.* at 381, 932 P.2d at 709.

287. 195 Ill. 2d 257, 746 N.E.2d 254 (2001).

288. *Id.* at 277, 746 N.E.2d at 266.

When courts confuse impact fees with tax-like revenue-raising techniques, the results can be confusing, particularly with respect to vested rights. Thus, for example, in *New Castle Investments v. City of Lacenter*,[289] a Washington appellate court held that transportation impact fees were not "land use control ordinances," and therefore a vesting statute did not apply to them.[290] The developer had applied for plat approval two days before an impact fee ordinance became effective.[291] The plat was approved and the impact fee waived because the preliminary plat application had been "perfected" before the city established the fee.[292] The court of appeals examined the definition of "land use control ordinances" to decide whether the land use vesting statute, which allowed perfection of a subdivision when the application for a preliminary plat approval was complete, applied.[293] The court stopped short of defining the relevant impact fees as "taxes," but did not find them to be "land use control ordinances" because they did not "control," zone, or limit land use—all elements of certainty that a developer requires from vesting.[294] As the transportation impact fee was a fee, the court noted that the vesting doctrine does not apply to fees,[295] and upheld the city's right to charge the fees after completion of the preliminary plat application.

A federal court in New Jersey has upheld a requirement that developers dedicate and improve access across private property to public trust lands along the shore.[296] The court cited New Jersey precedent for the protection of the public trust lands for public use,[297] and it cited *Ehrlich* in support of the requirement

---

289. 98 Wash. App. 224, 989 P.2d 542 (1999).

290. *Id.* at 236, 989 P.2d at 576.

291. *Id.* at 227, 989 P.2d at 571.

292. *Id.*

293. *Id.*

294. *Id.* at 229, 989 P.2d at 572.

295. *Id.* at 231, 989 P.2d at 573; *see* Lincoln Shiloh Assocs. v. Mukilteo Water Dist., 45 Wash. App. 123, 724 P.2d 1083, *review denied*, 107 Wash. 2d 1014 (1986).

296. National Ass'n of Homebuilders v. New Jersey Dep't of Envtl. Protection, 64 F. Supp. 2d 354 (D.N.J. 1999), challenged a rule promulgated by the department. The court described the portions of the rule at issue in the case:

> Specifically, Plaintiffs allege that the Rule is unconstitutional because it requires all owners of property within the Hudson River Waterfront Area desiring a New Jersey Department of Environmental Protection (hereinafter "NJDEP") waterfront development permit to, without compensation: (1) construct and maintain, at the owner's expense, a thirty-foot wide walkway along the entire waterfront of the property, to be build to standards specified in NJDEP regulations (hereinafter "Walkway"); (2) convey to NJDEP a conservation easement for the Walkway; and (3) allow perpendicular public access to the Walkway.

> *Id.* at 355.

297. *Id.* at 359 (citing Matthews v. Bay Head Improvement Ass'n, 95 N.J. 306, 326, 471 A.2d 355 (1984), *cert. denied*, 469 U.S. 821, 105 S. Ct. 93, 83 L. Ed. 2d 39 (1984)).

that the developers improve the walkways, noting that the imposition of some costs are typical of land development regulations and "well within the state's land use police power."[298]

In sum, cases upholding the validity of impact fees and other exactions for road improvements indicate that such exactions can be upheld even without specific enabling legislation. Fees should conform to the rational nexus test discussed previously that requires (1) a showing that the development will generate a need and that the amount exacted bears a roughly proportional relationship to the share of need that is contributed by the development, and (2) funds or property exacted must be earmarked for the purpose collected and must, at least in part, benefit the development which paid the exaction.[299]

2. Water and Sewer Improvements

Fees imposed to fund capital improvements to a local government's water or sewer system have been upheld in a number of jurisdictions. In most cases, the fees are called "connection fees," or "tap-in" fees. However, the fees are used to fund expansion or improvement of the water or sewer system necessitated by increases in population and new development. As with other types of impact fees, courts first inquire if the local government has sufficient authority in its enabling legislation to impose a fee. If so, the court then addresses the issue of whether the impact fee is a valid regulatory measure rather than an illegal tax or a taking without compensation. Most jurisdictions apply the rational nexus test to determine the reasonableness of the fee. This test requires first, a showing that the fee is related to a real need created by the new development, and second, that the funds collected are sufficiently "earmarked" for the benefit of the development paying the fee.[300]

The Florida Supreme Court upheld the concept of impact fees for funding capital improvements to municipal water and sewer systems in the landmark case of *Contractors & Builders Ass'n of Pinellas County v. City of Dunedin.*[301] The city enacted an ordinance imposing a fee to defray the cost of production, distribution, transmission, and treatment facilities for water and sewer provided at city expense. The fee was payable prior to issuance of a building permit, or, for existing structures, upon connection with the system. Fees were charged according to three classifications of users: dwelling units, transient units, and business units.[302] Although the ordinance in question was held invalid for failing to articulate necessary restrictions on the use of fees collected, the court stated, "in principle, however, we see nothing wrong with transferring

---

298. *National Ass'n of Homebuilders,* 64 F. Supp. 2d at 359 (citing Ehrlich v. City of Culver, 12 Cal. 4th 854, 886, 911 P.2d 429, 450 (1996)).

299. Bosselman & Stroud, *Mandatory Tithes, supra* note 3, at 397-98.

300. *Id.*

301. 329 So. 2d 314 (Fla. 1976).

302. *Id.* at 316-17 n.1.

to the new user of a municipally owned water or sewer system a fair share of the costs new use of the system involves."[303] The court continued:

> Water and sewer rates and charges do not, therefore, cease to be "just and equitable" merely because they are set high enough to meet the system's capital requirements, as well as to defray operating expenses. . . . The weight of authority supports the view that raising capital for future outlay is a legitimate consideration in setting rates and charges.[304]

The plaintiffs challenged the ordinance as an ultra vires attempt by the city to impose taxes. The court held that the city had authority to enact the ordinance and that the fees were not taxes. A key factor in rejecting characterization of the impact fee as a tax was evidence that the fees were less than costs the city would incur in accommodating new users of its water and sewer systems.[305]

Following *Dunedin*, the Florida Court of Appeals broadly interpreted a water district's enabling legislation to find authority to impose impact fees for water.[306] In order to meet expected costs of expansion, the district assessed a "capital contribution charge" on a per unit basis. The enabling statute authorized the district to "fix and collect rates, fees, and other charges for the use of the facilities and services provided by any water system or sewer system."[307] Even though impact fees were not an accepted method of financing expansion in Florida at the time of the enactment of this statute, the court held that the phrase "rates, fees, and other charges" was broad enough to include impact fees.[308] The court stated that, "the imposition of an impact fee is consistent with the statutory purpose of authorizing charges sufficient to ensure the maintenance of an adequate water system."[309] The South Carolina high court has similarly found that an impact fee for connecting to a sewer or water system is simply part of the charge for service.[310] Conversely, a Washington appellate court held that a city had no statutory authority to impose the impact fee specified in an agreement to extend sewer and water service and released the city from the agreement because of the failure of consideration.[311]

Once impact fees are an accepted method of payment for public improvements serving new developments, they are more likely to be upheld. When developers bought an abandoned auto repair business with the intent to convert it into a sports bar, connection fees for the plumbing changes required by a bar were up-

---

303. *Id.* at 317-18.

304. *Id.* at 319-20.

305. *Id.* at 318.

306. Englewood Water Dist. v. Halstead, 432 So. 2d 172 (Fla. Dist. Ct. App. 1983).

307. *Id.* at 173 (quoting ch. 59-931, §4(f), Laws of Florida).

308. *Id.*

309. *Id.* at 173.

310. J.K. Constr., Inc. v. Western Carolina Reg'l Sewer Auth., 336 S.C. 162, 519 S.E.2d 561 (1999). *Accord* Ford v. Georgetown County Water & Sewer Dist., 341 S.C. 10, 532 S.E.2d 873 (2000).

311. Nolte v. City of Olympia, 96 Wash. App. 944, 982 P.2d 659 (1999).

held.[312] The city imposed these impact fees because of the change of use, not because of increased use or new ownership, and the structural changes involved significantly impacted the existing water and sewer systems. The appellate court took this evidence to prove that the impact fees helped defray the costs of a new user of a municipal water or sewer system, rather than an illegal tax.[313]

After establishing the general validity of water and sewer connection fees in *Home Builders*, the Utah Supreme Court promulgated its oft-cited test of the reasonableness of such fees in *Banberry Development Corp. v. South Jordan City*.[314] As a condition of plat approval, a city ordinance required all subdividers to pay the entire cost of all water lines required to service the subdivision, including extensions from existing water mains. It also imposed a connection fee for each dwelling unit payable prior to connection to the city water system. The purpose of the fees was to enlarge water lines and storage and pumping facilities.[315] The court upheld the general legality of water impact fees designed to raise funds to enlarge and improve the water system, as well as the legality of conditioning water hook-ups or plat approval on their collection.[316]

The court stated: "Precise mathematical equality is neither feasible nor constitutionally vital," recognizing the flexibility needed by municipalities to deal with this difficult issue.[317] However, the fee payer must not be charged more than his "fair share":

> [T]o comply with the standard of reasonableness, a municipal fee related to services like water and sewer must not require newly developed properties to bear more than their equitable share of the capital costs in relation to benefits conferred.... The fee in question should not exceed the amount sufficient to equalize the relative burdens of newly developed and other properties.[318]

In *Lafferty v. Payson City*,[319] the city enacted ordinances imposing impact fees as a condition of issuing building permits, as well as increased connection fees for sewer, water, and electricity. The city claimed the impact fee was needed to finance improvements in the city's water and sewer systems necessitated by new home construction. The fee was struck down by the Utah Supreme Court because the ordinance did not specify what the funds collected would be used for.[320] The court remanded the case for a determination whether the fees were reasonable in accordance with seven factors identified in its prior decision

---

312. City of Zephyrhills v. Wood, 831 So. 2d 223 (Fla. Dist. Ct. App. 2002).

313. *Id.* at 225.

314. 631 P.2d 899 (Utah 1981).

315. *Id.* at 900-02.

316. The case was remanded, however, to determine the "reasonableness" of the fees in this case.

317. *Banberry Dev. Corp.*, 631 P.2d at 904.

318. *Id.* at 903.

319. 642 P.2d 376 (Utah 1982).

320. *Id.* at 378.

*Banberry Development Corp.*[321] The court summarized those factors to be applied in determining an equitable fee:

> (1) the cost of existing capital facilities;
> (2) the means by which those facilities have been financed;
> (3) the extent to which the properties being charged the new fees have already contributed to the cost of the existing facilities;
> (4) the extent to which they will contribute to the cost of existing capital facilities in the future;
> (5) the extent to which they should be credited for providing common facilities that the municipality has provided without charge to other properties in its service area;
> (6) extraordinary costs, if any, in serving the new property; and
> (7) the time-price differential inherent in fair comparisons of amounts paid at different times.[322]

In *Hillis Homes, Inc. v. Public Utility District No. 1 of Snohomish County,*[323] the Washington Supreme Court upheld a "general facilities charge" imposed for the purpose of funding capital improvements to the water system. There, the court held that the fee was authorized by statute, was not invalid as a tax, and was neither unreasonable, nor discriminatory, since it resulted from a classification based upon relative benefits received by each like group of customers. The general facilities charge was based on a detailed long range plan identifying facilities needed for the water system to serve anticipated new customers for the next 10 years. Based on this analysis, a series of projects were identified and the cost allocated to the new customers. A separate charge was developed for each class of customer: single-family, multi-family, commercial/industrial, and other.

> The monies collected are restricted to paying for the new customers' share of the improvements, either directly to fund the construction of the improvements or indirectly to pay for the new customers' share of the debt service of the revenue bonds.[324]

The court relied on the reasoning of *Dunedin* in concluding that the fee was not a tax, but a valid regulatory measure: "The District has exacted a connection charge from its new water system customers as part of an overall plan to regulate the use of water . . . . The fact that the connection charge necessarily imposes some burden on new customers does not make it an invalid tax."[325] The fee met the "benefit" portion of the rational nexus test because the amount of charges was calculated by using a "proportionate share analysis." The fees pay for only those improvements to the water system necessitated by the new cus-

---

321. 631 P.2d at 899.

322. *Lafferty,* 642 P.2d at 379.

323. 105 Wash. 2d 288, 714 P.2d 1163 (1986).

324. *Id.* at 295, 714 P.2d at 1167.

325. *Id.* at 299-300, 714 P.2d at 1169.

tomers, and hence will benefit them alone, and the remaining improvements are paid for by rate increases imposed on all customers.[326]

A Michigan appellate court has used logic and language much like that of the Washington court in upholding a fee charged for the extension of a sewer system by a township.[327] The township initially levied special assessments that would have totaled more than $9,000 on a parcel owned by one of the plaintiffs. A state tax review board ruled against the township on the ground that the installation of the sewers would increase the value of the affected property by far less than the amount of the assessment; on that basis, the board held that the assessment should have been limited to not more than $2,000 on the same property.[328] The township then enacted a new ordinance, establishing a sewer connection fee to be collected only from the property owners who successfully protested the special assessment.[329] The property owners then challenged the new connection fee, this time alleging that it was beyond the authority of the township and that it was simply a disguised assessment, essentially identical to the one struck down by the tax board. The court held for the township on both issues.[330]

The South Carolina Supreme Court has upheld a sewer system's "new account fee," holding that it was a legitimate charge and not a tax.[331] The Wyoming high court has also upheld a growth-related connection fee in *Coulter v.*

---

326. *Id.* at 300-01, 714 P.2d at 1170.

327. Graham v. Township of Kochville, 236 Mich. App. 141, 599 N.W.2d 793 (1999).

328. *Id.* at 143-44, 599 N.W.2d at 795.

329. *Id.* at 144-45, 599 N.W.2d at 795-96. The court described the fee system this way:

> The ordinance applied only to the affected property owners who had appealed the amount of the special assessment and to possible future owners of property not yet developed in the district. The fee was in the amount of $9,187.50, less any part of the $9,187.50 previously paid pursuant to the special assessment. Apparently, this fee would cover the cost of construction, engineering, testing, and administration costs of the system over twenty years, which is the "useful life of the watermain." The fees are assessed according to the individual measurements of each parcel of land with access to the watermain and the use of the land.

> *Id.*

330. *Id.* at 152-53, 599 N.W.2d at 799-80.

331. J.K. Constr., Inc. v. Western Carolina Reg'l Sewer Auth., 336 S.C. 162, 519 S.E.2d 561 (1999). Appellant paid, under protest, a "new account fee" imposed by respondent sewer authority. Appellant then brought a declaratory judgment action, challenging the validity of the fee and asking the circuit court to enjoin respondent from imposing the fee and order respondent to reimburse everyone who had paid the fee. The circuit court's master-in-equity granted respondent's motion for summary judgment. The South Carolina Supreme Court affirmed, holding that the required payment was a charge, not a tax, and respondent had uniformly imposed the charge upon those who were required to pay it. Moreover, the court held that the new account fee did not violate the Equal Protection Clause, because the classification was reasonably related to the legislative purpose to be achieved.

*City of Rawlins.*[332] Population projections indicated a dramatic increase in growth necessitating increased demand for city services such as water, sewer, and park facilities. The city enacted impact fee ordinances to offset the projected demand, pursuant to the city plan. The ordinances required that fees collected must be deposited to a sewer or water development fund, and expended only for the purpose of paying sewer or water development debt service.[333] The court held that the fees were (1) authorized by enabling legislation, (2) were not invalid taxes (relying on *Dunedin*), and (3) were "reasonable." Addressing the reasonableness or rational nexus issue, the court said:

> Such charges are earmarked for the specific purpose of assisting Rawlins in the payment of Rawlins' bonded indebtedness which has been in response to a continuing need to update its water and sewerage disposal system. Water and sewer line connection charges are a fair and reasonable means for the City to offset the impact placed on its system by the influx of new users.[334]

In *Amherst Builders*,[335] the Ohio Supreme Court upheld a similar ordinance. "In attempting to equalize the burden of the cost of constructing an adequate sewage system between present users and new users, a municipality . . . may impose upon new users a tap-in or connection fee which bears a reasonable relationship to the entire cost of providing service to those users."[336] The ordinance imposed a tap-in charge upon anyone desiring to connect to the city sewage system. A schedule of fees was based on average sewage flow for various types of structures, as estimated by EPA, resulting in a charge of $400 for single-family homes.[337] The court interpreted Ohio's state constitution broadly to find authorization for a municipality to impose "connection" fees to fund capital improvements to the city sewer system, stating[338]:

> It is well-settled that Section 4, Article XVIII, grants a municipality broad power to own and operate public utilities, and that a municipal sewage system is a type of "public utility" by that constitutional provision. There can be no doubt that, in order to exercise that power, a municipality must be able to impose charges upon the users of the system to defray the costs of both its construction and operation. . . . When this unimproved land is developed, the tap-in charge is imposed so that these new users will now assume a fair share of the original construction costs, thereby reimbursing the community for the previous benefit received.[339]

The court also found that the fees were substantially related to the entire cost of providing sewer service to the new user, because the fee charged was far less

---

332. 662 P.2d 888 (Wyo. 1983).

333. *Id.* at 890-93.

334. *Id.* at 900.

335. 61 Ohio St. 2d at 345, 402 N.E.2d at 1181.

336. *Id.* at 346, 402 N.E.2d at 1182.

337. *Id.*

338. *Id.* at 345, 402 N.E.2d at 1181.

339. *Id.* at 347, 402 N.E.2d at 1183.

than the cost of facilities required to serve each new user of the system.[340] Thus, the fees met the rational nexus test by adequately benefitting the fee payers. The *Amherst Builders* court distinguished an earlier case, *Waterbury Development Co. v. Witten,*[341] which invalidated a water connection fee as a tax because the ordinance did not provide for earmarking of the funds. The court found that, "[t]he fees collected pursuant to Ordinance 913.07 are earmarked specifically for a Sewer Revenue Fund, while the tap-in fees in *Waterbury* were not so earmarked for use."[342]

Relying on *Amherst Builders,* the Ohio Court of Appeals in *Haymes v. Holzemer*[343] held that a municipality may use connection or tap-in charges to recoup costs of construction of a sewage treatment plant without assessment procedures being implemented first. However, the tap-in fee was held invalid because the enabling statute required the charge to be paid *prior* to tap-in. The court upheld the principle of using connection fees to recoup the costs of construction of a new sewer system.

As in *Amherst Builders,* earmarking of funds was the issue in *Hayes v. City of Albany,*[344] challenging a city ordinance providing for sewer connection charges to be used for the construction and expansion of the city sewer system. The ordinance survived a challenge that it was an illegal tax because it properly limited the use of funds. The Oregon Court of Appeals relied on a section of the ordinance requiring all funds to be deposited in a "Sanitary Sewer Capital Reserve Fund," and limited expenditures to specific uses tied directly to the development and maintenance of the sewer system.[345] Thus, the ordinance ensured that the fees "can be used only in furtherance of the specified purposes and cannot be diverted to general public uses."[346]

In *Home Builders Ass'n of Greater Salt Lake v. Provo City,*[347] the Utah Supreme Court held that a sewer connection fee imposed to improve and enlarge the sewer system was a reasonable charge for use of the system and within the city's power to exact. The funds obtained were restricted to the enlargement, improvement, and operation of the sewer system and to the retirement of indebtedness incurred in its construction.[348] The court distinguished an earlier decision, *Weber Basin Home Builders Ass'n v. Roy City,*[349] in which the court invalidated a city ordinance increasing the cost of building permits from $12 to $112. In *Weber,* the city claimed that the increase was necessary to improve the

---

340. *Id.* at 349, 402 N.E.2d at 1184.

341. 54 Ohio St. 2d 412, 377 N.E.2d 505 (1978).

342. *Amherst Builders,* 61 Ohio St. 2d at 347 n.2, 402 N.E.2d at 1183 n.2.

343. 3 Ohio App. 3d 377, 445 N.E.2d 681 (1981).

344. 7 Or. App. 277, 490 P.2d 1018 (1971).

345. *Id.* at 281, 490 P.2d at 1020.

346. *Id.*

347. 28 Utah 2d 402, 503 P.2d 451 (1972).

348. *Id.*

349. 26 Utah 2d 215, 487 P.2d 866 (1971).

water and sewer system because of the construction of new homes; however, the fees collected went into the general fund. Thus, there was the danger that the funds might be used for purposes wholly unrelated to the purpose of the charge. In contrast, stated the court in *Provo City*, the charge in the instant case "is for a service rendered and not a revenue measure."[350]

Promptness pays in seeking relief from water taxes masquerading as impact fees. For example, in Rhode Island, plaintiffs who had been required to pay a water connection fee sued the city for recovery of the fees, which they depicted as illegal taxes.[351] The ordinance required a tapping fee, in addition to other water-connection fees, before any connection to the city's water main. Landowners paid the additional charges for six years, until the Public Utilities Commission found the fees to be illegal. At that point a class of plaintiffs sued to get back its money, but the trial court found that because plaintiffs had voluntarily paid the fees, no recovery was possible. On appeal, the state supreme court found that even if the tapping fee was a tax, their claims were time barred by a statute giving people 90 days or 3 months from the last payment's due date to file for recovery.[352]

In *City of Arvada v. City & County of Denver*,[353] the Colorado Supreme Court held that the city was authorized to enact an ordinance imposing a "development fee" on all new users connecting into the city water system for the purposes of future development. The court relied on enabling legislation giving municipalities the power to collect from users any rates, fees, or charges for services furnished in connection with water facilities[354]:

> While the imposition of a development fee as such is not authorized in this section, we hold that such a charge is within the general contemplation of this broadly worded statute ... these provisions reveal that the General Assembly intended to give municipalities broad, general powers to construct, improve and extend all the facilities necessary to operate a viable water system, and that this power includes authorization to accumulate a fund for future development.[355]

Relying on the rationale of *Arvada*, the Colorado Supreme Court upheld the constitutionality of a municipal ordinance imposing "facilities development fees" as a condition to connection with the sewer system.[356] The plaintiffs, owners of apartment buildings, challenged the ordinance as an invalid tax and a violation of equal protection since it required only new customers to pay the fees. The court held that since new connections are more directly related to the

---

350. 28 Utah 2d at 405, 503 P.2d at 452.

351. Paul v. City of Woonsocket, 745 A.2d 169 (R.I. 2000).

352. *Id.* at 170.

353. 663 P.2d 611 (Colo. 1983).

354. *Id.* at 614.

355. *Id.* at 615.

356. Loup-Miller Constr. Co. v. City & County of Denver, 676 P.2d 1170 (Colo. 1984). For a later case reaching the same conclusion, see Krupp v. Breckenridge Sanitation Dist., 19 P.3d 687 (Colo. 2001).

need for increased capacity than old connections, there is a rational basis for the distinction made by the ordinance.[357] Therefore, the court held that the ordinance did not impose taxes, but set fees, authorized by statute.[358]

In *Harbours Pointe of Nahotah, Ltd. Liability Corp. v. Village of Nahotah*,[359] a village entered into an agreement with the operators of the regional system, and attempted to levy assessments on every plot of land in the village to fund the project. After a public hearing, the assessments for the project began in 1980. The entire project had been paid for by 1996, but the assessments continued against new buyers. Harbours Pointe, a new purchaser, entered into a development agreement that it would pay for whatever percentage of the sewage system benefitted that property. Almost one-half of that payment went toward the 1980 reserve capacity assessment, for which the village had already collected sufficient funds, so the developer filed suit for compensation under 42 U.S.C. §1983. The U.S. Court of Appeals for the Seventh Circuit found that Harbours Pointe did not avail itself of state remedies supplied by a Wisconsin statute that allows property owners to contest just this sort of situation.[360] Therefore, the court found that plaintiffs had forfeited their rights to a remedy by not pursuing the state remedies.[361] Plaintiffs also were time barred from a new attempt because of their two-year delay in filing any complaint.[362]

In *Home Builders Ass'n of Central Arizona v. City of Scottsdale*,[363] the city imposed a "water resource development fee" as a condition to issuance of a building permit. The fee was for the purpose of providing water to the specific development. The court first addressed whether the fees were a tax and, therefore, not subject to the Takings Clause, or a regulatory fee that must meet the *Dolan* essential nexus test.[364] The court likened the development fee to a land use regulation, and concluded that the fees were subject to the Takings Clause.[365] However, the court concluded that because the fees involved a legis-

---

357. *Loup-Miller Constr. Co.*, 676 P.2d at 1174-75.

358. *Id.* at 1175-76; *see also City of Arvada*, 663 P.2d at 615.

359. 278 F.3d 701, 32 ELR 20421 (7th Cir. 2002).

360. *Id.* at 705, 32 ELR at 20422 (quoting WIS. STAT. §66.60(11)):

> [I]f the cost of the project shall be less than the special assessments levied, the governing body . . . shall reduce each special assessment proportionately and where any assessments . . . have been paid the excess over cost shall be applied to reduce succeeding unpaid installments . . . or refunded to the property owner.

361. *Id.* at 706, 32 ELR at 20422.

362. *Id.*

363. 902 P.2d 1347 (Ariz. Ct. App. 1995).

364. *Id.* at 1350.

365. *Id.*

lative, rather than adjudicative, determination, *Dolan* did not control the case, and therefore upheld the fees as a valid land use regulation.[366]

Largely following the analysis in *Ehrlich*, a Colorado court ruled a legislatively created wastewater impact fee on all building projects within a district not subject to *Nollan/Dolan* heightened scrutiny.[367] Several ski resorts, river drainage, and a large reservoir serving much of Denver are included in the wastewater district's area, for which the district assesses connection fees, monthly usage fees, and plant investment fees (PIFs). PIFs are one-time fees put toward any necessary expansion of the treatment service and must be paid before a building permit issues. The district determines the PIFs by calculating the estimated peak flow from the new building and then using a set formula for the rate incurred by that particular project, therefore making the fees neither individual nor discretionary, potentially taking them out of the *Nollan/Dolan* analysis.[368] Different rates apply to different types of buildings.

The service fee was intended to defray service costs, and the individual fee was proportionally related to the cost of the service.[369] Also, citing to *Del Monte Dunes*,[370] Colorado's Supreme Court clarified that "a *Nollan/Dolan* analysis is appropriate in the narrow circumstance where the government conditions development on the forfeiture of private property for public use."[371] The court allowed that "a very narrow class of purely monetary exactions" could be subjected to *Nollan/Dolan* analysis, but did not find that PIFs fit in that class because the PIFs are created legislatively and are generally applicable to any developer.[372]

Because water and sewer systems are typically operated as enterprises or proprietary departments, the courts may have less difficulty in recognizing the charges as fees rather than taxes. A California court has squarely held that connection fees payable to a water district are not subject to the refund provisions of California's Act on "development fees."[373]

A state appellate court upheld a town's right to collect water and sewer connection fees from builders at the permitting stage.[374] Town ordinances required one-time tap-in charges to new customers for water and sewer use and improve-

---

366. *Id.* at 1352. This decision was later upheld by the Arizona Supreme Court in Home Builders Ass'n of Cent. Ariz. v. City of Scottsdale, 187 Ariz. 479, 930 P.2d 993 (Ariz. 1997). *Accord* Krupp v. Breckenridge Sanitation Dist., 19 P.3d 687 (Colo. 2001).

367. *See* Krupp v. Breckenridge Sanitation Dist., 19 P.3d 687 (Colo. 2001).

368. *Id.* at 695-96.

369. *Id.* at 693-94.

370. 526 U.S. at 687, 119 S. Ct. at 1624, 143 L. Ed. 2d at 882, 29 ELR at 21133.

371. *Krupp*, 19 P.3d at 697.

372. *Id.* at 698.

373. Capistrano Beach Water Dist. v. Taj Dev. Corp., 72 Cal. App. 4th 524, 85 Cal. Rptr. 2d 382 (1999). The act interpreted in the case was the Mitigation Fee Act, CAL. GOV'T CODE §66000.

374. Burke v. Town of Shererville, 739 N.E.2d 1086 (Ind. Ct. App. 2000).

ments, including both a flat fee and a fee based on a proportionate capacity share of necessary extensions and expansions for new users. Builders argued that the town had enacted illegal impact fees that shifted the cost of services from general tax collection to new developments.[375] The town countered that the state legislature allowed them to charge sewer and water connection fees without enacting specific impact fee enabling ordinances, and that these charges were not impact fees because they applied to all new customers, not just new developments.[376] The court found that the town had followed appropriate avenues to charge these fees, and upheld the town's right to do so.[377]

Likewise, the South Carolina Supreme Court found water and sewer district fees were not taxes, but simply charges for services rendered.[378] Here, a district had agreed to build, operate, and maintain a public water and a sewer system, and charged for those services.[379] Upon connecting to the system, and as a condition for obtaining permits to build septic tanks, plaintiffs were charged impact and connection fees, which they contended were taxes.[380] The appellate court disagreed because the fees were specific to the services rendered.[381]

On the other hand, a state appellate court found that a municipal water authority's attempt to add water source and storage fees to the regular tap-in, turn-on fees for two new office buildings in order to pay for water infrastructure improvements for everyone was an invalid state tax.[382] Because the fees did not relate to any particular benefit for the commercial buildings themselves, or represent the cost of any particular impact on the water system from the buildings, and because the fees were only charged to newcomers but benefitted the whole community by improving the whole water district's system, the charges were really a tax.[383]

Remedies involving credits and refunds are often a matter of some complexity. To pay for water utility expansion, a Texas town enacted an ordinance charging all new water and sewer customers a one-time impact fee to the com-

---

375. *Id.* at 1089.

376. *Id.* The town argued, and the court agreed, that the Municipal Sewage Works Act (IC 36-9-23-25) grants municipalities broad discretion to establish sewer fees, preempting the Home Rule Statute and the Indiana Impact Fee Statute. The court also found that the Municipal Sewage Works Act contained an exclusive statutory procedure for objecting to the sewage connection charges, with which the builders did not comply. *Id.* at 1090.

377. *Id.* at 1092.

378. Ford v. Georgetown County Water & Sewer Dist., 341 S.C. 10, 532 S.E.2d 873 (2000).

379. *Id.* at 12, 532 S.E.2d at 874.

380. *Id.* at 13, 532 S.E.2d at 875.

381. *Id.*

382. Phillips v. Town of Clifton Park Water Auth., 730 N.Y.S.2d 565, 286 A.D.2d 834 (2001).

383. *Id.* at 567, 286 A.D.2d at 835.

munity upon connection of a subdivision to the city water and wastewater lines.[384] A developer helped pay to construct the three required connecting lines for a phase one subdivision, and then requested and received a refund from the impact fee reflecting the connection fees payment.[385] After the second phase, he made the same request, but the city refused to pay cash, offering instead a credit toward "future fees," apparently of no use to the developer as this second phase was the final one. The court remanded the case for more facts about the construction of each connector line, which normally would have been paid for by an impact fee in the form of a line of credit created by the developer.[386]

In another case of paying attention to details that come with traditionally accepted impact fees, a state supreme court found that a city ordinance requiring a water connection fee (tapping fee) may have been illegal, but the plaintiffs lost their chance to collect because the statute of limitations barred them.[387] The mandatory tapping fee had to be paid before the city would connect to the development and supply water, and the plaintiffs paid without protest. While the city had the right to make such a law, it did not seek or gain the required approval from the Public Utilities Commission, so the city council repealed the law, and plaintiffs sought to be reimbursed. The council reimbursed all who applied for reimbursement within the statutory period, but the plaintiffs had missed the deadline, which ended three years after each individual paid their fee, and the court saw no reason to bend the rules.[388]

Not all such fees go to support water and sewer "hardware." In Hawaii, water use fees include a pro rata charge toward studying and monitoring the streams from which water is diverted.[389] Because the studies helped the plaintiffs by letting them continue to use the water, aiding them in their quest for proof that diverting the water was not causing harm, and by giving information to the public as a whole, the court found that plaintiffs should pay their share for that benefit.[390] The court noted that the money is directly allocated to the studies, although no determination could be made about the proportionality of the fees because the studies had not yet begun, nor had the calculations for the fees been determined.[391] Thus, the court held that conditioning the permits on compliance with the paying of the study fees was neither an illegal taking nor an illegal tax, and the court reserved the right to decide on the proportionality of the fee until after the fee schedule had been created.[392]

---

384. *See* Jamail v. City of Cedar Park, No. 03-00-00795-CV, 2001 WL 726475 (Tex. App. June 29, 2001).

385. *Id.* at *1.

386. *Id.* at *4-*6.

387. Paul v. City of Woonsocket, 745 A.2d 169 (R.I. 2000).

388. *Id.* at 172.

389. In the Matter of the Water Use Permit Application, 94 Haw. 97, 184, 9 P.3d 409, 496 (2000).

390. *Id.* at 185, 9 P.3d at 497.

391. *Id.*

392. *Id.* at 186, 9 P.3d at 498.

## II. LAND DEVELOPMENT CONDITIONS

In sum, fees imposed on new development to fund capital improvements for water and sewer systems are widely accepted. Many communities continue to refer to such fees as "system development charges" or something similar, generally distinguishing them both from the plumbing and inspection fees charged for physical connection to the system (often called "tap" or connection fees or charges) and from impact or development fees imposed under more general regulatory authority. Most courts have had no difficulty in finding either express or implied authority for municipalities to impose such capital fees for water and sewer system capital facilities. This is probably because these areas have traditionally been regulated by local government, and most states have statutes empowering their municipalities to regulate their water and sewer systems.

### 3. Housing

There is some authority for the use of set-asides and other housing exactions and fees to provide needed low-income housing,[393] but whether this is a sufficient basis for nexus, let alone proportionality, to stave off a constitutional challenge, is not clear. Some flavor for the issues is derived from New Jersey cases suggesting that mandatory set-asides are constitutional under certain circumstances.

In *Southern Burlington County National Ass'n for the Advancement of Colored People v. Mount Laurel*,[394] builders attempted to remove the restrictive land controls of a recalcitrant municipality, which excluded the building of low- and moderate-income housing. The New Jersey Supreme Court held that a zoning ordinance which excluded lower income people from housing was unconstitutional because this violated the municipality's mandate to affirmatively afford a realistic opportunity for the construction of its fair share of low- and moderate-income housing. If local governments cannot meet their fair share requirement after removing all zoning restrictions and exactions that are not necessary to protect health and safety, a local government must then adopt mandatory set-asides to meet its constitutional obligations.[395] The court in dicta stated that municipalities who could not satisfy their "obligation" by removing restrictive zoning laws had the authority to require mandatory set-asides and density bonuses tied to lower income housing.[396] The court reasoned that the exercise of zoning power "directly tied to the physical use of the property," as opposed to the exercise of zoning power tied to income of those who used the property, was artificial.[397] Since all zoning has potentially significant "socioeconomic impacts," why not let the municipality do directly what it can do indirectly?[398]

---

393. *See* Linda Bozung, *A Positive Response to Growth Control Plans: The Orange County Inclusionary Housing Program*, 9 Pepp. L. Rev. 819 (1982); Bosselman & Stroud, *Mandatory Tithes, supra* note 3, at 405.

394. 92 N.J. 158, 456 A.2d 390 (1983).

395. *Id.* at 258, 267-68, 456 A.2d at 441, 446.

396. *Id.* at 271, 456 A.2d at 448.

397. *Id.*

398. *Id.*

This case was shortly followed by *In re Egg Harbor Associates*,[399] upholding the principle of mandatory set-asides. The New Jersey Department of Environmental Protection (DEP) conditioned its approval of a new development, which included 1,530 units, a 500-room hotel, a 300-slip marina, 22-story office building, and 4,200 parking spaces within a coastal zone upon the setting aside of 10% of the residential units for low-income housing and 10% for moderate-income housing. The court held that these requirements were neither arbitrary nor unreasonable.

*Egg Harbor* represents an example of the *Mount Laurel* mandate that municipalities have an affirmative duty to use their police power to create housing for the poor. This obligation is predicated upon the proposition that government controls all land for the health, safety, and welfare of the public. Since housing is a fundamental right in New Jersey and the poor are an element of society, the municipalities may use their police power to promote the building of housing for the poor.

Two experts cautiously predict that housing linkage programs will be upheld under the rational nexus test.[400] They recognize that the key issue is whether commercial development causes the need for new housing. Linkage programs are justified by the argument that new commercial development creates jobs. This attracts new residents to the area, increasing the demand for housing, which increases the price of housing, creating a need for low- and moderate-income housing.

Inclusionary housing requirements generally mean that a developer must provide a percentage of new homes for low- to moderate-income households. Such requirements are enacted because not enough affordable housing exists in the area and/or to counteract perceived and real exclusionary zoning practices. Communities provide inclusionary housing by requiring developers to create a percentage of rentals, low-priced sale units, off-site land dedication, off-site units, or in lieu fees. Common provisions include 10% to 15% of market-rate units being provided for low- to medium-income housing; small projects getting exemptions; on-site units or off-site units or land meeting the requirement; set unit size, type, price, location, timing, and long-term affordability; and in lieu fees, calculations of which vary.

Dozens of California counties and cities have enacted ordinances that allow for inclusionary housing. These ordinances are based on statutes explaining that "the development of a sufficient supply of housing to meet the needs of all Californians is a matter of statewide concern"[401] and that local governments have "a responsibility to use the powers vested in them to facilitate the improvement and development of housing to make adequate provision for the housing needs of all economic segments of the community."[402]

---

399. 94 N.J. 358, 464 A.2d 1115 (1983).

400. Bosselman & Stroud, *Mandatory Tithes*, *supra* note 3, at 411.

401. CAL. GOV'T CODE §65913.9.

402. *Id.* §65580(d).

## II. LAND DEVELOPMENT CONDITIONS

One such case upholding housing linkage fees is *Commercial Builders of Northern California*.[403] The city of Sacramento enacted a city ordinance conditioning certain nonresidential building permits on the payment of a fee to offset the burdens caused by low-income workers who were likely to move to the city to work at the commercial development. Commercial Builders challenged the ordinance, claiming that the fee was an uncompensated taking. The court upheld the ordinance, holding that the city had satisfied the essential nexus test under *Nollan* because the fee was designed to further the city's legitimate interest in housing low-income workers. The dissent, however, argued that the fees had little relationship to the impact of commercial development. The dissent further noted that if the fee imposed was sufficiently connected to the development, other more tenuously connected fees will also be upheld, such as exactions to subsidize small businesses, child care centers, food services, and health-care delivery systems.

In *Home Builders Ass'n of Northern California v. City of Napa*,[404] a California appellate court upheld a 10% inclusionary housing plan, saying that such a plan would only be facially invalid if it did not allow administrators to avoid unconstitutional applications.[405] Napa's City Council adopted its Inclusionary Ordinance in 1999 because Napa's Rural Urban Limit had created a limit on developable land, increasing land prices and creating what the city saw as an affordable housing crisis. Under the ordinance, 10% of all new residential dwellings must be affordable.[406] The ordinance provides for "alternative equivalents": land dedication, units off-site, or an in lieu fee.[407] Any in lieu fees go into a Housing Trust Fund that can only be used to increase and improve the affordable housing supply. The Napa City Council also created incentives for developers who met the 10% inclusionary requirement, giving them expedited processing, deferrals of fee payments, marketing help, waiver of expensive building standards, and density bonuses. Although Napa's inclusionary zoning ordinance was burdensome, the court found that the benefits created a safety valve for developers. Thus, there was no facial taking.[408] The court also found that providing affordable housing was a legitimate state interest, substantially advanced by the ordinance.[409]

---

403. 941 F.2d at 872.

404. 108 Cal. Rptr. 2d 60, 90 Cal. App. 4th 188 (Cal. App. 2001).

405. *Id.* at 64, 90 Cal. App. 4th at 194 (stating: "Here, City's inclusionary zoning ordinance imposes significant burdens on those who wish to develop their property. However the ordinance also provides significant benefits to those who comply with its terms.").

406. NAPA, CALIFORNIA, MUNICIPAL CODE ch. 15.94, *available at* http://www.cityofnapa.org/MunicipalCode/Default.htm (last visited Feb. 18, 2003).

407. *City of Napa*, 108 Cal. Rptr. 2d at 63, 90 Cal. App. 4th at 192.

408. *Id.* at 64, 90 Cal. App. 4th at 194.

409. *Id.* at 65, 90 Cal. App. 4th at 195-96.

In a related development, some local governments have found the need to balance local resident housing with tourist accommodation. To prevent negative impacts on communities from the displacement of those requiring low- and moderate-income housing, some cities, like San Francisco, have enacted ordinances to maintain a fixed percentage of such housing. In *San Remo Hotel Ltd. Partnership v. City & County of San Francisco*,[410] a residential hotel sought to convert all of its rooms to tourist hotel rooms but could not do so without obtaining a conditional use permit. The court found that housing replacement fees or replacement development requirements were constitutional. Because the ordinance allows for no discretion in determining whether it is applied or how to calculate the formula-based fees to a designated housing fund (if the applicant chooses to pay them instead of building a replacement housing development or sponsoring such construction), the court further found that the fees did not require the heightened scrutiny of *Nollan, Dolan,* or *Ehrlich*.[411] The court instead examined whether the legislatively enacted fees were reasonably related to the intended use and to the impact of the development, and found that they were so related to the cost of converting housing to hotels.[412]

A similar question arose in Seattle, where low-income tenants lost housing to a 1980s redevelopment market, and the state adopted enabling legislation in the 1990s to allow municipal governments to enact relocation provisions for low-income tenants ousted by demolition or redevelopment.[413] Seattle's subsequent Tenant Relocation Assistance Ordinance (TRAO) calls for landlords and the city to evenly split a $2,000 payment to displaced low-income tenants.[414] Some owners of units rented to low-income people challenged the constitutionality of the ordinance, calling it both a facial and as-applied taking.

The Ninth Circuit followed the regulatory takings analysis of *Agins*[415] in determining that the TRAO was constitutionally valid. The court found that the TRAO substantially advanced legitimate state interests, did not result in a physical invasion of property, and did not deny owners of all economically viable use of their properties.[416] Plaintiffs also did not meet their burden in proving a facial taking; they did not show that the ordinance went too far in regulating their property by proving that the ordinance diminished the value of their property so much as to have "essentially expropriated their property for public use."[417] In fact, plaintiffs did not submit evidence of any economic impact. The court also examined the case under *Nollan* and *Dolan*, finding that a $1,000 per

---

410. 27 Cal. 4th 643, 41 P.3d 87, 32 ELR Digest 20533 (Cal. 2002).

411. *Id.* at 669, 41 P.3d at 104, 32 ELR Digest at 20533.

412. *Id.* at 671, 672, 41 P.3d at 105, 106, 32 ELR Digest at 20533.

413. *See* Garneau v. City of Seattle, 147 F.3d 802, 804 (9th Cir. 1998).

414. SEATTLE, WASH., MUNICIPAL CODE 22.210.130.

415. 447 U.S. at 255, 100 S. Ct. at 2138, 65 L. Ed. 2d at 106, 10 ELR at 20361.

416. *Garneau,* 147 F.3d at 807.

417. *Id.* at 807-08.

tenant fee could not be considered a taking, and therefore found no reason to continue with the nexus or rough proportionality analysis, neither of which the court thought would come out in plaintiffs' favor anyway.[418] In a concurrence, one Justice explained that he found plaintiffs' argument completely disingenuous because the TRAO did not take any property, tangible or intangible,[419] from anyone. While he allowed that sometimes monetary charges could be takings, "[i]n the present case, however, appellants have made no showing that the TRAO either forces them to retain tenants against their wishes or disables them from using their land."[420]

The dissent argued that *Nollan* and *Dolan* are applicable because any amount, even $1,000, can be analyzed as being either proportional or not to the harm being remedied: moving costs. The dissent also stated that no harm is done by removing a tenant, because moving expenses "should come as no surprise to tenants, who, *by definition*, are legally obliged to move out eventually, perhaps involuntarily."[421] The dissenting judge notes that the landlord's right to remove a tenant falls under the "right to exclude" element of property ownership, and that by charging landlords for removing certain tenants, the TRAO "is *tantamount to* a physical occupation of land because it has the effect of depriving landowners—without just compensation—of their constitutional right to exclude."[422] The dissent pointed out that the question is whether a monetary exaction can be a taking, and, although *Nollan* and *Dolan* do not speak to that question, that does not mean the question cannot be answered.[423] The dissent would have answered yes, because the landlords receive nothing for the money they must spend. "Because the TRAO is not a 'user fee,' but rather a device for compelling landlords to bear a public burden, the TRAO cannot pass constitutional muster."[424]

## 4. Parks and Recreation

While courts have found providing open space and recreation to be valid exercises of the police power, like other impact fees, the amount of space required from the developer must be proportional to the amount required by the subsequent development. Local governments may require dedication of specific amounts of land, or in lieu fees that will be earmarked in a special fund to be used to purchase open space. Much of the litigation over exactions has involved park dedication and fee requirements, as discussed in this section. However, professional work in this field has evolved significantly in ways that are likely to affect local exaction practices.

---

418. *Id.* at 812.

419. *Id.* at 815 (Williams, J., concurring).

420. *Id.*

421. *Id.* at 818, (O'Scannlain, J., dissenting) (emphasis in original).

422. *Id.* at 818, 820 (emphasis in original).

423. *Id.* at 819.

424. *Id.* at 820.

Today, the thinking about a community's use of open space is much broader than it once was. Greenways along streams and rivers, passive open space, wildlife habitat and travel corridors, and a variety of other undeveloped lands may be significant parts of a community's overall plan for open space.[425] The focus of most of the case law and many of the local programs tested in these cases has been on achieving a "rational nexus" and "rough proportionality" between the dedication or fee requirements and the impacts of residential development. The need for greenways and general open space is one that relates to the entire community and to all types of development. There is little doubt that some communities will attempt to exact a share of the cost of such general open space from nonresidential development and, with a proper showing of nexus and proportionality, may succeed.[426]

Typical is *Hollywood Inc.*,[427] where the court held that a Broward County ordinance requiring subdividers and developers to dedicate land, or pay an in lieu fee or an impact fee to be used to acquire more park lands, was a reasonable exercise of the police power. Although the county charter did not specifically authorize the county to levy an impact fee for the expansion of parks, the court construed the charter liberally, holding that the county commission had the authority to impose an impact fee derived from the platting ordinance.[428] Among the factors that led the court to uphold the validity of the park impact fee were that the cost of the proposed park land exceeded the amount generated by the ordinance, and the funds would be used to acquire new parks or improve existing parks within 15 miles of the development that paid the exaction.[429]

Since impact fees evolved from the dedication requirements and in lieu fees by serving the same purpose, the rationales generally supporting a dedication requirement or in lieu fee thereof, for the purpose of acquiring park land or playgrounds as a condition to development, support the levying of an impact fee.[430] Courts have rejected both the "specifically attributable test" and the "direct benefit test" in measuring the reasonableness of a municipality's requiring park and recreation exactions from developing under the police power. In the landmark case of *Jordan v. Village of Menomonee Falls*,[431] the court upheld the

---

425. *See* JAMES D. MERTES & JAMES R. HALL, PARK, RECREATION, OPEN SPACE, AND GREENWAY GUIDELINES (National Recreation & Park Ass'n, 1996); ERIC DAMIAN KELLY & BARBARA BECKER, COMMUNITY PLANNING: AN INTRODUCTION TO THE COMPREHENSIVE PLAN ch. XX (Island Press 1999).

426. Note that one of the critical issues in Dolan v. City of Tigard, 512 U.S. 374, 114 S. Ct. 2309, 129 L. Ed. 2d 304, 24 ELR 21083 (1994), was a requirement for the dedication and improvement of a greenway along a creek and a related trail.

427. 431 So. 2d at 606.

428. *Id.* at 606, 609-10.

429. *Id.* at 606, 612.

430. *See* JAMES C. NICHOLAS, THE CHANGING STRUCTURE OF INFRASTRUCTURE FINANCE 23, 42 (Lincoln Institute of Land Policy, Monograph No. 85-5, 1985).

431. 28 Wis. 2d 608, 137 N.W.2d 442 (1965).

payment of a $5,000 in lieu fee that would be used to acquire lands for schools, parks, and recreational areas, by stating:

> We conclude that a required dedication of land for school, park or recreational sites as a condition for approval of the subdivision plat should be upheld as a valid exercise of police power if the evidence reasonably establishes that the municipality will be required to provide more land for schools, parks and playgrounds as a result of approval of the subdivision.[432]

The *Jordan* court challenged the logic of a more restrictive (and largely disregarded) Illinois decision:

> We deem this to be an acceptable statement of the yardstick to be applied, provided the words "specifically and uniquely attributable to his activity" are not so restrictively applied as to cast an unreasonable burden of proof upon the municipality which has enacted the ordinance under attack. In most instances it would be impossible for the municipality to prove that the land required to be dedicated for a park or a school site was to meet a need solely attributable to the anticipated influx of people into the community to occupy this particular subdivision. On the other hand, the municipality might well be able to establish that a group of subdivisions approved over a period of several years had been responsible for bringing into the community a considerable number of people making it necessary that the land dedications required of the subdividers be utilized for school, park and recreational purposes for the benefit of such influx. In the absence of contravening evidence this would establish a reasonable basis for finding that the need for the acquisition was occasioned by the activity of the subdivider. Possible contravening evidence would be a showing that the municipality prior to the opening up of the subdivisions, acquired sufficient lands for school park and recreational purposes to provide for future anticipated needs including such influx, or that the normal growth of the municipality would have made necessary the acquisition irrespective of the influx caused by opening up of subdivisions...
> * * *
> We do not consider the fact that other residents of the village as well as residents of the subdivision may make use of a public site required to be dedicated by subdivider for school, park or recreational purposes is particularly material to the constitutional issue. This is particularly true for land required to be dedicated for public street purposes.[433]

In *Aunt Hack Ridge Estates, Inc. v. Planning Commission*,[434] the court upheld as a valid exercise of the police power the city planning commission's regulation, which required a subdivider to dedicate no more than 4% of the total area of proposed subdivision, but not less than 10,000 square feet, as a prerequisite to plan approval.[435] A number of jurisdictions have established formulas to determine the dedication or in lieu fee requirements in exchange for residential development approval. In *Coulter*,[436] the court held that the city's authority to require the dedication of 6 acres per 1,000 people in the subdivision or in lieu

---

432. *Id.* at 618, 137 N.W.2d at 448.

433. *Id.* at 617-19, 137 N.W.2d at 447-48.

434. 160 Conn. 109, 273 A.2d 880 (1970).

435. *Id.* at 111, 273 A.2d at 886.

436. 662 P.2d at 888.

fees thereof was implied from state enabling legislation.[437] "Direct benefit," according to this court, was overcome by earmarking the funds: "The limitation on this power is the requirement that any fees collected in lieu of raw land dedication must be earmarked to accounts for the purposes of acquiring needed park land and maintenance of existing park facilities."[438]

Other courts have held that if a county has the power to reject a plat because of the inadequacy of park and recreational space, a county has the power to levy a fee in lieu of dedication. In *Jenad Inc. v. Village of Scarsdale*,[439] the New York Court of Appeals held that the planning board's requirement that a subdivider dedicate land within the subdivision for a park or pay a fee in lieu of such dedication was a valid exercise of the police power. The court rejected the argument that the fees were a tax, and analogized them to a type of zoning, like setback and side yard regulations. If counties have the power to zone lands for recreational purposes, they certainly should have the power to exact fees to accomplish the same purpose. As the court stated:

> This is not a tax at all but a reasonable form of village planning for the general community good . . . . This was merely a kind of zoning, like setback and side yard-regulations, minimum size lots, etc., and akin also to other reasonable requirements necessary sewers, water mains, lights, sidewalks, etc. If the developer did not provide for parks . . . the municipality would have to do it.[440]

Jenad's rationale supports the general proposition that the authority to enact an impact fee springs from the discretion to deny subdivision approval, unless parks were suitably located. The power to restrict includes the power to compel:

> We find in section 179-1 of the Village Law a sufficient grant to villages of power to make such exactions. In specific terms the statute validates "in proper case" requirements by village planning boards that a subdivision map, to obtain approval, must show "a park or parks suitably located for playground and recreational purposes." There is, to be sure, no such specificity as to a village rule setting up a "money in lieu of land system." However, section 179-1 says that a village planning board, when specific circumstances of a particular plat are such that park lands therein are not requisite, may "waive" provisions therefor, "subject to appropriate conditions and guarantees."[441]

Noting that California courts have repeatedly declared development to be a privilege, not a right, the court in *Associated Home Builders of the Greater Eastbay v. City of Walnut Creek*[442] upheld a state statute permitting cities to enact ordinances requiring the dedication of land or payment of fees for park and recreational purposes.[443] To validly attach the dedication or fees as a condition

---

437. *Id.* at 893, 901.

438. *Id.*

439. 18 N.Y.2d 78, 218 N.E.2d 673 (1966).

440. *Id.* at 84, 218 N.E.2d at 676.

441. *Id.* at 83, 218 N.E.2d at 675.

442. 4 Cal. 3d 633, 484 P.2d 606, 1 ELR 20223 (1971).

443. Currently codified at CAL. GOV'T CODE §66477.

to the approval of a subdivision map, however, the land or fees must be used only for the purpose of developing new or rehabilitating existing park or recreational facilities to serve the subdivision, and the amount and location of land to be dedicated or amount of fees paid must bear a reasonable relationship to the use of the park and recreational facilities by future inhabitants of the subdivision.[444] The dedication or fees are justified if the resulting facilities are generally, but not exclusively, available to those inhabitants.[445]

Finally, in *Cimarron Corp. v. Board of County Commissioners*,[446] the court held that the city could require the dedication or payment of an in lieu fee "when such are reasonably necessary to serve the proposed subdivision *and the future residents thereof*."[447] This approach was followed in *Messer v. Town of Chapel Hill*,[448] which held that "[the] selection of a location for a recreational area as a condition of approving plaintiff's subdivision plan was a valid exercise of its police power."[449] The court noted that the ordinance did not rely upon an arbitrary percentage, which other courts have found objectionable.[450]

Traditionally, in lieu fees were limited to those dedication requirements predicated on the subdivision code. Consequently, developments that do not require the subdivision of land have traditionally escaped such subdivision exactions.[451] Recently, however, in lieu fees for park land have even been extended to apartment buildings. In *Black v. City of Waukesha*,[452] the court held that the city was authorized to condition the securing of a building permit upon the payment of in lieu park fees, after the city agreed to rezone the property from a business to residential use.[453] In reaching its result, the court rejected the argument that the zoning ordinances applied only to subdivisions. The court reasoned that since the zoning ordinance tracked the platting ordinance in *Jordan*, the city had the authority by incorporating the requirement of payment of in lieu fees by reference.[454]

Dedication of park land as a prerequisite to plat approval is generally accepted by most courts. *Billings Properties, Inc. v. Yellowstone County*,[455] is noted for its expansive interpretation of the police power. The court held: "[T]he requirement that the subdivider dedicate a portion of his land for parks and playgrounds as a

---

444. *City of Walnut Creek*, 4 Cal. 3d at 637, 484 P.2d at 609-10, 1 ELR at 20224.

445. *Id.* at 640 n.5, 484 P.2d at 612 n.5, 1 ELR at 20227 n.5.

446. 193 Colo. 164, 563 P.2d 946 (1977).

447. *Id.* at 168, 563 P.2d at 948 (emphasis in original).

448. 59 N.C. App. 692, 297 S.E.2d 632 (1982).

449. *Id.* at 696, 297 S.E.2d at 635.

450. *Id.*

451. NICHOLAS, *supra* note 430.

452. 125 Wis. 2d 254, 371 N.W.2d 389 (Wis. Ct. App. 1985).

453. *Id.* at 256, 371 N.W.2d at 390-91.

454. *Id.* at 256-57, 371 N.W.2d at 391.

455. 144 Mont. 25, 394 P.2d 182 (1964).

condition precedent to approval of the plat is not an unreasonable exercise of the police power."[456] *Billings* invoked the fiction that the court granted the privilege to subdivide as a quid pro quo in exchange for the dedication requirements. "[I]t should be noted that appellant's act of attempting to secure approval of the plat was voluntary . . . . In theory at least, the owner of a subdivision voluntarily dedicates sufficient land for streets in return for the advantage and privilege of having his plat recorded."[457] Furthermore, the court rejected a distinction that the dedication of streets and alleys would be valid, as opposed to the dedication of parks and playgrounds, which are inherently different.[458]

Similarly, *City of College Station v. Turtle Rock Corp.*[459] abandoned the notion that park dedications were per se invalid. The court held the dedication requirement of one acre of land for each 133 proposed dwelling units for park purposes, or an in lieu fee if less than 133 units are proposed, as a condition to plat approval, was not unconstitutionally arbitrary on its face.[460] While the case was remanded to the lower court for trial with instructions to apply the diminution of value test to the issue of whether there had been a taking, the Texas Supreme Court would likely reverse, since in dicta the court noted that the developer chose to develop, and the funds were earmarked with the limitation that they were to be spent within two years.[461]

In 1996, a California court struck down an in-lieu recreation fee imposed upon a landowner who sought an amendment to the general plan and rezoning to allow a condominium project on his lot on which he had operated a private tennis club.[462] The city conditioned approval of the requested change on the owner's paying a $280,000 recreation fee to mitigate the loss of recreational facilities in the city, as well as an art fee imposed on all new developments. The owner challenged the recreational fee, and the case made its way to the court, which remanded the case to the California appeals court in light of *Dolan*. The California court upheld the fees, holding that the fees passed the *Dolan* test, and the owner appealed to the California Supreme Court.

The California Supreme Court reversed, holding that the recreation fee was not roughly proportional to the impact of the proposed development. The court first addressed the city's contention that *Dolan* does not apply to monetary exactions and held that, when monetary exactions are imposed in an individual and discretionary manner, the heightened scrutiny of *Dolan* does apply. The court then applied the dual-pronged test from *Nollan/Dolan*, holding that, although the city had a legitimate state interest in imposing a recreational fee, and

456. *Id.* at 32, 394 P.2d at 186.

457. *Id.* at 33, 394 P.2d at 187 (quoting Ridgefield Land Co. v. City of Detroit, 241 Mich. 468, 472, 217 N.W. 58, 59 (1928)).

458. *Id.*

459. 680 S.W.2d 802 (Tex. 1984).

460. *Id.* at 804, 806.

461. *Id.*

462. Ehrlich v. City of Culver, 911 P.2d 429 (Cal. 1996).

the fee itself was related to the loss of recreational facilities by the new development, the amount of the fee failed to be proportional to the development's impact. Under *Dolan*, the fee was an uncompensated taking.

Relying on principles of state law, a Washington appellate court has reached a conclusion similar to that in *Ehrlich* in striking down a land dedication requirement while upholding a separate exaction requiring that the developer of the project construct a secondary access road.[463] The court made this distinction:

> Because there is no evidence that the set-aside ordinance is roughly proportional to the impact of the proposed development, we agree that it is constitutionally defective. But the record does indicate that legitimate fire safety concerns led to the road requirement and that the road is reasonably necessary for public safety. Further, the developer failed to show that the requirement is unduly oppressive. Thus, this requirement violates neither the constitution nor statute.[464]

In a "clarification" to the opinion, issued together with a denial of a motion for reconsideration, the court held that the requirement for the transfer of open space "to the subdivision homeowner's association to meet the general public's perceived need for open space" was an exaction subject to the application of the *Nollan/Dolan* tests.[465] Similarly, the Washington Court of Appeals has applied the "rough proportionality" test in striking down an open space set-aside ordinance that required that a developer reserve 30% of its site as open space.[466]

In Ohio, an improvement fee for creation or improvement of park and recreation facilities was found to be an unconstitutional tax because the burden fell solely on developers and purchasers of new construction, with current residents gaining the benefits but paying nothing.[467] The Ohio appellate court held that the charge was not for a specific service provided by the government, but to help support the government in providing public services.[468] The Ohio Supreme Court reversed, remanding it to be examined in light of the newly decided *Home Builders Ass'n of Dayton & the Miami Valley v. City of Beavercreek*.[469] The latter case had upheld a local road impact fee, noting a local government's inherent ability to enact an impact fee ordinance, and reversing the appellate court's application of the tax/fee distinction, which had been similar to the appellate court analysis in the instant case.[470]

---

463. *Isla Verde Int'l Holdings v. City of Camas*, 99 Wash. App. 127, 990 P.2d 429 (1999).

464. *Id.* at 129-30, 990 P.2d at 432.

465. *Isla Verde Int'l Holdings*, 99 Wash. App. at 127, 990 P.2d at 429.

466. *Id.* at 132, 990 P.2d at 432.

467. *A&M Builders, Inc. v. City of Highland Heights*, No. 75676, 2000 WL 45859 (Ohio Ct. App. Jan. 20, 2000).

468. *Id.* at *6-*8.

469. 89 Ohio St. 3d 121, 729 N.E. 2d 349 (2000), *cited in* A & M Builders, Inc. v. City of Highland Heights, 89 Ohio St. 3d 279, 730 N.E. 2d 986 (2000).

470. *See City of Beavercreek*, 89 Ohio St. 3d at 121, 729 N.E. 2d at 349.

When a Vermont city gave final subdivision map approvals for two residential developments, it did so with the condition that the developer would pay a total fee, representing each unit, for building a recreation path on each property.[471] In both instances, the fee was credited against the city's regular recreation impact fee.[472] Two years after the first fee, and one year after the second, the city amended the ordinance to increase the recreation impact fees per unit of development, and required the developer to pay the difference, arguing that the fees it had paid were only credits toward whatever fee the city had in place at the time of actual development.[473] The court found that the credit was an "in-kind contribution," and the developer was thus exempt from paying the new fees.[474]

In Washington, a park impact fee may satisfy a city code's requirement for providing parks and recreation.[475] When the developer of a proposed subdivision submitted the required environmental checklist, the city responded that the development needed to consider alterations to accommodate stormwater runoff, drinking water, land stability, sewer lines, and traffic implications.[476] The city council approved the development's preliminary plat application after the developer revised its environmental checklist, even though the planning commission had advised against it.[477] The court agreed that the city council could examine the facts on its own and decide against the commission's recommendation, as long as the plat application met the necessary requirements such as adequate drainage, provisions for public roads and slope stability, and parks and recreation. In this case, the court found all of the above to be sufficient, with a park impact fee fulfilling the parks and recreation requirement.[478]

Also in Washington, another appellate court found that when a city assessed mitigation fees for a subdivision's impact on public parks, the city did not have to calculate the effects of the subdivisions' private recreational facilities that the residents might use.[479] The city's formula for assessing subdivisions' impacts on public parks involves charging a fee for each potential resident, and that mitigation fee is a condition of development approvals.[480] Even though the developer in this case had dedicated more than two acres of what became parkland to the city as a condition for another phase of the development, that dedication could not count for the current development's mitigation requirements.[481]

---

471. MBL Assocs. v. City of S. Burlington, 172 Vt. 297, 298, 776 A.2d 432, 433 (2001).

472. *Id.* at 298, 776 A.2d at 434.

473. *Id.* at 300, 776 A.2d at 435.

474. *Id.* at 301, 776 A.2d at 435-36.

475. Concerned Citizens for Buckley Planning v. City of Buckley, No. 25587-1-II, 2001 WL 112322 (Wash. Ct. App. Feb. 9, 2001).

476. *Id.* at *2-*3.

477. *Id.* at *3-*4.

478. *Id.* at *12-*13.

479. United Dev. Corp. v. City of Mill Creek, 106 Wash. App. 681, 26 P.3d 943 (2001).

480. *Id.* at 948.

481. *Id.*

## II. LAND DEVELOPMENT CONDITIONS

Also, just because future residents of the subdivision would be members of a homeowners' association that would be providing private recreational facilities inside the development, those facilities would not meet the city's recreational requirements of the comprehensive plan.[482] The city had no control over the type and quality of facilities within the development, nor any control over whether the development's residents would still use public parks.[483] The court held that all of the above would be pure speculation and therefore not what is required by law.[484]

The analysis changes significantly if a court finds elements of "agreement" in the providing of open space.[485] As part of a first (of three) phase subdivision approval, developers agreed to later provide at least 2,375 square feet of recreational space for the residents of the first phase's use, in addition to whatever was required for the later phases. No space was allocated during the second phase, so during approval proceedings for the third and final phase, the developers presented plans to allocate 4,598 square feet of recreational space. The planning and zoning commission denied the application, saying, among other things, that not enough space was set aside. After much litigation, the city council approved the third phase on the condition that the developer convey 2,375 square feet of common use land on Lot One of the third phase, on which there could not be a dwelling. The trial judge found that such a condition deprived the property owners of the right to exclude and of the ability to make any viable economic use of that lot, but the appellate court overturned on the basis that one cannot mix regulatory taking claims with exactions.[486] Because the recreational space was a previously agreed upon condition, the court pointed out that the court's analysis should not be based on dedications or exactions, but on the regulatory takings standard.[487] Using the court's standard of whether there was a loss of all viable economic use, the court held that one cannot look at a total taking of Lot One, but must consider Lot One in reference to at least all of phase three, if not to the total the subdivision.[488] The court found that no unconstitutional taking of property had occurred.[489]

Precision also counts in drafting open space exactions. In Simsbury, Connecticut, subdivision regulations required 20% of an 89-residence development be left as open space. While some of that open space could be used to also fulfill requirements for adequate drainage, road setbacks, and land buffer zones, "open space" was not actually defined in the regulations, nor were guidelines provided for developers to determine what was required of them

---

482. *Id.* at 950.

483. *Id.* at 951.

484. *Id.*

485. *See* City of Annapolis v. Waterman, 357 Md. 484, 745 A.2d 1000 (2000).

486. *Id.* at 523, 745 A.2d at 1020.

487. *Id.* at 525, 745 A.2d at 1022.

488. *Id.*

489. *Id.* at 531, 745 A.2d at 1025.

when providing that "open space."[490] The vague language gave the commission too much discretion: "[T]he commissioner may not adopt subdivision regulations simply so that the town will not be overburdened financially."[491] Because the court found that it could not determine the commission's intentions from its regulations' language, it could not expect a developer to do so either.[492] Thus, the court found that the regulation could not meet *Dolan*'s rough proportionality test, that it did not have *Nollan*'s essential nexus, and that the plaintiff met the burden of proof overcoming the presumption of constitutionality.[493] The court held that the commission "had no authority to enact [the subdivision] regulation" and that the regulation itself was unconstitutional.[494]

Also in Connecticut, a developer filed a complaint[495] against a planning commission for amending a section of its subdivision regulations, changing the percentage of open space that a subdivision must set aside from 10% to 15%.[496] The commission had some discretion over the 15% requirement. For example, if the subdivision is in an area with a suitable number of open spaces, parks, and playgrounds, it need not add more; nor must the subdivider provide open space where there is none because of the property's contours, or if the minimum amount of space would be less than an acre.[497] In some cases, an in lieu fee may be more applicable than a land set aside, and that in lieu fee, according to the regulations, cannot be more than 10% of the property's fair market value.[498] Plaintiffs argued that the new 15% land requirement exceeded the original legislative intent. The court found that the commission, acting as a legislative body, had the right and discretion to amend its regulations, and that the 15% of land had nothing to do with the fee's value percentage.[499] Relying on *Aunt Hack*,[500] the court did not find the amended regulation to be a facial taking, especially when none of the plaintiffs had yet subdivided their property.[501]

---

490. Culbro Corp. v. Town of Simsbury, No. CV 960559508, 1999 WL 162761, at *3 (Conn. Super. Ct. Mar. 2, 1999).

491. *Id.* (citing Beach v. Planning Zoning Comm'n, 141 Conn. 79, 84-85, 103 A.2d 814 (1954)).

492. *Id.* at *4.

493. *Id.*

494. *Id.* at *1. For a different treatment of "discretion" exercised to deny plat approval for lack of open space, see Watt v. Planning & Zoning Comm'n of the Town of Kent, 2000 Conn. Super. LEXIS 2312 (Conn. Super. Ct. 2000).

495. *See* Hardy Farm Ltd. v. Southbury Planning Comm'n, 2001 Conn. Super. LEXIS 1221 (Conn. Super. Ct. 2001).

496. *Id.* at *2.

497. *Id.* at *3.

498. *Id.* at *23.

499. *Id.* at *22 & *24.

500. 160 Conn. at 109, 273 A.2d at 880.

501. *See* 2001 Conn. Super. LEXIS 1221, at *29-*31. "The test which has been generally applied in determining whether a requirement that a developer set aside land for

## II. LAND DEVELOPMENT CONDITIONS

In Wisconsin, the state supreme court found that an open space corridor condition placed on a preliminary plat could be allowable, but an annexation condition was not.[502] The court pointed out that annexation includes political as well as property rights, so a municipality cannot in any way coerce a voting sector or landowner into annexation.[503] The open space issue was not yet ripe for adjudication, however, because it was intended for a future recreational trail that may or may not come about. The city said it may not need the corridor, but that if it did, it would justly compensate the landowner for the property. While the condition may be a temporary regulatory taking, because plaintiffs did not avail themselves of the statutorily created option for inverse condemnation, the claim was not ripe.[504] The court noted that "it is unreasonable to require the Hoepkers to wait until the final plat approval process for details as to the size and location of the open space corridor," and ordered the city, on remand, to provide the specific details of the corridor.[505]

### 5. Schools

The use of impact fees and other exactions to fund the construction of schools is a relatively common practice and has been the subject of frequent litigation. School impact fees also must be necessitated by, and provide a specific service for, the development charged. For example, a retirement community should not have to pay into a fund for a school that its residents neither drove the need for, nor benefit from.[506] A rapidly growing community's overwhelming need for adequate school facilities to meet the demand of its burgeoning population does not always provide a basis for an impact fee, either. Local governments use a variety of methods to help finance this particular public facility.

Among the most noteworthy cases is *St. Johns County*.[507] There, the Florida Supreme Court held that a fee of $448 per single-family dwelling met a rational nexus test when applied to a 100-unit subdivision, but failed a pre-*Dolan* proportionality standard because it was not clear the money collected would necessarily benefit those who paid the fee. The same court later held that a school im-

---

parks and playgrounds as a prerequisite to the approval of a subdivision plan is whether the burden cast upon the subdivider is specifically and uniquely attributable to his own activity." *Id.* at *29 (quoting *Aunt Hack*, 160 Conn. at 117-18, 273 A.2d at 885).

502. *See* Hoepker v. City of Madison Planning Comm'n, 209 Wis. 2d 633, 563 N.W.2d 145 (Wis. 1997).

503. *Id.* at 646-47, 563 N.W.2d at 150.

504. *Id.* at 652-53, 563 N.W.2d at 153.

505. *Id.*

506. *See* Volusia County v. Aberdeen at Ormond Beach Ltd. Liab. Partnership, 25 Fla. L. Weekly 390, 760 So. 2d 126 (Fla. Dist. Ct. App. 2000).

507. 16 Fla. L. Weekly at 264, 583 So. 2d at 635.

pact fee as applied to a retirement community, which had covenants prohibiting minors from residing in the development, failed the dual rational nexus test.[508]

In *Board of County Commissioners v. Bainbridge*,[509] the Colorado Supreme Court considered consolidated appeals regarding the authority of counties to levy school impact fees. The Colorado General Assembly had amended the county subdivision control act to allow a school impact fee limited to the "full market value" of sites that counties can require developers to reserve for schools in their subdivisions.[510] Both Boulder and Douglas counties adopted impact fee resolutions requiring "a second payment as a prerequisite to issuance of a building permit or certificate of occupancy above and beyond the required zoning and subdivision approvals."[511] Although the opinion is lengthy, the court's holding striking down the fees was simple: "Since we find no express or implied authority for the Counties to override the legislature's choice to specify both the maximum amount and the timing of the school fee, we find that the imposition of an additional school fee was without authority."[512]

Similarly, the Arizona Court of Appeals has narrowly construed municipal enabling legislation for development fees in Arizona and struck down a development fee levied by the city of Apache Junction under an intergovernmental agreement with the Apache Junction School District.[513] The court held that schools did not fall under the "necessary public services" language of the enabling act.[514] The court emphasized throughout its analysis the independence of the school financing system from municipal finance and other municipal authority.[515] The court rejected the city's argument that the "necessary public ser-

---

508. *Aberdeen at Ormond Beach*, 25 Fla. L. Weekly at 390, 760 So. 2d at 126. After a lengthy discussion of the legal and factual issues, the court held simply: "In sum, Aberdeen neither contributes to the need for additional schools nor benefits from their construction. Accordingly, the imposition of impact fees as applied to Aberdeen does not satisfy the dual rational nexus test." *Id.* at 410, 760 So. 2d at 137.

509. 929 P.2d 691 (Colo. 1996). In a later proceeding, the Colorado Court of Appeals held that the developers who won the suit were entitled not only to a refund of the fees paid, but to interest on the refund. Bainbridge, Inc. v. Douglas County Sch. Dist. RE-1, 973 P.2d 684 (Colo. Ct. App. 1998), *cert. denied*, 1999 Colo. LEXIS 331 (Colo. 1999).

510. COLO. REV. STAT. §30-28-133(4)(a)(I) and (II) (1986, 1996 Supp.). This 4-3 decision has more to do with the powers of counties in Colorado than with the national evolution of the law of impact fees. Counties in Colorado lack ordinance power and true home-rule power, and the Colorado high court has consistently construed their powers narrowly, in land use as in other fields.

511. *Bainbridge*, 929 P.2d at 695.

512. *Id.*

513. Home Builders Ass'n of Cent. Ariz. v. City of Apache Junction, 2000 Ariz. App. LEXIS 152 (Ariz. Ct. App. 2000).

514. ARIZ. REV. STAT. §9-463.05.A. The section reads: "A municipality may assess development fees to offset costs to the municipality associated with providing necessary public services to a development." *Id.*

515. 2000 Ariz. App. LEXIS 152, at *15-18.

vices" language should be broadly construed to include schools, which are an obvious necessity for a real community.[516] Although the state legislature had not specifically denied a city's right to create such a fee, it had provided that the state should support the public school system, and school districts could help finance their needs, but made no mention of a role for municipalities.[517] The statute upon which the city relied allowed a municipality to assess development fees to offset its costs in providing "necessary public services to a development."[518] The court noted that although the state supreme court had found "necessary public services" to at least include water service, and probably sewer,[519] because the legislature did not require municipalities to pay for schools, it had no such costs to offset in that arena.[520] Thus, the city had no authority to enact the ordinance.

Similarly, in Illinois, a court found that a statute allowing a municipality to implement a comprehensive plan for future development did not authorize a municipality to collect money for significant capital improvements like schools without specific statutory language.[521] When the landowners attempted to obtain a building permit for a single-family home, the village told them they had to pay the impact fees required by the village ordinance. The ordinance required a land acquisition fee and included calculation equations for determining the fees applicable to each proposed development. The landowners paid $3,924.54 under protest and built their home. They then instituted a complaint to get the money back, claiming that the ordinance was unconstitutional and not authorized by statute. The court never reached the constitutional question, but found that a statute authorizing requirements governing streets, parks, playgrounds,

---

516. The court held:

> Because nothing in the constitution or statutes giving powers to cities and towns suggests that cities have any authority over or responsibility for public school matters that, by implication, would provide authority to raise revenue to support them, we do not construe "necessary public services" to include the funding of public schools. Further, "costs to the municipality" must be caused by the direct provision of a "necessary public service" such as educational services or facilities, something for which the City has no legal responsibility. It would seem incongruous to conclude, therefore, that "necessary public services" in §9-463.05(A) includes funding the capital needs of public schools so as to permit municipal imposition of a development fee to do so, particularly in the absence of constitutional or statutory authorization for municipal expenditures or action in this area.

Id. at 121-22.

517. Home Builders Ass'n of Cent. Ariz. v. City of Apache Junction, 198 Ariz. 493, 198 Ariz. 493, 499, 11 P.3d 1032, 1038 (Ariz. Ct. App. 2000).

518. ARIZ. REV. STAT. §9-463.05(A).

519. See Home Builders Ass'n of Cen. Ariz. v. City of Scottsdale, 187 Ariz. 479, 930 P.2d 993 (1997).

520. City of Apache Junction, 198 Ariz. at 500, 11 P.3d at 1039.

521. See Thompson v. Village of Newark, 329 Ill. App. 3d 536, 768 N.E.2d 856 (2002).

school grounds, lot sizes, drainage, water supply, sewers, lighting, and sidewalks did not authorize impact fees for school construction.[522]

In a unique decision from California, a court upheld the application of a school development fee levied against Loyola Marymount University, a private college, on its construction of a business school.[523] The court determined that such development was "commercial" under the applicable county ordinance and that religious and governmental exemptions were inapplicable. Turning to whether the fees corresponded to a need incurred by the construction of the building,[524] the court noted that Loyola had not challenged the fees on that basis.[525] The court then found that the development fees were voluntary because the university chose to develop,[526] and valid.[527] Other California cases have upheld school impact fees for temporary or permanent facilities necessitated by rapid growth,[528] and when levied against a project designed to attract weekend or retirement home purchasers where school-age children were not prohibited from residing in the units.[529]

In a surprising spin, a Massachusetts appellate court found that because school fee improvements benefitted more people than those paying the fee, providing school facilities is a governmental obligation to the general public. Because the fees were not paid by choice, that fee was really a tax, which Massachusetts towns are not allowed to levy.[530] To create its fee formula, the town subtracted all other funding sources, then estimated how many children would be added by each new apartment and single-family dwelling, charging the respective unit its respective percentage of the remaining cost.[531] The collected funds stay in the development's part of town, paying only for school expansion projects in the representative area, not maintenance, with any remainder left after eight years being returned, in proportion, to those who paid the fee.[532] Nevertheless, the court found that the fees for improved schools did not so much provide a special ser-

---

522. *Id.* at 541-42, 768 N.E.2d at 860.

523. Loyola Marymount Univ. v. Los Angeles Unified Sch. Dist., 53 Cal. Rptr. 2d 424, 45 Cal. App. 4th 1256 (1996).

524. *Id.* at 430, 45 Cal. App. 4th at 1262-63.

525. *Id.* at 430, 45 Cal. App. 4th at 1264.

526. *Id.* at 432, 45 Cal. App. 4th at 1267-68.

527. *Id.* at 434-35, 45 Cal. App. 4th at 1271.

528. Candid Enters., Inc. v. Grossmont Union High Sch. Dist., 39 Cal. App. 3d 878, 705 P.2d 878 (1985).

529. McLain Western #1 v. San Diego County, 194 Cal. Rptr. 594 (1983). California statutory authorization and limitations on school fees is contained in CAL. GOV'T CODE §65995. *See also* CURTIN & TALBERT, *supra* note 51.

530. *See* Greater Franklin Devs. Ass'n, Inc. v. Town of Franklin, 730 N.E.2d 900, 902-03 (Mass. App. Ct. 2000).

531. *Id.*

532. *Id.*

vice to the developers by making their developments more attractive to buyers, but simply provided improved schools to the community at large.[533]

One of the more comprehensive school impact fee programs comes from Washington. Each school district is statutorily required to qualify annually for mitigation or impact fees.[534] To qualify, the district estimates the area growth and subsequent need, then calculates a dollar amount per unit of new development that would partially fulfill the monetary need created by that development, either for school improvements or new construction.[535] When a developer submits a preliminary plat for approval, it must include a letter from the impacted school district to the county, agreeing on an impact fee, and the county then decides whether the amount is adequate.[536] If the developer does not appeal the fees in a timely manner, one state appellate court found that simply naming a request to remove those fees a "plat revision" does not make it one.[537] By not appealing or contesting the fees, the developer entered a contractual agreement to pay them, and was bound by that agreement.[538]

Each Washington school district has statutory authority to impose school impact fees on new property developments, and each jurisdiction may use different methods of calculating those fees. One developer argued that the school impact fees in his area were miscalculated and that the school district did not correctly apply the fees under the ordinance, so he should not have to pay any.[539] On the miscalculation claim, the deputy hearing examiner had already reduced plaintiffs' fees by one-half, and the court found that the examiner had the authority to make that adjustment.[540] In checking the district's method of assessing fees, the court noted that the method used fit within the countywide average required by the ordinance.[541] The court also found that because "the school impact fees are to ensure adequate facilities for the school district as new students enroll," the students from plaintiffs' development need not be the only ones who benefit from the fees paid by that developer.[542] However, if plaintiffs' funds are not used by the school district within six years, a total refund may be requested. Plaintiffs did not meet their burden of proof of unusual circumstances that might render the fees unjust, that their development would not im-

---

533. *Id.* at 904.

534. *See* West Coast, Inc. v. Snohomish County, 104 Wash. App. 735, 738, 16 P.3d 30, 31-32 (2000).

535. *Id.* at 738, 16 P.3d at 32.

536. *Id.*

537. *Id.* at 740, 16 P.3d at 33.

538. *Id.* at 742-43, 16 P.3d at 34.

539. *See* Wellington River Hollow, Ltd. Liab. Corp. v. King County, 113 Wash. App. 574, 578-79, 54 P.3d 213, 215-16 (2002).

540. *Id.* at 580-81, 54 P.3d at 216.

541. *Id.* at 582-83, 54 P.3d at 217-18.

542. *Id.* at 587, 54 P.3d at 219-20.

pact the school district, or that they should not pay into school system improvements that would reasonably benefit its development.[543]

A county in Maryland enacted an ordinance providing that a final subdivision plat cannot be approved unless the residential developers can assure that the county's public facilities, including schools, can keep up with the population growth spurred by the development.[544] The public facility construction or in lieu fee must be paid within two years of the plat approval but may be waived, on the developer's request, if the waiver would not impact public health, safety, and welfare, and if the development does not impact that particular facility or the requirement would cause undue hardship, aside from financial concerns.[545] The county also allowed for specific agreements between the developer and county before the plat approval. In one case, developers agreed to pay waiver fees, based on a fee schedule in the ordinance, toward school facilities in order to get their plat approvals. The developers later claimed that the agreements were illegal, and that the fees were taxes. The court found that such agreements were valid contracts, and that the ordinance allowing for development impact fees, although not so called, also was valid and constitutional.[546]

## 6. Fire Protection

A town in Maine required a fire prevention easement for subdivision approval. The ordinance conditioned approval of the subdivision on construction of a 250,000-gallon fire pond within 2,000 feet of the development, if no other water supply existed, and an access easement for firefighters to maintain the pond and to pump the water to their hoses.[547] Developers charged that the ordinance was an unconstitutional taking. Maine's Supreme Court, following *Nollan*[548] and *Dolan*,[549] found that the ordinance was constitutional because the proposed development would be far from an adequate water source and in a town with no public water system, and that the access easement was no greater than that required.[550]

## 7. Historic Preservation

When a hydroelectric dam owner in Vermont, OMYA, Inc., applied for a second 30-year operating license, the Federal Energy Regulating Commission

---

543. *Id.* at 587-88, 54 P.3d at 220.

544. *See* Halle Dev., Inc. v. Anne Arundel County, 141 Md. App. 542, 545, 786 A.2d 48, 50 (2001).

545. *Id.*

546. *Id.* at 555, 786 A.2d at 55-56.

547. Curtis v. Town of S. Thomaston, 708 A.2d 657, 659 (Me. 1998).

548. 483 U.S. at 825, 107 S. Ct. at 3141, 97 L. Ed. 2d at 677, 17 ELR at 20918.

549. 512 U.S. at 374, 114 S. Ct. at 2309, 129 L. Ed. 2d at 304, 24 ELR at 21083.

550. *Curtis*, 708 A.2d at 659-60.

(FERC) granted the license with some conditions.[551] The conditions included historic preservation, off-street parking, landscaping, a footpath, a canoe portage route, and signs. FERC required the conditions under the authority of the Federal Power Act, which allows for conditions to protect fish and wildlife, public use, and recreation.[552] The license also cited the authority of a Programmatic Agreement among FERC, the Vermont State Historic Preservation Office for the Management of Historic Properties, and the Advisory Council on Historic Preservation. Under the agreement, OMYA had to protect the historic and archaeological elements of its property, with "a permanent exhibit, brochure, slide presentation, and outdoor signage."[553] FERC preserved the right to alter the requirements at any time during the license's term. OMYA argued that all the conditions made running the dam uneconomical, and that FERC had given more weight to the historical and recreational elements than to the business elements of the dam. The court found that the issue was not ripe because the conditions had not yet been implemented, and that the conditions did not cause a facial taking.[554]

The New York Landmarks Preservation Commission began allowing, on a permit basis, owners of historical landmarks to renovate their landmarks in 1986.[555] If the owner went beyond the permit and damaged the landmark, all work must cease. When RKO Delaware, Inc. went beyond its specified permit, the commission issued a stop work order. RKO Delaware submitted several proposals to fix the violations, all of which the commission rejected, and, because the violation remained, RKO could not do any work on the building. Upon inspection, however, the commission found that work had continued, to the detriment of the building's landmark status, and requested a financial promise that the originally permitted restoration work would be completed. Despite a number of communications between both parties, RKO contended that no work occurred for 13 years, constituting a taking. The court found, however, that RKO had not met the futility requirement under *Williamson*'s final decision requirement because no certainty existed that all of its proposed applications would be denied, and that RKO had not tried for and then been denied just compensation.[556] The court dismissed the claim, but left open the possibility that RKO could refile if and when it had enough facts to support the final decision requirement.[557]

---

551. *See* OMYA, Inc. v. Federal Energy Regulatory Comm'n, 111 F.3d 179, 324 U.S. App. D.C. 137 (D.C. Cir. 1997).

552. 16 U.S.C. §803(a), *cited by OMYA, Inc.*, 111 F.3d at 180, 324 U.S. App. D.C. at 138.

553. *OMYA, Inc.*, 111 F.3d at 181, 324 U.S. App. D.C. at 138 (quoting Programmatic Agreement at 6 (Apr. 6, 1993)).

554. *Id.* at 181-82, 324 U.S. App. D.C. at 139.

555. *See* RKO Delaware, Inc. v. City of New York, 2001 U.S. Dist LEXIS 17644 (E.D.N.Y. 2001).

556. *Id.* at *12-13 (citing Williamson County Reg'l Planning Comm'n v. Hamilton Bank, 473 U.S. 172, 195, 105 S. Ct. 3108, 3121, 87 L. Ed. 2d 126, 144 (1985)).

557. *Id.* at *16.

## F. Segregation of Funds, Credits, and Refunds

Typically, a statute or impact fee ordinance requires that funds collected by local governments as impact fees be placed in separate bank accounts relating to the public facility for which the fee is collected, and then used only for that kind or type of public facility.[558] For example, California authorizes the imposition of impact fees but requires the local agency to deposit the fee "in a separate capital facilities account or fund in a manner to avoid any commingling of the fees with other revenues and funds of the local agency" and restricts the use of these fees "solely for the purpose for which the fee was originally collected."[559] Similarly, the village of Northbrook, Illinois, authorizes the imposition of road impact fees and requires that such fees be deposited into the "village transportation impact fee account."[560] Moreover, the village restricts the use of these funds only "for those transportation facilities, controls and improvements set forth in the comprehensive road improvement plan."[561] Thus, under the provisions of most statutes and ordinances authorizing impact fees, it would be illegal to use road impact fees for the construction of schools.

In addition to requiring segregation of fees into separate accounts, the California statute also requires, "within 180 days after the last day of each fiscal year," that local agencies make the following information pertaining to the account available to the public:

(A) A brief description of the type of fee in the account or fund;

(B) The amount of the fee;

(C) The beginning and ending balance of the account or fund;

(D) The amount of the fees collected and the interest earned;

(E) An identification of each public improvement on which fees were expended and the amount of the expenditures on each improvement, including the total percentage of the cost of the public improvement that was funded with fees;

(F) An identification of an approximate date by which the construction of the public improvement will commence if the local agency determines that sufficient funds have been collected to complete financing on an incomplete public improvement, as identified in paragraph (2) of subdivision (a) of Section 66001, and the public improvement remains incomplete;

(G) A description of each interfund transfer or loan made from the account or fund, including the public improvement on which the transferred or loaned fees will be expended, and, in the case of an interfund loan, the date on which the loan will be repaid, and the rate of interest that the account or fund will receive on the loan; and

---

558. *See, e.g.*, ARIZ. REV. STAT. ANN. §9-463.05; CAL. GOV'T CODE §66000; COLO. REV. STAT. §29-1-801; GA. CODE ANN. §36-71-2(16); HAW. REV. STAT. §46-141; IDAHO CODE §67-8201; 605 ILL. COMP. STAT. ANN. §5-901; IND. CODE. ANN. §36-7-4-1300; ME. REV. STAT. ANN. tit. 30-A §4354; N.H. REV. STAT. ANN. §674:21; N.M. LAWS ch. 122; OR. REV. STAT. §223.297; PA. STAT. ANN. tit. 53, §10501-A; TEX. LOCAL GOV'T CODE ANN. §395.001; VA. CODE ANN. §15.1-498.1; WASH. REV. CODE ANN. §82.02.050; W. VA. CODE §7-20-1.

559. CAL. GOV'T CODE §66006.

560. NORTHBROOK, ILL., MUNICIPAL CODE §19-103(a).

561. *Id.* at §19-103(b).

(H) The amount of refunds made pursuant to subdivision (e) of Section 66001 and any allocations pursuant to subsection (f) of Section 66001.[562]

Not only must funds be segregated into separate accounts and used only for the purposes for which they are imposed, but also many statutes and impact fee ordinances impose a time limitation on the spending of these funds by the local government.[563] A typical provision from the Illinois impact fee statute requires that these fees be expended within five years of collection or refunded to the developer.[564]

Recall from an earlier section entitled *Cost and Calculation of Fees* that public facilities or improvements constructed with impact fees must "adequately" benefit the new development upon which the fee was imposed. By segregating fees into separate accounts apart from general funds, and spending those funds reasonably quickly, local governments avoid claims that the fees are merely veiled attempts at taxation for which they must have specific statutory authority. In *Board of County Commissioners of Palm Beach County*,[565] the court held that benefits accruing to the community generally do not adversely affect the validity of a development regulation provided the fee does not exceed the cost of the public facilities and improvements serving the development and the improvements adequately benefit the development that is the source of the fee. Similarly, the court in *Amherst Builders*[566] upheld a sewer tap-in charge that the city required be placed into a separate "sewer fund" apart from the city's general fund. Courts, however, have been reluctant to uphold impact fees that are collected and deposited into the general fund.[567]

If the local agency fails to use the fee collected and deposited in the appropriate separate account within a reasonable period of time, many statutes and ordinances provide that the fee must be refunded to the developer.[568] The rationale

---

562. CAL. GOV'T CODE §66006(b)(1).

563. *See, e.g.*, CAL. GOV'T CODE §66001(d) & (e); GA. CODE ANN. §36-71-9(1); HAW. REV. STAT. §46-144(5); IDAHO CODE §67-8210(4) & 8211; 605 ILL. COMP. STAT. ANN. §5-916; IND. CODE. ANN. §36-7-4-1332; ME. REV. STAT. ANN. tit. 30-A §4354(2)(D); N.H. REV. STAT. ANN. §674:21(V)(e); N.M. LAWS ch. 122, §17; PA. STAT. ANN. tit. 53, §10505-A(g); TEX. LOCAL GOV'T CODE ANN. §395.025; VT. STAT. ANN. tit. 24, §5203(e); VA. CODE ANN. §15.1-498.10; WASH. REV. CODE ANN. §82.02.070(1); W. VA. CODE §7-20-9(a).

564. 605 ILL. COMP. STAT. 5-916.

565. 446 So. 2d at 140.

566. 61 Ohio St. 2d at 349, 402 N.E.2d at 1184.

567. Lafferty v. Payson City, 642 P.2d 376 (Utah 1982); Waterbury Dev. Co. v. Witten, 54 Ohio St. 2d 412, 377 N.E.2d 505 (1978); Hayes v. City of Albany, 7 Or. App. 277, 490 P.2d 1018 (1971); Weber Basin Home Builders Ass'n v. Roy City, 26 Utah 2d 215, 487 P.2d 866 (1971).

568. *See, e.g.*, CAL. GOV'T CODE §66001(d) & (e); GA. CODE ANN. §36-71-9(1); HAW. REV. STAT. §46-144(5); IDAHO CODE §67-8210(4) & 8211; 605 ILL. COMP. STAT. ANN. §5-916; IND. CODE. ANN. §36-7-4-1332; ME. REV. STAT. ANN. tit. 30-A §4354(2)(D); N.H. REV. STAT. ANN. §674:21(V)(e); N.M. LAWS ch. 122, §17; PA. STAT. ANN. tit. 53, §10505-A(g); TEX. LOCAL GOV'T CODE ANN. §395.025;

is that since such fees are development-driven, they must not have been necessary in the first place. For example, the transportation impact fee ordinance of Northbrook, Illinois, reads:

Sec. 19-105. Return of funds.

It is the intent of this article that all village transportation impact fees and state transportation impact fees collected shall be encumbered for the uses respectively specified in sections 19-103 and 19-104 above within five (5) years following the date of collection. In determining whether the transportation impact fees have been encumbered, the transportation impact fees shall be accounted for on a first-in first-out (FIFO) basis. In the event any transportation impact fee collected is not encumbered within five (5) years following the date of the issuance of the occupancy permit for such development, such transportation impact fee, along with accrued interest, shall be refunded to the then current owner of the zoning lot with respect to which the transportation impact fee was collected; provided that the then current owner of such zoning lot files a petition with the village seeking a refund within one (1) year from the date that the transportation impact fee was required to be encumbered. Such transportation impact fee, assessed after January 28, 1992, shall bear interest at seventy (70) percent of the prime commercial rate in effect at the time of assessment of the transportation impact fee.[569]

However, at least two courts have upheld "no refund" provisions contained in impact fee laws. A Texas court held that a city could retain $1.3 million in community impact fees paid by a developer even after the developer abandoned the development.[570] The court relied on the fact that the ordinance was silent on refunds, and that the city had already spent the money to construct the water and sewer improvements that would benefit the developer's property. Similarly, a Florida court upheld an impact fee statute that provides that all impact fees are nonrefundable per se, although the court required the governmental entity to refund $33,000 in impact fees paid by a developer whose building permit is rescinded.[571] Moreover, if the developer has already made contributions in the form of money, land, or facilities, or if the development property taxes are intended to pay for part of the new facility or improvement, the developer is usually credited against the fee normally levied for these amounts.[572]

---

VT. STAT. ANN. tit. 24, §5203(e); VA. CODE ANN. §15.1-498.10; WASH. REV. CODE ANN. §82.02.070(1); W. VA. CODE §7-20-9(a).

569. NORTHBROOK, ILL., MUNICIPAL CODE §19-105.

570. McNair v. City of Cedar Park, Tex., 993 F.2d 1217 (5th Cir. 1993).

571. Cardillo v. Florida Keys Aqueduct Auth., 20 Fla. L. Weekly 1258, 654 So. 2d 1062 (Fla. Dist. Ct. App. 1995).

572. NICHOLAS & DAVIDSON, IMPACT FEES IN HAWAII, *supra* note 157.

## III. Development Agreements

### A. Why Development Agreements?

Recall that developer and local government face two difficult problems in the land development approval process. Local governments are unable to exact dedications of land or fees of the "impact" or "in lieu" variety without establishing a clear connection or nexus between the proposed development and the dedication or fee.[573] The developer is unable to "vest" or guarantee a right to proceed with a project until that project is commenced.[574] The development agreement offers a solution to both landowner/developer and local government. Often authorized by statute to help avoid reserved power and Contracts Clause problems discussed below, a well-structured agreement can be drafted to deal with a variety of common issues which arise in the land development process between landowner and local government.[575]

### B. The Basic Problem: Bargaining Away the Police Power and Reserved Power

The first issue is whether the local government has bargained away its police power by entering into an agreement under which it promises not to change its land use regulations during the life of the agreement. Specific statutory authori-

---

573. *See* Judith Welch Wegner, *Moving Toward the Bargaining Table: Contract Zoning, Development Agreements, and the Theoretical Foundations of Government Land Use Deals*, 65 N.C. L. REV. 957, 1017-20 (1987) (describing the "rational nexus" test adopted by a majority of jurisdictions to assess the reasonableness of provisions requiring exactions of property in development agreements, and the expansion of the doctrine governing exactions to address the use of "impact fees"); Lyle S. Hosada, *Development Agreement Legislation in Hawaii: An Answer to the Vested Rights Uncertainty*, 7 U. HAW. L. REV. 173 (1985); TAKINGS: LAND-DEVELOPMENT CONDITIONS AND REGULATORY TAKINGS AFTER *Dolan* and *Lucas* chs. 4, 9, 10, 11 (David L. Callies ed., 1996).

574. *See* John J. Delaney, *Vesting Verities and the Development Chronology: A Gaping Disconnect?*, 3 WASH. U. J.L. & POL'Y 603, 607-08 (2000) (noting that many states require action such as construction or expenditure of funds in reliance on a development permit for the permit to be valid).

575. *See generally* DEVELOPMENT AGREEMENTS, ANALYSES, COLORADO CASE STUDIES, COMMENTARY (Erin J. Johnson & Edward H. Ziegler eds., 1993); DEVELOPMENT AGREEMENTS, PRACTICE, POLICY AND PROSPECTS (Douglas R. Porter & Lindell L. Marsh eds., 1989); DAVID J. LARSEN, DEVELOPMENT AGREEMENTS MANUAL: COLLABORATION IN PURSUIT OF COMMUNITY INTERESTS (2002) (prepared for the Institute for Local Self Government, League of California Cities, Sacramento, California). For commentary on the British experience with development agreements, see David L. Callies & Malcolm Grant, *Paying for Growth and Planning Gain: An Anglo American Comparison of Development Conditions, Impact Fees, and Development Agreements*, 23 URB. LAW. 221 (1991). See Appendix XV for a checklist on drafting agreements, and Appendices X, XIII, and XIV for sample development and annexation agreements.

zation is helpful so as to make clear that these agreements effectuate a public purpose recognized by the state. Thirteen states have so far adopted legislation enabling local governments to enter into development agreements with landowner/developers.[576]

## 1. "Freezing" and the "Contracting Away" Issue

It is a black-letter law that local governments may not contract away the police power,[577] particularly in the context of zoning decisions.[578] Stated another way, government cannot bind itself to not exercise its police powers. It is thus considered to be against public policy to permit the bargaining of zoning and subdivision regulations for agreements and stipulations on the part of developers to do or refrain from doing certain things. Because land use and development regulations represent exercises of police power, a development or annexation agreement binding a local government not to exercise these regulatory powers arguably violates the reserved powers doctrine,[579] and is, therefore, ultra vires.

Under this doctrine, bargaining away the police power is the equivalent of a current legislature attempting to exercise legislative power reserved to later

---

576. *See* ARIZ. REV. STAT. ANN. §9-500.05; CAL. GOV'T CODE §65864; COLO. REV. STAT. §§24-68-101 to -106; FLA. STAT. ANN. §163.3220; LA. REV. STAT. ANN. §33:4780.22; NEV. REV. STAT. §278.0201; N.J. STAT. ANN. §40:55D-45.2; OR. REV. STAT. §94.504; VA. CODE ANN. §15.2-2303.1 (applies only to counties with a population between 10,300 and 11,000 and developments consisting of more than 1,000 acres); WASH. REV. CODE ANN. §36.70B.170.

577. *See* Carlino v. Witpain Investors, 499 Pa. 498, 504, 453 A.2d 1385, 1388 (1982) (noting that "individuals cannot, by contract, abridge police powers which protect the general welfare and public interest").

578. *See* Cederberg v. City of Rockford, 8 Ill. App. 3d 984, 986-87, 291 N.E.2d 249, 251-52 (1972) (voiding restrictive covenant and rezoning ordinance because the law "condemns the practice of regulating zoning through agreements or contracts between the zoning authorities and property owners"); Houston Petroleum Co. v. Automobile Prods. Credit Ass'n, 9 N.J. 122, 87 A.2d 319, 322 (N.J. 1952) ("Contracts thus have no place in a zoning plan and a contract between a municipality and a property owner should not enter into the enactment or enforcement of zoning regulations."); V.F. Zahodiakin Eng'g Corp. v. Zoning Bd. of Adjustment, 8 N.J. 386, 384, 86 A.2d 127, 131 (N.J. 1952) ("Zoning is an exercise of the police power to serve the common good and general welfare. It is elementary that the legislative function may not be surrendered or curtailed by bargain or its exercise controlled by the considerations which enter into the law of contracts.").

579. *See, e.g.*, Robert M. Kessler, *The Development Agreement and Its Use in Resolving Large-Scale, Multi-Party Development Problems: A Look at the Tool and Suggestions for Its Application*, 1 J. LAND USE & ENVTL. L. 451, 464-69 (1985) (discussing the reserved powers doctrine and the inability of local governments to contract away police powers); Bruce M. Kramer, *Development Agreements: To What Extent Are They Enforceable?*, 10 REAL EST. L.J. 29, 37-45 (1981) (discussing the history and current viability of the reserved powers doctrine in the context of development agreements).

legislatures.[580] However, an analysis of the cases indicates that what the courts generally inveigh against is such bargaining away forever, or at least for a very long time. The source of the doctrine, *Corporation of the Brick Presbyterian Church v. Mayor of New York*,[581] involved the municipal abrogation of a lease executed over 50 years before. While some later cases do involve invalidation of municipal action just a few years old,[582] the majority deals with behavior further back in time. The dominant view is that development agreements, drafted to reserve some governmental control over the agreement, do not contract away the police power, but rather constitute a valid present exercise of that power. Good analogous authority exists for the premise.[583]

A subsidiary question under the reserved powers doctrine is whether a city council, in exercising its power to contract, can make a contract that binds its successors. In *Carruth v. City of Madera*,[584] the city contended that obligations under an annexation agreement executed by a predecessor council were invalid because they deprived the successor city council of the power to determine city policy and act in the public interest. The court, however, held that the city was bound, and that a contract was made by the council or other governing body of a municipality and was fair, just, and reasonable at the time of its execution. The court concluded that the contract was neither void nor voidable merely because some of its executory features may operate to bind a successor council.[585]

---

580. *See* Stone v. Mississippi, 101 U.S. 814, 817-18, 25 L. Ed. 1079, 1079 (1880) (noting that "no legislature can curtail the power of its successors to make such laws as they may deem proper in matters of police"); Corporation of the Brick Presbyterian Church v. Mayor of N.Y., 5 Cow. 538, 542 (N.Y. Sup. Ct. 1826) (noting that local governments have "no power to limit their legislative discretion by covenant"), *discussed in* Kramer, *supra* note 579, at 37-39.

581. 5 Cow. 538 (N.Y. Sup. Ct. 1826).

582. *See, e.g.*, Hartnett v. Austin, 93 So. 2d 86, 89-90 (Fla. 1956) (affirming lower court's permanent injunction of a proposed revision of a zoning ordinance that had not yet taken effect); *V.F. Zahodiakin*, 8 N.J. at 395, 86 A.2d at 131-32 (affirming lower court's invalidation of a decision made earlier by the local board of adjustment that purported to grant a "variance" from zoning requirements).

583. *See, e.g.*, Morrison Homes Corp. v. City of Pleasanton, 130 Cal. Rptr. 196, 202, 58 Cal. App. 3d 724, 734-35 (1976) (holding that the effect of the general rule is to void only a contract which amounts to a city's "surrender" or "abnegation" of its *control* of a properly municipal function, and that the city's reservations of control over the land subject to an annexation agreement, as well as the "just, reasonable, fair and equitable" nature of the agreement, rendered the agreement valid and enforceable against the city).

584. 43 Cal. Rptr. 855, 233 Cal. App. 2d 688 (1965).

585. *Id.* at 860-61, 233 Cal. App. 2d at 695-96; *see also* Denio v. City of Huntington Beach, 22 Cal. 2d 580, 590, 140 P.2d 392, 397 (1943) (holding that a "fair, just and reasonable contract entered into by a governing body of a municipality . . . is neither void nor voidable merely because some of its executory features may extend beyond the terms of office of the members of [the governing] body"), *overruled by* Fracasse v. Brent, 6 Cal. 3d 784, 494 P.2d 9 (1972).

One of the clearest rejections of the application of reserved power and bargaining away the police power comes from the wide-ranging Nebraska Supreme Court opinion upholding development agreements in *Giger v. City of Omaha*.[586] The objectors to the agreement claimed that development agreements were a form of contract zoning and, therefore, illegal on their face. The Nebraska Supreme Court, however, preferred to characterize such agreements as a form of conditional zoning that actually increased the city's police power, rather than lessened it, by permitting more restrictive zoning (attaching conditions through agreement) than a simple *Euclidean* rezoning to a district in which a variety of uses would be permitted of right.[587]

Similarly, a recent California appeals court squarely upheld a development agreement that was challenged directly on "surrender of police power" grounds, holding that a "zoning freeze in the Agreement is not . . . a surrender or abnegation [of the police power]."[588] In *Santa Margarita Area Residents Together (SMART) v. San Luis Obispo County Board of Supervisors*,[589] an area residents' association contended that because San Luis Obispo County had entered into a development agreement for a project before the project was ready for construction, freezing zoning for a five-year period, the county improperly contracted away its zoning authority. In holding for the county, the court noted that land use regulation is an established function of local government, providing the authority for a local government to enter into contracts to carry out the function. The county's development agreement required that the project be developed in accordance with the county's general plan, did not permit construction until the county had approved detailed building plans, retained the county's discretionary authority in the future, and allowed a zoning freeze of limited duration only. The court found that the zoning freeze in the county's development agreement was not a surrender of the police power but instead "advance[d] the public interest by preserving future options."

In *Stephens v. City of Vista*,[590] the Stephenses purchased property in 1973 to develop an apartment complex of approximately 140 to 150 units. Subsequently, the city of Vista lowered the access street to the property, frustrating the Stephens' contemplated use, and downzoned the property. The Stephenses

---

586. 232 Neb. 676, 442 N.W.2d 182 (1989).

587. *Id.* at 687-88, 442 N.W.2d at 192. The court reasoned:

> In sum, we find that there is not clear and satisfactory evidence to support the appellants' contention that the city has bargained away its police power. The evidence clearly shows that the city's police powers are not abridged in any manner and that the agreement is expressly subject to the remedies available to the city under the Omaha Municipal Code. Further, we find that the agreement actually enhances the city's regulatory control over the development rather than limiting it.

> *Id.*

588. Santa Margarita Area Residents Together v. San Luis Obispo County Bd. of Supervisors, 100 Cal. Rptr. 2d 740, 748, 84 Cal. App. 4th 221, 233 (2000).

589. 100 Cal. Rptr. 2d 740, 748, 84 Cal. App. 4th 221, 223 (2000).

590. 994 F.2d 650 (9th Cir. 1993).

sued. The city and the Stephenses eventually entered into a settlement agreement providing for a specific plan and zoning that permitted construction of a maximum of 140 units. After rezoning the property, the city denied a site development plan, in part because it wanted the Stephenses to reduce the density. The Stephenses then renewed their lawsuit against the city.

The city argued that the settlement agreement unlawfully contracted away its police power. The court disagreed. The court first noted that when the city entered into the settlement agreement, it understood it was obligated to approve 140 units. Further, relying on *Morrison Homes Corp. v. City of Pleasanton,*[591] which upheld the validity of an annexation agreement, the court held that while generally a local government cannot contract away its legislative and governmental functions, this rule only applies to void a contract which amounts to a "surrender" of the local government's control of a municipal function.[592] Therefore, the city could contract for a guaranteed density and exercise its discretion in the site development process without surrendering control of all of its land use authority. The court awarded $727,500 in damages for breaching the agreement based on the difference between the value of the property with an entitlement of 140 units and the value of the property with a developable density of 55 units (the current zoning).[593] Similarly, a development agreement that obligates a local government to permit a certain density and type of development should be enforceable by the developer.

In sum, the current application of the reserved powers clause to abrogate government/private contracts has been rare and courts have attempted to find other grounds to uphold those contracts which are fair, just, reasonable, and advantageous to the local government.[594] It is unlikely that courts will fall back on the reserved powers clause to invalidate development agreements passed pursuant to state statute, especially if the agreements have a fixed termination date and that date is not decades away.

## 2. The Contracts Clause and Reserved Powers

It is also arguable that the Contracts Clause of the Constitution provides protection for development and annexation agreements in the face of a reserved power challenge: "No State shall . . . pass any . . . Law impairing the Obligation of Contracts."[595] Although statutorily defined as either a legislative or administrative act, a development agreement will be treated as a contract "when the lan-

---

591. 130 Cal. Rptr. 196, 58 Cal. App. 3d 724 (1976).

592. *Stephens*, 994 F.2d at 655.

593. *Id.* at 657.

594. *See, e.g.*, Carruth v. City of Madera, 43 Cal. Rptr. 855, 860-61, 233 Cal. App. 2d 688, 695-96 (1965) (holding contract entered into by city can be enforced, even if it extends beyond the legislative term, if the contract is fair, just reasonable, and advantageous to the city); *see also* Kramer, *supra* note 579, at 41 (discussing *Carruth*).

595. U.S. Const. art. I, §10, cl. 1.

guage and circumstances evince a legislative intent to create private rights of a contractual nature enforceable against the State."[596]

Once the parties enter into a development agreement, strict application of the Contracts Clause would prohibit government from passing any law or regulation that would subsequently impair the resulting contractual obligations. Further, any such act would be unconstitutional, notwithstanding the fact that the new regulation may be required by a genuine health, safety, or welfare crisis. Certainly, this result would not be tolerated, and, therefore, one must conclude that if a development agreement, subject to the Contracts Clause, irrevocably binds government to not exercise its police power in promotion of the public interest, then the agreement violates the reserved powers doctrine and is ultra vires.

The limitation of the Contracts Clause is, however, neither literal nor absolute.[597] The Court has held that the Contracts Clause limitation cannot operate to eclipse or eliminate "'essential attributes of sovereign power' . . . necessarily reserved by the States to safeguard the welfare of their citizens."[598] The test in *United States Trust Co.*, as refined in *Allied Structural Steel Co. v. Spannus*,[599] ultimately requires a balancing of the exercise of the police power against the impairment resulting from the exercise of such police power. The decisions suggest that any exercise of the police power that impairs any obligations under a development agreement would be subject to strict scrutiny, and, therefore, must be justifiable as an act "reasonable and necessary to serve an important public purpose."[600] Just what constitutes an "important public purpose" sufficient to justify the impairment of contract obligations is a factual determination. In *United States Trust Co.*, bondholders' security interests outweighed the state's interest in pollution control, rapid transit, and resource conservation. Similarly, in *Allied Structural Steel*, the state's interest in protecting its citizens' pensions failed to prevail over a private company's rights in its own pension plan.[601]

---

596. United States Trust Co. v. New Jersey, 431 U.S. 1, 17 n.14, 97 S. Ct. 1505, 1515 n.14, 52 L. Ed 2d 92, 106 n.14 (1977). For a full discussion, see Wegner, *supra* note 573, at 995-1003 (making the case that although writers have simply assumed that development agreements are contractual in nature, it would be more correct to characterize development agreements as possessing a hybrid contractual-regulatory nature).

597. *See* Eric Sigg, *California's Development Agreement Statute*, 15 S.W. U. L. Rev. 695, 720-22 (1985) (discussing tension between the Contracts Clause and the "reserved powers" doctrine, and describing various tests to determine whether a particular contract surrenders an essential attribute of a state's sovereignty).

598. *United States Trust Co.*, 431 U.S. at 21, 97 S. Ct. at 1517, 52 L. Ed. 2d at 109 (quoting Home Bldg. & Loan Ass'n v. Blaisdell, 290 U.S. 398, 435 (1934)).

599. 438 U.S. 234 (1978).

600. *United States Trust Co.*, 431 U.S. at 25, 97 S. Ct. at 1519, 52 L. Ed. 2d at 112.

601. For a thorough discussion of the *United States Trust Co.-Allied Structural Steel Co.* test, see Anthony v. Kualoa Ranch, Inc., 69 Haw. 112, 736 P.2d 55 (1987), in which the Hawaii Supreme Court applied the Contracts Clause doctrine to strike down a state statute requiring landlords to pay for leasehold improvements, at the

# III. DEVELOPMENT AGREEMENTS

## C. Statutory Authority: Critical for Development Agreements

Courts that condemn zoning by agreement inveigh against the abridgment of powers protecting the general welfare and the "bartering . . . [of] legislative discretion for emoluments that had no bearing on the merits of the requested amendment."[602] This makes statutory authority important, if not critical. Indeed, an Iowa court held that a city's promise to later widen a street and construct a sidewalk amounted to an illegal contract to perform a governmental function in the future.[603] This it could not do without statutory authority. The court opined that the same reasoning would also apply to the city's exercise of its police power.

### 1. Protection of General Welfare

The first issue—protection of general welfare—is probably disposed of by strong public purpose-serving language. California,[604] Florida,[605] and Hawaii[606] all have such language in their development agreement statutes.

---

tenant's option, as an unconstitutional impairment of contractual rights. *See also* Quality Refrigerated Serv., Inc. v. City of Spencer, 908 F. Supp. 1471 (N.D. Iowa 1995) (granting city's motion to dismiss, in part because plaintiff failed to state a cause of action under the Contracts Clause of the Constitution where it failed to show that city zoning ordinance substantially impaired a contractual relationship, or that legitimate government interests would not justify such an impairment if it existed); William G. Holliman, *Development Agreements and Vested Rights in California*, 13 URB. LAW. 44, 52-53 (1981) (concluding that "*United States Trust* and *Allied Structural Steel* suggest that any subsequent exercise of the police power which impairs the obligations under a development agreement would be subjected to a strict scrutiny test for reasonableness and necessity"); Kramer, *supra* note 579, at 35 (concluding that "[s]ubsequent legislative action seeking to amend, modify, or repeal [a] development agreement would undoubtedly impair the obligation of the contract and if less onerous alternatives were available to the legislature to achieve the same policy goals they would have to be taken"); Sigg, *supra* note 597, at 720-22 (concluding "it would appear that impairment by a city or country of its own development agreement would have to survive the heightened scrutiny of a 'reasonable and necessary to serve important state purposes' test"). For an exhaustive discussion of the reserved powers doctrine and its applicability to local government contracts (and its Contracts Clause limitations), see Janice C. Griffith, *Local Government Contracts: Escaping From the Governmental/Proprietary Maze*, 75 IOWA L. REV. 277 (1990).

602. Hedrich v. Village of Niles, 250 N.E.2d 791, 796 (Ill. App. Ct. 1969).

603. *See* Marco Dev. Corp. v. City of Cedar Falls, 473 N.W.2d 41, 44 (Iowa 1991) (holding that the same limitation that prohibits a legislature from binding successive legislative bodies applies to a legislature's grant to a city, through a home-rule amendment to the state constitution, of "the power to contract for a the exercise of its governmental or legislative authority").

604. The California Code provides:

The Legislature finds and declares that:

(a) The lack of certainty in the approval of development projects can re-

## 2. Requirements

As to the bartering away of unrelated (to land use) emoluments, a well-drafted statute generally limits such agreements to specific land use matters, with a

---

> sult in a waste of resources, escalate the cost of housing and other development to the consumer, and discourage investment in and commitment to comprehensive planning which would make maximum efficient utilization of resources at the least economic cost to the public.
>
> (b) Assurance to the applicant for a development project that upon approval of the project, the applicant may proceed with the project in accordance with existing policies, rules and regulations, and subject to conditions of approval, will strengthen the public planning process, encourage private participation in comprehensive planning, and reduce the economic costs of development.
>
> (c) The lack of public facilities, including, but limited to, streets, sewerage, transportation, drinking water, school, and utility facilities, is a serious impediment to the development of new housing. Whenever possible, applicants and local governments may include provisions in agreements whereby applicants are reimbursed over time for financing public facilities.

CAL. GOV'T CODE §65864 (West 1997). See Appendix VII for the full text of the California statute.

605. The Florida Code provides:

> (2) The Legislature finds and declares that:
>
> (a) The lack of certainty in the approval of development can result in a waste of economic and land resources, discourage sound capital improvement planning and financing, escalate the cost of housing and development, and discourage commitment to comprehensive planning.
>
> (b) Assurance to a developer that upon receipt of his or her development permit or brownfield designation he or she may proceed in accordance with existing laws and policies, subject to the conditions of a development agreement, strengthens the public planning process, encourages sound capital improvement planning and financing, assists in assuring there are adequate capital facilities for the development, encourages private participation in comprehensive planning, and reduces the economic costs of development.
>
> (3) In conformity with, in furtherance of, and to implement the Local Government Comprehensive Planning and Land Development Regulation Act and the Florida State Comprehensive Planning Act of 1972, it is the intent of the Legislature to encourage a stronger commitment to comprehensive and capital facilities planning, ensure the provision of adequate public facilities for development, encourage the efficient use of resources, and reduce the economic cost of development.
>
> (4) This intent is effected by authorizing local governments to enter into development agreements with developers, subject to the procedures and requirements of §§163.3220-163.3243.

FLA. STAT. ANN. §163.3220 (West 2000).

606. The Hawaii Code provides:

# III. DEVELOPMENT AGREEMENTS

catchall for related matters. Florida's development agreement statute contains such language.[607] What the statutes contemplate is the trade off of zoning for de-

---

Findings and purpose. The legislature finds that with land use laws taking on refinements that make the development of land complex, time consuming, and requiring advance financial commitments, the development approval process involves the expenditure of considerable sums of money. Generally speaking, the larger the project contemplated, the greater the expenses and the more time involved in complying with the conditions precedent to filing for a building permit.

The lack of certainty in the development approval process can result in a waste of resources, escalate the cost of housing and other development to the consumer, and discourage investment in and commitment to comprehensive planning. Predictability would encourage maximum efficient utilization of resources at the least economic cost to the public.

Public benefits derived from development agreements may include, but are not limited to, affordable housing, design standards, and on- and off-site infrastructure and other improvements. Such benefits may be negotiated for in return for the vesting of development rights for a specific period.

Under appropriate circumstances, development agreements could strengthen the public planning process, encourage private and public participation in the comprehensive planning process, reduce the economic cost of development, allow for the orderly planning of public facilities and services and the allocation of cost. As an administrative act, development agreements will provide assurances to the applicant for a particular development project, that upon approval of the project, the applicant may proceed with the project in accordance with all applicable statutes, ordinances, resolutions, rules, and policies in existence at the time the development agreement is executed and that the project will not be restricted or prohibited by the county's subsequent enactment or adoption of laws, ordinances, resolutions, rules, or policies.

Development agreements will encourage the vesting of property rights by protecting such rights from the effect of subsequently enacted county legislation which may conflict with any term or provision of the development agreement or in any way hinder, restrict, or prevent the development of the project. Development agreements are intended to provide a reasonable certainty as to the lawful requirements that must be met in protecting vested property rights, while maintaining the authority and duty of government to enact and enforce laws which promote the public safety, health, and general welfare of the citizens of our State. The purpose of this part is to provide a means by which an individual may be assured at a specific point in time that having met or having agreed to meet all of the terms and conditions of the development agreement, the individual's rights to develop a property in a certain manner shall be vested.

HAW. REV. STAT. §46-121 (1993). See Appendix VII for the full text of the Hawaii statute.

607. The Florida Code provides:

(1) A development agreement shall include the following:

(a) A legal description of the land subject to the agreement, and the names of its legal and equitable owners;

---

velopment-generated public infrastructure needs (whether or not, it should be added, such public infrastructure needs are generated by the instant development). This is confirmed by cases upholding cooperative and annexation agreements,[608] low-rent housing for zoning,[609] annexation, zoning, and sewer connections for annexation and annexation fees,[610] and redevelopment agreements.[611]

---

(b) The duration of the agreement;

(c) The development uses permitted on the land, including population densities, and building intensities and height;

(d) A description of public facilities that will service the development, including who shall provide such facilities; the date any new facilities, if needed, will be constructed; and a schedule to assure public facilities are available concurrent with the impacts of the development;

(e) A description of any reservation or dedication of land for public purposes;

(f) A description of all local development permits approved or needed to be approved for the development of the land;

(g) A finding that the development permitted or proposed is consistent with the local government's comprehensive plan and land development regulations;

(h) A description of any conditions, terms, restrictions, or other requirements determined to be necessary by the local government for the public health, safety, or welfare of its citizens; and

(i) A statement indicating that the failure of the agreement to address a particular permit, condition, term, or restriction shall not relieve the developer of the necessity of complying with the law governing said permitting requirements, conditions, term, or restriction.

(2) A development agreement may provide that the entire development or any phase thereof be commenced or completed within a specific period of time.

FLA. STAT. ANN. §163.3227 (West 2000).

608. *See* Housing Redevelopment Auth. v. Jorgensen, 328 N.W.2d 740, 742-43 (Minn. 1983) (holding that cooperation agreement entered into between city and housing and redevelopment authority required city to issue conditional permits for development of low-income housing project).

609. *See* Housing Auth. v. City of Los Angeles, 38 Cal. 2d 853, 870, 243 P.2d 515, 524 (1952) (holding that city was bound by cooperative agreement with housing authority that approved development and construction of low-rent housing project).

610. *See* Morrison Homes Corp. v. City of Pleasanton, 130 Cal. Rptr. 196, 201-02, 58 Cal. App. 3d 724, 733-34 (1976) (holding that annexation agreements entered into between the city and the developer that required the city to provide sewage service to the planned development were binding and enforceable against the city); Meegan v. Village of Tinley Park, 52 Ill. 2d 354, 359, 288 N.E.2d 423, 426 (1972) (dismissing developer's mandamus action for issuance of building permit to build a gasoline station pursuant to annexation agreement within a reasonable time after expiration of annexation agreement's statutory five-year period of validity).

611. *See* Mayor of Baltimore v. Crane, 277 Md. 198, 208-09, 352 A.2d 786, 791-92 (1976) (holding that where a developer conveyed a strip of property to the city for highway purposes under zoning ordinance that allowed developer's proposed development to contain the same density of dwelling units as if the land had not been

# III. DEVELOPMENT AGREEMENTS

The California, Florida, Hawaii, and Nevada statutes contain minimum standards for describing the basic character of a proposed development subject to a development agreement. These include the size and shape of buildings. In a decision that clearly signals the extent of flexibility possible in California, a California court of appeals recently upheld a development agreement containing no such precise standards.[612] According to the court, it was sufficient that the zoning ordinance contained height and use limitations in the zone where the proposed project was to be constructed.[613]

This clearly indicates the importance of a well-drafted statute in advancing the legality of the development agreement, particularly in the face of a reserved powers/bargaining away of the police power challenge. Indeed, there is only one significant case upholding a development agreement against this and other challenges without the benefit of such a statute.[614] It is, therefore, worth noting what other basic provisions are contained in a typical development agreement statute. Thirteen states[615] presently have such statutes. The most detailed comes from Hawaii, and so the citations that follow are primarily to that statute. However, California remains the state in which the vast majority of development agreements appear to be negotiated and are in effect.

## D. A Statutory Checklist

### 1. Enabling Ordinance

A preliminary issue is whether an enabling statute is sufficient to grant local government the authority to enter into development agreements. There is some authority for requiring a local government to pass an enabling ordinance setting out the details of development agreement/annexation agreement procedures and requirements. Thus, the Hawaii[616] and Florida[617] statutes appear to require

---

conveyed, the developer acquired vested contractual rights that were enforceable against the city).

612. *See* Santa Margarita Area Residents Together v. San Luis Obispo County Bd. of Supervisors, 100 Cal. Rptr. 2d 740, 743, 84 Cal. App. 4th 221, 225-26 (2000) (upholding development agreement that froze zoning on the proposed development property in exchange for developer's commitment to submit a specific construction plan in compliance with county land use requirements).

613. *Id.* at 747, 84 Cal. App. 4th at 231.

614. *See* Giger v. City of Omaha, 232 Neb. 676, 442 N.W.2d 182 (1989).

615. *See supra* note 576.

616. The Hawaii Code provides:

General authorization. Any county by ordinance may authorize the executive branch of the county to enter into a development agreement with any person having a legal or equitable interest in real property, for the development of such property in accordance with this part; provided that such an ordinance shall:

(1) Establish procedures and requirements for the consideration of development agreements upon application by or on behalf of per-

that local governments desiring to negotiate development agreements first pass a local resolution or ordinance to that effect. In Hawaii, the state legislature has delegated the authority to the county to enter into development agreements, provided, however, that the county first passes an enabling ordinance establishing the procedures that the county executive branch must follow. While the language of the Hawaii statute does not clearly require such an ordinance, three out of Hawaii's four counties have drafted them.

2. Approval and Adoption

Although one governmental body may enter into the negotiation stage of the development agreement, another may be authorized to approve the final product. In Hawaii, for example, the mayor is the designated negotiator, with the final agreement presented to the county legislative body (city council) for approval. If approved, the city council must then adopt the development agreement by resolution.[618] In California, a development agreement must be approved by ordinance.

---

sons having a legal or equitable interest in the property, in accordance with this part;

(2) Designate a county executive agency to administer the agreements after such agreements become effective.

(3) Include provisions to require the designated agency to conduct a review of compliance with the terms and conditions of the development agreement, on a periodic basis as established by the development agreement; and

(4) Include provisions establishing reasonable time periods for the review and appeal of modifications of the development agreement.

Negotiating development agreements. The mayor or the designated agency appointed to administer development agreements may make such arrangements as may be necessary or proper to enter into development agreements; provided that the county has adopted an ordinance pursuant to section 46-123.

The final draft of each individual development agreement shall be presented to the county legislative body for approval or modification prior to execution. To be binding on the county, a development agreement must be approved by the county legislative body and executed by the mayor on behalf of the county. County legislative approval shall be by resolution adopted by a majority of the membership of the county legislative body.

HAW. REV. STAT. §§46-123 to -124 (1993).

617. See FLA. STAT. ANN. §163.3223 (West 2000) ("Any local government may, *by ordinance*, establish procedures and requirements, as provided in §§163.320-163.3243, to consider and enter into a development agreement with any person having a legal or equitable interest in real property located within its jurisdiction.") (emphasis added).

618. The Hawaii Code provides:

Negotiating development agreements. The mayor or the designated agency appointed to administer development agreements may make

# III. DEVELOPMENT AGREEMENTS

A development agreement may also be entered into early in the planning process.[619] In *SMART*, an association comprised of area residents contended that a development agreement entered into by San Luis Obispo County was invalid because the project in contention had not been approved for actual construction. In rejecting this contention and holding for the county, the court stated that the development agreement statute should be liberally construed to permit "local government to make commitments to developers at the time the developer makes a substantial investment in the project."

The court found that the agreement entered into by the county conformed to the statute because, by focusing on the planning state of the project, the agreement met rather than evaded the purpose of the statute. The county's agreement maximized the public's role in final development, increased control over the inclusion of public facilities and benefits, and permitted the county to monitor the planning of the project to assure compliance with its existing land use regulations.

## 3. Conformance to Plans and Other Reviews

Development agreements must often comply with local government plans as a condition of enforceability, either by statute or because of the rubric that the zoning bargained-for must accord with comprehensive plans. The Hawaii[620] and California[621] development agreement statutes both so require. In California, the development agreement must be consistent with the general plan and

---

such arrangements as may be necessary or proper to enter into development agreements, including negotiating and drafting individual development agreements; provided that the county has adopted an ordinance pursuant to section 46-123.

The final draft of each individual development agreement shall be presented to the county legislative body for approval or modification prior to execution. To be binding on the county, a development agreement must be approved by the county legislative body and executed by the mayor on behalf of the county. County legislative approval shall be by resolution adopted by a majority of the membership of the county legislative body.

HAW. REV. STAT. §46-124 (1993).

619. Santa Margarita Area Residents Together v. San Luis Obispo County Bd. of Supervisors, 100 Cal. Rptr. 2d 740, 84 Cal. App. 4th 221 (2000).

620. *See* HAW. REV. STAT. §46-129 (1993) ("No development agreement shall be entered into unless the county legislative body finds that the provisions of the proposed development agreement are consistent with the county's general plan and any applicable development plan, effective as of the effective date of the development agreement.").

621. *See* CAL. GOV'T CODE §65867.5 (West 1997) ("A development agreement is a legislative act which shall be approved by ordinance and is subject by referendum. A development agreement shall not be approved unless the legislative body finds that the provisions of the agreement are consistent with the general plan and any applicable specific plan.").

any applicable specific plans.[622] A fully negotiated development agreement is a "project" under the California Environmental Quality Act,[623] and as such is subject to environmental review. This is true even when the development agreement is not directly approved by the local government but is instead submitted to the voters for approval.[624]

If, prior to incorporation of a new city or annexation to an existing city, a county has entered into a development agreement with the developer, the development agreement remains valid for the duration of the agreement, or for eight years from the effective date of the incorporation or annexation, whichever is earlier, or for up to 15 years upon agreement between the developer and the city.[625] This statute applies to incorporations where the development agreement was applied for prior to circulation of the incorporation petition and entered into between the county and the developer prior to the date of the incorporation election. The statute also allows the incorporating or annexing city to modify or suspend the provisions of the development agreement if it finds an adverse impact on public health or safety in the jurisdiction. However, as to annexations, if the proposal for annexation is initiated by a petitioner other than a city, the development agreement is valid unless the city adopts written findings that implementation of the development would create a condition injurious to the public health, safety or welfare of the city's residents.[626]

The importance of the plan is demonstrated by the Idaho Supreme Court in *Sprenger, Grubb & Associates v. City of Hailey.*[627] There, the court upheld a rezoning over the objections of the developers of property subject to what the court called a development agreement (arguably an annexation agreement), on the ground that the applicable plan was sufficiently broad in that it supported the contested downzoning.[628] Largely to the same effect is a recent California court of appeals decision where the existence of, and need to conform to, applicable plans, was critical in upholding a development agreement in the face of a broad and direct challenge to such agreements generally.[629]

---

622. Cal. Gov't Code §65867.5(c).

623. Cal. Pub. Res. Code §21000 et seq.

624. Citizens for Responsible Gov't v. City of Albany, 66 Cal. Rptr. 2d 102, 56 Cal. App. 4th 1199 (1997).

625. Cal. Gov't Code §65865.3.

626. *Id.*

627. 127 Idaho 576, 903 P.2d 741 (1995).

628. *Id.* at 585, 903 P.2d at 750 ("The Council's conclusion that the 'downsizing' . . . is consistent with Hailey's comprehensive plan is not clearly erroneous, and is affirmed.").

629. *See* Santa Margarita Area Residents Together v. San Luis Obispo County Bd. of Supervisors, 100 Cal. Rptr. 2d 740, 84 Cal. App. 4th 221 (2000).

# III. DEVELOPMENT AGREEMENTS

## 4. The Legislative/Administrative Issue

One of the thorniest problems in land use regulation is whether the amendment or changing of such a regulation is legislative or quasi-judicial/administrative.[630] Legislative decisions like zoning amendments are subject to initiative and referendum, whereas quasi-judicial decisions like the granting of a special use permit are not. Legislative decisions like rezonings are, when appealed, usually heard de novo whereas quasi-judicial decisions, like the granting of a special use permit, are decided on the record made before the permitting agency, usually under a state's administrative procedure code.[631] What about the development agreement? On this issue, California and Hawaii appear to differ—in the former, it is a legislative act,[632] whereas it is an administrative act in the latter.[633]

As with zoning, what follows from the statutory declarations—legislative in California, administrative (quasi-judicial) in Hawaii—is more than a matter of form. Legislative decisions are subject to referendum.[634] Quasi-judicial ones are not.[635] Given the common use of the referendum in both California and Hawaii to address land use issues, development agreements in Hawaii, at least, are likely to be "referendum-proof," as well as protected against government change, during the life of a development agreement. However, California limits the opportunity to repeal a development agreement to 30 days from the date the local government approved the agreement.[636] Thereafter, both the agreement and the proposed land development are immune from subsequent changes by referendum.[637] Moreover,

---

630. *See, e.g.*, Town v. Land Use Comm'n, 55 Haw. 538, 547-48, 524 P.2d 84, 90-91 (1974) (holding a reclassification of land by a state land use commission to be quasi-judicial); Fasano v. Board of County Comm'rs, 264 Or. 574, 579-80, 507 P.2d 23, 26 (1973) (holding a rezoning to be the same, despite the general rule that such "rezonings" are generally held to be legislative in character).

631. *See* JULIAN CONRAD JUERGENSMEYER & THOMAS E. ROBERTS, LAND USE PLANNING CONTROL LAW §§531, 533, 538 (1998); *see also* David Callies et al., *Ballot Box Zoning: Initiative, Referendum, and the Law*, 39 WASH. U. J. URB. & CONTEMP. L. 53 (1991). But as to federal due process, both administrative and legislative decisions appear to be referendable following the Court's decision in *City of Cuyahoga Falls v. Buckeye Community Hope Found.*, 123 S. Ct. 1389 (2003).

632. *See* SMART, 100 Cal. Rptr. 2d at 740, 84 Cal. App. 4th at 227.

633. *See* HAW. REV. STAT. §46-131 (1993) ("Each development agreement shall be deemed an administrative act of the government body made party to the agreement.").

634. *See* CAL. GOV'T CODE §65867.5 (West 1997) ("A development agreement is a legislative act . . . and is subject to the referendum.").

635. JUERGENSMEYER & ROBERTS, *supra* note 631, §§5.5 and 5.9. *But see City of Cuyahoga Falls*, 123 S. Ct. at 1389.

636. *See* Midway Orchards v. County of Butte, 269 Cal. Rptr. 796, 804-06, 220 Cal. App. 3d 765, 778-82 (1990) (holding that where development agreements are approved by legislative act of resolution that do not include referendum mechanism, constitutional right to referendum requires 30-day delay in effectiveness of the agreement to allow for referendum procedure).

637. *See* CURTIN & TALBERT, *supra* note 51, at 219.

in *Midway Orchards v. County of Butte*,[638] a California court held a development agreement was invalid because the general plan amendment relied on for consistency was timely referended.[639] The court stated:

> The development agreement was therefore unlawfully approved and executed. A contract entered into by a local government without legal authority is "wholly void," ultra vires and unenforceable. Such a contract can create no valid rights. Therefore, Midway can claim no right to develop its property based on a development agreement void from the beginning.[640]

Since a development agreement is a legislative act, a local government's decision not to enter into a development agreement need not be supported by findings.[641]

Under the California development agreement statute, mutuality of consideration is not required. As a practical matter, however, it is usually present as the developer obtains a "freeze" on applicable land use regulations while the public often obtains increased control over the development, certain assurances that the project will go forward, and perhaps other concessions from the developer that could not be obtained through the standard land use exaction process.

Finally, there is the question in California of whether the legislature can declare something to be a legislative act if it is not one anyway, even though this might "take away a right reserved in the California Constitution to the people of a city to rezone by initiative."[642] A California appellate court has declared that a development agreement is a legislative act.[643] This issue does not arise in Hawaii, both because the state constitution does not so provide, and because the Hawaii statute expresses a preference against such agreements being legislative acts. Other states have decided the question in the courts alone.[644]

---

638. 269 Cal. Rptr. 796, 220 Cal. App. 3d 765 (1990).

639. *Id.* at 804-06, 220 Cal. App. 3d at 778-82.

640. *Id.* at 783, 220 Cal. Rptr. at 807 (internal citations omitted). *See also* 216 Sutter Bay Assocs. v. County of Sutter, 58 Cal. App. 4th 860 (1997) (holding that an interim urgency zoning ordinance and a parallel "ordinary" urgency ordinance, adopted by a newly elected board of supervisors within the 30-day "referendum period," successfully stopped a development agreement adopted by the preceding, lame-duck board).

641. Native Sun/Lyon Communities v. City of Escondido, 19 Cal. Rptr. 2d 344, 15 Cal. App. 4th 892 (1993).

642. HAGMAN & JUERGENSMEYER, *supra* note 635, at 70. CAL. GOV'T CODE §65867.5 is the statute declaring a development agreement to be a legislative act.

643. Santa Margarita Area Residents Together v. San Luis Obispo County Bd. of Supervisors, 100 Cal. Rptr. 2d 740, 744, 84 Cal. App. 4th 221, 227 (2000).

644. *See, e.g.*, Geralnes B.V. v. City of Greenwood Village, 583 F. Supp. 830, 835 (D. Colo. 1984) (holding that city's zoning actions are quasi-judicial).

# III. DEVELOPMENT AGREEMENTS

## 5. Public Hearing

Another issue arising frequently is whether a public hearing is required before a development agreement can be entered into, and, if so, what proceedings are required. Both Hawaii[645] and California[646] explicitly require that a public hearing be held prior to adoption of the development agreement.

## 6. Binding of State and Federal Agencies

Hawaii and California diverge on another key point: the binding inclusion of state or federal agencies. Hawaii seeks to bind them[647]; California does not.[648] California initially appears to limit agreements to cities and counties, though it contemplates coastal commissions as parties under certain circumstances. Hawaii, on the other hand, appears determined to include state and federal agencies in development agreements.

---

645. *See* HAW. REV. STAT. §46-128 (2002) (stating: "No development agreement shall be entered into unless a public hearing on the application therefor first shall have been held by the county legislative body.").

646. The California Code provides:

> A public hearing on an application for a development agreement shall be held by the planning agency and by the legislative body. Notice of intention to consider adoption of a development agreement shall be given as provided in Section[s] 65090 and 65091 in addition to any other notice required by law for other actions to be considered concurrently with the development agreement.

CAL. GOV'T CODE §65867.

647. The Hawaii Code provides:

> In addition to the county and principal, any federal, state, or local government agency or body may be included as a party to the development agreement. If more than one government body is made party to an agreement, the agreement shall specify which agency shall be responsible for the overall administration of the agreement.

HAW. REV. STAT. §46-126(d) (1993).

648. The California Code provides:

> A development agreement shall not be applicable to any development project located in an area for which a local coastal program is required to be prepared and certified pursuant to the requirements of Division 20 (commencing with Section 30000) of the Public Resources Code, unless: (1) the required local coastal program has been certified as required by such provisions prior to the date on which the development agreement is entered into, or (2) in the event that the required local coastal program has not been certified, the California Coastal Commission approves such development agreement by formal commission action.

CAL. GOV'T CODE §65869 (West 1997).

### 7. Amendment or Cancellation of the Agreement

Generally, mutual consent of both parties is needed to amend or cancel the agreement.[649] In Hawaii, if the proposed amendment would substantially alter the original agreement, a public hearing must be held.[650] In California, a city or county may terminate or modify a development agreement if it finds and determines, on the basis of substantial evidence, that the applicant or successor in interest thereto has not complied in good faith with its terms or conditions.[651]

### 8. Breach

There are essentially two kinds of breaches that commonly occur during the period of an agreement: change in land use rules by local government and failure to provide a bargained-for facility, dedication, or hook-up by either party.

#### a. When Local Government Changes the Land Development Rules

Recall that the overriding concern of the landowner in negotiating an annexation or development agreement is the vesting of development rights or the freezing of land development regulations during the term of the agreement. Whether these regulations are changed just prior to the execution of the agreement, and whether the landowner may need further permits which are not subject to a particular agreement, raise different, but related, questions. Here, we deal only with the effect on the landowner and the agreement should the local government change development regulations during the term of the agreement. Development agreement statutes usually contemplate a freeze of development regulations.[652]

---

649. *See* CAL. GOV'T CODE §65868 (West 1997) ("A development agreement may be amended, or canceled, in whole or in part, by mutual consent of the parties to the agreement or their successors in interest . . . ."); HAW. REV. STAT. §46-130 (1993) ("A development agreement may be amended or canceled, in whole or in part, by mutual consent of the parties to the agreement, or their successors in interest.").

650. *See* HAW. REV. STAT. §46-130 (1993) ("[I]f the county determines that a proposed amendment would substantially alter the original development agreement, a public hearing on the amendment shall be held by the county legislative body before it consents to the proposed amendment.").

651. CAL. GOV'T CODE §65865.1.

652. For example, the California Code provides:

> Unless otherwise provided by the development agreement, rules, regulations, and official policies governing permitted uses of the land, governing density, and governing design, improvement, and construction standards and specifications, applicable to development of the property subject to a development agreement, shall be those rules, regulations, and official policies in force at the time of execution of the agreement. A development agreement shall not prevent a city, county, or city and county, in subsequent actions applicable to the property, from applying new rules, regulations, and policies which do not conflict with those

## III. DEVELOPMENT AGREEMENTS

The California Supreme Court, in *City of West Hollywood v. Beverly Towers*,[653] made it abundantly clear in a footnote that landowner protection from development regulation changes is a major factor in executing development agreements:

> Development agreements . . . between a developer and a government limit the power of that government to apply newly enacted ordinances to ongoing developments. Unless otherwise provided in the agreement, the rules, regulations, and official policies governing permitted uses, density, design, improvement, and construction are those in effect when the agreement is executed.[654]

The purpose of a development agreement, said the court, was "to allow a developer who needs additional discretionary approvals to complete a long-term development project as approved, regardless of any intervening changes in local regulations."[655]

The few courts that have dealt with local government changes in land use regulations have no difficulty in finding them inapplicable to the property subject to the agreement, provided the agreement itself is binding. Thus, in *Meegan v. Village of Tinley Park*,[656] the Illinois Supreme Court held that the original zoning of the subject property was valid during the term of the annexation agreement and any change by the village was void during that time. Indeed, since the village's attempted zoning change was void, said the court, there was no breach by the village.[657]

On the other hand, careful drafting is necessary to avoid the later application of land development regulations of a different sort than those contemplated in the agreement. Thus, in the California case of *Pardee Construction Co. of Nevada v. City of Camarillo*,[658] the court held applicable to the subject property a

---

rules, regulations, and policies applicable to the property as set forth herein, nor shall a development agreement prevent a city, county, or city and county from denying or conditionally approving any subsequent development project application on the basis of such existing or new rules, regulations, and policies.

Cal. Gov't Code §65866 (West 1997).

653. 52 Cal. 3d 1184, 805 P.2d 329 (1991).

654. *Id.* at 1191 n.6, 805 P.2d at 334 n.6. *See also* Daniel J. Curtin Jr., *Protecting Developers' Permits to Build: Development Agreement in Practice in California and Other States*, 18 Zoning & Plan. L. Rep. 85, 85092 (1995) (discussing various tests for determining when a developer's rights have vested and local government is estopped "from enacting or applying subsequent zoning changes to prevent the completion of the project or substantially reduce the return upon the developer's investment").

655. *Beverly Towers*, 52 Cal. 3d at 1191, 805 P.2d at 334-35.

656. 288 N.E.2d 423 (Ill. 1972).

657. *Id.* at 426; *cf.* Cummings v. City of Waterloo, 683 N.E.2d 1222, 1230 (Ill. App. Ct. 1997) (holding the city's amendment to its zoning ordinance that was contrary to the provisions of an annexation agreement was unenforceable against property subject to the annexation agreement).

658. 37 Cal. 3d 465, 690 P.2d 701 (1984).

transportation impact fee on the ground that it was different from the land development regulations listed in the agreement as frozen. While this seems to require a certain amount of prescience from the landowner at first blush, a local government can hardly be estopped from exercising its police power in enforcing a new breed of land development regulations that was not contemplated years before by either party, under the exercise of its police power. *Country Meadows West Partnership v. Village of Germantown*[659] represents an entirely different perspective. There, the court struck down the village's imposition of a new impact fee against a subdivider, holding that because of a subdivision agreement between the village and the subdivider, the subdivider was not obligated to pay the impact fee.

While most development agreement statutes either contain a limitation on the duration of such agreements,[660] or provide that the agreement must recite one,[661] many states appear to permit annexation agreements (and some states like Nebraska and California, development agreements) without the benefit of such a statutory construction. It is, therefore, theoretically possible for an agreement to be relatively open-ended with respect to matters such as the zoning of the subject property. The results can be unfortunate for the landowner since it is, of course, black letter law that a landowner has no vested right in a zoning classification absent activity that vests such rights.[662] Thus, where the agreement is silent on the time period, at least one court has held that a landowner is without remedy if, a few years after annexation pursuant to an annexation agreement, the annexing local government changes the zoning to a classification which makes the originally contemplated land development impossible.[663]

---

659. 237 Wis. 2d 290, 614 N.W.2d 498 (Wis. App. Ct. 2000).

660. *See, e.g.*, 65 ILL. COMP. STAT. 5/11-15.1-1 (West 1993) ("The agreement shall be valid and binding for a period of not to exceed 20 years from the date of its execution."); *id.* 5/11-15.1-5 ("Any annexation agreement executed prior to October 1, 1973 ... is hereby declared valid and enforceable as to such provisions for the effective period of such agreement, or for 20 years from the date of execution thereof, whichever is shorter.").

661. *See, e.g.*, CAL. GOV'T CODE §65865.2 (West 1997) ("A development agreement shall specify the duration of the agreement . . . ."); HAW. REV. STAT. §46-126 (1993) ("A development agreement shall ... (4) Provide a termination date ....").

662. *See infra* Part IV and David L. Callies, *Land Use: Herein of Vested Rights, Plans, and the Relationship of Planning and Controls*, 2 U. HAW. L. REV. 167, 168 (1979) ("While it is fair to say that most jurisdictions are satisfied with an expenditure of funds in reliance upon a preexisting zone classification to support a claim for these so-called vested rights, some jurisdictions have disregarded all together fairly large amounts so expended.") (footnote omitted).

663. *See* Carty v. City of Ojai, 143 Cal. Rptr. 506, 513, 77 Cal. App. 3d 329, 341 (1978) ("The reliance of the Cartys on the conduct of the city in the case before us has most tenuous predicates. No representations were made by any public official from the city as to the length of the time that the zone 'C-1' would continue.").

## III. DEVELOPMENT AGREEMENTS

### b. Nonperformance of a Bargained-For Act: Dedications, Contributions, and Hook-Ups

Equally common is the failure of a landowner or local government to live up to the other terms of the agreement, generally by failing to provide a public facility or money therefor, or by refusing to provide utility services to the subject property.[664] Under such circumstances, the courts have been strict in forcing the parties to live up to their bargains, even when unusual difficulties would appear to render such performance nearly impossible. Thus, in the California case of *Morrison Homes Corp.*, the court of appeals directed the local government to provide sewer connections to the landowner's property, as agreed in an annexation agreement, even though a superior governmental entity, a state regional water quality control board, ordered the local government not to do so.[665] After deciding that the agreement did not amount to the city's illegally contracting away its police power, the court stated: "The onset of materially changed conditions is not a ground for voiding a municipal contract which was valid when made, nor is the contracting city's failure to have foreseen them."[666]

### E. Limits on Local Government Conditions, Exactions, and Dedications Pursuant to Development Agreements

While every governmental action must be invested with a public purpose, there are few conditions, exactions, or dedications that a local government may not legitimately bargain for in negotiating such agreements. Certainly, local governments may require landowners and developers to make reasonable contributions toward whatever services and other resources the government will need to provide as a result of an a proposed development.[667] But this is so under existing law on development conditions and exactions entirely apart from such agreements.[668] The question is whether the local government may go further since

---

664. For other items bargained for and litigated, see Van Cleave v. Village of Seneca, 165 Ill. App. 3d 410, 411, 519 N.E.2d 63, 64 (1988) (exemptions from real estate taxes), and O'Malley v. Village of Ford Heights, 633 N.E.2d 848, 849 (Ill. App. Ct. 1994) (exemption from environmental ordinances, which did not survive legal challenge).

665. 130 Cal. Rptr. at 196, 58 Cal. App. 3d at 724; *but cf.* Keystone Bituminous Coal Ass'n v. DeBenedictis, 480 U.S. 470, 492, 107 S. Ct. 1232, 1246, 94 L. Ed. 2d 472, 492, 17 ELR 20440, 20450 (1987) (upholding governmental refusal to perform development agreement when health and safety issue is involved); Goldblatt v. Town of Hempstead, 369 U.S. 590, 593-94, 82 S. Ct. 987, 990, 8 L. Ed. 2d 130, 134 (1962) (same).

666. *Morrison Homes Corp.*, 130 Cal. Rptr. at 202, 58 Cal. App. 3d at 735.

667. *See, e.g.*, Village of Orland Park v. First Fed. Sav. & Loan Ass'n, 135 Ill. App. 3d 520, 526, 481 N.E.2d 946, 950 (1985) ("Additional positive effects of such agreements include controls over health sanitation, fire prevention, and police protection, which are vital to governing communities.").

668. *See supra* Part II and David L. Callies, *Exactions, Impact Fees, and Other Land Development Conditions, in* ZONING AND LAND USE CONTROLS ch. 9 (Eric Damian

the development agreement is indeed a voluntary agreement which neither government nor landowner is compelled to either negotiate or execute. So long as the agreement is indeed voluntary, the answer is almost certainly yes.[669]

Whether or not development agreements successfully avoid or survive nexus and proportionality challenges may depend, however, upon how willing the courts are to accept the underlying "voluntary" rationale. Nevertheless, some argue that exactions agreed to under a voluntary development agreement must bear a rational nexus to the needs created by the development.[670] The argument states that the "rational nexus" and "substantial advancement" standards of *Nollan* are not limited to just those instances where the municipality requires an exaction from an uncooperative landowner, but also apply to voluntary permit conditions. Under this view, the type and extent of exactions permissible under development agreements would not differ from the type and extent available under other traditional exaction mechanisms such as impact fees.

The rationale supporting such a view is that requiring the *Nollan* standard to be satisfied serves to prevent governmental abuse of the mechanism, as it is "difficult to tell whether a landowner's acceptance of a condition is truly voluntary or is instead a submission to government coercion."[671] Thus:

> A municipality could use . . . regulations to exact land or fees from a subdivider far out of proportion to the needs created by his subdivision in order to avoid imposing the burden of paying for additional services on all citizens via taxation.

Kelly ed., 2001); *see also* Dolan v. City of Tigard, 512 U.S. 374, 391, 114 S. Ct. 2309, 2319-20, 129 L. Ed. 2d 304, 320, 24 ELR 21083, 21087 (1994) (holding that the Takings Clause of the Fifth Amendment requires that "the city must make some sort of individualized determination that the required dedication is related both in nature and extent to the impact of the proposed development"); Nollan v. California Coastal Comm'n, 483 U.S. 825, 834-35, 107 S. Ct. 3141, 3147, 97 L. Ed. 2d 677, 688, 17 ELR 20918, 20920 (1987) ("We have long recognized that land use regulation does not effect a taking if it substantially advances legitimate state interests and does not deny an owner economically viable use of his land. . . . [A] broad range of governmental purposes and regulations satisfies these requirements.") (internal quotations omitted).

669. *See* City of Annapolis v. Waterman, 745 A.2d 1000, 1025 (Md. 2000) (conditions agreed to by the subdivider as part of an earlier subdivision agreement were not an unconstitutional taking of the subdivider's property). For a contrary view which would impose the same strict nexus and proportionality requirements upon such agreements as upon "free-standing" local government development dedications, exactions, and other conditions, see generally Sam D. Starritt & John H. McClanahan, *Land-Use Planning and Takings: The Viability of Conditional Exactions to Conserve Open Space in the Rocky Mountain West After Dolan v. City of Tigard, 114 S. Ct. 2309 (1994)*, 30 LAND & WATER L. REV. 415 (1995).

670. *See* Michael H. Crew, *Development Agreements After Nollan v. California Coastal Commission, 483 U.S. 825 (1987)*, 22 URB. LAW. 23, 27 (1990) ("In applying this standard, courts considered . . . the cost of existing public facilities and their manner of financing, the extent to which existing development has already contributed to the cost of these facilities, and the extent to which the proposed project will contribute to the cost of the existing facilities in the future.").

671. *Id.* at 46.

# III. DEVELOPMENT AGREEMENTS

To tolerate this situation would be to allow an otherwise acceptable exercise of police power to become grand theft.[672]

The Hawaii development agreement statute provides that, "[p]ublic benefits derived from development agreements may include, but are not limited to, affordable housing, design standards, and on- and off-site infrastructure and other improvements. Such benefits may be negotiated for in return for the vesting of development rights for a specific period."[673] According to one commentator:

> [T]he government can require the developer to provide public benefits unrelated to the proposed project in exchange for the municipality granting her the right to develop.... [T]he statute leads municipalities to believe that the granting of development rights confers a governmental benefit on the developer. This is not the case. *Nollan* clearly holds that "the right to build on one's own property—even though it's exercise can be subjected to legitimate permitting requirements—cannot remotely be described as a 'governmental benefit.'"[674]

However, while it is true that the right to develop on one's own land is not a governmental benefit, the right to develop is not the bargaining chip being tendered by the government in a development agreement. The authorities cited in support of the above-quoted argument concern exactions imposed as required conditions to development. In the case of a development agreement, the municipality is not granting the landowner the right to develop nor imposing conditions on such development, but instead is promising to protect the developer's investment by not enforcing any subsequent land use regulation that may burden the project. Because the developer does not require any such guarantee to exercise his right or privilege to build, and may certainly choose to avail himself of such a guarantee and to negotiate for it, it could be argued that the development agreement does indeed convey a "governmental benefit" upon the developer, since "[i]t is well established that there is no federal Constitutional right to be free from changes in land use laws."[675] The municipality should therefore be free to negotiate its best terms in exchange for the benefit conferred, regardless of nexus. Because development agreements are adopted as a result of negotiations between a local government and a developer, they are not subject to the *Dolan* or *Nollan* decisions.[676]

---

672. Collis v. City of Bloomington, 310 Minn. 5, 17, 246 N.W.2d 19, 26 (1976) (upholding statute authorizing municipalities to require dedication of land or payment of fees as condition of subdivision approval as constitutional since enabling legislation and implementing ordinance limited the amount of land to be dedicated to a "reasonable" percentage of the property).

673. HAW. REV. STAT. §46-121 (1993).

674. Crew, *supra* note 670, at 49 (quoting Nollan v. California Coastal Comm'n, 483 U.S. 826, 833 n.10, 107 S. Ct. 3141, 3148, 97 L. Ed. 2d 677, 688 n.10, 17 ELR 20918, 20929 n.10 (1987)).

675. Lakeview Dev. Corp. v. City of S. Lake Tahoe, 915 F.2d 1290, 1295 (9th Cir. 1990).

676. *See* Leroy Land Dev. Corp. v. Tahoe Reg'l Planning Agency, 939 F.2d 696, 21 ELR 21376 (9th Cir. 1991) (holding settlement agreement not subject to *Nollan*); *see also* David L. Callies & Julie A. Tappendorf, *Unconstitutional Land Development*

In *Hermosa Beach Stop Oil Coalition v. City of Hermosa Beach*,[677] the court held that the developer, who had failed to establish entitlement to vested rights to develop an oil business on property leased from the city, could have protected itself from subsequent regulatory changes by asking that the city enter into a development agreement. The court noted that it was likely that the city would have demanded additional consideration for either a risk-adjustment provision in the existing lease or a separate development agreement, and that having at least implicitly decided to forego such protection against future regulatory changes, the developer must accept the consequences of its judgment to do so.[678]

A trial court held that developers' rights vested at the time of signing a development agreement, and thus a city could not use wording within the agreement to allow it to raise sewer connection fees.[679] Developers and the city entered into a 15-year written agreement allowing for the development of a residential subdivision, allowing the city to charge any "new taxes, assessments, or development impact fees on the implementation of the Project" only if those same charges are levied on all other similar developments within the city.[680] Six years after the parties signed the contract, the city raised the monthly wastewater connection fees and initial capital surcharge for each residential unit during the period covered by the contract, and the developers sued for breach of contract because their development rights had vested at the time of the initial agreement. A trial court agreed, but said that plaintiffs could not challenge the increased costs for potential future homeowners.[681]

In *City of North Las Vegas v. Pardee Construction Co. of Nevada*,[682] a developer lost the appeal to define a cost-based fee as an impact fee in order to invalidate it through the parties' development agreement, which only prohibited impact fees. The municipality in this case regulated water issues on a regional level, and to respond to Nevada's growth spurt, the region passed a capital improvements plan to supplement the existing, overstrained water supply system.[683] The city had to join the regional water authority because its own water supply did not accommodate for any more growth. Upon joining, the city had to pay for the connection to the new system through citywide assessments and water delivery, connection, and commodity fees.[684] To meet these payments, the

---

*Conditions and the Development Agreement Solution: Bargaining for Public Facilities After* Nollan *and* Dolan, 51 CASE W. RES. L. REV., Summer 2001.

677. 103 Cal. Rptr. 2d 447, 86 Cal. App. 4th 534 (2001).

678. *Id.* at 464, 86 Cal. App. 4th at 558.

679. Referred to in the subsequent unpublished appeal, Operating Eng'rs Funds, Inc. v. City of Thousand Oaks, 2002 WL 44253 (Cal. Ct. App. 2d 2002) (holding that because the plaintiffs did not succeed in each of its claims, they could not qualify for attorneys fees).

680. *Id.* at *1.

681. *Id.* at *2.

682. 21 P.3d 8 (Nev. 2001).

683. *Id.* at 9.

684. *Id.*

city passed the costs on to the consumers at a direct rate—not making any profit.[685] Plaintiffs contended that these new charges were really impact fees and violated the terms of their development agreement.[686] Because the city does not make a profit, but bases the charges on those charges it must pay to the regional authority, with no money going toward capital improvements, the court found that the charge was simply cost-based and within the parameters of the development agreement.[687]

Courts regularly label sewer systems as a typical government function, but consider general water and stormwater systems to be proprietary. Thus, on balance, a development agreement often provides that the subdivision developer install the water and sewer lines needed both within the subdivision and to connect the subdivision to existing lines. Sometimes the development agreement also requires payments for upgrades to the city's water facilities to manage the greater flow requirements of the new development. In return for the improvements, the city agrees to maintain the pipe infrastructure within and connected to the subdivision.

## IV. Annexation Agreements

### A. Introduction

As discussed above, a developer desires to protect its ability to develop its property once it has obtained all land use and discretionary approvals. One way to protect the developer from changes in land use and zoning laws and permit the developer to complete its development is for the developer to enter into an agreement with the local government to freeze these regulations. One type of agreement used frequently, particularly in Illinois, is the annexation agreement.

### B. Bargaining Away Police Power

The issue of whether a local government bargains away its police power by entering into an agreement under which it promises not to change its land use regulations during the life of the agreement is the same for annexation agreements as it is for development agreements. Although specific statutory authorization is helpful to show the necessary public purpose that is recognized by the state, only a handful of states appear to have adopted legislation enabling local governments to enter into annexation agreements.[688] Apparently, the prevalence of statutory annexation provisions, together with a recognition that local governments have the powers they need to exercise their authorized powers (such as

---

685. *Id.* at 10.

686. *Id.*

687. *Id.* at 11.

688. Ariz. Rev. Stat. Ann. §9-500.05; 65 Ill. Comp. Stat. 5/11-15.1-1; Minn. Stat. §414.0325; N.C. Gen. Stat. §160A-58.21 (1989); Wash. Rev. Code §36.70B.170.

annexation), has convinced most courts considering the matter to uphold the annexation agreement in the absence of enabling statutes. For example, a California court of appeals held that the statutory sources of a city's authority to discharge its annexation and sewage functions, while not expressly vesting it with the authority to contract for either purpose by means of an annexation agreement, have that effect by necessary implication: "[A] city has authority to enter into contracts which enable it to carry out its necessary functions, and this applies to powers expressly conferred upon a municipality and to powers implied by necessity."[689]

Local governments may not "contract away the police power,"[690] particularly in the context of zoning decisions.[691] In other words, government cannot bind itself to not exercise its police powers. Because land use and development regulations represent exercises of police power, an annexation agreement binding a local government not to exercise these regulatory powers arguably violates the reserved powers doctrine, and is, therefore, ultra vires.

It is also considered to be against public policy to permit the bargaining of zoning and subdivision regulations for agreements and stipulations on the part of developers to do or refrain from doing certain things. The prohibition against bargaining away the police power finds its source in the so-called reserved power doctrine.[692] Under this doctrine, bargaining away the police power is the equivalent of a current legislature attempting to exercise legislative power reserved to later legislatures.[693] However, an analysis of the cases indicates that what the courts have generally struck down is the bargaining away forever of legislative powers, or at least for a very long time. Notwithstanding such limitations, if an annexation agreement is drafted to reserve some governmental control over the agreement, it does not contract away the police power, but rather constitutes a valid present exercise of that power.[694]

---

689. Morrison Homes Corp. v. City of Pleasanton, 130 Cal. Rptr. 196, 202, 58 Cal. App. 3d 724, 734 (1976) (citing Carruth v. City of Madera, 43 Cal. Rptr. 855, 860, 233 Cal. App. 2d 688, 695 (1965)).

690. Carlino v. Whitpain Investors, 499 Pa. 498, 453 A.2d 1385 (1982).

691. Cederberg v. City of Rockford, 8 Ill. App. 3d 984, 291 N.E.2d 249 (1972). *See also* Houston Petroleum Co. v. Automotive Prods. Credit Ass'n, 9 N.J. 122, 87 A.2d 319 (N.J. 1952): "Contracts thus have no place in a zoning plan and a contract between a municipality and a property owner should not enter into the enactment or enforcement of zoning regulations"; *see also* V.F. Zahodiakin Eng'g Corp. v. Zoning Bd. of Adjustment, 8 N.J. 386, 86 A.2d 127 (1952).

692. *See supra* Part III.A; Kramer, *supra* note 579; Kessler, *supra* note 579.

693. *See* Stone v. Mississippi, 101 U.S. 814, 25 L. Ed. 1079 (1880); Corporation of the Brick Presbyterian Church v. Mayor of New York, 5 Cow. 538 (N.Y. 1826), discussed in Kramer, *supra* note 579, at 37-39.

694. *See, e.g., Morrison Homes Corp.*, 130 Cal. Rptr. at 196, 58 Cal. App. 3d at 724 (holding that the effect of the general rule is to void only a contract which amounts to a city's "surrender" or "abnegation" of its *control* of a properly municipal function, and that the city's reservations of control over the land subject to an annexation agreement, as well as the "just, reasonable, fair and equitable" nature of the agreement, rendered the agreement valid and enforceable against the city).

# IV. ANNEXATION AGREEMENTS

This leads to the follow-up question: in exercising their power to contract, can the current corporate authorities make a contract that binds its successors? In *Carruth*,[695] the city contended that obligations under an annexation agreement executed by a predecessor council were invalid because they deprived the successor city council of the power to determine city policy and act in the public interest. The court, however, held that the contract entered into by the council was fair, just, and reasonable at the time of its execution and, therefore, the city was bound to its terms. In so holding, the court concluded that the contract was neither void nor voidable merely because some of its executory features may operate to bind a successor council.[696]

Similarly, in *Village of Orland Bank v. Federal Savings & Loan Ass'n of Chicago*,[697] a bank attempted to avoid obligations contained in an annexation agreement executed pursuant to the statutory authority contained in that state's preannexation agreement statute. Noting that the bank's cited authority involved agreements that proceeded without statutory authority, the Illinois Appellate Court observed:

> The authorization of preannexation agreements by statute, such as 11-15.1-1, serves to further important governmental purposes, such as the encouragement of expanding urban areas and to do so uniformly, economically, efficiently and fairly, with optimum provisions made for the establishment of land use controls and necessary municipal improvements including streets, water, sewer systems, schools, parks, and similar installations. This approach also discourages fragmentation and proliferation of special districts. Additional positive effects of such agreements include controls over health, sanitation, fire prevention and police protection, which are vital to governing communities.[698]

---

695. 43 Cal. Rptr. at 855.

696. *See supra* Part III.A; *Carruth*, 43 Cal. Rptr. at 855, 233 Cal. App. 2d at 688; *see also* Denio v. Huntington Beach, 22 Cal. 2d 580, 590, 140 P.2d 392, 397 (1943). Development agreement cases are largely in accord. One of the clearest rejections of the application of reserved power and bargaining away the police power comes from the wide-ranging Nebraska Supreme Court opinion upholding development agreements in Giger v. City of Omaha, 232 Neb. 676, 442 N.W.2d 182 (1989). The objectors to the agreement claimed that development agreements were a form of contract zoning and, therefore, illegal on their face. The Nebraska Supreme Court, however, preferred to characterize such agreements as a form of conditional zoning which actually increased the city's police power, rather than lessened it, by permitting more restrictive zoning (attaching conditions through agreement) than a simple Euclidean rezoning to a district in which a variety of uses would be permitted of right:

> In sum, we find that there is not clear and satisfactory evidence to support the appellants' contention that the city has bargained away its police power. The evidence clearly shows that the city's police powers are not abridged in any manner and that the agreement is expressly subject to the remedies available to the city under the Omaha Municipal Code. Further, we find that the agreement actually enhances the city's regulatory control over the development agreement rather than limiting it.

*Id.* at 192.

697. 135 Ill. App. 3d 520, 481 N.E.2d 946 (1985).

698. *Id.* 526, 481 N.E.2d at 950.

Also, where a foreign corporation attempted to disconnect its territory from the city of Greenwood Village, Colorado, in part on the ground that the annexation agreement under which the property was first annexed inhibited the city's future zoning power, the federal district court held that preannexation agreements imposing certain zoning classifications as conditions of annexation "have been upheld as valid and enforceable" in Colorado.[699] The court found that the city of Greenwood Village's zoning in this case fell into that category. To the same effect are several state court decisions upholding annexation agreements restricting a local government's power to later change zoning that was granted and guaranteed during the life of the agreement.[700]

Where a developer sued to recover payment to Colorado Springs for the acquisition of public parks made under an annexation agreement, the majority held that since the developer had obtained water and sewer services for its development under the agreement, as well as annexation to the city, it could not now seek to set aside the agreement.[701] The court stated that the parties "each got what it bargained for": the city wanted the property annexed and the property owners wanted water and sewer services.[702] The court emphasized that a "municipality is under no legal obligation in the first instance to annex contiguous territory, and may reject a petition for annexation for no reason at all." Thus, the court held that in an annexation agreement, a municipality "may impose such conditions by way of agreement as it sees fit."[703] Opining that "the majority opinion amounts to the longest and most dangerous step yet taken by this court in the general direction of emasculation of property rights,"[704] the dissent suggests that annexation agreements cannot require of a landowner that which the city could not constitutionally exact under the police power if the subject territory were already within the city's jurisdiction, even if that exaction is a trade off for that which the developer seeks, such as the discretionary annexation of its land.

Today, courts have little difficulty in upholding annexation agreements against any reserved powers/bargaining away the police power argument, particularly if supported by state legislation.[705] The current application of the re-

---

699. Geralnes B.V. v. City of Greenwood Village, Colo., 583 F. Supp. 830, 839 (D. Colo. 1984).

700. Rockville v. Brookeville Turnpike Constr. Co., 246 Md. 117, 228 A.2d 263 (1967); Union Nat'l Bank v. Glenwood, 38 Ill. App. 3d 469, 348 N.E.2d 226 (1976); French v. Lincolnshire, 31 Ill. App. 3d 537, 335 N.E.2d 29 (1975); Beshore v. Town of Bel Air, 237 Md. 398, 206 A.2d 678 (1965).

701. City of Colorado Springs v. Kitty Hawk Dev. Co., 154 Colo. 535, 392 P.2d 467 (1964).

702. *Id.* at 544, 392 P.2d at 472.

703. *Id.*

704. *Id.* at 547, 392 P.2d at 473 (Moore, J., dissenting).

705. Kessler, *supra* note 579; Donald G. Hagman, *Development Agreements*, 3 ZONING & PLAN. L. REP. 65 (1980); Callies & Tappendorf, *supra* note 676; David L. Callies, *Land Development Regulations*, §16.55, *in* LOCAL GOVERNMENT LAW ch. 16 (C. Dallas Sands & Michael E. Libonati eds., 1981); WILLIAM W. ABBOT ET AL.,

# IV. ANNEXATION AGREEMENTS

served powers clause to abrogate government-private contracts has been rare, and courts have attempted to find other grounds to uphold those contracts that are fair, just, reasonable, and advantageous to the local government.[706] It is unlikely that courts will fall back on the reserved powers clause in invalidating annexation agreements if the agreements have a fixed termination date—and that date is not decades away (the Illinois annexation agreement statute restricts the term of any annexation agreement to 20 years).[707]

## C. Enabling Act

While statutory authority is critical in the context of development agreements,[708] annexation agreement statutes appear to be less important.[709] Although not as prevalent as development agreement statutes, statutes authorizing a local government to enter into an annexation or preannexation agreement do exist.[710] For example, Illinois statutes provide:

> § 11-15.1-1. The corporate authorities of any municipality may enter into an annexation agreement with one or more of the owners of record of land in unincorporated territory. That land may be annexed to the municipality in the manner provided in Article 7 at the time the land is or becomes contiguous to the municipality. The agreement shall be valid and binding for a period of not to exceed 20 years from the date of its execution.[711]

Similarly, North Carolina authorizes local governments to enter into annexation agreements pursuant to the following statute:

---

DEVELOPMENT AGREEMENTS AND VESTED RIGHTS: A SECOND LOOK (1983); William G. Holliman, *Development Agreements and Vested Rights in California*, 13 URB. LAW. 44 (1981); Barbara Zeid, *Land Use Planning by Agreement: The Practice in England and California* (Draft L. Rev. note); MANDELKER, *supra* note 5, at §6.21 (1982); Kramer, *supra* note 579; DEVELOPMENT AGREEMENT MANUAL: COLLABORATION IN PURSUIT OF COMMUNITY INTERESTS, INSTITUTE FOR LOCAL SELF-GOVERNMENT (2002).

706. *See* Kramer, *supra* note 579; *see also* Carruth v. City of Madera, 43 Cal. Rptr. 855, 233 Cal. App. 2d 688 (1965).

707. 65 ILL. COMP. STAT. 5/11-15.1-1 et seq. See Appendix XII for the full text of the Illinois statute.

708. Marco Dev. Corp. v. City of Cedar Falls, 473 N.W.2d 41 (Iowa 1991) (holding that a city's promise to later widen a street and construct a sidewalk amounted to an illegal contract to perform a governmental function in the future).

709. Morrison Homes Corp. v. City of Pleasanton, 130 Cal. Rptr. 196, 202, 58 Cal. App. 3d 724, 734 (1976).

710. ARIZ. REV. STAT. ANN. §9-500.05; 65 ILL. COMP. STAT. 5/11-15.1-1; MINN. STAT. §414.0325; N.C. GEN. STAT. §160A-58.21 (1989); WASH. REV. CODE §36.70B.170.

711. 65 ILL. COMP. STAT. 5/11-15.1-1. This statute authorizes annexation agreements between municipalities and owners of property not contiguous to the municipality and was recently upheld by an Illinois appellate court in city of Springfield v. Judith Jones Dietsch Trust, 746 N.E.2d 1272 (Ill. App. Ct. 2001).

§160A-58.21. Purpose. It is the purpose of this Part to authorize cities to enter into binding agreements concerning future annexation in order to enhance orderly planning by such cities as well as residents and property owners in areas adjacent to such cities.[712]

Both Arizona and Washington authorize municipalities and owners to enter into "development agreements" relating to property located outside of the municipality's boundaries. Arizona's statute provides as follows:

§9-500.05 Development Agreements; public safety; definitions

A. A municipality, by resolution or ordinance, may enter into development agreements relating to property in the municipality and to property located outside the incorporated area of the municipality. If the development agreement relates to property located outside the incorporated area of the municipality, the development agreement does not become operative unless annexation proceedings to annex the property to the municipality are completed within the period of time specified by the development agreement or any extension of such time.[713]

Washington's statute states the following:

§36.70B.170 Development agreements—Authorized

(1) A local government may enter into a development agreement with a person having ownership or control of real property within its jurisdiction. A city may enter into a development agreement for real property outside its boundaries as part of a proposed annexation or a service agreement. A development agreement must set forth the development standards and other provisions that shall apply to and govern and vest the development, use, and mitigation of the development of the real property for the duration specified in the agreement. A development agreement shall be consistent with applicable development regulations adopted by a local government planning under chapter 36.70A RCW.[714]

## D. Issues

### 1. Enabling Ordinance

While the passage of an enabling ordinance setting out the procedures and requirements for entering into a development agreement may be a requirement for development agreements, such an ordinance does not appear to be required for annexation agreements. Thus, for example, Illinois does not require local enabling legislation and many communities in Illinois enter into annexation agreements based simply on the authority granted to the local government by Illinois statute.[715]

---

712. N.C. Gen. Stat. §160A-58.21. See Appendix XIII for the full text of the North Carolina statute.

713. Ariz. Rev. Stat. Ann. §9-500.05.

714. Wash. Rev. Code §36.70B.170.

715. 65 Ill. Comp. Stat. 5/11-15.1-1 et seq.

## 2. Approval and Adoption of the Agreement

Typically, an annexation agreement is approved through some formal action of the corporate authorities such as by the adoption of a resolution or ordinance. For example, in Illinois, an annexation agreement must be approved by either resolution or ordinance and must be passed by a vote of two-thirds of the corporate authorities then holding office, as set forth in the following statutory provision:

§11-15.1-3 Procedure
* * *

The annexation agreement or amendment shall be executed by the mayor or president and attested by the clerk of the municipality only after such hearing and upon the adoption of a resolution or ordinance directing such execution, which resolution or ordinance must be passed by a vote of two-thirds of the corporate authorities then holding office.[716]

Both Arizona[717] and Washington[718] require that development and annexation agreements be approved by resolution or ordinance and that they be recorded in the county in which the property is located. For example, the Washington statute provides:

§36.70B.190 Development Agreements—Recording—Parties and Successors Bound.

A development agreement shall be recorded with the real property records of the county in which the property is located. During the term of the development agreement, the agreement is binding on the parties and their successors, including a city that assumes jurisdiction through incorporation or annexation of the area covering the property covered by the development agreement.[719]

## 3. Public Hearing

States that have adopted statutes authorizing annexation agreements typically require that the local government entering into such an agreement hold a public hearing. For example, the Illinois, North Carolina, and Washington annexation agreement statutes all require that a public hearing be held prior to the approval of an annexation agreement:

Illinois:

§11-15.1-3. Any such agreement executed after July 31, 1963 and all amendments of annexation agreements, shall be entered into in the following manner. The corporate authorities shall fix a time for and hold a public hearing upon the

---

716. *Id.* 5/11-15.1-3. *See also* WASH. REV. CODE §36.70B.200, which provides as follows: "A county or city shall only approve a development agreement by ordinance or resolution after a public hearing."

717. ARIZ. REV. STAT. ANN. §9-500.05.

718. WASH. REV. CODE §36.70B.190.

719. *Id.*

proposed annexation agreement or amendment, and shall give notice of the proposed agreement or amendment not more than 30 nor less than 15 days before the date fixed for the hearing. This notice shall be published at least once in one or more newspapers published in the municipality, or, if no newspaper is published therein, then in one or more newspapers with a general circulation within the annexing municipality. After such hearing the agreement or amendment may be modified before execution thereof. The annexation agreement or amendment shall be executed by the mayor or president and attested by the clerk of the municipality only after such hearing and upon the adoption of a resolution or ordinance directing such execution, which resolution or ordinance must be passed by a vote of two-thirds of the corporate authorities then holding office.[720]

North Carolina:

§160A-58-24. Contents of agreements; procedure
* * *
(a) No agreement may be entered into under this Part unless each participating City has held a public hearing on the agreement prior to adopting the ordinance approving the agreement.[721]
* * *

Washington:

§36.70B.200 Development Agreement—Public Hearing

A county or city shall only approve a development agreement by ordinance or resolution after a public hearing. The county or city legislative body or a planning commission, hearing examiner, or other body designated by the legislative body to conduct the public hearing may conduct the hearing. If the development agreement relates to a project permit application, the provisions of chapter 36.70C RCW shall apply to the appeal of the decision on the development agreement.[722]

4. Conformance to Plans

Annexation agreements must often comply with local government plans as a condition of enforceability because the zoning that is bargained for in the agreement must accord with comprehensive plans. Thus, the Idaho Supreme Court in *Sprenger, Grubb & Associates*,[723] upheld a rezoning over the objections of the developers of property subject to an annexation agreement on the ground that the applicable plan was sufficiently broad in support of the contested downzoning. Arizona's statute explicitly requires that an agreement be consistent with the municipality's general plan.[724]

---

720. 65 ILL. COMP. STAT. 5/11-15.1-3.

721. N.C. GEN. STAT. §160A-58.24.

722. WASH. REV. CODE §36.70B.200.

723. 127 Idaho at 576, 903 P.2d at 741.

724. ARIZ. REV. STAT. §9-500.05B.

## 5. Amendment or Cancellation

Generally, both parties must mutually consent to amend or cancel the agreement.[725] In Illinois, an amendment to an annexation agreement must follow the same procedures as required for the original approval.[726] In North Carolina, an annexation agreement may be modified or terminated by a subsequent agreement by all parties and must be approved by ordinance and public hearing.[727]

## 6. Breach

There are essentially two kinds of breaches which commonly occur during the period of an agreement: change in land use rules by local government and failure by either party to live up to its obligations under the agreement. While provisions relating to breach and remedies therefor are typically negotiated between the parties, statutory provisions can provide some guidance in these matters.

### a. When Local Government Changes the Land Development Rules

As noted previously, the overriding concern of the landowner in negotiating an annexation agreement (besides the annexation itself) is the vesting of development rights or the freezing of land development regulations during the term of the agreement.

The Illinois annexation agreement statutes contemplates such a freeze:

§11-15.1-2 Contents and scope of agreements

Any such agreement may provide for the following as it relates to the land which is the subject of the agreement:
(a) The annexation of such territory to the municipality, subject to the provisions of Article 7.
(b) The continuation in effect, or amendment, or continuation in effect as amended, of any ordinance relating to subdivision controls, zoning, official plan, and building, housing and related restrictions; provided, however, that any public hearing required by law to be held before the adoption of any ordinance amendment provided in such agreement shall be held prior to the execution of the agreement, and all ordinance amendments provided in such agreement shall be enacted according to law.
(c) A limitation upon increases in permit fees required by the municipality.
(d) Contributions of either land or monies, or both, to any municipality and to other units of local government having jurisdiction over all or part of land that is the subject matter of any annexation agreement entered into under the provisions of this Section shall be deemed valid when made and shall survive the expiration date of any such annexation agreement with respect to all or any part of the land that was the subject matter of the annexation agreement.
* * *

---

725. *See, e.g.*, ARIZ. REV. STAT. §9-500.05C.

726. 65 ILL. COMP. STAT. 5/11-15.1-3.

727. N.C. GEN. STAT. §160A-58.2.4(d).

> Any action taken by the corporate authorities during the period such agreement is in effect, which, if it applied to the land which is the subject of the agreement, would be a breach of such agreement, shall not apply to such land without an amendment of such agreement.
>
> After the effective term of any annexation agreement and unless otherwise provided for within the annexation agreement or an amendment to the annexation agreement, the provisions of any ordinance relating to the zoning of the land that is provided for within the agreement or an amendment to the agreement, shall remain in effect unless modified in accordance with law. This amendatory Act of 1995 is declarative of existing law and shall apply to all annexation agreements.[728]

The few courts that have dealt with local government changes in land use regulations have had no difficulty in finding them inapplicable to the property subject to the agreement, provided the agreement itself is binding. Thus, in *Village of Tinley Park*,[729] the Illinois Supreme Court held that the original zoning of the subject property was valid during the term of the annexation agreement, and any change by the village was void during that time. Indeed, since the village's attempted zoning change was void, said the court, there was no breach by the village.[730]

However, Illinois courts have also held that the expiration of an annexation agreement results in the expiration of whatever zoning classification the landowner had bargained for in the agreement. In *Bank of Waukegan v. Village of Vernon Hills*,[731] the landowner sued for the benefits of a zoning classification and special use permit passed and granted under an expired annexation agreement. The court held that the zoning and permits that were enacted the same day as the expired agreement "were provisions of the annexation agreement," and thus only enforceable "during the life of the annexation agreement." The court concluded that any other result would evade the term limits of annexation agreements as set out in the applicable statute.[732] It is not clear how a legislative act of a local government can be so automatically terminated by the expiration of an agreement. Surely the inapplicability of zoning changes in the *Village of Tinley Park* case, due to the shield provided by the annexation agreement, does not lead to the broad conclusion that any zoning resulting from such an agreement terminates when the agreement does. In attempting to address the inherent problems created by the *Bank of Waukegan* decision, the Illinois General Assembly adopted the following amendatory language in 1995:

> After the effective term of any annexation agreement and unless otherwise provided for within the annexation agreement or an amendment to the annexation agreement, the provisions of any ordinance relating to the zoning of the land that is

---

728. 65 ILL. COMP. STAT. 5/11-15.1-2.

729. 52 Ill. 2d at 354, 288 N.E.2d at 423.

730. *Id.*; *see also* Cummings v. City of Waterloo, 683 N.E.2d 1222 (Ill. 1997) (city's amendment to its zoning ordinance that was contrary to the provisions of an annexation agreement was unenforceable against property subject to the annexation agreement).

731. 254 Ill. App. 3d 24, 626 N.E. 2d 245 (1993).

732. *Id.*

provided for within the agreement or an amendment to the agreement, shall remain in effect unless modified in accordance with law. This amendatory Act of 1995 is declarative of existing law and shall apply to all annexation agreements.[733]

While some annexation agreement statutes either contain a limitation on the duration of such agreements,[734] or provide that the agreement must recite one, many states, including California, appear to permit annexation agreements without the benefit of a statute. It is, therefore, theoretically possible for an annexation agreement to be relatively open-ended with respect to matters such as the zoning of the subject property. The results can be unfortunate for the landowner because a landowner usually has no vested right in a zoning classification absent activity that vests such rights.[735] Thus, where the agreement is silent on the time period, at least one court has held that a landowner is without remedy if, a few years after annexation pursuant to an annexation agreement, the annexing local government changes the zoning to a classification which makes the originally contemplated land development impossible.[736]

*b. Nonperformance of a Bargained-For Act: Dedications, Contributions, and Hook-Ups*

Another common breach involves the failure of a landowner or local government to live up to the other terms of the agreement. This generally results from a developer failing to provide a public facility or money therefore,[737] or a local government refusing to provide utility or other services to the property to be annexed. Under such circumstances, the courts have been strict in forcing the parties to live up to their bargains, even when unusual difficulties would appear to render such performance nearly impossible. Thus, in the California case of *Morrison Homes Corp.*,[738] the court of appeals directed the local government to provide sewer connections to the landowner's property, as agreed in an annexation agreement, even though a superior governmental entity, a state regional water quality control board, ordered the local government not to do so. After deciding that the city had not illegally contracted away its police power through the agreement, the court said:

> The onset of materially changed conditions is not a ground for voiding a municipal contract which was valid when made, nor is the contracting city's failure to have foreseen them.[739]

---

733. 65 ILL. COMP. STAT. 5/11-15.1-2.

734. *Id.* 5/11-15.1-1 et seq.

735. Callies, *supra* note 662.

736. Carty v. City of Ojai, 143 Cal. Rptr. 506, 77 Cal. App. 3d 329 (1978).

737. Other items bargained for and litigated: exemptions from real estate taxes, Van Cleave v. Village of Seneca, 165 Ill. App. 3d 410, 519 N.E.2d 63 (1988); exemption from environmental ordinances (which did not survive legal challenge), O'Malley v. Village of Ford Heights, 633 N.E.2d 848 (Ill. 1994).

738. 130 Cal. Rptr. at 196, 58 Cal. App. 3d at 724.

739. *Id.*

In much the same vein, the Colorado Supreme Court refused a landowner's request that roughly $25,000 in payments to a local government for acquisition of parks, playgrounds, and schools be returned on the ground that the annexation agreement requiring such payment was ultra vires:

> The plaintiff wanted water and sewer services; the City required annexation and a sum of money equal to eight percent of the appraised value of the property. Each got what it bargained for.... We see no reason, legal or moral, why plaintiff should have all of the benefits of its bargain by which it obtained the water and sewer services it needed in order to carry out its plans, and yet receive back from the city a portion of the consideration which it gave in order to obtain these services.[740]

Of course, as intimated in the foregoing case, the agreement itself must be binding. Thus, the Illinois Appellate Court in *Village of Lisle v. Outdoor Advertising Co.*,[741] refused to enforce a local government ordinance banning certain signs and billboards on the property subject to an annexation agreement, on the ground that the property was not contiguous to the village, and therefore the annexation agreement was invalid and unenforceable.

## 7. Limits on Conditions

Under existing law on development conditions and exactions, local governments have broad authority to require landowners and developers to make reasonable contributions toward whatever services and other resources the government will need to provide as a result of an annexation.[742] May a local government go further than what is permitted under exactions law based on an argument that the annexation agreement is a voluntary agreement that neither government nor landowner is compelled to either negotiate or execute? Provided the agreement is indeed voluntary, the answer is almost certainly yes.[743] Perhaps the best judicial support for this proposition comes from the Colorado

---

740. City of Colorado Springs v. Kitty Hawk Dev. Co., 154 Colo. 535, 544, 392 P.2d 467, 472 (1964).

741. 188 Ill. App. 3d 751, 758, 544 N.E.2d 836, 839 (1989).

742. Village of Orland Bank v. Federal Savings & Loan Ass'n of Chicago, 135 Ill. App. 3d 520, 481 N.E.2d 946 (1985). *See* Patrick J. Rohan, *in* ZONING AND LAND USE CONTROLS, *supra* note 668; *see also* Dolan v. City of Tigard, 512 U.S. 374, 114 S. Ct. 2309, 129 L. Ed. 2d 304, 24 ELR 21083 (1994); Nollan v. California Coastal Comm'n, 483 U.S. 825, 107 S. Ct. 3141, 97 L. Ed. 2d 677, 17 ELR 20918 (1987).

743. *See, e.g.*, City of Annapolis v. Waterman, 357 Md. 484, 745 A.2d 1000 (2000) (conditions agreed to by the subdivider as part of an earlier subdivision agreement were not an unconstitutional taking of the subdivider's property). For a contrary view which would impose the same strict nexus and proportionality requirements upon such agreements as upon "free-standing" local government development dedications, exactions, and other conditions, see Starritt & Mcclannahan, *Land-Use Planning and Takings: The Viability of Conditional Exactions to Conserve Open Space in the Rocky Mountain*, 30 LAND & WATER L. REV. 415 (1995).

# IV. ANNEXATION AGREEMENTS

Supreme Court.[744] In upholding the levying of a fee as a condition of annexation under an annexation agreement, the court held:

> A municipality is under no legal obligation in the first instance to annex contiguous territory, and may reject a petition for annexation for no reason at all. It follows then that if the municipality elects to accept such territory solely as a matter of its discretion, it may impose such conditions by way of agreement as it sees fit. If the party seeking annexation does not wish to annex under the conditions imposed, he is free to withdraw his petition to annex and remain without the city.[745]

One legislature has, however, limited the authority of local governments to impose what would otherwise be unauthorized impact fees or dedications as part of an annexation or development agreement:

> Nothing in [the development/annexation agreement statute] is intended to authorize local government to impose impact fees, inspection fees, or dedications or to require any other financial contributions or mitigation measures except as expressly authorized by other applicable provisions of state law.[746]

The validity of traditional exaction ordinances concerns the purposes to which the exaction will be put and the relationship of the exaction to the need created by the development. A discussion of the "rational nexus" standard is contained in an earlier section entitled *Enabling Act*, but a collateral issue is raised when determining the municipal authority to extract exactions pursuant to an annexation agreement.

The "reasonable relationship," "specifically and uniquely attributable," and "rational nexus" tests that have been developed in the courts to determine the constitutionality of development exactions have been used to assess the validity of both on-site and off-site impact fees and may be relied upon to challenge annexation agreements. Whereas off-site impact fees and linkage regulations are used to fund improvements necessitated by development in the region as a whole, rather than for needs more directly attributable to the new development, annexation agreements seeking to extract funds for tenuously related off-site benefits are sufficiently analogous to invite challenge under the same standards.[747] Whether or not annexation agreements successfully avoid or survive such challenges may depend upon how willing the courts are to accept a return to the underlying "voluntary" rationale.

Some have argued that exactions agreed to under a voluntary annexation agreement must bear a rational nexus to the needs created by the develop-

---

744. *Kitty Hawk Dev. Co.*, 154 Colo. at 535, 392 P.2d at 467.

745. *Id.* at 545, 392 P.2d at 472.

746. WASH. REV. CODE §36.70B.210.

747. *See* John Delaney, *Development Agreements: The Road From Prohibition to "Let's Make a Deal,"* 25 URB. LAW. 49 (1993); *see also* Donald L. Connors & Michael E. High, *The Expanding Circle of Exactions: From Dedication to Linkage*, 50 LAW & CONTEMP. PROBS. 69, 82 (1987) (concluding that even if Boston's linkage exactions are viewed as regulatory fees, they are vulnerable to being invalidated as not reasonably related to needs created by the regulated development).

ment.[748] The argument states that the "rational nexus" and "substantial advancement" standards of *Nollan* are not limited to just those instances where the municipality requires an exaction from an uncooperative landowner, but also apply to voluntary permit conditions. Under this view, the type and extent of exactions permissible under annexation agreements would not differ from the type and extent available under other traditional exaction mechanisms such as impact fees.

The rationale supporting such a view is that requiring the *Nollan* standard to be satisfied serves to prevent governmental abuse of the mechanism, as it is "difficult to tell whether a landowner's acceptance of a condition is truly voluntary or is instead a submission to government coercion."[749] In the case of annexation agreements, however, it is the developer's choice to annex and protect itself by attempting to freeze zoning or land use regulations. The developer does not require annexation or any guarantee in order to exercise his right or privilege to build, and may certainly choose to proceed without it. To the extent that the developer chooses to annex its property to the local government and to negotiate for any regulatory freezes, arguably the annexation agreement does convey a "governmental benefit" upon the developer, since "[i]t is well established that there is no federal Constitutional right to be free from changes in land use laws."[750] The municipality should therefore be free to negotiate its best terms in exchange for the benefit conferred, regardless of nexus.

## V. Vested Rights

This section discusses the principles of law and equity that permit a landowner to continue with or complete a land development or land use activity in the face of a change in regulations that would otherwise prohibit or limit that development or activity. Although typically the issue of continuing a use is covered by the general topic of "nonconforming uses" and the issue of completing a development falls under "vested rights," the two are closely related in equity if not always in law. This issue most typically arises in litigation, either raised as a defense against an enforcement action or used as the basis for a claim for relief.

Of course, to the extent that landowner and local government execute a development agreement or annexation agreement, as described in parts III and IV, the issue of vested rights ought not to arise. After all, a principal purpose of a development agreement is to vest the rights of a landowner to proceed with whatever development is the subject of the agreement, as many development agreement statutes clearly contemplate.[751] The so-called common law of vesting de-

---

748. *See* Crew, *supra* note 670.

749. *Id.* at 46. *See also* Collis v. City of Bloomington, 310 Minn. 5, 17-18, 246 N.W.2d 19, 26 (1976) (upholding as constitutional a statute authorizing municipalities to require dedication of land or payment of fees as condition of subdivision approval since enabling legislation and implementing ordinance limited the amount of land to be dedicated to a "reasonable" percentage of the property).

750. Lakeview Dev. Corp. v. City of S. Lake Tahoe, 915 F.2d 1290 (9th Cir. 1990).

751. *See, e.g.*, CAL. GOV'T CODE §65864.

velopment rights in the absence of such an agreement, much as the section on land development conditions deals with the common law of such conditions in the absence of a development agreement or annexation agreement on the sound legal ground that the presence of such an agreement renders the application of a nexus or proportionality theory moot.[752]

## A. Introduction and Background

The point at which a landowner may continue with a land development project despite new land development regulations that now prohibit such development generates an inquiry into vested rights and its close cousin, equitable estoppel. The two legal doctrines arise from very different principles.[753] Vested rights technically focuses only upon whether a landowner has acquired sufficient real property rights to proceed with a development project, or some phase thereof, unaffected by subsequently promulgated government regulation. Equitable estoppel, sometimes also called zoning estoppel, focuses on the conduct of government and whether it would be equitable under the circumstances to permit government to repudiate some official action upon which the landowner has relied to proceed with a land development project.[754] The former is often said to be based upon common law and constitutional principles dealing with rights in property, whereas the latter is said to be derived from equitable principles.

As appears below, the results may often be the same whichever doctrine is applied, leading most courts to treat the two doctrines as interchangeable.[755] However, there is a critical difference between the two doctrines that should significantly affect the pleading and trial of cases where either might apply, if not their outcomes: good faith. Obviously a landowner proceeding on the basis of equitable estoppel must be proceeding in "good faith." He who seeks equity must do equity. Pursuing an equitable remedy requires "clean hands," as every first-year law student knows. But what of vested property rights based upon common law and constitutional principles? Do we legally care whether such a landowner has clean hands?[756] Does it matter, legally, what a landowner knows,

---

752. *See, e.g.*, David L. Callies & Julie A. Tappendorf, *Unconstitutional Land Development Conditions and the Development Agreement Solution: Bargaining for Public Facilities After* Nollan *and* Dolan, 51 CASE W. RES. L. REV. 663 (2001).

753. Robert M. Rhodes & Cathy M. Sellers, *Vested Rights: Establishing Predictability in a Changing Regulatory System*, 20 STETSON L. REV. 475, 476 (1991); MANDELKER, *supra* note 5; CHARLES L. SIEMON ET AL., VESTED RIGHTS: BALANCING PUBLIC AND PRIVATE DEVELOPMENT EXPECTATIONS 9 (ULI 1982).

754. Rhodes & Sellers, *supra* note 753, at 476; David G. Heeter, *Zoning Estoppel: Application of the Principles of Equitable Estoppel and Vested Rights to Zoning Disputes*, 1971 URB. L. ANN. 65; MANDELKER, *supra* note 5, §6.13.

755. *Id.*

756. For a discussion of the distinction between equitable or zoning estoppel and vested rights, particularly the elimination of equitable principles, including reliance, from the latter, see Morgan R. Bentley, *Effects of Equitable Estoppel and Substantial De-*

or should have known, if his theory of the case rests on vested rights and not estoppel? After all, no less an authority than the Court recently held that "notice" of a strict land use regulation does not prevent a purchaser of land so restricted from challenging the restriction as a regulatory taking of property without compensation.[757] It would, therefore, seem reasonable to keep the theories separate, though it is likely the case law is too far gone in joining the two, as appears in the sections below. Therefore, except where noted, the term vested rights will include, for all practical purposes, equitable estoppel for the remainder of this section.

After a brief description of the elements necessary to establish vested rights, the remainder of this section sets out the common circumstances under which claims for vested rights arise, together with a selection of cases illustrating each circumstance or situation. Since an increasing number of states have passed statutes codifying vested rights in their jurisdiction, the statutes of California and Colorado are appended for further information and guidance. For a list of those states that have chosen to deal with vested rights by passing development agreement legislation, and for a discussion generally of development agreements and annexation agreements, see parts III and IV on development agreements and annexation agreements, and Appendices VII, VIII, IX, and X.

### B. Elements of Vested Rights

There are essentially three parts to a vested rights claim against government interference with respect to a land development project:

1. a governmental act or omission;
2. landowner change of position or reliance upon that governmental act or omission; and (in the case of estoppel)
3. in good faith.[758]

### 1. Governmental Act or Omission

Nearly all commentators and cases are agreed that there must be some governmental act or omission upon which a landowner relies to his detriment in order for there to be a legitimate claim for vested rights,[759] and the more recent that act or omission the better. It is, therefore, generally considered to be a matter of black letter law in this area that a landowner has no vested right in a zoning classification[760] unless the classification is either relatively recent, passed at the

---

viations to Vested Rights in DRI Projects: A New Approach, 43 FLA. L. REV. 767, 774 (1991).

757. Palazzolo v. Rhode Island, 533 U.S. 606, 32 ELR 20516 (2001). See, for comment, David L. Callies & Calvert G. Chipchase, Palazzolo v. Rhode Island: Ripeness and "Notice" Rule Clarified and Statutory "Background Principles" Narrowed, 33 URB. LAW. 907 (2001).

758. MANDELKER, supra note 5, §6.13; Rhodes & Sellers, supra note 753, at 478.

759. MANDELKER, supra note 5, §6.14; Rhodes & Sellers, supra note 753, at 482-86.

760. MANDELKER, supra note 5, §6.14.

request of the landowner, or passed or created principally to frustrate a land development project.[761] However, a variety of other acts or omissions by government often serve to vest rights in a landowner with respect to a particular land development project. There are significant differences among the states concerning the kind of governmental action reliance upon which will result in such vesting. These range from the necessity of a building permit, which virtually every jurisdiction recognizes as sufficient,[762] to an appropriate letter from a city official.[763] Even a zone classification has been deemed sufficient.[764] From the most secure to the least secure in terms of vested rights, these are:

1. a building permit;
2. final subdivision plat approval;
3. preliminary subdivision plat approval;
4. final planned development plan approval;
5. preliminary planned development plan approval;
6. submission of an application for approval of the above;
7. special use or conditional use permit;
8. site plan approval;
9. grading or other site preparation, by itself; and
10. newly-enacted zoning classification, particularly if upon application or request of landowner claiming vested rights.

All of the above are discussed in more detail in a later section entitled *What Constitutes Sufficient Governmental Action.*

2. Detrimental Reliance

Virtually all commentators and cases agree that a landowner must change position or rely on an act or omission of government, however weak, in order to claim vested rights. Most agree, however, that the reliance or change in position must have economic consequences for the landowner, which usually means the expenditure of money. Indeed, the amount spent in reliance upon such a government act or omission is often a major factor in deciding whether there has been sufficient reliance to justify a finding of vested rights.[765] Thus, for exam-

---

761. *Id.* §6.16. *See* Western Land Equities, Inc. v. City of Logan, 617 P.2d 388 (Utah 1980). In a very few jurisdictions, some measure of vested rights results from a "new" zoning classification, particularly if sought by the landowner now claiming such rights.

762. MANDELKER, *supra* note 5, §6.21.

763. Rhodes & Sellers, *supra* note 753, 482.

764. *See* Texas Co. v. Town of Miami Springs, 44 So. 2d 808 (Fla. 1950); Hough v. Amato, 212 So. 2d 662 (Fla. 1968).

765. MANDELKER, *supra* note 5, §6.20; Rhodes & Sellers, *supra* note 753, at 486-88; SIEMON ET AL., *supra* note 753, at 32.

ple, Florida courts have required expenditures in amounts from $8,000 to $600,000 sufficient for "equitable estoppel" to apply, in some instances before the landowner had made any physical changes to the land.[766]

Other jurisdictions have held expenditures in the millions of dollars to be insufficient, without a building permit. The most egregious example of such jurisdictions is California. Thus, in *Oceanic California, Inc., v. North Central Coast Regional Commission*,[767] the court found expenditure of $26.9 million in direct costs insufficient. Also, in the case of *Avco Community Developers v. South Coast Regional Commission*,[768] which eventually led to the passage of California's development agreement statute. There, despite having all necessary permits but a building permit and having spent over $2 million in grading, infrastructure, and associated costs for a residential housing development, the California Supreme Court held that Avco still needed a permit from the California Coastal Commission under later-applied coastal regulations. Similarly, in *Pete Drown Inc. v. Town of Ellenburg*,[769] a New York court held that $850,000 was insufficient under the circumstances to vest development rights.

The *Avco* case illustrates the history of the doctrine of vested rights in land use and development. Early cases focused on the question of whether a builder or owner could complete a building that had proceeded to some stage of planning or actual construction. The necessary governmental action in such a case was, of course, the issuance of a building permit. Thus, the issuance of a building permit was an absolute prerequisite for a determination of vested rights in the early cases. In *Avco*, the California Supreme Court applied that test mechanically, without considering the policy behind the test. Clearly Avco had met the intent of the test—obtaining a valid government approval and proceeding with substantial expenditures in good-faith reliance on that approval.

3. Good Faith

Though technically not part of a vested rights theory, many courts require a landowner to have relied, changed position, or otherwise acted "in good faith" in order for property rights to develop or continue developing a particu-

---

766. *See* Bregar v. Britton, 75 So. 2d 753 (Fla. 1954) ($28,000 for land preparation); Project Home, Inc., v. Town of Astatula, 373 So. 2d 710 (Fla. 1979) ($8,000 for water and sewer improvements); Town of Longboat Key v. Mezrah, 10 Fla. L. Weekly 1015, 467 So. 2d 488 (Fla. Dist. Ct. App. 1985) ($40,000 for plans and permit procurement); Board of Comm'rs v. Lutz, 314 So. 2d 815 (Fla. 1975) ($100,000 for planning and other preparatory fees); Town of Largo v. Imperial Homes Corp., 309 So. 2d 571 (Fla. 1975) ($379,000 for land, architectural fees, interest, taxes, and sewer permits); City of N. Miami v. Margulies, 289 So. 2d 424 (Fla. 1974) ($600,000 for planning, architectural, engineering, and surveying fees).

767. 133 Cal. Rptr. 664, 66 Cal. App. 3d 57 (1976).

768. 17 Cal. 3d 785, 553 P.2d 546 (1976).

769. 229 A.D.2d 877, 646 N.Y.S.2d 205 (N.Y. 1996).

lar project to vest.[770] Thus, for example, rushing to complete or begin a project in order to knowingly avoid a possible change in zone classification has been held to constitute bad faith.[771] So has notice of a pending election and a similar rush to complete.

On the other hand, landowners have a right to expect fair dealing on the part of elected and appointed officials. Thus, where a local government approved a request for rezoning with knowledge that a landowner's purchase of the subject property was contingent on that rezoning and then attempted to downzone the land to prevent the development, the court held that the local government had acted in bad faith.[772] A more difficult case is the issuance of an illegal building permit—or other clear error in official assurance of the legality of a proposed development—upon which a landowner in good faith relies. Allowing the development to proceed may raise significant health and safety issues, as well as violate a "fundamental canon" of local government law that provides wrongfully issued or approvals wrongfully given are void ab initio.[773] Therefore, many courts will not permit the illegal development to proceed.[774]

On the other hand, some jurisdictions estop local government from interfering with a land development project even if proceeding upon invalid assurances and permits provided the landowner reliance is substantial and in good faith, and the permission or approval is sufficiently definite and precise. In *Abbeville Arms v. City of Abbeville*,[775] the court directed the city to issue a building permit for a project on land erroneously zoned. There, the developer had both purchased the property and made substantial additional expenditures in reliance on both a defective zoning map and a letter of approval from the city's zoning administrator.[776]

California's experience is instructive. The California Supreme Court held that a developer could not claim a vested right in reliance upon a permit he had reason

---

770. MANDELKER, *supra* note 5, §6.18; Rhodes & Sellers, *supra* note 753, at 478-82; SIEMON ET AL., *supra* note 753, at 29-32.

771. Smith v. City of Clearwater, 383 So. 2d 681 (Fla. 1980); Morris v. Postma, 41 N.J. 354, 196 A.2d 792 (1964); Clackamas County v. Holmes, 265 Or. 193, 508 P.2d 190 (1973); Boron Oil Co. v. L.C. Kimple, 445 Pa. 327, 284 A.2d 744 (1971).

772. Town of Largo v. Imperial Homes Corp., 309 So. 2d 571 (Fla. 1975).

773. SIEMON ET AL., *supra* note 753, at 27; *see, e.g.*, Hunt v. Caldwell, 222 Va. 91, 279 S.E.2d 138 (1981); Town of Blacksburg v. Price, 221 Va. 168, 266 S.E.2d 899 (1980); State v. Missoula, 166 Mont. 385, 533 P.2d 1087 (Mont. 1975).

774. MANDELKER, *supra* note 5, §6.17. *Contra*, permitting the development to proceed anyway: Town of W. Hartford v. Rechel, 190 Conn. 114, 459 A.2d 1015 (1983); Saah v. District of Columbia Bd. of Zoning Adjustment, 433 A.2d 1114 (D.C. Cir. 1981); City of Peru v. Querciagrossa, 73 Ill. App. 3d 1040, 392 N.E.2d 778 (1979); City of Berea v. Wren, 818 S.W.2d 274 (Ky. 1991); Petrosky v. Zoning Hearing Bd., 485 Pa. 501, 402 A.2d 1385 (1979); Abbeville Arms v. City of Abbeville, 273 S.C. 491, 257 S.E.2d 716 (1979).

775. 273 S.C. 491, 257 S.E.2d 716 (1979).

776. *See also* City of Peru v. Querciagrossa, 73 Ill. App. 3d 1040, 392 N.E. 778 (1979) (setbacks); City of Coral Gables v. Puiggros, 376 So. 2d 281 (Fla. 1979).

to know might be defective.[777] In *Pettitt v. City of Fresno*,[778] the court further held that a property owner who had constructed improvements in reliance upon an invalid building permit could be required to remove the structure, even though the permit was regular on its face and the property owner acted without actual knowledge of any defect in it. The following year, another court held that a property owner could not obtain vested rights in reliance upon an approval obtained in accordance with the requirements of the county where the rules and practices adopted by the county did not conform strictly to the clear requirements of law.[779]

A property owner or applicant also cannot rely on written statements made by a public official unless the official is authorized to make them. In *Burchett v. City of Newport Beach*,[780] the petitioner alleged a breach of a "written agreement with Defendant City of Newport Beach whereby said City agreed to allow Plaintiffs to improve said real property with a two story condominium structure and retain the existing driveway to said property . . . ."[781] The allegation was based on a letter from the Burchetts to the planning department asking for a permit to use an existing, nonconforming driveway, on which letter an assistant planner had marked a notation that the facts were "correct." The court first noted that the city's charter provided that it could not be bound by any contract "unless the same shall be in writing, approved by the city council and signed on behalf of the city by the mayor and the city clerk or by such officer or officers as shall be designated by the City Council."[782] Second, the assistant planner was neither the person to contact for an "encroachment permit," nor a member of the correct department. The court cited *Horsemen's Benevolent & Protective Ass'n v. Valley Racing Ass'n*,[783] for the proposition that "no government, whether state or local, is bound to any extent by an officer's acts in excess of his authority."[784] The court held that "one who deals with a public officer stands presumptively charged with a full knowledge of that officer's powers, and is bound at his peril to ascertain the extent of his powers to bind the government for which he is an officer, and any act of an officer to be valid must find express authority in the law or be necessarily incidental to a power expressly granted."[785]

---

777. Strong v. County of Santa Cruz, 15 Cal. 3d 720, 543 P.2d 264 (1975).

778. 110 Cal. Rptr. 262, 34 Cal. App. 3d 813 (1973).

779. People v. County of Kern, 115 Cal. Rptr. 67, 39 Cal. App. 3d 830 (1974).

780. 40 Cal. Rptr. 2d 1, 33 Cal. App. 4th 1472 (1995).

781. *Id.* at 4, 33 Cal. App. 4th at 1479.

782. *Id.*

783. 6 Cal. Rptr. 2d 698, 4 Cal. App. 4th 1538 (1992).

784. 40 Cal. Rptr. 2d at 4, 33 Cal. App. 4th at 1479.

785. *Id.* (quoting *Horsemen's*, 36 Cal. Rptr. 2d at 713, 4 Cal. App. 4th at 1564) (general law city was not bound by oral contract because it did not comply with California Governmental Code §40602 and relevant city code provisions).

# V. VESTED RIGHTS

## C. What Constitutes Sufficient Governmental Action

There are a variety of acts and omissions by government that have been held sufficient to support a claim of vested rights, assuming that the landowner meets any applicable good-faith standard in relying on such act or omission.

### 1. Building Permit

Virtually all authorities agree that the granting of a building permit vests the land development rights of a landowner.[786] This is so because in most jurisdictions, the building permit cannot issue unless the land is otherwise ripe for development and all zoning and other land use permits have been granted. Therefore, for the pertinent government to change its mind at this stage in the land development process is generally considered at least inequitable under an estoppel theory, and except for the fact that the development project is uncompleted, arguably in the same legal category as a nonconformity, as discussed above.[787] Thus, for example, in *Town of Orangetown v. Magee*,[788] Bradley Industrial Park, Inc., acquired 34 acres in order to construct an industrial building. The town's building inspector approved Bradley's plan and issued a building permit. However, as the construction progressed, opposition to the project materialized, and the inspector revoked the permit after Bradley had incurred nearly $4 million in post-permit expenses, and the town rezoned the property to make such industrial use impossible. Holding that a vested right is acquired when, pursuant to a legally issued permit, the landowner "demonstrates a commitment to the purpose for which the permit was granted by effecting substantial changes and incurring substantial expenses to further the development,"[789] the court held that Bradley had acquired vested rights. The South Dakota Supreme Court applied the doctrine of equitable estoppel in holding that a property owner's purchase of $4,197 in materials constituted sufficient reliance on a building permit to estop the city from then revoking the permit.[790]

The corollary of the rule that issuance of a building permit may vest certain rights is that application for a building permit is typically a prerequisite for a vested rights claim.[791] Courts requiring the acquisition of a building permit before a landowner obtains vested rights to proceed can be quite strict about the

---

786. MANDELKER, *supra* note 5; SIEMON ET AL., note 738, at 26.

787. For discussion and a contrary view on this point, however, see SIEMON ET AL., *supra* note 753, at 54-56.

788. 665 N.E.2d 1061 (N.Y. 1996).

789. *Id.* at 1064.

790. Even v. City of Parker, 1999 S.D. 72, 597 N.W.2d 670 (1999).

791. *See* Lake Bluff Housing Partners v. City of S. Milwaukee, 197 Wis. 2d 157, 540 N.W.2d 189 (1995), *rev'g*, 188 Wis. 2d 230, 525 N.W.2d 59 (1994), in which a developer of proposed low-income housing challenged a downzoning of the property from multi-family to single-family but lost a vested rights claim because the partners had not applied for a building permit.

application of this requirement. Thus, in the aforementioned *Avco* decision from California, even though the developer had spent hundreds of thousands of dollars in reliance upon grading and other permits, and even though the regulations requiring a shoreline development permit from a state agency were not in effect at the time the landowner made these expenditures, the court held that in absence of a building permit, the landowner had no vested right to proceed and therefore the expenditures and grading operations conducted in reliance on these other permits were irrelevant.[792]

California courts have applied the *Avco* doctrine in a number of later cases, including *Davidson v. County of San Diego*.[793] In *Davidson*, although the property owner had applied for a building permit, submitted site plans, and made various expenditures in reliance on the building permit, the court declined to find a vested right to continue with the development based on the developer's lack of a building permit. Under the judicial vested rights doctrine in *Avco*, the property owner did not have a right to have his application considered under regulations as they existed at the time he applied for the building permit. The court noted, however, that the county ordinance did, in fact, grant a vested right to the developer. The court emphasized that local ordinances may confer vested rights earlier than available under the judicial vested rights doctrine.

Maryland has adopted a vested rights doctrine similar to that created in the California courts. In *Town of Sykesville v. West Shore Communications*,[794] the court set out the law of vested rights as follows:

> For a right to proceed with construction under existing zoning to vest, three conditions must be satisfied: 1) there must be actual physical commencement of some significant and visible construction; 2) the commencement must be undertaken in good faith, to wit, with the intention to continue with the construction and to carry it through to completion; and 3) the commencement of construction must be pursuant to a validly issued building permit.[795]

The court applied the rule in *Town of Sykesville* to confer a vested right on the developer of a communications tower who had significantly commenced construction, in good faith, pursuant to a valid building permit. Therefore, the court held, a newly enacted ordinance, which effectively invalidated West Shore's site plan for the tower, did not apply to the subject property. The Maryland courts apply this vested rights rule strictly, so that if one element is lacking, the court will not confer a vested right. For example, in *Prince George's County, Maryland v. Sunrise Development Partnership*,[796] the Maryland court applied the above vested rights rule to hold that, although the developer had obtained a valid building permit, it had failed to commence construction of the proposed apartment building, even though the developer had poured concrete, installed

---

792. Avco Community Developers v. South Coast Reg'l Comm'n, 17 Cal. 3d 785, 553 P.2d 546 (1976).

793. 56 Cal. Rptr. 2d 617, 49 Cal. App. 4th 639 (1996).

794. 110 Md. App. 300, 677 A.2d 102 (1996).

795. *Id.* at 305, 677 A.2d at 104.

796. 330 Md. 297, 623 A.2d 1296 (1993).

snow fencing, cut down trees, and begun constructing the retaining walls before the county downzoned the property.

If a local government issues a building permit based on a mistake of fact, such as an erroneous plan, much will turn on whether the developer or the local government made the error, and whether the error will result in health or safety hazards. In *Rivera v. City of Phoenix*,[797] the developer submitted plans that were later found to contain incorrect information. The city council issued the building permit, but subsequently revoked it due to zoning violations. The developer claimed that he had a vested right to continue his project, based on the state vested rights doctrine which vests a property right when a building or special use permit is legitimately issued, and the permittee relies on the permit. The court noted that since the developer did not have a "legitimately issued" permit, it could not argue that it had a vested right to continue with its project.[798]

Some jurisdictions hold that a completed building application is sufficient, but it is important that in those jurisdictions requiring a building permit before rights vest, the application be free of conditions that could be construed as discretionary permits or decisions. Moreover, many such jurisdictions also require that the building permit eventually be issued.[799] Thus, in *Aspen v. Marshall*,[800] the Colorado Supreme Court held a landowner was not entitled to vested rights for a hot tub building permit, due to the need to obtain other appropriate permits which were prerequisites to the issuance of the building permit. Under such circumstances, the building permit was neither automatic nor the final permit needed.

Additionally, if a regulation is not newly enacted, but instead a proceeding authorized by regulations existing prior to a building permit application, the Ninth Circuit has held that it will not interfere with a developer's vested right. In *R.C. Hedreen Co. v. City of Seattle*,[801] a developer applied for a building permit for a property that was designated as a landmark. The city made a decision not to act on landmark designations for a four-year period, and the developer sought to have this moratorium extended to allow him to develop the property. The court recognized that Washington has a vested rights doctrine that vests the right to develop upon the filing of the permit application. Although the developer was protected from newly enacted regulations, the court found that the landmark ordinance was in place prior to the application, and could not interfere with his vested right.

Applying the Washington vested rights doctrine to find a vested right to develop upon the filing of the permit application is *Mercer Enterprises, Inc. v.*

---

797. 186 Ariz. 600, 925 P.2d 741 (1996).

798. *Id.* at 601, 925 P.2d at 742. The court cited a number of cases that support its view that a building permit that is issued under a mistake of fact or in violation of an ordinance does not vest a developers rights. *See, e.g.*, Matheson v. De Kalb County, 354 S.E.2d 121 (Ga. 1987); Miller v. Board of Adjustment, 521 A.2d 642 (Del. 1986).

799. *See, e.g.*, Smith v. Winhall Planning Comm'n, 140 Vt. 178, 436 A.2d 760 (1981); Ready-to-Pour v. McCoy, 95 Idaho 510, 511 P.2d 792 (1973).

800. 912 P.2d 56 (Colo. 1996).

801. 74 F.3d 1246 (9th Cir. 1996).

*City of Bremerton.*[802] The defendant applied for a building permit in order to construct a condominium project in Bremerton. Three months later, before any action had been taken on the application, the city placed a moratorium on all permit processing under a previous ordinance allowing condominium developments in residential areas, including Mercer's land. The city repealed the earlier ordinance, and failed to act on Mercer's permit. Mercer brought an action to compel the city to process its permit application under the ordinance in effect at the time of its application. The court applied the Washington vested rights rule to hold that Mercer's rights vested at the time of the application. Therefore, the city's repeal of the ordinance allowing condominium developments did not apply to Mercer's development.

The building permit application situation described above should be distinguished from the conditional building permit, which may lead courts to vest rights depending upon the conditions. Thus, in *Browning-Ferris Industries v. Wake County,*[803] a federal district court found that the landowner acquired vested rights under at least two theories, one of which was the granting of a building permit and change of position and expenditure of funds based thereon. Although the landowner had not acquired a national pollutant discharge elimination system (NPDES) permit for the operation of its facility at the time the building permit was issued, the court nevertheless was

> convinced that, under North Carolina common law, plaintiffs' rights to develop the subject tract had vested. Plaintiffs incurred substantial expenditures in reliance on the site plan approval and issuance of the building permit. Plaintiffs' efforts following the site plan approval were undertaken in good faith and under reasonable reliance on the validity of the approvals they had been granted. It is of no consequence that the building permit was conditional in nature . . . .[804]

Of course, a statute may also provide for vesting upon reliance on a building permit. In the above *Browning-Ferris* case, a North Carolina statute forbids the application of changes in zoning restrictions and boundaries to uses for which either building permits have been issued or a vested right has been established. Further statutory provisions establish a vested right in the landowner after approval of a site specific development plan, whether or not conditional, provided the conditions are eventually met.[805]

Lastly, some courts have held landowner rights to vest upon the probability of the issuance of a building permit.[806] Much depends on the extent of reliance of the landowner, coupled with the kinds of official assurances provided by government. Thus, for example, Illinois courts have found vested rights when a landowner has purchased land, applied for a building permit, and demolished a

---

802. 93 Wash. 2d 624, 611 P.2d 1237 (1980).

803. 905 F. Supp. 312 (E.D.N.C. 1995).

804. *Id.* at 319.

805. N.C. GEN. STAT. §160A-385(b) and (c), *cited in* Browning-Ferris Indus. v. Wake County, 905 F. Supp. at 317, 318.

806. *See* SIEMON ET AL., *supra* note 753, at 26-27.

relatively valuable building,[807] or when another landowner had spent substantial funds on architectural, legal, and organizational fees.[808] Although Hawaii now follows a more strict rule (as noted below), a series of earlier cases also held vested rights might be found upon the probability of the issuance of a building permit, based upon official assurances.[809]

In one such case, a Nevada district court found for a large company in a vested rights case worth millions of dollars even though the building permits had not been officially issued.[810] In 1999, a Nevada county ordinance precluded businesses larger than 110,000 square feet from having more than 7.5% of their retail space allocated to food. Wal-Mart had begun planning a year before to build two "Supercenters" in the county that would occupy 205,000 square feet with more than 25% of the space for groceries. Wal-Mart had obtained unanimous zoning approval from the Clark County Commission eight months before the passage of the new ordinance, and, after gaining zoning approval, had spent more than $5 million on the property for one site alone, and paid for architects, engineers, utilities, and grading permits. On Oct. 14, 1999, the Clark County District Attorney's office directed the Building Department not to issue the building permits for the two sites, the same day that Wal-Mart had been told that the permits were ready. Thus, without that directive from the district attorney, a final building permit for one site and the foundation permits for the other site would have been issued, all before the ordinance became effective. The court took into account the fact that Wal-Mart had received all the needed discretionary approvals before the ordinance took effect, while the building permits were merely ministerial.[811] "It would be a perversion of the pending ordinance doctrine if it could be used once rights to a particular piece of property had vested."[812] The court granted a preliminary injunction on the new ordinance for Wal-Mart's two projects, noting that monetary damages would not be an adequate remedy when the company was unlikely to recover what could well be a billion dollars of damages from the county, and that the balance of hardships fell on Wal-Mart's side.[813]

---

807. Mattson v. City of Chicago, 89 Ill. App. 3d 378, 411 N.E.2d 1002 (1980).

808. Cos Corp. v. City of Evanston, 27 Ill. 2d 570, 190 N.E.2d 364 (1963).

809. Denning v. Maui, 52 Haw. 653, 485 P.2d 1048 (1971); Allen v. Honolulu, 58 Haw. 432, 571 P.2d 328 (1977); Life of the Land v. Honolulu, 60 Haw. 446, 592 P.2d 26 (1979). For discussion of these cases and the general principles applicable to vested rights, see David L. Callies, *Herein of Vested Rights, Plans, and the Relationship of Planning and Controls*, 2 U. HAW. L. REV. 167 (1979).

810. *See* Walmart Stores, Inc. v. County of Clark, 125 F. Supp. 2d 420 (D. Nev. 1999).

811. *Id.* at 427.

812. *Id.* at 428.

813. *Id.* at 429.

2. Subdivision Plats or Plans

As the case that ended the previous section demonstrates, courts often look to other than a building permit to vest land development rights in a landowner, particularly if the permission granted is of a more ministerial nature, even if tinged with some discretion.[814] Although there are certainly cases to the contrary (particularly with respect to old plats),[815] many courts will vest land development rights upon actions taken in reliance on final plats of subdivision. Increasingly, courts will do so with respect to preliminary plat approvals as well, though obviously a landowner can expend less in reliance thereon.

*a. Final Plats*

Government approval of a final subdivision plat is often a ministerial act, and therefore similar to a building permit for the purposes of vested rights. Thus, in *Board of Commissioners of South Whitehall Township, Lehigh County v. Toll Brothers*,[816] the court held that final subdivision approval vested the property owners' right to continue with their development. In *Toll Brothers*, the developers had submitted their final subdivision plan for the township's approval, which the township subsequently granted. The township ordinance, in effect at the time the subdivision was approved, required a $500 payment for water and sewer connection to each lot in the subdivision. Subsequent to approving the developer's final subdivision plan, however, the township amended the ordinance, increasing the water and sewer connection fees for each lot to $4,000. Following the amendment, the developer applied for building permits, which the township refused to grant unless the developer paid the new $4,000 fee for each lot. The developer challenged the fee, arguing that the township was prohibited from applying the new ordinance to the developer's subdivision because the ordinance in effect at the time the township approved its subdivision plan governed the development. The court agreed, holding that "a municipality may not apply a new ordinance increasing fee schedules to a development for which it has previously granted subdivision approval."[817] The court concluded

---

814. As appears in other subsections of the section entitled *What Constitutes Sufficient Governmental Action*, many jurisdictions require that a landowner obtain the last discretionary—as opposed to a ministerial—permit before rights to develop vest. Some, like Hawaii, make this requirement explicit. *See* County of Kauai v. Pacific Standard Life Ins. Co., 65 Haw. 318, 653 P.2d 766 (1982). Others do so by implication.

815. *See, e.g.*, R.A. Vachon & Son, Inc., v. City of Concord, 112 N.H. 107, 289 A.2d 646 (1972). *See* commentary in SIEMON ET AL., *supra* note 753, at 24-25.

816. 147 Pa. Commw. 298, 607 A.2d 824 (1992).

817. *Id. See also* Raum v. Board of Supervisors of Tredyffrin Township, 29 Pa. Commw. 9, 370 A.2d 777 (1977). In Raum, a township approved a developer's subdivision plans, but subsequently enacted a new ordinance that increased fee schedules. The court stated, "landowners whose developments have been approved by a municipality have the right to rely upon the fee schedules in effect at the time of the approval of the plan," and held that the township could not apply the new ordinance to the approved development.

that the township's new ordinance would not apply to the new development and directed the township to issue building permits based on the terms of the ordinance in effect when it granted final subdivision plan approval.

Similarly, in *Ramapo 287 Ltd. Partnership v. Village of Montebello*,[818] the New York Supreme Court, appellate division, held that a developer who received subdivision approval to improve his property may acquire a vested right in continuing approval, notwithstanding a subsequent zoning change. In *Ramapo*, the original property owner had applied for and received permission to subdivide its property into four commercial lots. Ramapo purchased the property, and the village subsequently enacted a zoning regulation increasing yard requirements for the subject property. Ramapo commenced construction on one of the four lots and submitted preliminary site plan applications for the other three lots. The village rejected the plans, however, because they did not conform to the new zoning regulations regarding yard-size requirements. The plaintiff submitted new site plan applications that met the amended zoning requirements that the village approved. The plaintiff subsequently challenged the village's new ordinance, arguing that the new requirements should not apply to its property because it had acquired a vested right to develop the subdivision based on the previously granted subdivision approval.

The court examined the state's vesting rights cases, and concluded, "a developer who improves his property pursuant to original subdivision approval may acquire a vested right in continued approval despite subsequent zoning changes."[819] Although the court recognized that the developer had acquired final subdivision approval, it declined to decide whether plaintiff had a vested right to continue its development, and remanded. The court did note, however, that if the proposed development would be "equally useful under the new zoning requirements, a vested right in the already approved subdivision may not be claimed based on the alterations."[820] Elsewhere, landowners have successfully resisted lot size increases after spending substantial sums on approved subdivision plats,[821] and after installation of water, drainage, and road systems, and construction of model homes.[822]

Even with such final plat approval, lack of position change may prevent a vested right.[823] In *L.M. Everhart Construction Inc. v. Jefferson County Planning Commission*,[824] a construction company's predecessor submitted a

---

818. 165 A.D.2d 544, 568 N.Y.S.2d 492 (1991).

819. *Id.* at 547, 568 N.Y.S.2d at 494 (citing Matter of Ellington Constr. Corp. v. Zoning Bd. of Appeals, 152 A.D.2d 365, 549 N.Y.S.2d 405 (1989); Matter of Jaffee v. RCI Corp., 119 A.D.2d 854, 500 N.Y.S.2d 427 (1986)).

820. *Id.*

821. Kasparek v. Johnson County Bd. of Health, 288 N.W.2d 511 (Iowa 1980).

822. Tellimar Homes, Inc. v. Miller, 14 A.D.2d 586, 218 N.Y.S.2d 175 (1961).

823. L.M. Everhart Constr. Inc. v. Jefferson County Planning Comm'n, 2 F.3d 48 (4th Cir. 1993).

824. 2 F.3d 48 (4th Cir. 1993).

proposed plat to the planning commission that refused to approve it because it was not consistent with the comprehensive plan for the county. The company's predecessor challenged the commission's decision and ultimately the commission approved the subdivision plat. Three years later, however, the county commission, with the planning commission's recommendations, adopted a zoning ordinance, which, if applied to the property in question, would require a side setback that was not required prior to the ordinance enactment. After the ordinance was adopted, the construction company purchased the property and applied for building permits. The commission refused to issue building permits, however, based on the new ordinance's side setback requirement. The construction company challenged the ordinance, arguing that based on the earlier approval of the subdivision plans, it had a vested right to continue the development notwithstanding the ordinance's setback requirement.

The court disagreed, holding that a subdivision plat approval does not create a vested right to develop. Moreover, the court continued, "even the issuance of a building permit—a part of the construction process that occurs long after the approval of a subdivision plat—does not vest rights against future changes in zoning regulations."[825] The court noted that most jurisdictions require that a landowner make substantial expenditures on a subdivision before rights to complete the subdivision will vest. Since the construction company had expended no resources before the zoning ordinance took effect (in fact it had not even purchased the property before the commission enacted the ordinance), the court concluded that it had no vested right to develop the subdivision without complying with the setback requirements.

The Colorado Supreme Court also rejected a vested rights claim based on final approval for a two-lot subdivision, with one large apartment building proposed for each lot in *P.W. Investments, Inc. v. City of Westminster.*[826] The developer more or less completed one building, defaulted, and left a lender with the problem of completing the first building and then deciding what to do with the rest of the project. Faced with accelerating growth, the city adopted a growth management program several years after the default that required the developer to obtain an allocation of "service commitments" sufficient to support services to a proposed building before obtaining a building permit. Eager to market the property as fully developable, the foreclosing lender claimed that the final subdivision approval and construction of the first apartment building vested rights to complete the project as planned. The court ruled for the city, holding that tap permits did not represent assurances of future availability of water and sewer services and that any such belief was unreasonable.

### b. Preliminary Plats

In most jurisdictions, the approval of a preliminary plat or plan of subdivision is a discretionary act. In those jurisdictions in which final discretionary approval

---

825. *Id.* at 52.

826. 655 P.2d 1365 (Colo. 1982).

vests development rights,[827] the approval of a preliminary plat of subdivision is sufficient to vest such development rights, provided it is indeed the last discretionary permit needed.

California courts in particular have vested land development rights following government approval of so-called vesting tentative maps, particularly in the face of changes in local government comprehensive plans.[828] In California at least, this common-law rule is now recognized by statute[829] in what one commentator views as a response to the above-discussed *Avco* decision. Upon approval of a vesting tentative map, a landowner has vested rights to proceed with the land development in accordance with local ordinances, policies, and standards in existence at the time the application for the map is accepted as complete or is deemed complete.[830]

A more difficult situation arises when a landowner submits a preliminary subdivision plat in reliance on existing zoning, but the approving body refuses to approve it after delay and intermediate passage of regulations that would make the plat as submitted nonconforming. At least one court[831] has held that when a landowner's proposed plat conforms to then-existing ordinances, the local planning commission must approve the plat, even though there was some evidence that a number of landowners were submitting plats on "dormant" projects in order to "beat the clock" with respect to new planning regulations. This is, of course, a recognition that action and good faith have little to do with vested rights, but rather with estoppel, an equitable action.

A few states have enacted legislation protecting a property owner's right to continue with his development once a governing authority has approved the developer's preliminary subdivision plan. In New Jersey, for example, the statute confers upon the applicant a vested right to develop for three years, following either preliminary approval of a major subdivision plan or site plan. The court applied the New Jersey statute in *B&W Associates v. Planning Board of the Town of Hackettstown*,[832] and held that B&W Associates had a vested right to continue its development. The town had granted preliminary major subdivision approval to B&W to allow the company to build a warehouse. Subsequently, the town amended the zoning ordinance and eliminated warehousing as a permitted use on B&W's property. The court concluded that the statute clearly intended to vest a developer's right to continue its project once the governing authority had approved its preliminary plan, and no subsequent zoning change would apply to the property.

---

827. *See, e.g.*, Hawaii, *as held in* County of Kauai v. Pacific Standard Life Ins. Co., 65 Haw. 318, 653 P.2d 766 (1982).

828. *See* Youngblood v. Board of Supervisors of San Diego County, 22 Cal. 3d 644, 586 P.2d 556 (1978); Smith v. Winhall Planning Comm'n, 140 Vt. 178, 436 A.2d 760 (1981).

829. CAL. GOV'T CODE §§66498.1-66498.9.

830. CURTIN & TALBERT, *supra* note 51, at 97. *See also* Bright Dev. v. City of Tracy, 24 Cal. Rptr. 2d 618, 620, 20 Cal. App. 4th 783, 788 (1993).

831. Lake City Corp. v. City of Mequon, 199 Wis. 2d 353, 544 N.W.2d 600 (1996).

832. 242 N.J. Super. 1, 575 A.2d 1371 (1990).

Pennsylvania has also enacted a statute protecting a property owner's right to develop once a preliminary application for subdivision approval has been obtained. The statute protects the property owner from any "subsequent change or amendment in the zoning, subdivision or other governing ordinance or plan . . . [for] five years." In *Harwick v. Board of Supervisors of the Township of Upper Saucon,*[833] a property owner had submitted a preliminary subdivision plan to the board of supervisors and received approval of the preliminary plan on July 12, 1983. In July 1984, the property owner had submitted its final subdivision plan, but it was not approved by the board until October 1993, nine years after the owner submitted it. In the interim, the township amended its zoning ordinance. The property owner argued that he was protected from the application of the new ordinance based on its statutorily protected vested right. The town objected to the vested rights argument, stating that since the property owner had failed to obtain final approval within the statutorily limited five-year period, its vested rights had expired. The court disagreed, holding that the town had granted an extension of the five-year period to the owner, and therefore he was not subject to the new ordinance enacted after he received preliminary plan approval. Although the town had not granted an explicit extension, the court found that the course of dealing between the parties evidenced an intent to extend the five-year period, so that the developer retained a vested right beyond the statutorily set time limit.

Although most courts require that the subdivision plan be *approved* to confer a vested right, at least two courts have vested the right to develop upon the *submission* of the subdivision plan. In *Noble Manor Co. v. Pierce County,*[834] the developer submitted a completed subdivision plat application to the county to build three multi-family residential units. At the time Noble Manor submitted its application, the applicable ordinance required a minimum lot size of 13,500 square feet for duplex developments. Before the subdivision plans were approved, however, the county enacted an interim zoning ordinance increasing the lot size for duplexes from 13,500 to 20,000 square feet. The county refused to issue building permits for the project based on the new ordinance's increased lot size requirement.

The court first examined the Washington State-vested rights law, noting it was a minority rule. The court observed that the state of Washington does not follow the "building permit" rule followed in many other jurisdictions, and that "[u]nder Washington law, property development rights vest at the time a developer files a complete and legally sufficient building permit or preliminary plat

---

833. Harwick v. Board of Supervisors of the Township of Upper Saucon, 663 A.2d 878 (Pa. 1995) (citing PA. MUNICIPALITIES PLANNING CODE §508(4)(ii)).

834. 81 Wash. App. 141, 913 P.2d 417 (1996). *See Harwick,* 663 A.2d at 878 (Pennsylvania statute protects property owner from newly enacted ordinance while application for approval of a plat is pending). *But cf.* Brazos Land, Inc. v. Board of County Comm'rs of Rio Arriba County, 115 N.M. 168, 848 P.2d 1095 (1993) (applicant for preliminary subdivision plat approval had no vested right and was subject to subsequently enacted regulations where no actual approval of application).

application."[835] Applying this minority rule to the facts in the case, the court concluded that once Noble Manor had submitted its subdivision plat application, its right to develop had vested and no subsequent ordinance would apply to its development.[836] It is, of course, critical in these cases that the application be complete for development rights to vest.[837]

### 3. Planned Development Plan Approval

The law with respect to planned development plan approval is largely the same as that which applies to subdivision plat approval, except that a sketch plan is almost certainly insufficient to vest land development rights. The usual order of planned development approval is sketch plan, preliminary plan, and final plan, with the latter often processed at the same time as subdivision plats, if any.[838]

One state has enacted a statute that protects a property owner's right to continue its planned development plan when a local government approves a PUD plan. In Colorado, the Vested Property Rights Act provides:

> A vested property right, once established as provided for in this article, precludes any zoning or land use action by a local government or pursuant to an initiated measure which would alter, impair, prevent, diminish, or otherwise delay the development or use of the property as set forth in a site specific development plan [PUD]. . . .[839]

In *Villa at Greeley, Inc. v. Hopper*,[840] a developer submitted a PUD plan to the Board of County Commissioners (Board) to develop a pre-parole facility in the county. The Board approved it, and subsequently a group opposed to the development called for a referendum to give voters special authority to review decisions on incarceration sites. The developer sought and obtained a ruling that it had a vested property right under the Vested Property Rights Act. The voters amended the home rule charter through the referendum to allow voters to preclude issuance of a certificate of occupancy for pre-parole facilities without

---

835. *Noble Manor Co.*, 81 Wash. App. at 146, 913 P.2d at 420 (citing Valley View Indus. Park v. Redmond, 107 Wash. 2d 621, 733 P.2d 182 (1987)).

836. *But cf.* Erickson & Assocs. v. McLerrran, 123 Wash. 2d 864, 872 P.2d 1090 (1994) (Washington vested rights doctrine does not apply to filing of a completed Master Use Permit application (similar to site plan) as it does to filing of building permit application).

837. Washington has emerged as one of the most liberal states in determining when one's development right has vested. *See, e.g.*, Friends of the Law v. King County, 123 Wash. 2d 518, 869 P.2d 1056 (1994) (holding that the developer's right to complete its project had vested at the time it submitted its "fully completed" application for preliminary plat approval); Adams v. Thurston County, 70 Wash. App. 471, 855 P.2d 284 (Wash. 1993) (vesting of development rights occurred at time developer filed a complete and legally sufficient preliminary plat application and subsequently enacted land use regulations do not apply to that development).

838. *See* CALLIES ET AL., CASES AND MATERIALS ON LAND USE, *supra* note 5.

839. Vested Rights Property Act, COLO. REV. STAT. §24-68-103 (1988).

840. 917 P.2d 350 (Colo. 1996).

voter approval. The developer sued, claiming that the charter amendment violated his statutorily protected vested property right.

The court agreed with the developer, holding that the Act, by its own terms, created a vested property right when the local government approved the developer's PUD plan. However, the court noted that the Act provides for an exception to the vested right's protection, if the governmental authority gives just compensation for costs incurred subsequent to the receipt of plan approval. Therefore, the court remanded the case to the trial court to determine the proper compensation.

In Washington State, when landowners filed applications for a PUD and an unclassified use permit (UUP) in 1991, the county's 1983 Zoning Ordinance was in effect. During environmental review for the recreational area's development, however, the Growth Management Act was amended, designating certain areas for interim urban growth. The interim zoning ordinance was invalidated in 1994 and revised in 1995, with the final zoning ordinance adopted in 1996. Because the County Hearing Examiner determined that the project had vested while the 1983 Zoning Ordinance was in effect, the examiner recommended approval of the applications subject to 25 conditions.[841] Following the Land Use Petition Act standard of review, a Washington appellate court found that the PUD had vested on the date of application, and that case law had established that a complete conditional use permit, which the court found to be similar enough to a UUP, also vests a project.[842]

The Washington Supreme Court has held that monetary liability may arise where a local government disregards a developer's vested rights.[843] The case involved vested rights arising under the Washington statute, and, specifically, a denial of a permit necessary to the construction of a recently approved PUD project that had vested rights under Washington law.[844] The developer did not

---

841. North Kitsap Coordinating Council v. Kitsap County, No. 46624-1-I, 2001 Wash. App. LEXIS 2232 (2001).

842. *Id.* at *20-*21.

843. Mission Springs, Inc. v. City of Spokane, 134 Wash. 2d 947, 954 P.2d 250 (1998), as corrected.

844. The court summarized the facts and related conclusions:

> On August 31, 1992, the Spokane City Council adopted Ordinance No. C-30529 approving Mission Springs' application for a planned unit development (PUD) comprised of 790 apartment units located within approximately 33 separate buildings. This final approval followed submittals by the developer setting forth the nature of the proposed development in sufficient detail to enable the city council to affirmatively determine pursuant to RCW 58.17.110 that the development made adequate provision for "the public health, safety, and general welfare and for such open spaces, drainage ways, streets or roads, alleys, other public ways, transit stops, potable water supplies . . . ," etc. RCW 58.17.110(2)(a). The record shows a public hearing was held on November 5, 1991, Clerk's papers (CP) at 202, wherein evidence was taken on these matters. Thereafter the hearing examiner concluded on November 25, 1991, that the PUD application should be granted, sub-

use the grading permits initially issued to it but applied for new grading permits well within the five-year period during which its development rights were vested. That application resulted in a hearing before the city council of which the developer was not apprised, although there were a number of opponents present. After discussion at the meeting, the council voted to delay the issuance of the grading permit until council could obtain additional traffic studies. The court ruled for the developer[845]: "Simply put, neither a grading permit, building permit, nor any other ministerial permit may be withheld at the discretion of a local official to allow time to undertake a further study."[846] It concluded:

> Mission Springs was entitled to regular administrative processing and issuance of the requested grading permit in accordance with ordinance criteria. The Spo-

---

> ject to various conditions. CP at 202.
>
> The record also demonstrates it was well known to the developer and local government officials the addition of a 790-unit apartment complex at this location would necessarily cause a predictable increase in traffic upon adjacent roads and highways subsequent to ultimate construction and occupancy. That this factor was fully considered by all concerned there can be no doubt as the developer submitted a traffic study detailing the likely traffic increase as a result of the apartment build-out with specific reference to the likely routes of travel. *See* CP at 245, 304 (describing 1991 traffic impact study). We also note that it was known, or should have been known, to all concerned as of the date of final approval of August 31, 1992, the developer was statutorily vested with the legal right to build out the planned improvements identified in the PUD for a period of five years under the ordinances, statutes, and regulations in effect at the time of the August 1992 approval "unless the legislative body finds that a change in conditions creates a serious threat to the public health or safety in the subdivision." RCW 58.17.170. No such finding, however, was ever made.

*Mission Springs, Inc.*, 134 Wash. 2d at 952-53 [footnote omitted]; internal references are to the Revised Code of Washington.

845. The court said:

> Without material dispute of fact it appears these defendants abrogated Mission Springs' right to obtain issuance of a grading permit when the City Council acted to deny issuance of this or any permit and the City Manager acquiesced in the council's demands.
>
> That the City Manager willfully withheld the permit from issuance upon, or in prevention of, satisfaction of ordinance criteria during the June through August 1995 period upon the motion of the City Council is not disputed. Nor is it denied the City Council acted contrary to the legal advice of its own city attorney, and in no uncertain terms. The issue here is not whether or not the Spokane City Council can lawfully request its city manager to perform at municipal expense such additional studies as it may see fit but rather is whether the statutory and constitutional rights of Mission Springs were violated when its right to obtain this grading permit upon satisfaction of ordinance criteria was abrogated pending the completion of such additional studies.

134 Wash. 2d at 959.

846. *Id.* at 961.

kane City Council, contrary to the advice of its own city attorney, deprived the permit applicant of that process lawfully due by instructing its city manager to withhold the permit for reasons extraneous to ordinance, or lawful, criteria. The City Manager did in fact suspend the required process and acceded to the City Council's demand to withhold the permit without lawful justification, thereby depriving Mission Springs of its property absent the lawful process due under the laws of this State and the ordinances of Spokane. The duration of the deprivation, and the ultimate issuance of the permit after suit had been commenced, does not change the fact that the legal rights of Mission Springs were violated in the first instance.

The trial court's summary judgment of dismissal is reversed, and the case is remanded for trial consistent with this opinion.[847]

## 4. Site Plan Approval

Some jurisdictions have equated the approval of a site plan with the issuance of a building permit.[848] In *Board of Supervisors v. Medical Structures, Inc.*,[849] the court so held, observing: "The site plan has virtually replaced the building permit as the most vital document in the development process."[850]

In New Jersey, the state vesting rights statute grants to the developer with preliminary site plan approval vested rights for a three-year period from the date of preliminary approval.[851] In *Bleznak v. Township of Evesham*,[852] a property owner applied for and received preliminary site approval to build a nursery school in Evesham Township. One week later, the owner obtained final site plan approval. At the time plaintiffs obtained their site plan approvals, the property was located in the general business zone under the applicable zoning ordinance. Subsequently, the township amended its ordinance, placing plaintiffs' property in a residential district. The township maintained that the ordinance applied to the plaintiff's property, and the nursery school was therefore a nonconforming use, which the plaintiffs could not expand or change unless they complied with the new zoning. Plaintiffs argued that the property was protected against newly enacted ordinances by the New Jersey statute, which confers vested rights for a period of three years upon preliminary approval of a site plan. The court agreed with the plaintiffs, holding that the statute clearly intends to protect properties from newly enacted regulations for a period of three

---

847. *Id.* at 971-72.

848. SIEMON ET AL., *supra* note 753, at 22-23.

849. 213 Va. 355, 192 S.E.2d 799 (1972).

850. *Id.* at 357, 192 S.E.2d at 801.

851. N.J. STAT. ANN. §§40:55D-49 and 52. See *infra* for discussion of the New Jersey vested rights statute in a section entitled Subdivision Plats or Plans. *See, e.g.*, Palatine I v. Planning Bd. of the Township of Montville, 133 N.J. 546, 628 A.2d 321 (1993) (holding that developer had protected vested right to continue with project following township's grant of preliminary site plan approval for period of five years. Once the time period expired, however, township was not equitably estopped from applying zoning amendments to property).

852. 170 N.J. Super. 216, 406 A.2d 201 (1979).

years, and therefore plaintiffs could continue with their nursery school project unaffected by the rezoning.

In *Village of Palatine v. LaSalle National Bank*,[853] an Illinois court held that a municipality may not deny a developer's application for a building permit once the governing authority has approved the site plan application and the property owner has made substantial expenditures or changed his position. There, developers obtained site plan approval for a development containing more than 500 multifamily units, to be completed in three phases. The developers completed Phase I in 1974, the same year that the village adopted a floodplain ordinance prohibiting virtually all construction in areas designated as floodplains. Almost all of the developers' project was located in the Flood Fringe, designated by the Illinois Department of Transportation as an area permitting development. In 1978, the developers applied for building permits for Phases II and III. The village refused to issue the permits, based on the floodplain ordinance. Then, the village also adopted a height ordinance, restricting the height of buildings within the development's zoning classification.

The village subsequently brought an action to have the court declare both ordinances enforceable against the development. The court noted that since the development was no longer in the floodplain, the question of the validity of the floodplain ordinance was moot. The issue, therefore, was whether the height ordinance would apply to the development in question. The court first addressed the developers' vested rights argument, concluding that the village's approval of the original site plan resulted in a vested right to continue with the project in accordance with the original site plan, and the village could not apply its newly enacted height ordinance to the development to divest the developers of that right.

Although site plan approval will vest the right to develop in some jurisdictions, others have refused to extend their vested rights rule to allow such protection to property owners. For example, in *American West Development v. City of Henderson*,[854] the Nevada Supreme Court refused to extend the state vested rights rule to include master plan (site plan) approval. The court emphasized that "[i]n order for rights in a proposed development project to vest, zoning or use approvals must not be subject to further governmental discretionary action affecting project commencement, and the developer must prove considerable reliance on the approvals granted."[855] Because the developer still had to submit applications for subdivision maps, building permits, and other discretionary approvals, no right to continue its development had as yet vested. The court noted that, notwithstanding the developer's lack of vested rights, the city was still required to give substantial deference to the master plan. Therefore, the court remanded the case to require the city to review the developer's project with the proper deference to the master plan.

---

853. 112 Ill. App. 3d 885, 445 N.E.2d 1277 (1983).

854. 111 Nev. 804, 898 P.2d 110 (1995).

855. *Id.* at 807, 898 P.2d at 112.

The submission of a site plan application will rarely result in vested rights. In *Town of Stephens City v. Russell*,[856] a developer submitted a site plan application to the town's planning commission, intending to build three apartment buildings on his property. The planning commission rejected the site plan, based on the developer's failure to comply with zoning regulations. The developer resubmitted the site plan, but it still failed to comply with the town's zoning ordinance. While the site plan approval process was pending, the town amended its zoning ordinance, which reduced the number of apartment units the developer could build on his site. The developer then sought a vested rights determination in court. The court reviewed the Virginia case law on vested rights, concluding that a property owner must obtain some type of government permit or approval to acquire a vested right. Since the developer's site plan had never been approved by the planning commission, the developer had not acquired a vested right, and therefore the amended zoning ordinance applied to the property.

5. Special or Conditional Use Permit

A number of jurisdictions have vested land development rights upon the issuance of a special use permit, particularly if it is the last discretionary permit issued by government.[857] Thus in *Graham Beach Partnership v. County of Kauai*,[858] the Hawaii Supreme Court held a shoreline management permit (SMP) under a state coastal zone management statute administered by Hawaii's counties constituted the last discretionary act necessary to vest land development rights. In a controversial decision, the court held that since objectors filed a certified petition for a referendum on underlying zoning before the county granted the SMP, the referendum itself became the final discretionary permit.

Equating a special use permit and a building permit, one court agreed with a landowner that his rights had vested after spending nearly $1.5 million after obtaining such a permit.[859] Similarly, in *Cardwell v. Smith*,[860] the court held that property owners who relied in good faith on a special use permit previously granted by the zoning board had a vested right to operate a rock quarry. The property owners had applied for a special use permit to operate a rock quarry on its property. The Forsyth County Zoning Board granted the special use permit and the plaintiffs, neighboring property owners, sought review of the Zoning Board's decision. While plaintiffs' suit was pending, the Forsyth County Commissioners adopted an amendment to the zoning ordinance prohibiting the operation of a quarry on property zoned R-6, like the subject property. The plain-

---

856. 241 Va. 160, 399 S.E.2d 814 (1991).

857. SIEMON ET AL., *supra* note 753, at 23-24.

858. 65 Haw. 318, 653 P.2d 766 (1982).

859. Town of Paradise Valley v. Gulf Leisure Corp., 27 Ariz. App. 600, 557 P.2d 532 (1976). *See also* Renieris v. Village of Skokie, 85 Ill. App. 2d 418, 229 N.E.2d 345 (1967); Elam v. Albers, 44 Colo. App. 281, 616 P.2d 168 (1980).

860. 106 N.C. App. 187, 415 S.E.2d 770 (1992).

tiffs argued that the amendment should apply to the property, and furthermore that the defendants had no vested right to operate a quarry since they did not have a building permit.

The court first examined the vested rights rule as adopted by the state supreme court:

> [O]ne who, in good faith and in reliance upon a permit lawfully issued to him, makes expenditures or incurs contractual obligations . . . may not be deprived of his right to continue such construction and use by the revocation of such permit, whether the revocation be by the enactment of an otherwise valid zoning ordinance or by other means . . . .[861]

Applying the rule to the facts in this case, the court found that the defendants had spent more than $1 million to begin quarry operations in reliance upon the special use permit. The court concluded that the defendants made substantial expenditures in good-faith reliance upon the special use permit, and plaintiffs could not now deprive them of their right to operate the quarry by applying the zoning ordinance amendment.

In *City of Miami v. 20th Century Club, Inc.*,[862] the city of Miami granted to a property owner a conditional use permit to allow the owner to operate a private club in an apartment building. Later, the owner sought to expand the club and applied for a building permit. The city refused to issue a building permit until the owner applied for another conditional use permit. The owner sued, arguing that the conditional use permit vested his right to expand his club. The court agreed, holding that "the city's resolution created a vested right of 'conditional use' zoning for the appellee and that the appellee had a right to rely on the existing zoning in seeking a building permit for expansion from the city."[863]

Other courts have held that a special use permit will suffice to vest land development rights. In *Town of Paradise Valley v. Gulf Leisure Corp.*,[864] the town of Paradise Valley issued a special use permit to a landowner, authorizing the development of his parcel as a resort hotel. In reliance upon the issuance of the permit, Gulf Leisure Corporation purchased the property from the landowner and obtained a significant loan from the bank. As allowed by the permit, Gulf Leisure filed an application to extend the special use permit, which the Paradise Valley Planning and Zoning Commission denied. Gulf Leisure sued, arguing that it had a vested right to construct the resort, based on the validly issued special use permit. The court set out the vested rights doctrine as follows:

> Once a building permit and/or a special use permit are issued as duly authorized by law, as in this case, and the permittee has materially acted in reliance thereon and the guidelines delimited therein, the right to continue under those rules is

---

861. *Id.* at 773, 415 S.E.2d at 191 (citing Town of Hillsborough v. Smith, 276 N.C. 48, 54-55, 170 S.E.2d 904, 909 (1969)).

862. 313 So. 2d 448 (Fla. 1975).

863. *Id.*

864. 27 Ariz. App. 600, 557 P.2d 532 (1976).

vested and a municipality may not arbitrarily revoke or change the rules under which the permit was issued.[865]

The court then noted that the landowner had been granted a valid special use permit, and had expended significant amounts of money in reliance of the permit, both in purchasing the property and in subsequent architectural fees, overhead expenses, and the clearing of the land. Based on these facts, the court concluded that Gulf Leisure had a vested right to continue construction under the special use permit.

One court has held that a special use permit *application* is not a cognizable property interest and therefore does not vest a right to develop.[866] A company sought to develop a rock quarry on 146 acres purchased in 1984. The property was zoned R-1, and mining was a permitted use in the area if the landowner obtained a special use permit. When county commissioners learned of Teer's mining plans, they moved to delete mining as a permitted use in all residential districts, including Teer's property. The county met with Teer, and told him that the county was preparing a comprehensive land use plan designating Teer's property as a rural industrial zone, and encouraged Teer to apply for a special use permit. One month later, however, the county commissioners changed the land use plan to designate Teer's property from R-1 to Rural Buffer, allowing no mining. Teer sued, claiming a vested right based on the special use permit application.

The court applied North Carolina law addressing "cognizable property interests," which states that if a local zoning authority possesses "[a]ny significant discretion in granting a permit, there is no cognizable property interest in the issuance of that permit."[867] Because North Carolina law gives the board of commissioners considerable discretion to grant or deny a special use permit, the court concluded that Teer had no assurance that the board of commisioners would grant its application for a special use permit and therefore no vested right.

*Town Pump, Inc. v. Board of Adjustment of Red Lodge*[868] involved the purchase of undeveloped property on which Town Pump planned to "operate a gas station, convenience store, and casino, and to sell beer and wine for consumption in the casino."[869] Apparently those uses were permitted by right, but the sale was conditioned on subdivision of the property by the seller. While the subdivision review was pending, the city rezoned the property to a "commercial highway" zoning district that allowed the sale of beer and wine only with a special exception. The board of adjustment denied the company's application for special exception, after which the company appealed to the trial court. While the trial was pending, the city adopted a new "development code," which imposed new restrictions on such applications and which by its terms was intended to apply to any new consideration of an application from Town Pump.

---

865. *Id.* at 607, 557 P.2d at 539.

866. Nello L. Teer Co. v. Orange County, 1993 U.S. App. LEXIS 12525 (4th Cir. 1993).

867. *Id.*

868. 292 Mont. 6, 971 P.2d 349 (1998).

869. *Id.* at 8, 971 P.2d at 350.

The Montana high court held that a local government has the authority to adopt new regulations and to apply them to "pending applications."[870] It rejected the company's argument that its application was no longer "pending," because the company asserted it had been wrongfully denied and thus should have been issued by the time the new code was adopted.[871]

One court has created a vested rights rule that requires *both* a validly issued special use permit and the filing of a site plan to vest a property owner's right to develop. In two factually similar cases decided on the same day, the Virginia Supreme Court addressed the issue of whether the issuance of a special use permit creates a vested right. First, in *Board of Supervisors of Fairfax County v. Medical Structures*,[872] the board of supervisors granted a special use permit to the original property owner to build a nursing home in a residential district of Fairfax County. Medical Structures purchased the property from the owner, and on March 7, 1969, filed a site plan as a prerequisite to the issuance of a building permit. The site plan was resubmitted several times, the last submission occurring on November 12, 1969. On October 8 and November 19, the board of supervisors amended the zoning ordinance to prohibit nursing homes with more than 50 beds in certain residential districts, including Medical Structures' property. Medical Structures argued that the issuance of a special use permit and the filing of a site plan created a vested right. The Virginia court agreed:

> Where, as here, a special use permit has been granted under a zoning classification, a bona fide site plan has thereafter been filed and diligently pursued, and substantial expense has been incurred in good faith before a change in zoning, the permittee then has a vested right to the land use described in the use permit and he cannot be deprived of such use by subsequent legislation.[873]

The court concluded that Medical Structures had a vested right, and the board of supervisors was ordered to approve Medical Structures' site plan and issue a building permit.

Similarly, in *Board of Supervisors of Fairfax County v. Cities Service Oil Co.*,[874] the landowner had applied for and was granted a special use permit authorizing a gasoline service station. Cities Service then filed a preliminary site plan as a prerequisite to the issuance of a building permit. Before final site plan approval, however, the board of supervisors rezoned the subject property to C-O. The board of supervisors refused to approve the final site plan or to issue a building permit because the service station was not a permitted use under the new zoning designation. Cities Service sued the board of supervisors, arguing that its substantial expenditure in reliance upon an existing zoning classification, together with the special use permit, created a vested property right. The board of supervisors, on the other hand, argued that no vested right arises until a building permit

---

870. *Id.* at 13, 971 P.2d at 353-54.

871. *Id.* at 14, 971 P.2d at 354.

872. 213 Va. 355, 192 S.E.2d 799 (1972); Board of Supervisors of Fairfax County v. Cities Serv. Oil Co., 193 S.E.2d 1 (1972).

873. *Medical Structures*, 213 Va. at 358, 192 S.E.2d at 801.

874. 193 S.E.2d 1 (Va. 1972).

has been issued and substantial expenditures have been made in reliance on the permit. Relying on its holding in *Medical Structures*, the court held that Cities Service had a vested right to the land use described in the use permit and was entitled to approval of the site plan and issuance of a building permit.[875]

More recently, the same Virginia court reiterated its vested rights rule to hold that a landowner who had failed to identify a significant official governmental act to support a vested rights claim had no vested right.[876] In *Notestein v. Board of Supervisors of Appomattox County*[877] a landowner challenged the validity of a newly enacted zoning ordinance that prohibited the development and operation of a solid waste landfill on their property. The Notesteins had filed an application for a landfill permit, but had not obtained a special use permit or building permit prior to the board of supervisor's enacting the zoning ordinance at question. The court cited *Medical Structures* and *Cities Service* for the rule that a landowner who is granted a special use permit, has filed a site plan, and incurred substantial expenses in good faith before the zoning change, will obtain a vested right to develop its property.[878] The court concluded that because a governmental entity had not acted officially (either issuing a special use permit or building permit), the Notesteins' vested rights argument must fail.

### 6. Grading and Other Site Preparation Permits

While many courts would be unlikely to confer a vested right based on the granting of preliminary approvals such as grading or other preparation permits, some commentators see a trend in finding such rights.[879] Thus, a landowner withstood a challenge to his proposed development under newly enacted zoning regulations because of actions taken in reliance upon a validly issued grading permit.[880] The court held that in the vested rights context, it could see "no rational distinction between building or conditional use permits and a grading

---

875. *Id.*

876. Notestein v. Board of Supervisors of Appomattox County, 240 Va. 146, 393 S.E.2d 205 (1990). *See also* Snow v. Amherst County Bd. of Zoning Appeals, 248 Va. 404, 448 S.E.2d 606 (1994) (reiterating the special use permit vested rights rule and holding that the issuance of a variance is not a "significant official governmental act within the meaning of our established precedent" and does not reach the level required to vest property rights in Virginia); Board of Supervisors of Chesterfield County v. Trollingwood Partnership, 248 Va. 112, 445 S.E.2d 151 (1994) (emphasizing that the special use permit must be followed by filing of a "bona fide site plan." Without detailed plans the court will not consider a special use permit sufficient to vest a developers' right to develop his property).

877. 240 Va. 146, 393 S.E.2d 205 (1990).

878. *Id.* at 151-52, 393 S.E.2d at 208 (citing *Medical Structures*, 213 Va. at 357-58, 192 S.E.2d at 801 and Board of Supervisors of Fairfax County v. Cities Serv. Oil Co., 193 S.E.2d 1, 3 (Va. 1972)).

879. SIEMON ET AL., *supra* note 753, at 22-23.

880. Juanita Bay Valley Community Ass'n v. City of Kirkland, 9 Wash. App. 59, 510 P.2d 1140 (1973).

permit."[881] Other jurisdictions have found such permits as a foundation permit sufficient to vest land development rights.[882]

Other jurisdictions, however, have been less responsive to vested rights claims based on such preliminary permits.[883] Certainly merely performing preparatory measures on the property, such as test drilling, would fail to rise to the level of vesting a property owner's right to develop. In *Bickerstaff Clay Products Co. v. Harris County*,[884] a brick manufacturing company purchased a 161-acre tract of land in Harris County, and conducted several test drills on the property to determine the extent of mylonite in the land. The company did not immediately mine the property, instead holding it for future use. More than 20 years later, the county board of commissioners adopted a countywide zoning ordinance and land use plan for the county. The ordinance zoned the subject property A-1, or vacant land, with agriculture and forestry as the permitted uses. In 1993, the mining company applied for a mining permit from the state Environmental Protection Department. The department granted the permit, and the mining company sought county rezoning to M-2, which would permit mining. The county denied the company's application, based on the zoning designation, and the company sued.

The court addressed the company's argument that it had a vested right to mine the property, and held that in order to acquire a vested right a governmental body must have acted in some way so that the company had a right to rely on the action. Here, the mining company had merely performed preliminary test drilling and had not obtained any permits upon which it could rely. Clearly, the court concluded, the company had no vested right to mine its property and the county's action in denying the rezoning application was valid.

## 7. Zoning Classifications

While it is generally true that there is no vested right in existing zoning,[885] several jurisdictions have held that it is a different matter entirely with respect to a newly enacted zoning classification, particularly if the new classification was recently

---

881. *Id.* at 84, 510 P.2d at 1155.

882. Sakolsky v. City of Coral Gables, 151 So. 2d 433 (Fla. 1963).

883. Siemon et al., *supra* note 753, at 21-22.

884. 89 F.3d 1481 (11th Cir. 1996).

885. *See, e.g.*, Gilliland v. County of Los Angeles, 179 Cal. Rptr. 73, 126 Cal. App. 3d 610 (1981); Town of Stephens v. Russell, 241 Va. 160, 399 S.E.2d 814 (1991); Zealy v. City of Waukesha, 201 Wis. 2d 356, 548 N.W.2d 528 (1996); Pasco County v. Tampa Dev. Corp., 364 So. 2d 850 (Fla. 1978); Beasley v. Potter, 493 F. Supp. 1059 (W.D. Mich. 1980); Golden Gate Corp. v. Town of Narragansett, 116 R.I. 552, 359 A.2d 321 (1976); City of University Park v. Benner, 485 S.W.2d 773 (Tex. 1972); City of Gainesville v. Cone, 365 So. 2d 737 (Fla. 1979); Town of Vienna Council v. Kohler, 218 Va. 966, 244 S.E.2d 542 (1978); Siemon et al., *supra* note 753, at 14-15.

obtained by the landowner claiming vested rights.[886] Thus, several Florida courts have found vested rights upon a landowner change in position following rezonings at the landowner's request. In one, the landowner had spent a year negotiating with the local government and incurred substantial expenditures.[887] In another, the developer had paid several times the pre-zoning value of the land, incurring substantial financial obligations to make the purchase.[888]

Of course, if the rezoning is accompanied by a plan or other similar document, the likelihood of a rezoning vesting land development rights is increased still further. Submission (though not necessarily separate approval) of a master plan[889] and a site development plan[890] with a successful rezoning request have both been held to vest such development rights. Thus, in *Resolution Trust Corp. v. Town of Highland Beach*,[891] property owners purchased 24.8 acres of land, intending to build a residential development. The town commission approved a residential plan unit development (RPUD-II) for the property in 1974. One year later, the town amended the PUD ordinance so that any real property zoned or classified RPUD would continue to be so classified for one year from the effective date of the ordinance. The ordinance further required the town to grant extensions of the time period upon a property owner's application showing evidence of governmental delay and required the property owners to complete all construction within 10 years. In 1980, the property owners formed a joint venture and redesigned the RPUD, reducing its density from 846 units to 620. The town subsequently issued construction permits for the RPUD, and approved the redesigned RPUD. The town also informed the joint venture that the RPUD would expire in 1990, 10 years after the town had issued the first construction permits as set out in the ordinance. In 1984, however, the planning board passed a resolution amending the RPUD's completion date, moving it to July 1, 1985. The joint venture argued against the planning board's interpretation of the ordinance and the new completion date, without avail, and subsequently failed to complete construction by the new completion date. In 1987, the town changed the land use designation of the property, downzoning the property to residential with a density of only eight units per acre. The joint venture sued the town, seeking to reinstate the RPUD and for damages in an inverse condemnation action.

The court first addressed the joint venture's vested rights argument, noting that although "there is no property right in possession of a building permit we have consistently held that property interests and vested rights may arise from zoning

---

886. SIEMON ET AL., *supra* note 753, at 15; Resolution Trust Corp. v. Town of Highland Beach, 18 F.3d 1536 (11th Cir. 1994).

887. Board of County Comm'rs of Metro. Dade County v. Lutz, 314 So. 2d 815 (Fla. 1975).

888. Jones v. U.S. Steel Credit Corp., 382 So. 2d 48 (Fla. 1980).

889. Town of Largo v. Imperial Homes Corp., 309 So. 2d 571 (Fla. 1975).

890. Hollywood Beach Hotel Co. v. City of Hollywood, 329 So. 2d 10 (Fla. 1976).

891. 18 F.3d 1536 (11th Cir. 1994).

and permit approvals."[892] The court concluded that the town's actions in interpreting the ordinance and its representations to the joint venture, coupled with the joint venture's acts of reliance on the completion date, rose to the level of a vested right. The court continued: "[T]he joint venture had a vested right in the beneficial use of the subject property granted under zoning ordinance 282 classifying the property as a residential [PUD] . . . and fixing the time of completion as August 8, 1990."[893] Moreover, the court emphasized that the town had the authority to interpret its own ordinance, and the joint venture should be able to reasonably rely on the town's interpretation. Therefore, the joint venture had a vested right in RPUD zoning through August 1990, not July 1985.

*D. Legislative Solutions*

Some legislatures have adopted laws addressing vested rights directly,[894] and others have provided alternative routes to certainty, as through development agreements.

---

892. *Id.* at 1545 (citing Marine Open, Inc. v. Manatee County, 877 F.2d 892, 894 (11th Cir. 1989); Wheeler v. City of Pleasant Grove, 896 F.2d 1347, 1351 (11th Cir. 1990); A.A. Profiles, Inc. v. City of Fort Lauderdale, 850 F.2d 1483 (11th Cir. 1988)).

893. *Id.* at 1545.

894. *See, e.g.*, Colorado: COLO. REV. STAT. §24-68-103, which provides:

(1)(a) Each local government shall specifically identify, by ordinance or resolution, the type or types of site specific development plan approvals within the local government's jurisdiction that will cause property rights to vest as provided in this article. Any such ordinance or resolution shall be consistent with the provisions of this article. Effective January 1, 2000, if a local government has not adopted an ordinance or resolution pursuant to section 24-68-102(4) specifying what constitutes a site specific development plan that would trigger a vested property right, then rights shall vest upon the approval of any plan, plat, drawing, or sketch, however denominated, that is substantially similar to any plan, plat, drawing, or sketch listed in section 24-68-102(4).

(b) A vested property right shall be deemed established with respect to any property upon the approval, or conditional approval, of a site specific development plan, following notice and public hearing, by the local government in which the property is situated.

(c) A vested property right shall attach to and run with the applicable property and shall confer upon the landowner the right to undertake and complete the development and use of said property under the terms and conditions of the site specific development plan including any amendments thereto. A local government may approve a site specific development plan upon such terms and conditions as may reasonably be necessary to protect the public health, safety, and welfare. Such conditional approval shall result in a vested property right, although failure to abide by such terms and conditions will result in a forfeiture of vested property rights. A site specific development plan shall be deemed approved upon the effective date of the local government legal action, resolution, or ordinance relating thereto. Such approval shall be subject to all rights of referendum and judicial review; except that the period of time permitted

Massachusetts has adopted a statute providing a developer with protection from zoning changes under specified circumstances:

> If a definitive plan, or a preliminary plan followed within seven months by a definitive plan, is submitted to a planning board for approval under the subdivision control law, and written notice of such submission has been given to the city or town clerk before the effective date of ordinance or by-law, the land shown on such plan shall be governed by the applicable provisions of the zoning ordinance or by-law, if any, in effect at the time of the first such submission while such plan or plans are being processed under the subdivision control law, and, if such definitive plan or an amendment thereof is finally approved, for eight years from the date of the endorsement of such approval . . . . [895]

The Massachusetts high court held that the zoning "freeze" applied even in a case where the town had the authority to "rescind" its approval of the subdivision plat; in short, the effect of the rescission, as interpreted by the court, was to eliminate the approval of the plat but to continue the zoning freeze that it established, apparently allowing the developer to apply again for subdivision approval under the original zoning.[896] The Massachusetts Appellate Court has also considered the statute and given effect to it in a case in which it directed approval of the subdivision by the planning board on remand.[897]

---

by law for the exercise of such rights shall not begin to run until the date of publication, in a newspaper of general circulation within the jurisdiction of the local government granting the approval, of a notice advising the general public of the site specific development plan approval and creation of a vested property right pursuant to this article. Such publication shall occur no later than fourteen days following approval.

(2) Zoning that is not part of a site specific development plan shall not result in the creation of vested property rights.

Idaho: Idaho Code §67-6511, which includes this language:

(d) If a governing board adopts a zoning classification pursuant to a request by a property owner based upon a valid, existing comprehensive plan and zoning ordinance, the governing board shall not subsequently reverse its action or otherwise change the zoning classification of said property without the consent in writing of the current property owner for a period of four (4) years from the date the governing board adopted said individual property owner's request for the zoning classification change. If the governing body does reverse its action or otherwise change the zoning classification of said property during the above four (4) year period without the current property owner's consent in writing, the current property owner shall have standing in a court of competent jurisdiction to enforce the provisions of this section.

See, for further commentary, Terry D. Morgan, *Vested Rights Legislation*, 34 URB. LAW. 131 (2002).

895. MASS. GEN. LAWS. ch. 40A, §6, ¶ 5.

896. Heritage Park Dev. Corp. v. Town of Southbridge, 424 Mass. 71, 674 N.E.2d 233 (1997).

897. Massachusetts Broken Stone Co. v. Planning Bd. of Weston, 45 Mass. App. Ct. 738, 701 N.E.2d 664 (1998).

# V. VESTED RIGHTS

The Colorado statute is interesting because it demands certainty from the process, but it allows local governments to choose the stage of the process at which they grant certainty.[898] Some may choose to grant vesting with a very early approval, such as a preliminary plat or even a grading permit. The disadvantage of that to the local government is that it has less data at that point, but it may be offset by the fact that the five-year vesting period will run out sooner. Other local governments may choose to grant vesting at the last possible moment, perhaps at the final plat or even site-plan review stage. That gives the local government much more data on which to base a decision and creates a greater likelihood that the developer will actually complete the project; it also extends the vesting period farther into the future. The Washington Supreme Court has held that a developer has "vested" rights under state statute to pursue an application under the rules in place when the application was filed.[899]

In a sense, the choice does not matter. The important thing to both parties is to have certainty for some specified period of time. The Colorado law provides such a specified period of time. Where permitted by law, development agreements also provide a specified period of time, as noted in part IV.

---

898. Colo. Rev. Stat. §24.68-103.

899. Association of Rural Residents v. Kitsap County, 141 Wash. 2d 185, 4 P.3d 115 (2000), where the court held: "This court has stated that '[i]n Washington, "vesting" refers generally to the notion that a land use application, under the proper conditions, will be considered only under the land use statutes and ordinances in effect at the time of the application's submission.'" *Id.* at 193, 4 P.3d at 119 (citing Noble Manor v. Pierce County, 133 Wash. 2d 269, 275, 943 P.2d 1378, 1381 (1997); Vashon Island Comm. for Self-Gov't v. Washington State Boundary Review Bd., 127 Wash. 2d 759, 767-68, 903 P.2d 953, 957 (1995)). The case had an unusual set of facts. The county had approved an urban growth area, which would have excluded the proposed development, but a state appellate board had remanded it to the county for further consideration and the county had failed to take timely action on the remand. On those facts, the court held that the former PUD regulations of the county were the applicable regulations, as the urban growth area regulations currently had no effect.

# Case List

## A

*A.A. Profiles, Inc. v. City of Fort Lauderdale*, 850 F.2d 1483 (11th Cir. 1988)

*A Local & Reg'l Monitor (ALARM) v. City of Los Angeles*, 20 Cal. Rptr. 2d 228, 16 Cal. App. 4th 630 (1993)

*A&M Builders, Inc. v. City of Highland Heights*, No. 75676, 2000 Ohio App. LEXIS 139 (Ohio Ct. App. Jan. 20, 2000)

*A&M Builders v. City of Highland Heights*, 89 Ohio St. 3d 279, 730 N.E.2d 986 (2000)

*Abbeville Arms v. City of Abbeville*, 273 S.C. 491, 257 S.E.2d 716 (1979)

*Adams v. Thurston County*, 70 Wash. App. 471, 855 P.2d 284 (1993)

*Agins v. Tiburon*, 447 U.S. 255, 100 S. Ct. 2138, 65 L. Ed. 2d 106, 10 ELR 20361 (1980)

*Ahamann-Yamane, Ltd. Liab. Corp. v. Tabler*, 105 Wash. App. 103, 19 P.3d 436 (2001)

*Allen v. Honolulu*, 58 Haw. 432, 571 P.2d 328 (1977)

*Allied Structural Steel Co. v. Spannus*, 438 U.S. 234 (1978)

*American Fabricare v. Township of Falls*, 101 F. Supp. 2d 301 (E.D. Pa. 2000)

*American W. Dev. v. City of Henderson*, 111 Nev. 804, 898 P.2d 110 (1995)

*Amherst Builders Ass'n v. City of Amherst*, 61 Ohio St. 2d 345, 402 N.E.2d 1181 (1980)

*Amoco Oil Co. v. Village of Schaumburg*, 277 Ill. App. 3d 926, 661 N.E.2d 380 (1995)

*Annapolis v. Waterman*, 357 Md. 484, 745 A.2d 1000 (2000)

*Anthony v. Kualoa Ranch, Inc.*, 69 Haw. 112, 736 P.2d 55 (1987)

*Arcadia Dev. Corp. v. City of Bloomington*, 552 N.W.2d 281 (Minn. Ct. App. 1996)

*Art Piculell Group v. Clackamas County*, 142 Or. App. 327, 922 P.2d 1227 (1996)

*Aspen v. Marshall*, 912 P.2d 56 (Colo. 1996)

*Associated Home Builders, Inc. v. City of Walnut Creek*, 4 Cal. 3d 637, 484 P.2d 606 (1971)

*Association of Rural Residents v. Kitsap County*, 141 Wash. 2d 185, 4 P.3d 115 (2000)

*Aunt Hack Ridge Estates, Inc. v. Planning Comm'n*, 273 A.2d 880 (Conn. 1970)

*Avco Community Developers Inc. v. South Coast Reg'l Comm'n*, 17 Cal. 3d 785, 553 P.2d 546 (1976)

*Ayres v. City Council of Los Angeles*, 34 Cal. 2d 31, 207 P.2d 1 (Cal. 1949)

# B

*B&W Assocs. v. Planning Bd. of the Town of Hackettstown*, 242 N.J. Super. 1, 575 A.2d 1371 (1990)

*Bainbridge, Inc. v. Douglas County Sch. Dist. RE-1*, 973 P.2d 684 (Colo. Ct. App. 1998)

*Baltica Constr. Co. v. Planning Bd. of Franklin Township.*, 222 N.J. Super. 428, 537 A.2d 319 (1987)

*Banberry Dev. Corp. v. South Jordan City*, 631 P.2d 899 (Utah 1981)

*Bank of Waukegan v. Village of Vernon Hills*, 254 Ill. App. 3d 24, 626 N.E.2d 245 (1993)

*Batch v. Town of Chapel Hill*, 326 N.C. 1, 387 S.E.2d 655 (1990)

*Beach v. Planning Zoning Comm'n*, 141 Conn. 79, 103 A.2d 814 (1954)

*Beasley v. Potter*, 493 F. Supp. 1059 (W.D. Mich. 1980)

*Beaver Meadows v. Board of County Comm'rs*, 709 P.2d 928 (Colo. 1985)

*Benchmark Land Co. v. City of Battle Ground*, 94 Wash. App. 537, 972 P.2d 944 (1999)

*Benchmark Land Co. v. City of Battle Ground*, 103 Wash. App. 721, 14 P.3d 172 (2000)

*Bercielli v. Zoning Bd. of Appeals*, 608 N.Y.S.2d 570 (App. Div. 1994)

*Beshore v. Town of Bel Air*, 237 Md. 398, 206 A.2d 678 (1965)

*Bethlehem Evangelical Lutheran Church v. City of Lakewood*, 626 P.2d 668 (Colo. 1981)

*Bexar County v. City of San Antonio*, 352 S.W.2d 905 (Tex. 1962)

*Bickerstaff Clay Prods. Co. v. Harris County*, 10 Fla. L. Weekly 172, 89 F.3d 1481 (11th Cir. 1996)

*Bill Stroop Roofing, Inc. v. Metropolitan Dade County*, 788 So. 2d 365 (Fla. Dist. Ct. App. 2001)

*Billings Properties, Inc. v. Yellowstone County*, 144 Mont. 25, 394 P.2d 182 (1964)

*Bixel Assocs. v. City of Los Angeles*, 216 Cal. App. 3d 1208, 265 Cal. Rptr. 347 (1989)

*Black v. City of Killeen*, 78 S.W.3d 686 (Tex. Crim. App. 2002)

*Black v. City of Waukesha*, 125 Wis. 2d 254, 371 N.W.2d 389 (Wis. Ct. App. 1985)

*Bleznak v. Township of Evesham*, 170 N.J. Super. 216, 406 A.2d 201 (1979)

*Bloom v. City of Fort Collins*, 13 Brief Times Rptr. 1548, 784 P.2d 304 (Colo. 1989)

*Blue Jeans Equities W. v. City & County of San Francisco*, 4 Cal. Rptr. 2d 114, 3 Cal. App. 4th 164 (1992)

*Board of Comm'rs of S. Whitehall Township, Lehigh County v. Toll Brothers*, 147 Pa. Commw. 298, 607 A.2d 824 (1992)

*Board of County Comm'rs v. Bainbridge, Inc.*, 929 P.2d 691 (Colo. 1996)

*Board of County Comm'rs of Metro. Dade County v. Lutz*, 314 So. 2d 815 (Fla. Dist. Ct. App. 1975)

*Board of Supervisors of Chesterfield County v. Trollingwood Partnership*, 248 Va. 112, 445 S.E.2d 151 (1994)

*Board of Supervisors of Fairfax County v. Cities Serv. Oil Co.*, 193 S.E.2d 1 (Va. 1972)

*Board of Supervisors of Fairfax County v. Medical Structures*, 213 Va. 355, 192 S.E.2d 799 (1972)

*Boron Oil Co. v. L.C. Kimple*, 445 Pa. 327, 284 A.2d 744 (1971)

*Brazos Land, Inc. v. Board of County Comm'rs of Rio Arriba County*, 115 N.M. 168, 848 P.2d 1095 (1993)

*Bregar v. Britton*, 75 So. 2d 753 (Fla. 1954)

*Breneric Assocs. v. City of Del Mar*, 81 Cal. Rptr. 2d 324, 69 Cal. App. 4th 166 (1998)

*Bright Dev. v. City of Tracy*, 24 Cal. Rptr. 2d 618, 20 Cal. App. 4th 783 (1993)

*Browning-Ferris Indus. v. Wake County*, 905 F. Supp. 312 (E.D.N.C. 1995)

*Buck Lake Alliance v. Board of County Comm'rs*, 25 Fla. L. Weekly 1493, 765 So. 2d 124 (Fla. 2000)

*Builder Indus. Ass'n v. City of Oceanside*, 33 Cal. Rptr. 2d 137, 27 Cal. App. 4th 744 (1994)

*Building Indus. Ass'n of Cleveland & Suburban Counties v. City of Westlake*, 103 Ohio App. 3d 546, 660 N.E.2d 501 (1995)

*Burchett v. City of Newport Beach*, 40 Cal. Rptr. 2d 1, 33 Cal. App. 4th 1472 (1995)

*Burke v. Town of Schererville*, 739 N.E.2d 1086 (Ind. Ct. App. 2000)

*Burton v. Clark County*, 91 Wash. App. 505, 958 P.2d 343 (1998)

## C

*C-470 Joint Venture v. Trizec Colo., Inc.*, 176 F.3d 1289 (10th Cir. 1999)

*Candid Enters., Inc. v. Grossmont Union High Sch. Dist.*, 39 Cal. 3d 878, 705 P.2d 876 (1985)

*Capistrano Beach Water Dist. v. Taj. Dev. Corp.*, 72 Cal. App. 4th 524, 85 Cal. Rptr. 2d 382 (1999)

*Cardillo v. Florida Keys Aqueduct Authority*, 20 Fla. L. Weekly 1258, 654 So. 2d 1062 (Fla. Dist. Ct. App. 1995)

*Cardwell v. Smith*, 106 N.C. App. 187, 415 S.E.2d 770 (1992)

*Carlino v. Whitpain Investors*, 499 Pa. 498, 453 A.2d 1385 (1982)

*Carruth v. City of Madera*, 43 Cal. Rptr. 855, 233 Cal. App. 2d 688 (1965)

*Carty v. City of Ojai*, 143 Cal. Rptr. 506, 77 Cal. App. 3d 329 (1978)

*Castle Homes & Dev., Inc. v. City of Brier*, 76 Wash. App. 95, 882 P.2d 1172 (1994)

*Cederberg v. City of Rockford*, 8 Ill. App. 3d 984, 291 N.E.2d 249 (1972)

*Cherokee County v. Greater Atlanta Homebuilders Ass'n*, 255 Ga. App. 764, 566 S.E.2d 470 (2002)

*Cherry Hills Farms, Inc. v. City of Cherry Hills*, 670 P.2d 779 (Colo. 1983)

*Chicago Title Ins. Co. v. Village of Bollingbrook*, No. 97 C 7055, 1999 WL 65054 (N.D. Ill. Feb. 5, 1999)

*Chicago Title Ins. Co. v. Village of Bollingbrook*, No. 97 C 7055, 1999 WL 259952 (N.D. Ill. Apr. 6, 1999)

*Christopher Lake Dev. Co. v. St. Louis County*, 35 F.3d 1269 (8th Cir. 1994)

*Cimarron Corp. v. Board of County Comm'rs*, 193 Colo. 164, 563 P.2d 946 (1977)

*Citizens for Responsible Gov't v. City of Albany*, 66 Cal. Rptr. 2d 102, 56 Cal. App. 4th 199 (1997)

*City & County of San Francisco v. Golden Gate Heights Invs.*, 18 Cal. Rptr. 2d 467, 14 Cal. App. 4th 1203 (1993)

*City of Arvada v. City & County of Denver*, 663 P.2d 611 (Colo. 1983)

*City of Annapolis v. Waterman*, 357 Md. 484, 745 A.2d 1000 (Md. 2000)

*City of Berea v. Wren*, 818 S.W.2d 274 (Ky. 1991)

*City of Chicago Heights v. Living Word Outreach Full Gospel Church & Ministries, Inc.*, 196 Ill. 2d 1, 749 N.E.2d 916 (2001)

*City of College Station v. Turtle Rock Corp.*, 680 S.W.2d 802 (Tex. 1984)

*City of Colorado Springs v. Kitty Hawk*, 154 Colo. 535, 392 P.2d 467 (1964)

*City of Coral Gables v. Puiggros*, 376 So. 2d 281 (Fla. 1979)

*City of Crowley v. Prejean*, 173 So. 2d 832 (La. Ct. App. 1965)

*City of DeSoto v. Centurion Homes, Inc.*, 1 Kan. App. 2d 634, 573 P.2d 1081 (1977)

*City of Fayetteville v. IBI*, 659 S.W. 505 (Ark. 1983)

*City of Gainesville v. Cone*, 365 So. 2d 737 (Fla. 1979)

*City of Irvine v. Irvine Citizens Against Overdevelopment*, 30 Cal. Rptr. 2d 797, 25 Cal. App. 4th 868 (1994)

*City of Miami v. 20th Century Club, Inc.*, 313 So. 2d 448 (Fla. 1975)

*City of Monterey v. Del Monte Dunes at Monterey, Ltd.*, 526 U.S. 687, 119 S. Ct. 1624, 143 L. Ed. 2d 882 (1999)

*City of N. Las Vegas v. Pardee Constr. Co.*, 21 P.3d 8 (Nev. 2001)

*City of N. Miami v. Margulies*, 289 So. 2d 424 (Fla. 1974)

*City of Peru v. Querciagrossa*, 73 Ill. App. 3d 1040, 392 N.E.2d 778 (1979)

*City of Portsmouth v. Schlesinger*, 57 F.3d 12 (1st Cir. 1995)

*City of San Diego v. Holodnak*, 203 Cal. Rptr. 797 (Cal. 1984)

*City of Springfield v. Judith Jones Dietsch Trust*, 746 N.E.2d 1272 (Ill. App. Ct. 2001)

# CASE LIST

*City of Univ. Park v. Benner*, 485 S.W.2d 773 (Tex. 1972)

*City of W. Hollywood v. Beverly Towers*, 52 Cal. 3d 1184, 805 P.2d 329 (1991)

*City of Zephyrhills v. Wood*, 831 So. 2d 223 (Fla. Dist. Ct. App. 2002)

*Clackamas County v. Holmes*, 265 Or. 193, 508 P.2d 190 (1973)

*Clark v. City of Albany*, 137 Or. App. 293, 904 P.2d 185 (1995)

*Cobb v. Snohomish County*, 64 Wash. App. 451, 829 P.2d 169 (1991)

*Collier County v. State*, 733 So. 2d 1012 (Fla. 1999)

*Collis v. City of Bloomington*, 310 Minn. 5, 246 N.W.2d 19 (1976)

*Commercial Builders of N. Cal. v. City of Sacramento*, 941 F.2d 872 (9th Cir. 1991)

*Concerned Citizens for Buckley Planning v. City of Buckley*, No. 25587-1-II, 2001 WL 112322 (Wash. Ct. App. Feb. 9, 2001)

*Continental Dev. Corp. v. Hart, Superior Court/California for County of Los Angeles*, No. C617808 (Cal. Oct. 21, 1986)

*Contractors & Builders Ass'n v. City of Dunedin*, 329 So. 2d 314 (Fla. 1976)

*Contractors & Builders Ass'n of Pinellas County v. City of Dunedin*, 444 U.S. 867, 100 S. Ct. 140, 62 L. Ed. 2d 91 (1979)

*Contracts Funding v. Maynes*, 527 P.2d 1073 (Utah 1974)

*Cook v. Clackamas County*, 50 Or. App. 75, 622 P.2d 1107, *review denied*, 290 Or. 853 (1981)

*Corcoran v. Village of Bennington*, 128 Vt. 482, 266 A.2d 457 (1970)

*Corporation of the Brick Presbyterian Church v. Mayor, Alderman & Commonalty of the City of N.Y.*, 5 Cowens (N.Y.) 538 (1826)

*Cos Corp. v. City of Evanston*, 27 Ill. 2d 570, 190 N.E.2d 364 (1963)

*Coulter v. City of Rawlins*, 662 P.2d 888 (Wyo. 1983)

*Country Joe, Inc. v. City of Eagan*, 560 N.W.2d 681 (Minn. 1997)

*Country Meadows W. Partnership v. Village of Germantown*, 237 Wis. 2d 290, 614 N.W.2d 498 (2000)

*County of Kauai v. Pacific Standard Life Ins. Co. (Nukolii)*, 65 Haw. 318, 653 P.2d 766 (1982)

*Culbro Corp. v. Town of Simsbury*, No. CV 960559508, 1999 WL 162761 (Conn. Super. Ct. 1999)

*Cummings v. City of Waterloo*, 683 N.E.2d 1222 (Ill. App. Ct. 1997)

*Curtis v. Town of S. Thomaston*, 1998 Me. 63, 708 A.2d 657 (1998)

## D

*David A. Ulrich, Inc., v. Town of Saukville*, 7 Wis. 2d 173, 96 N.W.2d 612 (Wis. 1959)

*Davidson v. County of San Diego*, 56 Cal. Rptr. 2d 617, 49 Cal. App. 4th 639 (1996)

*DeBottari v. City Council*, 217 Cal. Rptr. 790, 171 Cal. App. 3d 1024 (1985)

*Dellinger v. City of Charlotte*, 114 N.C. App. 146, 441 S.E.2d 626 (1994)

*Denio v. City of Huntington Beach*, 22 Cal. 2d 580, 140 P.2d 392 (1943)

*Denning v. Maui*, 52 Haw. 653, 485 P.2d 1048 (1971)

*Dolan v. City of Tigard*, 512 U.S. 374, 114 S. Ct. 2309, 129 L. Ed. 2d 304, 24 ELR 21083 (1994)

*Donwood, Inc. v. Spokane County*, 90 Wash. App. 389, 957 P.2d 775 (1998)

*Dowerk v. Charter Township of Oxford*, No. 204032, 1998 WL 842266 (Mich. App. Dec. 4, 1998)

**E**

*Eastern Enters. v. Apfel*, 524 U.S. 498, 118 S. Ct. 2131, 141 L. Ed. 2d 451 (1998)

*Edelbeck v. Town of Theresa*, 57 Wis. 2d 172, 203 N.W.2d 694 (1973)

*Ehrlich v. City of Culver*, 19 Cal. Rptr. 2d 468, 15 Cal. App. 4th 1737 (1993)

*Ehrlich v. City of Culver*, 12 Cal. 4th 854, 911 P.2d 429 (1996)

*Elam v. Albers*, 44 Colo. App. 281, 616 P.2d 168 (1980)

*Englewood Hills, Inc., v. Village of Englewood*, 14 Ohio App. 2d 195, 237 N.E.2d 621 (1967)

*Englewood Water Dist. v. Halstead*, 432 So. 2d 172 (Fla. Dist. Ct. App. 1983)

*Erickson & Assocs., Inc. v. McLerrran*, 123 Wash. 2d 864, 872 P.2d 1090 (1994)

*Estate of Crain v. City of Williams*, 192 Ariz. 342, 965 P.2d 76 (1998)

*Euclid v. Ambler Realty Co.*, 272 U.S. 365, 100 S. Ct. 2138, 65 L. Ed. 2d 106 (1926)

*Even v. City of Parker*, 1999 S.D. 72, 597 N.W.2d 670 (1999)

*Everett Sch. Dist. No. 2 v. Mastro*, 97 Wash. App. 1013 (1999)

*Ex rel. Waterbury Dev. Co. v. Witten*, 54 Ohio St. 2d 412, 377 N.E.2d 505 (1978)

**F**

*F&W Assocs. v. County of Somerset*, 276 N.J. Super. 519, 648 A.2d 482 (1994)

*Fairview Enters., Inc. v. City of Kansas City*, No. WD 58947, 2001 WL 967787 (Mo. Ct. App. Aug. 28, 2001)

*Fasano v. Board of Co. Comm'rs*, 264 Or. 574, 507 P.2d 23 (1973)

*Ford v. Georgetown County Water & Sewer Dist.*, 341 S.C. 10, 532 S.E.2d 873 (2000)

*Forseth v. Village of Sussex*, 20 F. Supp. 2d 1267 (E.D. Wis. 1998)

*Forseth v. Village of Sussex*, 199 F.3d 363 (7th Cir. 2000)

*Fracasse v. Brent*, 6 Cal. 3d 784, 494 P.2d 9 (1972)

*French v. Lincolnshire*, 31 Ill. App. 3d 537, 335 N.E.2d 29 (1975)

*Friends of the Law v. King County*, 123 Wash. 2d 518, 869 P.2d 1056 (1994)

*Frisella v. Town of Farmington*, 131 N.H. 78, 550 A.2d 102 (N.H. 1988)

# CASE LIST

## G

*GST Tucson Lightwave, Inc. v. City of Tucson*, 190 Ariz. 478, 949 P.2d 971 (Ariz. Ct. App. 1997)

*Gackler Land Co. v. Yankee Springs, Township*, 427 Mich. 562, 398 N.W.2d 393 (1986)

*Garneau v. City of Seattle*, 147 F.3d 802 (9th Cir. 1998)

*Garnick v. Zoning Hearing Bd. of Bridgeton Township*, 427 A.2d 310 (Pa. Commw. Ct. 1981)

*Gates v. Jarvis, Cornette & Payton*, 465 S.W.2d 278 (Ky. 1971)

*Geralnes B.V. v. City of Greenwood Village, Colo.*, 583 F. Supp. 830 (D. Colo. 1984)

*Giger v. City of Omaha*, 232 Neb. 676, 442 N.W. 2d 182 (1989)

*Gilliland v. County of Los Angeles*, 179 Cal. Rptr. 73, 126 Cal. App. 3d 610 (1981)

*Glencrest Realty Co. v. Zoning Hearing Bd. of Wash. Township*, 46 Pa. Commw. 177, 406 A.2d 836 (1979)

*Goldblatt v. Town of Hempstead*, 369 U.S. 590, 82 S. Ct. 987, 8 L. Ed. 2d 130 (1962)

*Golden Gate Corp. v. Town of Narragansett*, 116 R.I. 552, 359 A.2d 321 (1976)

*Graham v. Township of Kochville*, 236 Mich. App. 141, 599 N.W.2d 793 (1999)

*Graham Beach Partnership v. County of Kauai*, 653 P.2d 766 (Haw. 1982)

*Greater Franklin Developers Ass'n v. Town of Franklin*, 49 Mass. App. Ct. 500, 730 N.E.2d 900 (2000)

*Greater Yellowstone Coalition, Inc. v. Board of County Comm'rs of Gallatin County*, 305 Mont. 232, 25 P.3d 168 (2001)

*Gregory v. Board of Supervisors*, 257 Va. 530, 514 S.E.2d 356 (1999)

## H

*Hale v. Osborn Coal Enters.*, 729 So. 2d 853 (Ala. Civ. App. 1997)

*Halle Dev., Inc. v. Anne Arundel County*, 141 Md. App. 542, 786 A.2d 48 (2001)

*Halle Dev., Inc. v. Anne Arundel County*, 2002 Md. LEXIS 785 (2002)

*Harbour Village Apts. v. City of Mukilteo*, 139 Wash. 2d 604, 989 P.2d 542 (1999)

*Harbours Pointe of Nashotah, Ltd. Liab. Corp. v. Village of Nashotah*, 278 F.3d 701, 32 ELR 20421 (7th Cir. 2002)

*Hardy Farm Ltd. v. Southbury Planning Comm'n*, 2001 Conn. Super. LEXIS 1221 (Conn. Super. Ct. 2001)

*Harnett v. Austin*, 93 So. 2d 86 (Tex. 1956)

*Harris v. City of Wichita*, 862 F. Supp. 287, 294 (D. Kan. 1994)

# CASE LIST

*Home Builders Ass'n of Cent. Ariz. v. Riddel*, 109 Ariz. 404, 510 P.2d 376 (Ariz. 1973)

*Home Builders Ass'n of Dayton & the Miami Valley v. City of Beavercreek*, 89 Ohio St. 3d 121, 729 N.E.2d 349 (2000)

*Home Builders Ass'n of Greater Des Moines v. City of W. Des Moines*, 644 N.W.2d 339 (Iowa 2002)

*Home Builders Ass'n of Greater Salt Lake v. Provo City*, 28 Utah 2d 402, 503 P.2d 451 (1972)

*Home Builders Ass'n of Utah v. City of Am. Fork*, 361 Utah Adv. Rep. 46, 973 P.2d 425 (1999)

*Homebuilders Ass'n of Dayton v. City of Beavercreek*, Nos. 97-CA-113, 97-CA-115, 1998 WL 735931 (Ohio App. 2d 1998)

*Home Bldg. & Loan Ass'n v. Blaisdell*, 290 U.S. 398, 54 S. Ct. 231, 78 L. Ed. 413 (1934)

*Horsemen's Benevolent & Protective Ass'n v. Valley Racing Ass'n*, 6 Cal. Rptr. 2d 698, 4 Cal. App. 4th 1538 (1992)

*Hough v. Amato*, 212 So. 2d 662 (Fla. 1968)

*Housing Auth. v. City of Los Angeles*, 38 Cal. 2d 853, 243 P.2d 515 (1952)

*Housing Redevelopment Auth. v. Jorgensen*, 328 N.W.2d 740 (Minn. 1983)

*Houston Petroleum Co. v. Automotive Prods. Credit Ass'n*, 9 N.J. 122, 87 A.2d 319 (1952)

*Hunt v. Caldwell*, 222 Va. 91, 279 S.E.2d 138 (1981)

## I

*Illinois ex rel. Van Cleave v. Village of Seneca*, 519 N.E.2d 63 (Ill. 1988)

*In re Appeal of Taft Corners Assocs., Inc.*, 171 Vt. 135, 758 A.2d 804 (2000)

*In re Egg Harbor Assocs.*, 94 N.J. 358, 464 A.2d 1115 (1983)

*In the Matter of the Water Use Permit Applications (Waihole)*, 94 Haw. 97, 9 P.3d 409 (2000)

*Isla Verde Int'l Holdings, Inc. v. City of Camas*, 99 Wash. App. 127, 990 P.2d 429 (1999)

*Isla Verde Int'l Holdings v. City of Camas*, 49 P.3d 867 (Wash. 2002)

## J

*J.C. Reeves Corp. v. Clackamas County*, 131 Or. App. 615, 887 P.2d 360 (1994)

*J.K. Constr., Inc. v. Western Carolina Reg'l Sewer Auth.*, 336 S.C. 162, 519 S.E.2d 561 (1999)

*J.W. Jones Cos. v. City of San Diego*, 157 Cal. App. 3d 745, 203 Cal. Rptr. 580 (1984)

*Jackson County Citizen's League v. Jackson County*, 171 Or. App. 149, 15 P.3d 42 (2001)

*Jamail v. City of Cedar Park*, No. 03-00-00795-CV, 2001 Tex. App. LEXIS 4398 (2001)

*Juanita Bay Valley Community Ass'n v. City of Kirkland*, 9 Wash. App. 59, 510 P.2d 1140 (1973)

*Jenad, Inc. v. Village of Scarsdale*, 18 N.Y.2d 78, 218 N.E.2d 673 (1966)

*Johnson v. Metropolitan Gov't of Nashville & Davidson County*, 2002 Tenn. App. LEXIS 568 (2002)

*Jones v. U.S. Steel Credit Corp.*, 382 So. 2d 48 (Fla. 1980)

*Jordan v. Village of Menomonee Falls*, 28 Wis. 2d 608, 137 N.W.2d 442 (1965)

*Juanita Bay Valley Community Ass'n v. City of Kirkland*, 510 P.2d 1140 (Wash. 1973)

## K

*Kaiser Aetna v. United States*, 444 U.S. 164, 100 S. Ct. 383, 62 L. Ed. 2d 332 (1979)

*Kasparek v. Johnson County Bd. of Health*, 288 N.W.2d 511 (Iowa 1980)

*Kavanau v. Santa Monica Rent Control Bd.*, 16 Cal. 4th 761, 941 P.2d 851 (1997)

*Keystone Bituminous Coal Ass'n v. DeBenedictis*, 480 U.S. 470, 107 S. Ct. 1232, 94 L. Ed. 2d 472, 17 ELR 20440 (1987)

*Kiewit Constr. Group, Inc. v. Clark County*, 83 Wash. App. 133, 920 P.2d 1207 (1996)

*Krughoff v. City of Naperville*, 68 Ill. 2d 352, 369 N.E.2d 892 (1977)

*Krupp v. Breckenridge Sanitation Dist.*, 19 P.3d 687 (Colo. 2001)

*Kyrene Sch. Dist. v. Chandler*, 150 Ariz. 240, 722 P.2d 967 (Ariz. Ct. App. 1986)

## L

*L.M. Everhart Constr. Inc. v. Jefferson County Planning Comm'n*, 2 F.3d 48 (4th Cir. 1993)

*Lafferty v. Payson City*, 642 P.2d 376 (Utah 1982)

*Lake Bluff Hous. Partners v. City of S. Milwaukee*, 197 Wis. 2d 157, 540 N.W.2d 189 (1995), *rev'g* 188 Wis. 2d 230, 525 N.W.2d 59 (1994)

*Lake City Corp. v. City of Mequon*, 199 Wis. 2d 353, 544 N.W.2d 600 (1996)

*Lakeview Dev. Corp. v. South Lake Tahoe*, 915 F.2d 1290 (9th Cir. 1990)

*Lampton v. Pinaire*, 610 S.W.2d 915 (Ky. Ct. App. 1981)

*Lancaster Redevelopment Agency v. Dibley*, 25 Cal. Rptr. 2d 593 (1993)

*Landgate, Inc. v. California Coastal Comm'n*, 17 Cal. 4th 1006, 953 P.2d 1188 (1998)

*Land/Vest Properties v. Town of Plainfield*, 117 N.H. 817, 379 A.2d 200 (1977)

*Leroy Land Dev. Corp. v. Tahoe Reg'l Planning Agency,* 939 F.2d 696 (9th Cir. 1991)

*Lesher Communications, Inc. v. City of Walnut Creek,* 52 Cal. 3d 531, 802 P.2d 317 (1990)

*Lexington-Fayette Urban County Gov't v. Schneider & Hi Acres Dev. Co.,* 849 S.W.2d 557 (Ky. App. 1992)

*Life of the Land v. Honolulu,* 60 Haw. 446, 592 P.2d 26 (1979)

*Lincoln Property Co. v. City of Torrance, Superior Court/Cal. for County of Los Angeles,* No. C607339 (Cal. Nov. 4, 1986)

*Lincoln Shiloh Assocs. v. Mukilteo Water Dist.,* 45 Wash. App. 123, 724 P.2d 1083, *review denied,* 107 Wash. 2d 1014 (1986)

*Long Beach Equities, Inc. v. County of Ventura,* 231 Cal. App. 3d 1016 (1991)

*Loup-Miller Constr. Co. v. City & County of Denver,* 676 P.2d 1170 (Colo. 1984)

*Loyola Marymount Univ. v. Los Angeles Unified Sch. Dist.,* 53 Cal. Rptr. 2d 424, 45 Cal. App. 4th 1256 (1996)

*Lucas v. South Carolina Coastal Council,* 505 U.S. 1003, 112 S. Ct. 2886, 120 L. Ed. 2d 798 (1992)

*The Luxembourg Group, Inc. v. Snohomish County,* 887 P.2d 446 (Wash. 1995)

# M

*MBL Assocs. v. City of S. Burlington,* 172 Vt. 297, 776 A.2d 432 (2001)

*Magness v. Caddo Parish Police Jury,* 318 So. 2d 1172 (La. Ct. App. 1975)

*Manocherian v. Lenox Hill Hosp.,* 84 N.Y.2d 385, 643 N.E.2d 479 (1994)

*Marblehead v. City of San Clemente,* 277 Cal. Rptr. 550 (1991)

*Marco Dev. Corp. v. City of Cedar Falls,* 473 N.W.2d 41 (Iowa 1991)

*Marine Open, Inc. v. Manatee County,* 877 F.2d 892 (11th Cir. 1989)

*Marshall v. Board of County Comm'rs,* 912 F. Supp. 1456 (D. Wyo. 1996)

*Massachusetts Broken Stone Co. v. Planning Board of Weston,* 45 Mass. App. Ct. 738, 701 N.E.2d 664 (1998)

*Matheson v. De Kalb County,* 354 S.E.2d 121 (Ga. 1987)

*Matter of Ellington Constr. Corp. v. Zoning Bd. of Appeals,* 152 A.D.2d 365, 549 N.Y.S.2d 405 (1989)

*Matter of Jaffee v. RCI Corp.,* 119 A.D.2d 854, 500 N.Y.S.2d 427 (1986)

*Matthews v. Bay Head Improvement Ass'n,* 95 N.J. 306, 471 A.2d 355 (1984), *cert. denied,* 469 U.S. 821, 105 S. Ct. 93, 83 L. Ed. 2d 39 (1984)

*Mattson v. City of Chicago,* 89 Ill. App. 3d 378, 411 N.E.2d 1002 (1980)

*Mayor & the City Council of Baltimore v. Crane,* 277 Md. 198, 352 A.2d 786 (1976)

*McCarthy v. City of Leawood,* 257 Kan. 566, 894 P.2d 836 (1995)

*McClure v. City of Springfield,* 175 Or. App. 425, 28 P.3d 1222 (2001)

*McKenzie v. City of White Hall*, 112 F.3d 313 (8th Cir. 1997)

*McLain Western #1 v. San Diego County*, 146 Cal. App. 3d 772, 194 Cal. Rptr. 594 (1983)

*McNair v. City of Cedar Park*, 993 F.2d 1217 (5th Cir. 1993)

*Medical Ctr. at Princeton v. Township of Princeton Bd. of Adjustment*, 343 N.J. Super. 177, 778 A.2d 482 (2001)

*Meegan v. Village of Tinley Park*, 52 Ill. 2d 354, 288 N.E.2d 423 (1972)

*Mercer Enterprises, Inc. v. City of Bremerton*, 93 Wash. 2d 624, 611 P.2d 1237 (1980)

*Merrelli v. City of St. Clair Shores*, 96 N.W.2d 144 (Mich. 1959)

*Messer v. Town of Chapel Hill*, 59 N.C. App. 692, 297 S.E.2d 632 (1982)

*Midtown Properties, Inc. v. Township of Madison*, 172 A.2d 40 (N.J. 1961)

*Midway Orchards v. County of Butte*, 269 Cal. Rptr. 796, 220 Cal. App. 3d 765 (1990)

*Miller v. Board of Adjustment*, 521 A.2d 642 (Del. 1986)

*Miller v. City of Port Angeles*, 38 Wash. App. 904, 691 P.2d 229 (1984)

*Mission Springs, Inc. v. City of Spokane*, 134 Wash. 2d 947, 954 P.2d 250 (1998)

*Molgard v. Town of Caledonia*, 527 F. Supp. 1073 (E.D. Wis. 1981), *aff'd*, 696 F.2d 59 (7th Cir. 1982)

*Morris v. Postma*, 41 N.J. 354, 196 A.2d 792 (1964)

*Morrison Homes Corp. v. City of Pleasanton*, 130 Cal. Rptr. 196, 58 Cal. App. 3d 724 (1976)

# N

*N.E. Brickmaster v. Town of Salem*, 133 N.H. 655, 582 A.2d 601 (1990)

*National Ass'n of Homebuilders v. New Jersey Dep't of Envtl. Protection*, 64 F. Supp. 2d 354 (D.N.J. 1999)

*Native Sun/Lyon Communities v. City of Escondido*, 19 Cal. Rptr. 2d 344, 15 Cal. App. 4th 892 (1993)

*Nello L. Teer Co. v. Orange County*, 1993 U.S. App. LEXIS 12525 (4th Cir. 1993)

*New Castle Invs. v. City of Lacenter*, 98 Wash. App. 224, 989 P.2d 569 (1999)

*Nielson v. Merriam*, 91 Wash. App. 1049 (1998)

*Noble Manor Co. v. Pierce County*, 81 Wash. App. 141, 913 P.2d 417 (1996)

*Noble Manor v. Pierce County*, 133 Wash. 2d 269, 943 P.2d 1378 (1997)

*Nollan v. California Coastal Comm'n*, 483 U.S. 825, 107 S. Ct. 3141, 97 L. Ed. 2d 677 (1987)

*Nolte v. City of Olympia*, 96 Wash. App. 944, 982 P.2d 659 (1999)

*North Kitsap Coordinating Council v. Kitsap County*, 2001 Wash. App. LEXIS 2232 (Wash. Ct. App. 2001)

# CASE LIST

*Northern Ill. Home Builders Ass'n v. County of DuPage*, 251 Ill. App. 3d 494, 621 N.E.2d 1012 (1993), *aff'd in part, rev'd in part*, No. 76503, 1995 WL 123705 (Ill. Mar. 23, 1995)

*Northern Ill. Home Builders Ass'n v. County of DuPage*, 165 Ill. 2d 25, 649 N.E.2d 384 (1995)

*Northwestern Fin. Group, Inc. v. County of Gaston*, 329 N.C. 180, 405 S.E.2d 138 (N.C. 1991)

*Norwick v. Village of Winfield*, 225 N.E.2d 30 (Ill. 1967)

*Notestein v. Board of Supervisors of Appomattox County*, 240 Va. 146, 393 S.E.2d 205 (1990)

## O

*OMYA, Inc. v. Federal Energy Regulatory Comm'n*, 111 F.3d 179 (D.C. Cir. 1997)

*Oceanic Cal., Inc. v. North Cent. Coast Reg'l Comm'n*, 133 Cal. Rptr. 664, 63 Cal. App. 3d 57 (1976)

*O'Malley v. Village of Ford Heights*, 633 N.E.2d 848 (Ill. App. Ct. 1994)

*Operating Engineers Funds, Inc. v. City of Thousand Oaks*, 2002 WL 44253 (Cal. Ct. App. 2002)

*Overstreet v. Zoning Hearing Bd. of Schuykill Township*, 49 Pa. Commw. 397, 412 A.2d 169 (1980)

## P

*P.W. Invs., Inc. v. City of Westminister*, 655 P.2d 1365 (Colo. 1982)

*Palatine I v. Planning Bd. of the Township of Montville*, 133 N.J. 546, 628 A.2d 321 (1993)

*Palazzolo v. Rhode Island*, 533 U.S. 606, 121 S. Ct. 2448, 150 L. Ed. 2d 592 (2001)

*Pardee Constr. Co. v. City of Camarillo*, 37 Cal. 3d 465, 690 P.2d 701 (1984)

*Parking Ass'n of Georgia v. City of Atlanta*, 515 U.S. 1116, 115 S. Ct. 2268, 132 L. Ed. 2d 273 (1995)

*Pasco County v. Tampa Dev. Corp.*, 364 So. 2d 850 (Fla. 1978)

*Paul v. City of Woonsocket*, 745 A.2d 169 (R.I. 2000)

*Penn Cent. Transp. Co. v. City of N.Y.*, 438 U.S. 104, 98 S. Ct. 2646, 57 L. Ed. 2d 631, 8 ELR 20528 (1978)

*Pennsylvania Coal Co. v. Mahon*, 260 U.S. 393, 43 S. Ct. 158, 67 L. Ed. 322 (1922)

*People v. County of Kern*, 115 Cal. Rptr. 67, 39 Cal. App. 3d 830 (1974)

*People v. Van Cleave*, 519 N.E.2d 63 (Ill. 1988)

*Pete Drown Inc. v. Town of Ellenburg*, 229 A.D.2d 877, 646 N.Y.S.2d 205 (1996)

# CASE LIST

*Rivera v. City of Phoenix*, 186 Ariz. 600, 925 P.2d 741 (1996)

*Rockville v. Brookville Turnpike Constr. Co.*, 246 Md. 117, 228 A.2d 263 (1967)

*Rogers Mach. Inc. v. Washington County*, 181 Or. App. 369, 45 P.3d 966 (2002)

*Rohn v. City of Visalia*, 263 Cal. Rptr. 319, 214 Cal. App. 3d 1463 (1989)

*Rolling Pines Ltd. Partnership v. City of Little Rock*, 73 Ark. App. 97, 40 S.W.3d 828 (2001)

*Rue Lafayette Mortgage Corp. v. Wenger*, 366 So. 2d 1059 (La. 1979)

*Russell v. Palos Verdes Properties*, 32 Cal. Rptr. 488, 218 Cal. App. 2d 754 (1963)

## S

*SLS Partnership, Apple Valley v. City of Apple Valley*, 511 N.W.2d 738 (Minn. 1994)

*Saad v. City of Berkeley*, 30 Cal. Rptr. 2d 95, 24 Cal. App. 4th 1206 (1994)

*Saah v. District of Columbia Bd. of Zoning Adjustment*, 433 A.2d 1114 (D.C. Cir. 1981)

*Sakolsky v. City of Coral Gables*, 151 So. 2d 433 (Fla. 1963)

*Salt Lake County v. Board of Educ. of Granite Sch. Dist.*, 808 P.2d 1056 (Utah 1991)

*San Remo Hotel Ltd. Partnership v. City & County of San Francisco*, 27 Cal. 4th 643, 41 P.3d 87, 32 ELR 20533 (2002)

*Santa Margarita Area Residents Together (SMART) v. San Luis Obispo County*, 84 Cal. App. 4th 221, 100 Cal. Rptr. 2d 740 (2000)

*Santa Monica Beach, Ltd. v. Superior Court of Los Angeles County*, 19 Cal. 4th 952, 968 P.2d 993 (1999)

*Sarasota County v. Taylor Woodrow Homes*, 652 So. 2d 1247 (Fla. 1995)

*School Dist. of Scranton v. Dale & Dale Design & Dev.*, 559 Pa. 398, 741 A.2d 186 (1999)

*Schultz v. City of Grants Pass*, 131 Or. App. 220, 884 P.2d 569 (1994)

*2nd Roc-Jersey Assocs. v. Town of Morristown*, 158 N.J. 581, 731 A.2d 1 (1999)

*Seiler v. Charter Township of Northville*, 53 F. Supp. 2d 957 (E.D. Mich. 1999)

*Shapell Indus., Inc. v. Milipitas Unified Sch. Dist.*, 1 Cal. App. 4th 218, 1 Cal. Rptr. 2d 818 (1991)

*Simonsen v. Town of Derry*, 145 N.H. 382, 765 A.2d 1033 (2000)

*Smith v. City of Clearwater*, 383 So. 2d 681 (Fla. 1980)

*Smith v. Winhall Planning Comm'n*, 140 Vt. 178, 436 A.2d 760 (1981)

*Smith Chapel Baptist Church v. City of Durham*, 350 N.C. 805, 517 S.E.2d 874 (1999)

*Snider v. Board of County Comm'rs of Walla Walla County*, 85 Wash. App. 371, 932 P.2d 704 (1997)

*Snow v. Amherst County Bd. of Zoning Appeals*, 248 Va. 404, 448 S.E.2d 606 (1994)

*Soliday v. Haycock Township*, 785 A.2d 139 (Pa. Commw. Ct. 2001)

*Southern Burlington County National Association for the Advancement of Colored People v. Mount Laurel*, 92 N.J. 158, 456 A.2d 390 (1983)

*Sparks v. Douglas County*, 127 Wash. 2d 901, 904 P.2d 738 (Wash. 1994)

*Sprenger, Grabb & Assocs. v. City of Hailey*, 127 Idaho 576, 903 P.2d 741 (1995)

*St. Johns County v. Northeast Fla. Builders Ass'n*, 16 Fla. L. Weekly 264, 583 So. 2d 635 (Fla. 1991)

*State ex rel. Corning v. District Court*, 156 Mont. 81, 474 P.2d 701 (1970)

*State ex rel. Zupancic v. Schimenz*, 174 N.W.2d 533 (Wis. 1970)

*State v. Altimas*, 137 Or. App. 606, 905 P.2d 258 (1995)

*State v. Missoula*, 166 Mont. 385, 533 P.2d 1087 (1975)

*Steel v. Cape Corp.*, 111 Md. App. 1, 677 A.2d 634 (1996)

*Stephens v. City of Vista*, 994 F.2d 650 (9th Cir. 1993)

*Stewart v. Inhabitants of Town of Durham*, 451 A.2d 308 (Me. 1982)

*Stone v. Mississippi*, 101 U.S. 814, 25 L. Ed. 1079 (1879)

*Strong v. County of Santa Cruz*, 15 Cal. 3d 720, 543 P.2d 264 (1975)

*Sundance Homes, Inc. v. County of Du Page*, 195 Ill. 2d 257, 746 N.E.2d 254 (Ill. 2001)

## T

*Tahoe-Sierra Preservation Council, Inc. v. Tahoe Regional Planning Agency*, 535 U.S. 302, 122 S. Ct. 1465, 152 L. Ed. 2d 517, 32 ELR 20627 (2002)

*Tellimar Homes, Inc. v. Miller*, 14 A.D.2d 586, 218 N.Y.S.2d 175 (1961)

*Texas Co. v. Town of Miami Springs*, 44 So. 2d 808 (Fla. 1950)

*Texas Manufactured Hous. Ass'n v. City of Nederland*, 101 F.3d 1095 (5th Cir. 1996)

*Thompson v. Village of Newark*, 329 Ill. App. 3d 536, 768 N.E.2d 856 (2002)

*Timber Trails Corp. v. Planning and Zoning Comm'n of the Town of Sherman*, No. 272170, 1992 WL 239100 (Conn. Super. Ct. 1992)

*Town v. Land Use Comm'n*, 55 Haw. 538, 524 P.2d 84 (1974)

*Town of Blacksburg v. Price*, 221 Va. 168, 266 S.E.2d 899 (1980)

*Town of Flower Mound v. Stafford Estates Ltd. Partnership*, 71 S.W.3d 18 (Tex. Crim. App. 2d 2002)

*Town of Gloucester v. Olivo's Mobile Home Court, Inc.*, 111 R.I. 120, 300 A.2d 465 (1973)

*Town of Hillsborough v. Smith*, 276 N.C. 48, 170 S.E.2d 904 (1969)

*Town of Largo v. Imperial Homes Corp.*, 309 So. 2d 571 (Fla. 1975)

# CASE LIST

*Town of Longboat Key v. Lands End Ltd.*, 433 So. 2d 574 (Fla. Dist. Ct. App. 1983)

*Town of Longboat Key v. Mezrah*, 10 Fla. L. Weekly 1015, 467 So. 2d 488 (Fla. Dist. Ct. App. 1985)

*Town of Nottingham v. Lee Homes, Inc.*, 118 N.H. 438, 388 A.2d 940 (1978)

*Town of Orangetown v. Magee*, 665 N.E.2d 1061 (N.Y. 1996)

*Town of Paradise Valley v. Gulf Leisure Corp.*, 27 Ariz. App. 600, 557 P.2d 532 (1976)

*Town of Plaistow v. Nadeau*, 493 A.2d 1158 (N.H. 1985)

*Town of Stephens City v. Russell*, 241 Va. 160, 399 S.E.2d 814 (1991)

*Town of Sykesville v. West Shore Communications*, 110 Md. App. 300, 677 A.2d 102 (1996)

*Town of Vienna Council v. Kohler*, 218 Va. 966, 244 S.E.2d 542 (1978)

*Town of W. Hartford v. Rechel*, 190 Conn. 114, 459 A.2d 1015 (1983)

*Town Pump, Inc. v. Board of Adjustment of Red Lodge*, 292 Mont. 6, 971 P.2d 349 (1998)

*Towne Properties v. City of Fairfield*, 50 Ohio St. 2d 356, 364 N.E.2d 289 (1977)

*Trimen Dev. County v. King County*, 124 Wash. 2d 261, 877 P.2d 187 (1994)

*216 Sutter Bay Assocs. v. County of Sutter*, 58 Cal. App. 4th 860 (1997)

## U

*Union County v. Hoffman*, 512 N.W.2d 168 (S.D. 1994)

*Union Nat'l Bank v. Glenwood*, 38 Ill. App. 3d 469, 348 N.E. 2d 226 (1976)

*United Dev. Corp. v. City of Mill Creek*, 106 Wash. App. 681, 26 P.3d 943 (2001)

*United States Trust Co. v. New Jersey*, 431 U.S. 1, 97 S. Ct. 1505, 52 L. Ed 2d 92 (1977)

*Unlimited v. Kitsap County*, 50 Wash. App. 723, 750 P.2d 651 (1988)

## V

*V.F. Zahodiakin Corp. v. Zoning Bd. of Adjustment*, 8 N.J. 386, 86 A2d 127 (1952)

*Valley View Indus. Park v. Redmond*, 107 Wash. 2d 621, 733 P.2d 182 (1987)

*Van Cleave v. Village of Seneca*, 165 Ill. App. 3d 410, 519 N.E.2d 63 (1988)

*Vandergriff v. City of Chattanooga*, 44 F. Supp. 2d 927 (E.D. Tenn. 1998)

*Vashon Island Comm. for Self-Gov't v. Washington State Boundary Review Bd.*, 127 Wash. 2d 759, 903 P.2d 953 (1995)

*Villa at Greeley, Inc. v. Hopper*, 917 P.2d 350 (Colo. 1996)

*Village of Lisle v. Outdoor Adver. Co.*, 188 Ill. App. 3d 751, 544 N.E.2d 836 (1989)

*Village of Orland Park v. First Fed. Sav. & Loan Ass'n of Chicago*, 135 Ill. App. 3d 520, 481 N.E.2d 946 (1985)

*Village of Palatine v. LaSalle Nat'l Bank*, 112 Ill. App. 3d 885, 445 N.E.2d 1277 (1983)

*Village Pond Inc. v. Town of Darien*, 60 F.3d 1273 (7th Cir. 1995)

*Volusia County v. Aberdeen at Ormond Beach Ltd. Liab. Partnership*, 25 Fla. L. Weekly 390, 760 So. 2d 126 (Fla. 2000)

## W

*Walmart Stores, Inc. v. County of Clark*, 125 F. Supp. 2d 420 (D. Nev. 1999)

*Walz v. Town of Smithtown*, 46 F.3d 162, 25 ELR 20770 (2d Cir. 1995)

*Warmington Old Town Assocs. v. Tustin Unified Sch. Dist.*, 101 Cal. App. 4th 840 (2002)

*Waterbury Dev. Co. v. Witten*, 54 Ohio St. 2d 412, 377 N.E.2d 505 (Ohio 1978)

*Waters Landing Ltd. Partnership v. Montgomery County*, 337 Md. 15, 650 A.2d 712 (1994)

*Watt v. Planning & Zoning Comm'n of the Town of Kent*, 2000 Conn. Super. LEXIS 2312 (Conn. Super. Ct. 2000)

*Weber Basin Home Builders Ass'n v. Roy City*, 26 Utah 2d 215, 487 P.2d 866 (1971)

*Wellington River Hollow, Ltd. Liab. Corp. v. King County*, 113 Wash. App. 574, 54 P.3d 213 (2002)

*West Coast, Inc. v. Snohomish County*, 104 Wash. App. 735, 16 P.3d 30 (2000)

*Western Land Equities, Inc. v. City of Logan*, 617 P.2d 1073 (Utah 1980)

*Wheeler v. Armstrong*, 166 Mont. 363, 533 P.2d 964 (1975)

*Wheeler v. City of Pleasant Grove*, 896 F.2d 1347, 1351 (11th Cir. 1990)

*Williamson County Reg'l Planning Comm'n v. Hamilton Bank*, 473 U.S. 172 (1985)

## Y

*Yellow Lantern Kampground v. Town of Cortlandville*, 279 A.D.2d 6, 716 N.Y.S.2d 786 (2000)

*Youngblood v. Board of Supervisors of San Diego County*, 22 Cal. 3d 644, 586 P.2d 556 (1978)

## Z

*Zahodiakin Eng'g Corp. v. Zoning Board of Adjustment*, 86 A.2d 127 (N.J. 1952)

*Zealy v. City of Waukesha*, 201 Wis. 2d 356, 548 N.W.2d 528 (1996)

# APPENDICES

# Table of Contents

# APPENDICES

## I. CALIFORNIA MITIGATION ACT—GOVERNMENT CODE

**66000**. As used in this chapter:

(a) "Development project" means any project undertaken for the purpose of development. "Development project" includes a project involving the issuance of a permit for construction or reconstruction, but not a permit to operate.

(b) "Fee" means a monetary exaction other than a tax or special assessment, whether established for a broad class of projects by legislation of general applicability or imposed on a specific project on an ad hoc basis, that is charged by a local agency to the applicant in connection with approval of a development project for the purpose of defraying all or a portion of the cost of public facilities related to the development project, but does not include fees specified in Section 66477, fees for processing applications for governmental regulatory actions or approvals, fees collected under development agreements adopted pursuant to Article 2.5 (commencing with Section 65864) of Chapter 4, or fees collected pursuant to agreements with redevelopment agencies which provide for the redevelopment of property in furtherance or for the benefit of a redevelopment project for which a redevelopment plan has been adopted pursuant to the Community Redevelopment Law (Part 1 (commencing with Section 33000) of Division 24 of the Health and Safety Code.

(c) "Local agency" means a county, city, whether general law or chartered, city and county, school district, special district, authority, agency, any other municipal public corporation or district, or other political subdivision of the state.

(d) "Public facilities" includes public improvements, public services and community amenities.

**66000.5**. This chapter, Chapter 6 (commencing with Section 66010), Chapter 7 (commencing with Section 66012), Chapter 8 (commencing with Section 66016), and Chapter 9 (commencing with Section 66020) shall be known and may be cited as the Mitigation Fee Act.

**66001**. (a) In any action establishing, increasing, or imposing a fee as a condition of approval of a development project by a local agency on or after January 1, 1989, the local agency shall do all of the following:

(1) Identify the purpose of the fee.

(2) Identify the use to which the fee is to be put. If the use is financing public facilities, the facilities shall be identified. That identification may, but need not, be made by reference to a capital improvement plan as specified in Section 65403 or 66002, may be made in applicable general or specific plan requirements, or may be made in other public documents that identify the public facilities for which the fee is charged.

(3) Determine how there is a reasonable relationship between the fee's use and the type of development project on which the fee is imposed.

(4) Determine how there is a reasonable relationship between the need for the public facility and the type of development project on which the fee is imposed.

181

(b) In any action imposing a fee as a condition of approval of a development project by a local agency on or after January 1, 1989, the local agency shall determine how there is a reasonable relationship between the amount of the fee and the cost of the public facility or portion of the public facility attributable to the development on which the fee is imposed.

(c) Upon receipt of a fee subject to this section, the local agency shall deposit, invest, account for, and expend the fees pursuant to Section 66006.

(d) For the fifth fiscal year following the first deposit into the account or fund, and every five years thereafter, the local agency shall make all of the following findings with respect to that portion of the account or fund remaining unexpended, whether committed or uncommitted:

(1) Identify the purpose to which the fee is to be put.

(2) Demonstrate a reasonable relationship between the fee and the purpose for which it is charged.

(3) Identify all sources and amounts of funding anticipated to complete financing in incomplete improvements identified in paragraph (2) of subdivision (a).

(4) Designate the approximate dates on which the funding referred to in paragraph (3) is expected to be deposited into the appropriate account or fund. When findings are required by this subdivision, they shall be made in connection with the public information required by subdivision (b) of Section 66006. The findings required by this subdivision need only be made for moneys in possession of the local agency, and need not be made with respect to letters of credit, bonds, or other instruments taken to secure payment of the fee at a future date. If the findings are not made as required by this subdivision, the local agency shall refund the moneys in the account or fund as provided in subdivision (e).

(e) Except as provided in subdivision (f), when sufficient funds have been collected, as determined pursuant to subparagraph (F) of paragraph (1) of subdivision (b) of Section 66006, to complete financing on incomplete public improvements identified in paragraph (2) of subdivision (a), and the public improvements remain incomplete, the local agency shall identify, within 180 days of the determination that sufficient funds have been collected, an approximate date by which the construction of the public improvement will be commenced, or shall refund to the then current record owner or owners of the lots or units, as identified on the last equalized assessment roll, of the development project or projects on a prorated basis, the unexpended portion of the fee, and any interest accrued thereon. By means consistent with the intent of this section, a local agency may refund the unexpended revenues by direct payment, by providing a temporary suspension of fees, or by any other reasonable means. The determination by the governing body of the local agency of the means by which those revenues are to be refunded is a legislative act.

(f) If the administrative costs of refunding unexpended revenues pursuant to subdivision (e) exceed the amount to be refunded, the local agency, after a public hearing, notice of which has been published pursuant to Section 6061 and posted in three prominent places within the area of the development project, may determine that the revenues shall be allocated for some other purpose for which fees are collected subject to this chapter and which serves the project on which the fee was originally imposed.

**66002.** (a) Any local agency which levies a fee subject to Section 66001 may adopt a capital improvement plan, which shall indicate the approximate location, size, time of availability, and estimates of cost for all facilities or improvements to be financed with the fees.

(b) The capital improvement plan shall be adopted by, and shall be annually updated by, a resolution of the governing body of the local agency adopted at a noticed public hearing. Notice of the hearing shall be given pursuant to Section 65090. In addition, mailed notice shall be given to any city or county which may be significantly affected by the capital improvement plan. This notice shall be given no later than the date the local agency notices the public hearing pursuant to Section 65090. The information in the notice shall be not less than the information contained in the notice of public hearing and shall be given by first-class mail or personal delivery.

(c) "Facility" or "improvement," as used in this section, means any of the following:

(1) Public buildings, including schools and related facilities; provided that school facilities shall not be included if Senate Bill 97 of the 1987 -88 Regular Session is enacted and becomes effective on or before January 1, 1988.

(2) Facilities for the storage, treatment, and distribution of nonagricultural water.

(3) Facilities for the collection, treatment, reclamation, and disposal of sewage.

(4) Facilities for the collection and disposal of storm waters and for flood control purposes.

(5) Facilities for the generation of electricity and the distribution of gas and electricity.

(6) Transportation and transit facilities, including but not limited to streets and supporting improvements, roads, overpasses, bridges, harbors, ports, airports, and related facilities.

(7) Parks and recreation facilities.

(8) Any other capital project identified in the capital facilities plan adopted pursuant to Section 66002.

**66003.** Sections 66001 and 66002 do not apply to a fee imposed pursuant to a reimbursement agreement by and between a local agency and a property owner or developer for that portion of the cost of a public facility paid by the property owner or developer which exceeds the need for the public facility attributable to and reasonably related to the development. This chapter shall become operative on January 1, 1989.

**66004.** The establishment or increase of any fee pursuant to this chapter shall be subject to the requirements of Section 66018.

**66005**. (a) When a local agency imposes any fee or exaction as a condition of approval of a proposed development, as defined by Section 65927, or development project, those fees or exactions shall not exceed the estimated reasonable cost of providing the service or facility for which the fee or exaction is imposed.

(b) This section does not apply to fees or monetary exactions expressly authorized to be imposed under Sections 66475.1 and 66477.

(c) It is the intent of the Legislature in adding this section to codify existing constitutional and decisional law with respect to the imposition of development fees and monetary exactions on developments by local agencies. This section is declaratory of existing law and shall not be construed or interpreted as creating new law or as modifying or changing existing law.

**66006**. (a) If a local agency requires the payment of a fee specified in subdivision (c) in connection with the approval of a development project, the local agency receiving the fee shall deposit it with the other fees for the improvement in a separate capital facilities account or fund in a manner to avoid any commingling of the fees with other revenues and funds of the local agency, except for temporary investments, and expend those fees solely for the purpose for which the fee was collected. Any interest income earned by moneys in the capital facilities account or fund shall also be deposited in that account or fund and shall be expended only for the purpose for which the fee was originally collected.

(b) (1) For each separate account or fund established pursuant to subdivision (a), the local agency shall, within 180 days after the last day of each fiscal year, make available to the public the following information for the fiscal year:

(A) A brief description of the type of fee in the account or fund.

(B) The amount of the fee.

(C) The beginning and ending balance of the account or fund.

(D) The amount of the fees collected and the interest earned.

(E) An identification of each public improvement on which fees were expended and the amount of the expenditures on each improvement, including the total percentage of the cost of the public improvement that was funded with fees.

(F) An identification of an approximate date by which the construction of the public improvement will commence if the local agency determines that sufficient funds have been collected to complete financing on an incomplete public improvement, as identified in paragraph (2) of subdivision (a) of Section 66001, and the public improvement remains incomplete.

(G) A description of each interfund transfer or loan made from the account or fund, including the public improvement on which the transferred or loaned fees will be expended, and, in the case of an interfund loan, the date on which the loan will be repaid, and the rate of interest that the account or fund will receive on the loan.

(H) The amount of refunds made pursuant to subdivision (e) of Section 66001 and any allocations pursuant to subdivision (f) of Section 66001.

(2) The local agency shall review the information made available to the public pursuant to paragraph (1) at the next regularly scheduled public meeting not less than 15 days after this information is made available to the public, as re-

quired by this subdivision. Notice of the time and place of the meeting, including the address where this information may be reviewed, shall be mailed, at least 15 days prior to the meeting, to any interested party who files a written request with the local agency for mailed notice of the meeting. Any written request for mailed notices shall be valid for one year from the date on which it is filed unless a renewal request is filed. Renewal requests for mailed notices shall be filed on or before April 1 of each year. The legislative body may establish a reasonable annual charge for sending notices based on the estimated cost of providing the service.

(c) For purposes of this section, "fee" means any fee imposed to provide for an improvement to be constructed to serve a development project, or which is a fee for public improvements within the meaning of subdivision (b) of Section 66000, and that is imposed by the local agency as a condition of approving the development project.

(d) Any person may request an audit of any local agency fee or charge that is subject to Section 66023, including fees or charges of school districts, in accordance with that section.

(e) The Legislature finds and declares that untimely or improper allocation of development fees hinders economic growth and is, therefore, a matter of statewide interest and concern. It is, therefore, the intent of the Legislature that this section shall supersede all conflicting local laws and shall apply in charter cities.

(f) At the time the local agency imposes a fee for public improvements on a specific development project, it shall identify the public improvement that the fee will be used to finance.

**66006.5.** (a) A city or county which imposes an assessment, fee, or charge, other than a tax, for transportation purposes may, by ordinance, prescribe conditions and procedures allowing real property which is needed by the city or county for local transportation purposes, or by the state for transportation projects which will not receive any federal funds, to be donated by the obligor in satisfaction or partial satisfaction of the assessment, fee, or charge.

(b) To facilitate the implementation of subdivision (a), the Department of Transportation shall do all of the following:

(1) Give priority to the refinement, modification, and enhancement of procedures and policies dealing with right-of-way donations in order to encourage and facilitate those donations.

(2) Reduce or simplify paperwork requirements involving right-of-way procurement.

(3) Increase communication and education efforts as a means to solicit and encourage voluntary right-of-way donations.

(4) Enhance communication and coordination with local public entities through agreements of understanding that address state acceptance of right-of-way donations.

**66007.** (a) Except as otherwise provided in subdivision (b), any local agency that imposes any fees or charges on a residential development for the construction of public improvements or facilities shall not require the payment of those fees or charges, notwithstanding any other provision of law, until the date of the final inspection, or the date the certificate of occupancy is issued, whichever occurs first. However, utility service fees may be collected at the time an application for utility service is received. If the residential development contains more than one dwelling, the local agency may determine whether the fees or charges shall be paid on a pro rata basis for each dwelling when it receives its final inspection or certificate of occupancy, whichever occurs first; on a pro rata basis when a certain percentage of the dwellings have received their final inspection or certificate of occupancy, whichever occurs first; or on a lump-sum basis when the first dwelling in the development receives its final inspection or certificate of occupancy, whichever occurs first.

(b) Notwithstanding subdivision (a), the local agency may require the payment of those fees or charges at an earlier time if (1) the local agency determines that the fees or charges will be collected for public improvements or facilities for which an account has been established and funds appropriated and for which the local agency has adopted a proposed construction schedule or plan prior to final inspection or issuance of the certificate of occupancy or (2) the fees or charges are to reimburse the local agency for expenditures previously made. "Appropriated," as used in this subdivision, means authorization by the governing body of the local agency for which the fee is collected to make expenditures and incur obligations for specific purposes.

(c) (1) If any fee or charge specified in subdivision (a) is not fully paid prior to issuance of a building permit for construction of any portion of the residential development encumbered thereby, the local agency issuing the building permit may require the property owner, or lessee if the lessee's interest appears of record, as a condition of issuance of the building permit, to execute a contract to pay the fee or charge, or applicable portion thereof, within the time specified in subdivision (a). If the fee or charge is prorated pursuant to subdivision (a), the obligation under the contract shall be similarly prorated.

(2) The obligation to pay the fee or charge shall inure to the benefit of, and be enforceable by, the local agency that imposed the fee or charge, regardless of whether it is a party to the contract. The contract shall contain a legal description of the property affected, shall be recorded in the office of the county recorder of the county and, from the date of recordation, shall constitute a lien for the payment of the fee or charge, which shall be enforceable against successors in interest to the property owner or lessee at the time of issuance of the building permit. The contract shall be recorded in the grantor-grantee index in the name of the public agency issuing the building permit as grantee and in the name of the property owner or lessee as grantor. The local agency shall record a release of the obligation, containing a legal description of the property, in the event the obligation is paid in full, or a partial release in the event the fee or charge is prorated pursuant to subdivision (a).

(3) The contract may require the property owner or lessee to provide appropriate notification of the opening of any escrow for the sale of the property for which the building permit was issued and to provide in the escrow instruc-

tions that the fee or charge be paid to the local agency imposing the same from the sale proceeds in escrow prior to disbursing proceeds to the seller.

(d) This section applies only to fees collected by a local agency to fund the construction of public improvements or facilities. It does not apply to fees collected to cover the cost of code enforcement or inspection services, or to other fees collected to pay for the cost of enforcement of local ordinances or state law.

(e) "Final inspection" or "certificate of occupancy," as used in this section, have the same meaning as described in Sections 305 and 307 of the Uniform Building Code, International Conference of Building Officials, 1985 edition.

(f) Methods of complying with the requirement in subdivision (b) that a proposed construction schedule or plan be adopted, include, but are not limited to, (1) the adoption of the capital improvement plan described in Section 66002, or (2) the submittal of a five-year plan for construction and rehabilitation of school facilities pursuant to subdivision (c) of Section 17017.5 of the Education Code.

**66008.** A local agency shall expend a fee for public improvements, as accounted for pursuant to Section 66006, solely and exclusively for the purpose or purposes, as identified in subdivision (f) of Section 66006, for which the fee was collected. The fee shall not be levied, collected, or imposed for general revenue purposes.

## II. FLORIDA IMPACT FEE STATUTE

**163.3202 Land development regulations.**

(1) Within 1 year after submission of its revised comprehensive plan for review pursuant to s. 163.3167(2), each county and each municipality shall adopt or amend and enforce land development regulations that are consistent with and implement their adopted comprehensive plan.

(2) Local land development regulations shall contain specific and detailed provisions necessary or desirable to implement the adopted comprehensive plan and shall as a minimum:

(a) Regulate the subdivision of land;

(b) Regulate the use of land and water for those land use categories included in the land use element and ensure the compatibility of adjacent uses and provide for open space;

(c) Provide for protection of potable water wellfields;

(d) Regulate areas subject to seasonal and periodic flooding and provide for drainage and stormwater management;

(e) Ensure the protection of environmentally sensitive lands designated in the comprehensive plan;

(f) Regulate signage;

(g) Provide that public facilities and services meet or exceed the standards established in the capital improvements element required by s. 163.3177 and are available when needed for the development, or that development orders and permits are conditioned on the availability of these public facilities and services necessary to serve the proposed development. Not later than 1 year after its due date established by the state land planning agency's rule for submission of local comprehensive plans pursuant to s. 163.3167(2), a local government shall not issue a development order or permit which results in a reduction in the level of services for the affected public facilities below the level of services provided in the comprehensive plan of the local government.

(h) Ensure safe and convenient onsite traffic flow, considering needed vehicle parking.

(3) This section shall be construed to encourage the use of innovative land development regulations which include provisions such as transfer of development rights, incentive and inclusionary zoning, planned-unit development, impact fees, and performance zoning. These and all other such regulations shall be combined and compiled into a single land development code for the jurisdiction. A general zoning code shall not be required if a local government's adopted land development regulations meet the requirements of this section.

(4) The state land planning agency may require a local government to submit one or more land development regulations if it has reasonable grounds to believe that a local government has totally failed to adopt any one or more of the land development regulations required by this section. Once the state land planning agency determines after review and consultation with local government whether the local government has adopted regulations required by this section, the state land planning agency shall notify the local government in writing within 30 calendar days after receipt of the regulations from the local govern-

ment. If the state land planning agency determines that the local government has failed to adopt regulations required by this section, it may institute an action in circuit court to require adoption of these regulations. This action shall not review compliance of adopted regulations with this section or consistency with locally adopted plans.

(5) The state land planning agency shall adopt rules for review and schedules for adoption of land development regulations.

**History.**—s. 14, ch. 85-55; s. 12, ch. 86-191; s. 14, ch. 93-206; s. 7, ch. 95-322; s. 6, ch. 96-416; s. 5, ch. 98-146.

# APPENDICES

## III. ILLINOIS ROAD IMPACT FEE STATUTE

### DIVISION 9. ROAD IMPROVEMENT IMPACT FEES

(605 ILCS 5/5-901)

Sec. 5-901. Short title. This Division may be cited as the Road Improvement Impact Fee Law. (Source: P.A. 86-97.)

(605 ILCS 5/5-902)

Sec. 5-902. General purposes. The General Assembly finds that the purpose of this legislation is to create the authority for units of local government to adopt and implement road improvement impact fee ordinances and resolutions. The General Assembly further recognizes that the imposition of such road improvement impact fees is designed to supplement other funding sources so that the burden of paying for road improvements can be allocated in a fair and equitable manner. It is the intent of the General Assembly to promote orderly economic growth throughout the State by assuring that new development bears its fair share of the cost of meeting the demand for road improvements through the imposition of road improvement impact fees. It is also the intent of the General Assembly to preserve the authority of elected local government officials to adopt and implement road improvement impact fee ordinances or resolutions which adhere to the minimum standards and procedures adopted in this Division by the State. (Source: P.A. 86-97.)

(605 ILCS 5/5-903)

Sec. 5-903. Definitions. As used in this Division:

"Units of local government" mean counties with a population over 400,000 and all home rule municipalities.

"Road improvement impact fee" means any charge or fee levied or imposed by a unit of local government as a condition to the issuance of a building permit or a certificate of occupancy in connection with a new development, when any portion of the revenues collected is intended to be used to fund any portion of the costs of road improvements.

"Road improvements" mean the improvement, expansion, enlargement or construction of roads, streets, or highways under the jurisdiction of units of local government, including but not limited to bridges, rights-of-way, and traffic control improvements owned and operated by such units of local government. Road improvements may also include the improvement, expansion, enlargement or construction of roads, ramps, streets or highways under the jurisdiction of the State of Illinois, provided an agreement providing for the construction and financing of such road improvements has been reached between the State and the unit of local government and incorporated into the comprehensive road improvement plan. Road improvements shall not include tollways but may include tollway ramps.

"New development" means any residential, commercial, industrial or other project which is being newly constructed, reconstructed, redeveloped, structurally altered, relocated, or enlarged, and which generates additional traffic within the service area or areas of the unit of local government. "New development" shall not include any new development for which site specific development approval has been given by a unit of local government within 18 months before the first date of publication by the unit of local government of a notice of public hearing to consider the land use assumptions relating to the development of a comprehensive road improvement plan and imposition of impact fees; provided, however, that a building permit for such new development is issued within 18 months after the date of publication of such notice.

"Roads, streets or highways" mean any roads, streets or highways which have been designated by the unit of local government in the comprehensive road improvement plan together with all necessary appurtenances, including but not limited to bridges, rights-of-way, tollway ramps, and traffic control improvements.

"Comprehensive road improvement plan" means a plan prepared by the unit of local government in consultation with the Advisory Committee.

"Advisory Committee" means the group of members selected from the public and private sectors to advise in the development and implementation of the comprehensive road improvement plan, and the periodic update of the plan.

"Person" means any individual, firm, partnership, association, public or private corporation, organization or business, charitable trust, or unit of local government.

"Land use assumptions" means a description of the service area or areas and the roads, streets or highways incorporated therein, including projections relating to changes in land uses, densities and population growth rates which affect the level of traffic within the service area or areas over a 20 year period of time.

"Service area" means one or more land areas within the boundaries of the unit of local government which has been designated by the unit of local government in the comprehensive road improvement plan.

"Residential development" means a house, building, or other structure that is suitable or capable of being used for residential purposes.

"Nonresidential development" means a building or other structure that is suitable or capable of being used for all purposes other than residential purposes.

"Specifically and uniquely attributable" means that a new development creates the need, or an identifiable portion of the need, for additional capacity to be provided by a road improvement. Each new development paying impact fees used to fund a road improvement must receive a direct and material benefit from the road improvement constructed with the impact fees paid. The need for road improvements funded by impact fees shall be based upon generally accepted traffic engineering practices as assignable to the new development paying the fees.

"Proportionate share" means the cost of road improvements that are specifically and uniquely attributable to a new development after the consideration of the following factors: the amount of additional traffic generated by the new development, any appropriate credit or offset for contribution of money, dedication of land, construction of road improvements or traffic reduction techniques, payments reasonably anticipated to be made by or as a result of a new develop-

191

ment in the form of user fees, debt service payments, or taxes which are dedicated for road improvements and all other available sources of funding road improvements.

"Level of service" means one of the categories of road service as defined by the Institute of Transportation Engineers which shall be selected by a unit of local government imposing the impact fee as the adopted level of service to serve existing development not subject to the fee and new development, provided that the level of service selected for new development shall not exceed the level of service adopted for existing development.

"Site specific development approval" means an approval of a plan submitted by a developer to a unit of local government describing with reasonable certainty the type and intensity of use for a specific parcel or parcels of property. The plan may be in the form of, but need not be limited to, any of the following: a preliminary or final planned unit development plan, subdivision plat, development plan, conditional or special use permit, or any other form of development use approval, as utilized by a unit of local government, provided that the development use approval constitutes a final exercise of discretion by the unit of local government.

"Developer" means any person who undertakes new development.

"Existing deficiencies" mean existing roads, streets, or highways operating at a level of service below the adopted level of service selected by the unit of local government, as defined in the comprehensive road improvement plan.

"Assisted financing" means the financing of residential development by the Illinois Housing Development Authority, including loans to developers for multi-unit residential development and loans to purchasers of single family residences, including condominiums and townhomes.
(Source: P.A. 90-356, eff. 8-10-97.)

(605 ILCS 5/5-904)
Sec. 5-904. Authorization for the Imposition of an Impact Fee. No impact fee shall be imposed by a unit of local government within a service area or areas upon a developer for the purposes of improving, expanding, enlarging or constructing roads, streets or highways directly affected by the traffic demands generated from the new development unless imposed pursuant to the provisions of this Division. An impact fee payable by a developer shall not exceed a proportionate share of costs incurred by a unit of local government which are specifically and uniquely attributable to the new development paying the fee in providing road improvements, but may be used to cover costs associated with the surveying of the service area, with the acquisition of land and rights-of-way, with engineering and planning costs, and with all other costs which are directly related to the improvement, expansion, enlargement or construction of roads, streets or highways within the service area or areas as designated in the comprehensive road improvement plan. An impact fee shall not be imposed to cover costs associated with the repair, reconstruction, operation or maintenance of existing roads, streets or highways, nor shall an impact fee be used to cure existing deficiencies or to upgrade, update, expand or replace existing roads in order to meet stricter safety or environmental requirements; provided, however, that

such fees may be used in conjunction with other funds available to the unit of local government for the purpose of curing existing deficiencies, but in no event shall the amount of impact fees expended exceed the development's proportionate share of the cost of such road improvements. Nothing contained in this Section shall preclude a unit of local government from providing credits to the developer for services, conveyances, improvements or cash if provided by agreement even if the credits are for improvements not included in the comprehensive road improvement plan, provided the improvements are otherwise eligible for inclusion in the comprehensive road improvement plan. (Source: P.A. 88-470.)

(605 ILCS 5/5-905)
Sec. 5-905. Procedure for the Imposition of Impact Fees. (a) Unless otherwise provided for in this Division, an impact fee shall be imposed by a unit of local government only upon compliance with the provisions set forth in this Section.

(b) A unit of local government intending to impose an impact fee shall adopt an ordinance or resolution establishing a public hearing date to consider land use assumptions that will be used to develop the comprehensive road improvement plan. Before the adoption of the ordinance or resolution establishing a public hearing date, the governing body of the unit of local government shall appoint an Advisory Committee in accordance with this Division.

(c) The unit of local government shall provide public notice of the hearing date to consider land use assumptions in accordance with the provisions contained in this Section.

(d) The unit of local government shall publish notice of the hearing date once each week for 3 consecutive weeks, not less than 30 and not more than 60 days before the scheduled date of the hearing, in a newspaper of general circulation within the unit of local government. The notice of public hearing shall not appear in the part of the paper where legal notices or classified ads appear. The notice shall not be smaller than one-quarter page of standard size or tabloid-size newspaper.

(e) The notice shall contain all of the following information:

(1) Headline designated as follows: "NOTICE OF PUBLIC HEARING ON LAND USE ASSUMPTIONS RELATING TO THE DEVELOPMENT OF A COMPREHENSIVE ROAD IMPROVEMENT PLAN AND IMPOSITION OF IMPACT FEES".

(2) The date, time and location of the public hearing.

(3) A statement that the purpose of the hearing is to consider proposed land use assumptions within the service area or areas that will be used to develop a comprehensive road improvement plan.

(4) A general description of the service area or areas within the unit of local government being affected by the proposed land use assumptions.

(5) A statement that the unit of local government shall make available to the public upon request the following: proposed land use assumptions, an easily understandable and detailed map of the service area or areas to which the pro-

posed land use assumptions shall apply, along with all other available information relating to the proposed land use assumptions.

(6) A statement that any member of the public affected by the proposed land use assumptions shall have the right to appear at the public hearing and present evidence in support of or against the proposed land use assumptions.

(f) In addition to the public notice requirement, the unit of local government shall send a notice of the intent to hold a public hearing by certified mail, return receipt requested, to any person who has requested in writing by certified mail return receipt requested, notification of the hearing date, at least 30 days before the date of the adoption of the ordinance or resolution establishing the public hearing date.

(g) A public hearing shall be held for the consideration of the proposed land use assumptions. Within 30 days after the public hearing has been held, the Advisory Committee shall make a recommendation to adopt, reject in whole or in part, or modify the proposed land use assumptions presented at the hearing by written report to the unit of local government. Thereafter the unit of local government shall have not less than 30 nor more than 60 days to approve, disapprove, or modify by ordinance or resolution the land use assumptions proposed at the public hearing and the recommendations made by the Advisory Committee. Such ordinance or resolution shall not be adopted as an emergency measure.

(h) Upon the adoption of an ordinance or resolution approving the land use assumptions, the unit of local government shall provide for a comprehensive road improvement plan to be developed by qualified professionals familiar with generally accepted engineering and planning practices. The comprehensive road improvement plan shall include projections of all costs related to the road improvements designated in the comprehensive road improvement plan.

(i) The unit of local government shall adopt an ordinance or resolution establishing a date for a public hearing to consider the comprehensive road improvement plan and the imposition of impact fees related thereto.

(j) A public hearing to consider the adoption of the comprehensive road improvement plan and imposition of impact fees shall be held within the unit of local government subject to the same notice provisions as those set forth in the subsection (d). The public hearing shall be conducted by an official designated by the unit of local government.

(k) Within 30 days after the public hearing has been held, the Advisory Committee shall make a recommendation to adopt, reject in whole or in part, or modify the proposed comprehensive road improvement plan and impact fees. The unit of local government shall have not less than 30 nor more than 60 days to approve, disapprove, or modify by ordinance or resolution the proposed comprehensive road improvement plan and impact fees. Such ordinance or resolution shall not be adopted as an emergency measure.
(Source: P.A. 86-97.)

(605 ILCS 5/5-906)
Sec. 5-906. Impact Fee Ordinance or Resolution Requirements.

# APPENDICES

(a) An impact fee ordinance or resolution shall satisfy the following 2 requirements:

(1) The construction, improvement, expansion or enlargement of new or existing roads, streets, or highways for which an impact fee is imposed must be specifically and uniquely attributable to the traffic demands generated by the new development paying the fee.

(2) The impact fee imposed must not exceed a proportionate share of the costs incurred or the costs that will be incurred by the unit of local government in the provision of road improvements to serve the new development. The proportionate share is the cost specifically attributable to the new development after the unit of local government considers the following: (i) any appropriate credit, offset or contribution of money, dedication of land, construction of road improvements or traffic reduction techniques; (ii) payments reasonably anticipated to be made by or as a result of a new development in the form of user fees, debt service payments, or taxes which are dedicated for road improvements; and (iii) all other available sources of funding road improvements.

(b) In determining the proportionate share of the cost of road improvements to be paid by the developer, the following 8 factors shall be considered by the unit of local government imposing the impact fee:

(1) The cost of existing roads, streets and highways within the service area or areas.

(2) The means by which existing roads, streets and highways have been financed to cure existing deficiencies.

(3) The extent to which the new development being assessed the impact fees has already contributed to the cost of improving existing roads, streets or highways through taxation, assessment, or developer or landowner contributions paid in prior years.

(4) The extent to which the new development will contribute to the cost of improving existing roads, streets or highways in the future.

(5) The extent to which the new development should be credited for providing road improvements, without charge to other properties within the service area or areas.

(6) Extraordinary costs, if any, incurred in servicing the new development.

(7) Consideration of the time and price differential inherent in a fair comparison of fees paid at different times.

(8) The availability of other sources of funding road improvements, including but not limited to user charges, general tax levies, intergovernmental transfers, and special taxation or assessments.

(c) An impact fee ordinance or resolution shall provide for the calculation of an impact fee in accordance with generally accepted accounting practices. An impact fee shall not be deemed invalid because payment of the fee may result in a benefit to other owners or developers within the service area or areas, other than the person paying the fee.

(Source: P.A. 86-97.)

(605 ILCS 5/5-907)

Sec. 5-907. Advisory Committee. A road improvement impact fee advisory committee shall be created by the unit of local government intending to impose impact fees. The Advisory Committee shall consist of not less than 10 members and not more than 20 members. Not less than 40% of the members of the committee shall be representatives of the real estate, development, and building industries and the labor communities and may not be employees or officials of the unit of local government. The members of the Advisory Committee shall be selected as follows:

(1) The representatives of real estate shall be licensed under the Real Estate License Act of 2000 and shall be designated by the President of the Illinois Association of Realtors from a local Board from the service area or areas of the unit of local government.

(2) The representatives of the development industry shall be designated by the Regional Developers Association.

(3) The representatives of the building industry shall be designated representatives of the Regional Home Builders representing the unit of local government's geographic area as appointed from time to time by that Association's president.

(4) The labor representatives shall be chosen by either the Central Labor Council or the Building and Construction Trades Council having jurisdiction within the unit of local government.

If the unit of local government is a county, at least 30% of the members serving on the commission must be representatives of the municipalities within the county. The municipal representatives shall be selected by a convention of mayors in the county, who shall elect from their membership municipal representatives to serve on the Advisory Committee. The members representing the county shall be appointed by the chief executive officer of the county.

If the unit of local government is a municipality, the non-public representatives shall be appointed by the chief executive officer of the municipality.

If the unit of local government has a planning or zoning commission, the unit of local government may elect to use its planning or zoning commission to serve as the Advisory Committee, provided that not less than 40% of the committee members include representatives of the real estate, development, and building industries and the labor communities who are not employees or officials of the unit of local government. A unit of local government may appoint additional members to serve on the planning or zoning commission as ad hoc voting members whenever the planning or zoning commission functions as the Advisory Committee; provided that no less than 40% of the members include representatives of the real estate, development, and building industries and the labor communities.

(Source: P.A. 91-245, eff. 12-31-99.)

(605 ILCS 5/5-908)

Sec. 5-908. Duties of the Advisory Committee. The Advisory Committee shall serve in an advisory capacity and shall have the following duties:

(1) Advise and assist the unit of local government by recommending proposed land use assumptions.

(2) Make recommendations with respect to the development of a comprehensive road improvement plan.

(3) Make recommendations to approve, disapprove or modify a comprehensive road improvement plan by preparing a written report containing these recommendations to the unit of local government.

(4) Report to the unit of local government on all matters relating to the imposition of impact fees.

(5) Monitor and evaluate the implementation of the comprehensive road improvement plan and the assessment of impact fees.

(6) Report annually to the unit of local government with respect to the progress of the implementation of the comprehensive road improvement plan.

(7) Advise the unit of local government of the need to update or revise the land use assumptions, comprehensive road improvement plan, or impact fees.

The unit of local government shall adopt procedural rules to be used by the Advisory Committee in carrying out the duties imposed by this Division. (Source: P.A. 86-97.)

(605 ILCS 5/5-909)
Sec. 5-909. Unit of Local Government to Cooperate with the Advisory Committee. The unit of local government shall make available to the Advisory Committee all professional reports in relation to the development and implementation of land use assumptions, the comprehensive road improvement plan and periodic up-dates to the comprehensive road improvement plan. (Source: P.A. 86-97.)

(605 ILCS 5/5-910)
Sec. 5-910. Comprehensive Road Improvement Plan. Each unit of local government intending to impose an impact fee shall prepare a comprehensive road improvement plan. The plan shall be prepared by persons qualified in fields relating to engineering, planning, or transportation. The persons preparing the plan shall consult with the Advisory Committee. The comprehensive road improvement plan shall contain all of the following:

(1) A description of all existing roads, streets or highways and their existing deficiencies within the service area or areas of the unit of local government and a reasonable estimate of all costs related to curing the existing deficiencies, including but not limited to the upgrading, updating, improving, expanding or replacing of such roads, streets or highways and the current level of service of the existing roads, streets and highways.

(2) A commitment by the unit of local government to cure existing deficiencies where practicable relating to roads, streets, and highways.

(3) A description of the land use assumptions adopted by the unit of local government.

(4) A description of all roads, streets or highways proposed to be improved, expanded, enlarged or constructed to serve new development and a reasonable estimate of all costs related to the improvement, expansion, enlarge-

197

ment or construction of the roads, streets or highways needed to serve new development at a level of service not to exceed the level of service on the currently existing roads, streets or highways.

(5) Identification of all sources and levels of funding available to the unit of local government for the financing of the road improvements.

(6) If the proposed road improvements include the improvement of roads, streets or highways under the jurisdiction of the State of Illinois or another unit of local government, then an agreement between units of government shall specify the proportionate share of funding by each unit. All agreements entered into by the State must provide that the portion of the impact fees collected due to the impact of new development upon roads, streets, or highways under State jurisdiction be allocated for expenditure for improvements to those roads, streets, and highways under State jurisdiction.

(7) A schedule setting forth estimated dates for commencing construction of all road improvements identified in the comprehensive road improvement plan.

Nothing contained in this subsection shall limit the right of a home rule unit of local government from imposing conditions on a Planned Unit Development or other zoning relief which may include contributions for road improvements, which are necessary or appropriate for such developments, but are not otherwise provided for in the comprehensive
road improvement plan.
(Source: P.A. 86-97; 86-1158.)


(605 ILCS 5/5-911)
Sec. 5-911. Assessment of Impact Fees. Impact fees shall be assessed by units of local government at the time of final plat approval or when the building permit is issued when no plat approval is necessary. No impact fee shall be assessed by a unit of local government for roads, streets or highways within the service area or areas of the unit of local government if and to the extent that another unit of local government has imposed an impact fee for the same roads, streets or highways.
(Source: P.A. 86-97.)


(605 ILCS 5/5-912)
Sec. 5-912. Payment of Impact Fees. In order to minimize the effect of impact fees on the person paying the fees, the following methods of payment shall be used by the unit of local government in collecting impact fees. Impact fees imposed upon a residential development, consisting of one single family residence, shall be payable as a condition to the issuance of the building permit. Impact fees imposed upon all other types of new development, including multi-unit residential development, shall be payable as a condition to the issuance of the certificate of occupancy, provided that the developer and the unit of local government enter into an agreement designating that the developer notify the unit of local government that the building permit or the certificate of occupancy has been issued. For any development receiving assisted financing, including any development for which a commitment for assisted financing has

been issued and for which assisted financing is provided within 6 months of the issuance of the certificate of occupancy, the unit of local government shall provide for the payment of the impact fees through an installment agreement at a reasonable rate of interest for a period of 10 years after the impact fee is due. Nothing contained in this Section shall preclude the payment of the impact fee at the time when the building permit is issued or at an earlier stage of development if agreed to by the unit of local government and the person paying the fees. Nothing contained in this Section shall preclude the unit of local government from making and entering into agreements providing for the cooperative collection of impact fees but the collection of impact fees shall be the sole responsibility of the unit of local government imposing the impact fee. Such agreements may also provide for the reimbursement of collection costs from the fees collected.

At the option of the unit of local government, impact fees may be paid through an installment agreement at a reasonable rate of interest for a period of up to 10 years after the impact fee is due.

Nothing contained in this section shall be construed to give units of local government a preference over the rights of any purchaser, mortgagee, judgment creditor or other lienholder arising prior to the filing in the office of the recorder of the county or counties in which the property is located of notification of the existence of any uncollected impact fees.
(Source: P.A. 86-97.)

(605 ILCS 5/5-913)
Sec. 5-913. Impact Fees to be Held in Interest Bearing Accounts.
All impact fees collected pursuant to this Division shall be deposited into interest bearing accounts designated solely for such funds for each service area. All interest earned on such funds shall become a part of the moneys to be used for the road improvements authorized by this Division. The unit of local government shall provide that an accounting be made annually for any account containing impact fee proceeds and interest earned. Such accounting shall include, but shall not be limited to, the total funds collected, the source of the funds collected, the total amount of interest accruing on such funds, and the amount of funds expended on road improvements. Notice of the results of the accounting shall be published in a newspaper of general circulation within the unit of local government at least 3 times. A statement that a copy of the report is available to the public for inspection at reasonable times shall be contained in the notice. A copy of the report shall be provided to the Advisory Committee.
(Source: P.A. 86-97.)

(605 ILCS 5/5-914)
Sec. 5-914. Expenditures of Impact Fees. Impact fees shall only be expended on those road improvements within the service area or areas as specified in the comprehensive road improvement plan, as updated from time to time. Impact fees shall be expended in the same manner as motor fuel tax money allotted to the unit of local government solely for road improvement costs.
(Source: P.A. 86-97.)

(605 ILCS 5/5-915)
Sec. 5-915. Comprehensive Road Improvement Plan Amendments and Updates. The unit of local government imposing an impact fee may amend the comprehensive road improvement plan no more than once per year, provided the cumulative amendments do not exceed 10% of the total plan in terms of estimated project costs. If a proposed plan amendment will result in the cumulative amendments to the plan exceeding 10% of the total plan, then the unit of local government shall follow the procedures set forth in Section 5-905 of this Division. Regardless of whether the Comprehensive Road Improvement Plan has been amended, the unit of local government imposing an impact fee shall update the comprehensive road improvement plan at least once every 5 years. The 5 year period shall commence from the date of the original adoption of the comprehensive road improvement plan. The updating of the comprehensive road improvement plan shall be made in accordance with the procedures set forth in Section 5-905 of this Division.
(Source: P.A. 88-470.)

(605 ILCS 5/5-916)
Sec. 5-916. Refund of Impact Fees. All impact fees collected by a unit of local government shall be refunded to the person who paid the fee or to that person's successor in interest whenever the unit of local government fails to encumber by contract impact fees collected within 5 years of the date on which such impact fees were due to be paid.

Refunds shall be made in accordance with this Section provided that the person who paid the fee or that person's successor in interest files a petition with the unit of local government imposing the impact fee, seeking a refund within one year from the date that such fees were
required to be encumbered by contract.

All refunds made shall bear interest at a rate which is at least 70% of the Prime Commercial Rate in effect at the time of the imposition of the impact fee.
(Source: P.A. 86-97; 87-187.)

(605 ILCS 5/5-917)
Sec. 5-917. Appeals Process. Any person paying an impact fee shall have the right to contest the land use assumptions, the development and implementation of the comprehensive road improvement plan, the imposition of impact fees, the periodic updating of the road improvement plan, the refund of impact fees and all other matters relating to impact fees. The initial appeal shall be made to the legislative body of the unit of local government in accordance with the procedures adopted in the ordinance or resolution. Any subsequent relief shall be sought in a de novo proceeding in the appropriate circuit court.
(Source: P.A. 86-97.)

(605 ILCS 5/5-918)
Sec. 5-918. Transition Clauses.
(a) Conformance of Existing Ordinances. A unit of local government which currently has in effect an impact fee ordinance or resolution shall have

not more than 12 months from July 26, 1989 to bring its ordinance or resolution into conformance with the requirements imposed by this Act, except that a home rule unit of local government with a population over 75,000 and located in a county with a population over 600,000 and less than 2,000,000 shall have not more than 18 months from July 26, 1989, to bring that ordinance or resolution into conformance.

(b) Exemption of Developments Receiving Site Specific Development Approval. No development which has received site specific development approval from a unit of local government within 18 months before the first date of publication by the unit of local government of a notice of public hearing to consider land use assumptions relating to the development of a comprehensive road improvement plan and imposition of impact fees and which has filed for building permits or certificates of occupancy within 18 months of the date of approval of the site specific development plan shall be required to pay impact fees for permits or certificates of occupancy issued within that 18 month period.

This Division shall have no effect on the validity of any existing agreements entered into between a developer and a unit of local government pertaining to fees, exactions or donations made by a developer for the purpose of funding road improvements.

(c) Exception to the Exemption of Developments Receiving Site Specific Development Approval. Nothing in this Section shall require the refund of impact fees previously collected by units of local government in accordance with their ordinances or resolutions, if such ordinances or resolutions were adopted prior to the effective date of this Act and provided that such impact fees are encumbered as provided in Section 5-916.
(Source: P.A. 86-97; 86-1158.)

(605 ILCS 5/5-919)
Sec. 5-919. Home Rule Preemption. A home rule unit may not impose road improvement impact fees in a manner inconsistent with this Division. This Division is a limitation under subsection (i) of Section 6 of Article VII of the Illinois Constitution on the concurrent exercise by home rule units of powers and functions exercised by the State.
(Source: P.A. 86-97.)

## IV. MODEL IMPACT FEE ORDINANCE

The following impact fee ordinance was prepared by counsel[1] and recently adopted by a suburban local government located in the Chicago area.

### CHAPTER 160: DEVELOPMENT IMPACT FEES

SECTION

---

1    Prepared by Holland & Knight LLC, Chicago, Illinois.

# APPENDICES

## ARTICLE I

## GENERAL PROVISIONS

Sec. 160.101 Citation.

These regulations shall be known, cited, and referred to as the "Development Impact Fee Ordinance."

Sec. 160.102 Findings and Purpose.

(A) It is declared to be the policy of the City that the provision of various public facilities required to serve new residential development is subject to the control of the City in accordance with the comprehensive plan of the City for the orderly, planned, efficient, and economical development of the City.

(B) New residential developments cause and impose increased and excessive demands upon public facilities and services that are specifically and uniquely attributable to those new residential developments. Affected facilities and services include public schools, parks and library services.

(C) Planning projections indicate that new residential development shall continue and shall place ever-increasing demands on the school districts, the Park District, and the library to provide necessary public facilities.

(D) Development potential and property values are influenced and affected by City policy as expressed in the comprehensive plan and as implemented by the City zoning ordinance, the school districts, the Park District, and the library.

(E) To the extent that new residential developments place demands upon public facilities that are specifically and uniquely attributable to such developments, those demands should be satisfied by requiring that the new residential developments creating the demands pay the cost of meeting the demands.

(F) The amount of the development impact fees to be required of new residential developments shall be determined by a triennial needs assessment and, pursuant thereto, the proportionate share cost of the additional public facilities needed to support such developments shall be calculated. The additional public facilities shall be identified in capital improvement programs, thereby ensuring that new residential developments are required to pay only that portion of the costs of acquiring needed lands and only that portion of the costs of constructing needed capital facilities specifically and uniquely attributable to the new residential developments.

(G) The City Council, after careful consideration, hereby finds and declares that imposition of development impact fees upon new residential developments to finance specified public facilities, the demand for which is created by such developments within the City, is in the best interests of the general welfare of the City and its residents, is equitable, and does not impose an unfair burden on such developments. Therefore, the City Council deems it necessary and desirable to adopt this Chapter as herein set forth.

Sec. 160.103 Applicability.

This Chapter requires payment of development impact fees, payable at the time of issuance of a building permit, in an amount equal to the proportionate share of the cost of the various public facilities required to serve certain developments. The fees for school and park district capital improvements, school site development, park district site improvements, and library capital improvements shall be uniformly applicable to all residential development, as defined herein. (Ord. 49-97, J. 24, p. 297-299, passed 8/25/97; **Ord. 02-01, J. 27, p. 07-24, passed 01/08/01**)

ARTICLE II

DEFINITIONS

Sec. 160.201 Definitions and Interpretation.

(A) The language in the text of this Chapter shall be interpreted in accordance with the following rules of construction:

(1) The singular number includes the plural number, and the plural the singular;

(2) The word "shall" is mandatory; the word "may" is permissive; and

(3) The masculine gender includes the feminine and neuter.

(B) The following words and phrases shall, for the purposes of this Chapter, have the meanings respectively ascribed to them in this Subsection, except when the context otherwise indicates.

(1) **"Bedroom"** means any room in a dwelling unit that (a) is suitable for sleeping purposes, (b) is greater than 100 square feet in floor area, and (c) is not a living room, dining room, kitchen, or bathroom.

(2) **"Building Permit"** means the permit issued by the City for the construction, reconstruction, alteration, addition, repair, placement, removal or demolition of or to a building or structure within the corporate limits of the City. (Ord. 49-97, J. 24, p. 297-299, passed 8/25/97; **Ord. 02-01, J. 27, p. 07-24, passed 01/08/01**)

(3) **"Building Site"** means an area of land designed, intended or used as a location for a structure.

(4) **"Capital Budget"** means the portion of the City's, Park District's, school districts', and/or library's annual budget devoted to the funding of capital improvement projects.

(5) **"Capital Improvement"** means a project or piece of equipment with a useful life in excess of three years and limited to the following improvements to sites: newly constructed buildings; newly constructed structural improvements to buildings and permanent additions to buildings; systems that are being installed within newly constructed buildings or within permanent additions to buildings (including, but not limited to, electrical systems, plumbing systems, fire protection systems, and heating, ventilation, and air conditioning systems); additions to or replacements of systems within existing buildings to the extent necessary to meet the demands of development; grading, landscaping, seeding, and planting of shrubs and trees on sites and adjacent ways; and retaining walls and parking lots on sites; and the initial surfacing and soil treatment of athletic fields and tennis courts, when undertaken or constructed in connection with the construction of new school or Park District or permanent additions thereto; furnishing and installing for the first time fixed playground apparatus, flagpoles, gateways, fences, and underground storage tanks that are not part of building service systems; and demolition work.

(6) **"Capital Improvement Program"** means a multi-year plan of any school district, the Park District, and/or library that: (i) projects, for a planning period of at least 5 years, the need for capital improvements within the service area served by the public body; (ii) sets forth a schedule for the construction, acquisition, or leasing of the capital improvements to meet the projected need; (iii) indicates the size and general location of the needed capital improvements; (iv) identifies the estimated costs of constructing, acquiring, or leasing the needed capital improvements; and (v) sets forth the anticipated funding sources and funds to be received by the public body (including, but not limited to, funds that will be received from the sale of existing capital improvements) for the construction, acquisition, or leasing of the needed capital improvements.

(7) **"City"** means the City of Highland Park.

(8) **"City Council"** means the City Council of the City.

(9) **"Code"** means "The Highland Park Code of 1968", as amended.

(10) **"Comprehensive Plan"** means the official plan for the development of the City adopted by the City Council.

(11) **"Cost"** means expenditures incurred or estimated to be incurred to fund a capital improvement project. These costs include, without limitation, acquisition of land, construction of improvements, equipping of facilities, and administrative, engineering, architectural, and legal expenses incurred in connection therewith.

(12) **"Detention Area"** means a dry-bottom area of land which provides for the temporary storage of stormwater runoff.

(13) **"Developer"** means the person undertaking a residential development, which may, for purposes of this Chapter include, without limitation, the owner as well as the subdivider of the land on which the development is to take place.

(14) **"Development"** means any of the following activities occurring on or after July 1, 1995:

(a) any subdivision of land;

(b) any re-subdivision or modification of an existing subdivision;

(c) any planned unit development;

(d) any modification of an existing planned unit development; or

(e) any construction, reconstruction, alteration, addition, repair, or placement of or to a building, that requires the issuance of a building permit. (Ord. 49-97, J. 24, p. 297-299, passed 8/25/97; **Ord. 02-01, J. 27, p. 07-24, passed 01/08/01**)

(15) **"Development Impact Fee"** means a special and additional fee imposed pursuant to the provisions of this Chapter. (Ord. 49-97, J. 24, p. 297-299, passed 8/25/97; **Ord. 02-01, J. 27, p. 07-24, passed 01/08/01**)

(16) **"Development Impact Fee Schedule Resolution"** means the resolution to be adopted by the City Council establishing the development impact fee schedule pursuant to, and in accordance with, Section 160.301 (B) of this Chapter.

(17) **"Disbursement Agreement"** means that certain agreement, attached as Exhibit A to the intergovernmental agreement, entered into between the City and each public body, individually, for any residential development that the public body desires to receive development impact fees from and that serves as the public body's acknowledgement of the amount of development impact fees it is to receive from any such residential development, as well as the public body's agreement to indemnify the City in its administration of this Chapter.

(18) **"Dwelling Unit"** shall have the meaning ascribed to it in the Zoning Ordinance.

(19) **"Gross Acreage"** means the entire area of a parcel of real property or a building site expressed in acres or portions thereof.

(20) **"Intergovernmental Agreement"** means that certain agreement to be entered into between the City and each public body, individually, that affirms each public body's acknowledgement that this Chapter shall control the collection and distribution of development impact fees, or land in lieu of development impact fees, and that creates the responsibility for each public body to fully indemnify the City in connection with its administration of this Chapter.

(21) **"Library"** means the public library of the City.

(22) **"Lot"** shall have the meaning ascribed to it in the Zoning Ordinance.

(23) **"MAI"** means the professional designation "Member, Appraisal Institute" as conferred by The American Institute of Real Estate Appraisers.

(24) **"Park District"** means the Park District of Highland Park.

(25) **"Person"** means any individual, firm, partnership, association, corporation, organization or business, or charitable trust.

(26) **"Planned Unit Development"** shall have the same meaning ascribed to it in the Zoning Ordinance.

(27) **"Proportionate Share"** means the cost of a public facility specifically and uniquely attributable to a development; after the consideration of the generation of additional demand from the development, and any appropriate

credits for contribution of money, dedication of land, or taxes dedicated for such projects.

(28) **"Public Body"** means, collectively, the Park District, library, and school districts that have filed triennial needs assessments with the City Clerk of the City.

(29) **"Public Facility"** means any or all of the following facilities which may be financed in whole or in part by the requirement of a development impact fee:

(a) School sites and/or school district capital improvements;

(b) Park District sites and/or Park District capital improvements; and/or

(c) Library capital improvements.

(30) **"Residential Development"** means any development, as defined in this Chapter, that is (a) used, or is designed or intended to be used, entirely or in part, for residential purposes, and (b) contemplates, or results in, a net increase in the number of lots, dwelling units, or bedrooms over that which previously existed on the property on which the development is, or is to be, located.

(31) **"Retention Area"** means a wet-bottom area of land, which provides for the temporary storage of stormwater runoff.

(32) **"School District"** means the following public school districts:

(a) Bannockburn School District 106;

(b) Deerfield Public School District 109;

(c) North Shore School District 112; and

(d) Township High School District 113, situated wholly or partially within the corporate limits of the City.

(33) **"Service Standard"** means the existing level of service delivery associated with a public facility for which a development impact fee shall be required.

(34) **"Site Plan"** means a document prepared to scale indicating accurately the dimensions and boundaries of a site; and showing the location of all proposed buildings, structures, uses, and principal site development features for a parcel of land.

(35) **"Sites"** mean lands that are: (i) leased or owned, or to be leased or owned, by a public body: and (ii) used, to be used, or capable of being used for any purposes of the public body.

(36) **"Specifically and Uniquely Attributable"** means an identifiable portion of the need contained in the needs assessment for additional public facilities.

(37) **"Subdivision"** shall have the meaning ascribed to it in the Subdivision Ordinance.

(38) **"Subdivision Agreement"** means an agreement, entered into between a Developer and the City, approving and governing the subdivision of land pursuant to the Subdivision Ordinance.

(39) **"Subdivision Ordinance"** means Chapter 151 of this Code, regulating the processes and design standards applicable to the division of land within the City, as the same has been, and may from time to time hereafter be, amended.

(40) **"Table of Estimated Ultimate Population per Dwelling Unit"** means the most current version of the population projection table, by dwelling unit type and age categories, prepared by Associated Municipal Consultants, Inc., of Naperville, Illinois, a division of Ehlers & Associates, Inc., of Minneapolis, Minnesota.

(41) **"Triennial Needs Assessment"** means those certain assessments prepared, or to be prepared, by the Park District, the library, and the school districts, every three years, pursuant to which the Park District, the Library, and the School Districts plan and determine their respective needs for lands and capital improvements for which development impact fees are to be imposed for advancement of the legitimate governmental interests of the respective public bodies.

(42) **"Wetland"** means an area that is inundated or saturated by surface water or groundwater at a frequency and duration sufficient to support, and that under normal circumstances does support, a prevalence of vegetation typically adapted for life in saturated soil conditions.

(43) **"Zoning Ordinance"** means Chapter 150 of this Code, regulating the use of land within the City, as the same has been, and may from time to time hereafter be, amended.

ARTICLE III

ADMINISTRATION

Sec. 160.301 General Procedures for Development Impact Fees.

(A) Calculation of Development Impact Fees. Development impact fees established pursuant to this Chapter shall be calculated by the City Department of Community Development.

(B) Development Impact Fee Schedule Resolution. The development impact fees established pursuant to this Chapter shall be authorized annually by the City Council pursuant to a Development Impact Fee Schedule Resolution. The Development Impact Fee Schedule Resolution shall include:

(1) the Schedule of Development Impact Fees; and

(2) the effective date of the Schedule of Development Impact Fees.

(C) Review of Triennial Needs Assessment. Prior to and in its process of adopting its Development Impact Fee Schedule Resolution, the City Council shall consider and review the triennial needs assessments on file with the City Clerk to determine whether each given public body has made such modifications thereto as are deemed necessary as a result of (1) development occurring in the prior year, (2) public facilities actually constructed, (3) changing public facility needs, (4) inflation, (5) revised cost estimates for public facilities, (6) changes in the availability of other funding sources applicable to public facility projects, and (7) such other factors as may be relevant.

(D) Collection of Development Impact Fees. Development impact fees calculated and due pursuant to this Chapter shall be collected by the City Building Division prior to issuance of any building permit for a residential development, as defined herein. (Ord. 49-97, J. 24, p. 297-299, passed 8/25/97; **Ord. 02-01, J. 27, p. 07-24, passed 01/08/01**)

(E) Transfer of Funds to Accounts. Upon receipt of development impact fees, the City Building Division shall forward such fees to the City Finance Department.

(1) Establishment and Maintenance of Accounts.

(a) The City Finance Department shall establish interest-bearing accounts in a bank authorized to receive deposits of City funds.

(b) A separate account shall be established by each public body which has forwarded a copy of its needs assessment to the City Clerk of the City.

(c) Interest earned by each account shall be credited to that account and shall be used solely for the purposes specified for the funds of such account.

(d) The City Finance Department shall maintain and keep adequate financial records for each such account, which shall show the source and disbursement of all revenues, and which shall account for all moneys received.

(F) Disbursement of Funds. In order to ensure that each distribution of development impact fees from each account shall be used solely and exclusively for the provision of projects specified in a given needs assessment, prior to the City Council authorizing disbursement of any such funds in accord with Section 160.301, the City Clerk shall be in receipt of each of the following:

(1) A fully executed intergovernmental agreement between the City and the public body receiving such funds governing certain aspects of the implementation of this Chapter by the City and the public body; and.

(2) A fully executed disbursement agreement governing the specific development for which the funds are applicable; and

(3) If the development involves the division of land in accordance with the Subdivision Ordinance, a fully executed Subdivision Agreement. The pro rata share of the costs of public facilities servicing the development shall be incorporated into the Subdivision Agreement.

No Final Plat shall be approved for any development, and no impact fees shall be disbursed, without receipt by the City Clerk of the fully executed intergovernmental and disbursement agreements required pursuant to paragraphs (1) and (2) above, and the subdivision agreement required pursuant to paragraph (3) above.

Sec. 160.302 Use of Development Impact Fees.

Development impact fees paid pursuant to this Chapter shall be restricted to use solely and exclusively for paying the cost of public facilities, whether payment is made directly therefor, or as a pledge against bonds, revenue certificates, or other obligations of indebtedness.

Sec. 160.303 Effect of Development Impact Fees on Zoning and Subdivision Regulations.

This Chapter shall not affect, in any manner, the permissible use of property, density of development, design, and improvement standards and requirements; or any other aspect of the development of land or provision of public improvements subject to the zoning and subdivision regulations or other applicable regulations of the City, which shall be operative and remain in full force and effect without limitation with respect to all such development.

### Sec. 160.304 Development Impact Fees as Additional and Supplemental Requirement.

Development impact fees are additional and supplemental to, and not in substitution of, any other requirements imposed by the City on the development of land or the issuance of building permits. In no event shall a property owner be obligated to pay for public facilities in an amount in excess of the amount calculated pursuant to this Chapter; but, provided that a property owner may be required to pay, pursuant to City ordinances, regulations or policies, for other public facilities in addition to the development impact fees for public facilities as specified herein. (Ord. 49-97, J. 24, p. 297-299, passed 8/25/97)

### Sec. 160.305 Land in Lieu of Development Impact Fees.

(A) Each public body may make a request in writing to the City Council to allow for a donation of land in lieu of development impact fees related to any development. Such a request shall specifically itemize the public body's reasons for requesting land in lieu of development impact fees.

(B) Upon receipt of a request from a public body for land in lieu of development impact fees, the City Council shall consider and perform an analysis of such request, and make a determination thereon by resolution duly adopted. The resolution shall be based upon a review of the triennial needs assessment on file with the City Clerk for the public body making the request, as well as the following factors: (1) other developments occurring in the prior year within the surrounding area of the development, (2) public facilities actually constructed and servicing the surrounding area of the development, (3) changing public facility needs and capacity at existing public facilities servicing the surrounding area of the development, and (4) such other factors as the City Council may deem to be relevant.

(C) Requests of land in lieu of development impact fees shall be made specifically for the construction of public facilities or expansion of public facilities on adjacent parcels.

### ARTICLE IV

### STUDIES AND NEEDS ASSESSMENTS

### Sec. 160.401 Preparation of Triennial Needs Assessments.

Each public body shall prepare a study at least once every three years from which it shall develop its triennial needs assessment. The study may consist of a detailed examination or analysis of existing public facilities, capital improvement programs, service standards or research regarding sites, capital improvements and/or service standards.

# APPENDICES

Sec. 160.402 Use and Content of Triennial Needs Assessment.

(A) A single triennial needs assessment may be used for lands and capital facilities, and for two or more classifications of lands or buildings, if the service areas for these types of lands or buildings are congruent, and two or more public bodies join together in the preparation of a triennial needs assessment provided the assessment ultimately contains the information required under this Section for each service area served by each such public body. A triennial needs assessment shall contain the following information for each service area described in the assessment:

(1) An inventory of existing lands and buildings utilized by the public body to provide services within the service area;

(2) An identification of the area of each building within the service area and, in the case of schools, the number of students then enrolled in each school building;

(3) A projection of the character of development that is expected to occur within each service area during the succeeding 10-year period;

(4) An identification of the amount of lands that will be necessary within each service area in order to accommodate the demands of the projected development; and

(5) A general description of the total building area and, in the case of schools, temporary classrooms, if any, that will be necessary within each service area in order to provide capacity for the projected development.

(B) Public bodies that complete triennial needs assessments for the acquisition of lands; for the construction, leasing or acquisition of capital facilities; or, in the case of schools, for the leasing of temporary classrooms shall update those triennial needs assessments and shall amend their adopted lands acquisition plan and their adopted capital facilities plan based on those updated triennial needs assessments.

## ARTICLE V

## CALCULATIONS

Sec. 160.501 Source Information for Population Estimate Variable in Impact Fee Formulas.

(A) Calculation of required development impact fees or land dedication, as set forth in this Article V, shall be made in accordance with the population density projections contained in the most current version of the Table of Estimated Ultimate Population Per Dwelling Unit, as defined in this Chapter.

(B) In the event a developer files a written objection to the use of the Table of Estimated Ultimate Population Per Dwelling Unit, the developer shall obtain and submit, at his or her own cost, a demographic study showing the estimated population to be generated from the residential development; and in that event, final determination of the density formula to be used in such calculations shall be made by the City Council, in its sole discretion, based upon such demographic information submitted by the developer and from other sources which may be submitted to the City Council by a local public body.

211

Sec. 160.502 Determination of Land Value and Distribution of Development Impact Fees.

(A) Determination of Land Value. The development impact fees for schools, library and park sites shall be based on the fair market value of an acre of land for such facilities. The land value shall be used in making any calculations required in this Chapter unless the developer files a written objection thereto. In the event of any such objection, the developer, at his or her own cost, shall obtain and submit an independent appraisal from an MAI designated appraiser indicating the fair market value of such improved land in the area of the proposed development. Final determination of said fair market value per acre of such land shall be made by the City Council in its sole discretion based on such information submitted by the developer and from other sources which may be submitted to the City Council by the school district or others.

(B) Distribution of Development Impact Fees. The development impact fee for Park District capital improvements and school district capital improvements shall be collected by the City and shall be held by the City solely for the improvement of parks and schools and building sites as set forth in this Chapter to serve the immediate and future needs of the residential development. Provided the City Clerk has in his possession the respective agreements and indemnities of the Park District or school district as required by this Chapter, as the case may be, the development impact fees so collected and held shall be forwarded from time to time to the Park District and school district to be used in the funding of building sites, and for other capital improvements purposes as permitted by law. Provided the City Clerk has in his possession the agreements and indemnities of the library as required by this Chapter, the development impact fees for library capital improvement shall be collected by the City and forwarded from time to time to the library to be used in the funding of the construction of buildings, the acquisition of books, and for other purposes as permitted by law.

Sec. 160.503 Criteria for Determining School District Capital Improvement Development Impact Fee.

(A) Service Area Requirement and Population Ratio. The amount of the development impact fee required for school district capital improvement shall be directly related to the ultimate number of students estimated to be generated by the residential development. The school district capital improvement development impact fee requirement shall be determined by obtaining the product of the following: (1) the estimated number of new students to be generated by the residential development, as derived from the most current version of the Table of Estimated Ultimate Population per Dwelling Unit; times (2) the capital costs per student, as derived from the most current version of the school district's triennial needs assessment on file with the City Clerk's office; and (3) then adjusted for the school district capital improvement credit as established in this Section.

(B) School District Capital Improvement Credit. The school district capital improvement development impact fee shall be adjusted by reducing the calculated fee by 10 percent to compensate for:

(1) The present value of the future stream of real estate tax payments from the residential development allocated to the annual school district capital improvement budget; and

(2) The per student amount of state financial aid received by the school district and allocated to the annual school district capital improvement budget.

Sec. 160.504 Criteria for Determining School Site Development Impact Fee.

The following criteria shall govern the calculation of the school site development impact fee:

(A) Service Area Requirement and Population Ratio. The amount of land that would be required for a school site shall be directly related to the ultimate number of students to be generated by the residential development. The school site development impact fee requirement shall be determined by obtaining the product of the following: (1) estimated number of students to be generated by the residential development within each school classification, as derived from the most current version of the Table of Estimated Ultimate Population per Dwelling Unit; over (2) the maximum recommended number of students to be served in each such school classification as established in this Section; times (3) the recommended number of acres for a school site of each school classification as established in this Section. The product thereof shall be the acres of land deemed needed to have sufficient school site land to serve the estimated increased number of students in each such school classification. The school site development impact fee shall be the cash amount equal to the product of the number of acres required for school site times the fair market value of land per acre established in this Chapter.

(B) School Classification and Size of School Site. School classifications and the size of school building sites within the City shall be determined in accordance with the following criteria:

| School Classification by Grade | Land | | Facilities |
| --- | --- | --- | --- |
| | Capacity | Acres | Square Feet per Student |
| Elementary or Grade 0-5 | 350 | 8.5 | 105 |
| Junior High or Grades 6-8 | 600 | 26 | 162.5 |
| High School or Grades 9-12 | 1,500 | 24 | 263 |

(C) Location. Where land in lieu of development impact fees is requested, or required pursuant to Article VI of this Chapter, the comprehensive plan and the standards adopted by the affected school district shall be used as guidelines in locating sites.

213

**Sec. 160.505 Criteria for Determining Park District Capital Improvement Development Impact Fee.**

(A) Service Area Requirement and Population Ratio. The amount of the development impact fee required for Park District capital improvement shall be directly related to the ultimate number of residents estimated to be generated by the residential development. The Park District capital improvement development impact fee requirement shall be determined by obtaining the product of the following: (1) the estimated number of new residents to be generated by the residential development, as derived from the most current Table of Estimated Ultimate Population per Dwelling Unit; times (2) the capital costs per resident, as derived from the most current version of the Park District's triennial needs assessment on file with the City Clerk's office; and (3) then adjusted for the park district capital improvement credit as established in this Section.

(B) Park District Improvement Credit. The Park District capital improvement development impact fee shall be adjusted by reducing the calculated fee by 10 percent to compensate for the present value of the future stream of real estate tax payments from the residential development allocated to the annual Park District capital improvement budget.

**Sec. 160.506 Criteria for Determining Park District Site Improvement Fee.**

The following criteria shall govern the calculation of the Park District site improvement fee:

(A) Service Area Requirement and Population Ratio. The amount of land that would be required for a park site shall be directly related to the ultimate population to be generated by the residential development. The Park District site improvement fee requirement shall be determined by obtaining the product of the following: (1) estimated population to be served by the park system, as derived from the most current version of the Table of Estimated Ultimate Population per Dwelling Unit; over (2) one thousand; times (3) the sum of the recommended number of acres of park site for each park classification as established in this Section. The product thereof shall be the acres of land deemed needed to have sufficient park site land to serve the estimated increased population. The Park District site improvement fee shall be the cash amount equal to the product of the number of acres required for park site times the fair market value of land per acre established in this Chapter.

(B) Park Site Classification and Acreage per Population. Park site classifications and the minimum acres of park site per one thousand population shall be determined in accordance with the following criteria:

| Type of Park | Size Range in Acres | Minimum Acres per 1,000 Pop. |
|---|---|---|
| Mini-Park | 1 - 3 | .5 |
| Neighborhood park | 3 - 20 | 2.0 |
| Community park | 50 - 100 | 8.0 |
| Total | | 10.5 |

(C) Location. Where land in lieu of a development impact fees is requested, or required pursuant to Article VI of this Chapter, the comprehensive plan of the "Standards by Types of Recreation and Park Areas" as adopted by the City shall be used as guidelines in locating sites. Factors affecting the location of required park site dedication shall include but not be limited to:

(1) Accessibility to population served;

(2) Existence of mature vegetation;

(3) Proximity to permanent and seasonal waterways;

(4) Existence of or proximity to unique topographical features; and

(5) The value of the site as an extension of existing elements of the park system.

(D) Credit for Private Park Site. Where a private park site is included on a site plan, or in a proposed subdivision or planned unit development, and is designed to serve the immediate and future park needs of the residents of that subdivision or development; credit toward the required Park District site improvement fee may be given. The extent of such credit shall be at the sole discretion of the City Council and shall be based upon the needs of the projected residents in conformance with the total park plan for the general area. Where a private park site credit is given, the credit shall be subtracted from the Park District site improvement fee requirement as established in this Chapter. The developer shall guarantee that the private park shall be permanently maintained for such use by the execution of appropriate legal documents.

Sec. 160.507 Criteria for Determining Library Capital Improvement Impact Fee.

The following criteria shall govern the calculation of the library capital improvement development impact fee:

(A) Service Area Requirement and Population Factor. The development impact fee required for library capital improvements shall be directly related to the ultimate population to be generated by the residential development. The library development impact fee requirement shall be determined by obtaining the product of the following: (1) the estimated population generated by the residential development to be served by the library, as derived from the most current version of the Table of Estimated Ultimate Population Per Dwelling Unit; times (2) the cost per capita of library capital improvements required to serve the residential development, as derived from the Library's most current triennial needs assessment; and (3) then adjusting for library capital improvement credit as established in this Section.

(B) Library Capital Improvement Credit. The library capital improvement development impact fee shall be adjusted by reducing the calculated fee by 10 percent to compensate for:

(1) The present value of the future real estate tax payments from the residential development allocated to the annual library capital improvement budget; and

(2) The per capita amount of state financial aid received by the library and allocated to the annual library capital improvement budget.

### Sec. 160.508 Credit for Net Reduction of Any or All Lots, Dwelling Units or Bedrooms.

(A) Where a new residential development involves a net reduction in the number of any or all of the lots, dwelling units or bedrooms on the property on which the development is, or is to be, located, a credit for such net reduction shall be calculated on a "per unit of public body" basis. The amount of the credit for such net reduction shall not be less than zero and shall not be used to offset development impact fees due other public bodies calculated by reason of the new residential development.

(B) In the event a developer is entitled to a credit for the net reduction of the number of any or all of the lots, dwelling units or bedrooms on the property on which the development is, or is to be, located, and more than one lot is created from the property on which such unit or units were located, the credit shall be equally divided among all such newly created lots. The amount of such credit due per lot shall be determined at the time a new plat of subdivision is filed and the amount of the credit for each such lot shall be set forth in the Subdivision Agreement, or applicable agreement, prior to recordation.

### ARTICLE VI

### LAND CONTRIBUTIONS

### Sec. 160.601 Reservation of Additional Land.

Where land is requested in lieu of a development impact fee or in lieu of a portion of a development impact fee, and the comprehensive plan or the standards of the City call for a larger park site or school site in a particular residential development than the developer is required to dedicate, the land needed beyond the developer's dedication shall be reserved in accord with the Statutes of the State of Illinois for subsequent purchase by the City or other public body designated by the City; provided that a negotiated purchase is made within one year from the date of approval of the final plat, or if an agreement between the developer and the City is recorded outlining specific conditions for the conveyance of such property.

### Sec. 160.602 Combining with Adjoining Development.

Where land is requested in lieu of a development impact fee and the residential development is less than forty acres, where practical, a park site or school site should be combined with dedications from adjoining developments in order to produce a usable park site or school site without undue hardship on a particular developer.

### Sec. 160.603 General Site Standards.

The slope, topography and geology of the dedicated site as well as its surroundings must be suitable for its intended purpose. Wetlands shall not be accepted for City ownership and maintenance and shall not serve as a credit toward the required Park District capital improvement fee. Stormwater detention areas shall not be accepted for City ownership and maintenance, and the portion

216

of a detention area designed to function primarily as a component of the storm-water control system shall not serve as a credit toward the required Park District capital improvement fee. Retention areas shall not be accepted for City owner-ship and maintenance, and shall not serve as a credit toward the required Park District capital improvement fee. A park site shall be not less than one acre in area. Wetlands, detention areas, retention areas and areas of steep slope shall not be accepted as school sites; and shall not serve as a credit toward the re-quired school site development impact fee.

Sec. 160.604 School Site Standards.

A school site shall be dedicated in a condition ready for full infrastructure improvements as required by this Code, including but not limited to electrical service, water service, sanitary sewer, storm sewer and street improvements. Depending upon projected timing for the construction of school facilities, a cash contribution may be required in lieu of the sidewalk and street tree im-provements. The cash contribution shall be equal to the cost of such improve-ments consistent with approved engineering plans and estimates of cost.

## V. VILLAGE OF NORTHBROOK, ILLINOIS IMPACT FEE ORDINANCE

### SECTION 4-101 GENERAL SUBDIVISION AND DEVELOPMENT DESIGN AND IMPROVEMENT STANDARDS

G. Public Land Dedication and Contribution Standards.

1. General Requirement.

(a) Condition of Subdivision or Final Plat of Subdivision Approval. As a condition of approval of a Subdivision, or of a Final Plat therefor, located, entirely or in part, within a residential district, or is, or is intended to be, used, entirely or in part, for residential purposes, the Applicant therefor shall be required to dedicate land for park and recreational purposes and for school sites to serve the immediate and future needs of the residents of the proposed Subdivision, or to agree to the payment of a cash contribution in lieu of actual land dedication, or to provide a combination of land and cash contributions, at the option of the Village, in accordance with this Subsection G. *(Note: This Entire Section Revised by Ordinance No. 98-67)*

(b) Condition of Occupancy Permit. No occupancy permit shall be issued by the Village until (a) the dedication described in Subparagraph 1 (a) above has been received by the Village, or (b) the Northbrook Park District and the applicable school district delivers to the Village Manager a written acknowledgment that it has received the cash contribution described in Subparagraph 1(a) above.

(c) Applicability to All Subdivisions. As provided in Section 5-104 of this Code, the term Subdivision as used throughout this Subsection G, shall have the meaning as set forth in said Section 5-104, which meaning includes, without limitation, planned developments and developments, as such terms are defined in this Code.

(d) Applicability to Subdivisions With Existing Residential Dwelling Units. The calculation of the required dedication of land, or cash contribution in lieu thereof, shall be adjusted with respect to any new subdivision of land on which there exists, at the time of submission to the Village of an application for subdivision approval, one or more residential dwelling units. Such adjustment shall allow for the ultimate population density for such new subdivision to be reduced, proportionately, based on such existing dwelling units, irrespective of whether such existing dwelling units will remain in existence after approval of the new subdivision, or will be replaced by new dwelling units.

2. Density Formula.

(a) Population Table. The Table of Estimated Ultimate Population Per Dwelling Unit, set forth below as Table 4-1, shall be used as provided in this Subsection G to calculate the required dedication of land for park and recreational or school site purposes or for cash contributions in lieu thereof, unless a written objection thereto is filed by the Applicant with the Village Manager pursuant to Subparagraph (c) of this Paragraph 2.

218

(b) <u>Presumed Density Formula</u>. In applying Table 4-1 to a proposed Subdivision for which the types of units and number of bedrooms cannot reasonably be determined from the data and materials on file with the Village, the following types of units and bedroom data shall be used, unless a written objection thereto is filed by the Applicant with the Village Manager pursuant to Subparagraph (c) of this Paragraph 2:

|  |  |
|---|---|
| Single Family Detached: | Four bedroom unit per lot. |
| Single Family Attached: | Equal mix of two and three bedroom units at maximum unit density permitted by applicable zoning. |
| Multiple Family Dwellings in the R-6 District: | Equal mix of two and three bedroom units at maximum unit density permitted by applicable zoning. |
| Multiple Family Dwellings in the R-7 District or the R-8 District: | Equal mix of one and two bedroom units at maximum unit density permitted by applicable zoning. |

(c) <u>Objection to Density Formulae</u>. If the Applicant files a written objection with the Village Manager to the use of Table 4-1 or the presumed density formula set forth in Subparagraph (b) of this Paragraph 2, the Applicant shall submit, at the Applicants sole cost and expense, a thorough and comprehensive demographic study showing the estimated population to be generated by the proposed Subdivision. The Board of Trustees shall make the final determination as to the density formula and estimated population that shall apply to the proposed Subdivision, which final decision shall be based on the demographic study submitted by the Applicant and all other facts and circumstances relevant to the issue as determined and required by the Board of Trustees. Nothing in this Subparagraph (c) shall be construed as limiting or preventing the Board of Trustees from utilizing Table 4-1 or the presumed density formula set forth in Subparagraph (b) of this Paragraph 2 for any proposed Subdivision.

3. <u>Criteria For Park Land Dedication</u>.

(a) <u>Calculation Of Land Required To Be Dedicated</u>. The amount of land required to be dedicated for park and recreational purposes for a proposed Subdivision shall be a direct function of the ultimate population density of that Subdivision. The requirement shall be based on a standard of five acres of land per 1,000 ultimate population, computed in accordance with Paragraph and Table 4-1 of this Subsection.

(b) <u>Location Of Land To Be Dedicated</u>. The location of the land to be dedicated for park and recreational purposes for the proposed Subdivision pursuant to this Subsection G shall be determined by the Northbrook Park District Board of Commissioners. The determination shall be based on such factors as the Northbrook Park District shall deem appropriate, including specifically, but without limitation, the availability of land, the suitability of any particular land for park and recreational purposes as opposed to use for other development, the location of the land relative to population concentrations, and the proximity of the land to other park or recreational lands.

(c) Minimum Size of Dedicated Land. The minimum size of any land to be dedicated for park and recreational purposes shall be 87,120 square feet, and no dimension shall be less than 100 feet; provided, however, that the Board of Trustees may approve dedications of a smaller size or dimension when required by the specific plans of the proposed Subdivision and when the usefulness of the smaller area for park and recreational purposes is clearly demonstrated.

(d) On-Site Storage Prohibited. No materials, including, without limitation, top soil or other soil materials, shall be stored on any land that has been dedicated, or that has been designated for dedication, to the Village for park or recreational purposes pursuant to this Subsection G.

(e) Detention and Retention Areas Not Qualified. No stormwater detention or retention area shall qualify as land suitable for dedication for park and recreational purposes, unless the suitability of such land for park and recreational purposes as a secondary use is clearly demonstrated to the satisfaction of the Northbrook Park District Board of Commissioners.

4. Criteria for School Site Land Dedication.

(a) Calculation of Land Required to Be Dedicated. The amount of land required to be dedicated for school sites for a proposed Subdivision shall be a direct function of the ultimate number of students to be generated by the Subdivision. The school site land dedication requirement shall be determined in accordance with the following equation:

(1) Number of children from the proposed Subdivision to be served in each school classification (computed in accordance with Table 4-1)

*divided by:*

(2) Maximum number of students to be served in each such school classification (as stated in Subparagraph (b) of this Paragraph 4)

*multiplied by:*

(3) Minimum number of acres for each school site for each such school classification (as stated in Subparagraph (b) of this Paragraph 4)

The product of such calculation shall be the minimum acreage of land necessary for school sites to serve the children in the proposed Subdivision.

(b) School Classifications; Land Required. School classifications and the required minimum size of new school sites within the Village shall be determined in accordance with the following criteria:

| School Classification by Grades | Maximum Number of Students for Each Such Classification | Minimum Number of Acres Per Site of Such Classification |
|---|---|---|
| **Elementary Schools (K-8)** | | |
| Grades Kindergarten Through 8th | 900 Students | 14 Acres |
| **High Schools (9-12)** Grades 9th Through 12th | 2000 Students | 55 Acres |

(c) Location of Land to Be Dedicated. The location of each school site shall be determined by the Board of Trustees. The Villages official Comprehensive Plan and the standards adopted by the affected school district shall be used as guidelines in locating school sites.

(d) On-Site Storage Prohibited. No materials, including, without limitation, top soil or other soil materials, shall be stored on any land that has been dedicated, or that has been designated for dedication, to the Village for school site purposes pursuant to this Subsection.

(e) Detention and Retention Areas Not Qualified. No stormwater detention or retention area shall qualify as land suitable for dedication for a school site, unless the suitability of such land for such school site as a secondary use is clearly demonstrated to the satisfaction of the Board of Trustees.

5. Criteria for Payment in Lieu of Land Dedication.

(a) General Qualification. In the event that a proposed Subdivision is small and the resulting required land dedication is too small, in the determination of the Board of Trustees, to be practical, or when the Board of Trustees finds that the available land is inappropriate for park and recreational purposes or for a school site, then the Village shall have the authority to require the Applicant to pay a cash contribution in lieu of the otherwise required land dedications, in accordance with the standards of this Paragraph 5.

(b) Definition of Fair Market Value. The cash contributions in lieu of land shall be based on the fair market value of the acres of land in the proposed Subdivision, as determined by the Board of Trustees based on the value of improved land in and surrounding the Village. The fair market value figure shall be set forth in the Villages annual fee ordinance and shall be used in making any calculation required by this Subsection, unless the Applicant or other affected party files an objection pursuant to Subparagraph (c) of this Paragraph 5. The Village Manager shall periodically, but no less frequently than annually, survey surrounding communities, conduct discussions with the applicable Township Assessors office, affected school districts, and other interested parties, and shall report findings of such surveys and communications to the Board of Trustees with respect to the continued adequacy and reasonableness of the Villages determination of fair market value as set forth in the annual fee ordinance.

(c) Objection to Fair Market Value Determination. If the Applicant or any other affected person files a written objection with the Village Manager to the fair market value as established pursuant to Subparagraph (b) of this Paragraph 5, and as set forth in the annual fee ordinance, the Applicant or other affected person shall submit, at their sole cost and expense, a written appraisal professionally prepared by a Member of the Appraisal Institute of America (M.A.I). The appraisal shall show the fair market value of improved land in the area of the proposed Subdivision. Upon receipt of such objection, the Village Manager shall cause the same to be delivered to the Northbrook Park District and the applicable school district. The Northbrook Park District and the applicable school district shall have the right, but not the obligation, within 30 days after receipt of the objection from the Village Manager, to make a recommendation regarding the disposition of such objection. The Board of Trustees shall make the final determination as to the fair market value of such improved land, which final determination shall be based on the appraisal or other information submitted by the Applicant or other affected person, the recommendations, if any, received from the Northbrook Park District and the applicable school district, and all other facts and circumstances relevant to the issue as determined and required by the Board of Trustees. Nothing in this Subparagraph (c) shall be construed as limiting or preventing the Board of Trustees from utilizing the fair market value as established in Subparagraph (b) of this Paragraph for any proposed Subdivision.

(d) Disposition of Cash Contributions.

(1) Cash contributions in lieu of park land dedications shall be paid directly to the Northbrook Park District solely for use in the acquisition or development of park and recreational land to serve the immediate or future needs of the residents of the Proposed Subdivision or for the improvement of other existing local park and recreational sites.

(2) Cash contributions in lieu of school site land dedications shall be paid directly to the applicable school district or districts, as the case may be, solely for use in the acquisition of land for a school site to serve the immediate or future needs of students from the proposed Subdivision or for the improvement to any existing school site already serving such needs.

(3) All cash contributions made pursuant to this Subsection shall be held in trust by the public body to whom the cash contributions are paid and shall be kept separate from all other funds and shall be accounted for in the appropriate manner.

(e) Refund of Cash Contributions. If any portion of a cash contribution in lieu of a park land dedication, or a cash contribution in lieu of a school site land dedication, as the case may be, is not expended for the purposes set forth herein within seven years after the date of receipt of such contribution by the Northbrook Park District or applicable school district, then that cash contribution shall be refunded to the Applicant who made such contribution, or its successor or assign.

6. Criteria for Combination Land Dedication and Cash Payment. A combination of land dedication and cash contribution in lieu of land dedication may be required when appropriate as determined by the Board of Trustees, including, without limitation, in the following two circumstances:

(a) Inadequate Land. The proposed Subdivision has some but not enough adequate land to meet the dedication requirements of this Subsection. That portion of the land within the proposed Subdivision that is adequate for park land or a school site shall be dedicated as provided in this Subsection, and a cash contribution shall be required for any additional land that would have been required to be dedicated pursuant to this Subsection.

(b) Previous Acquisition. A major part of the local park or recreational site or school site already has been acquired and only a small parcel of land is needed from the proposed Subdivision to complete the site. Such parcel shall be acquired by dedication, and a cash contribution shall be required for any additional land that would have been required to be dedicated pursuant to this Subsection.

7. Reservation of Additional Land. When the Villages Official Comprehensive Plan or other applicable standard of the Village requires a larger amount of park and recreational land or a larger school site in a particular Subdivision than the Applicant is otherwise required to dedicate pursuant to the terms of this Subsection, then the land needed in excess of the otherwise required dedication shall be reserved by the Applicant for subsequent purchase by the applicable other public body, provided that such acquisition is started within one year after the date of approval of the Final Plat for the proposed Subdivision.

8. Combining With Adjoining Subdivisions. For proposed Subdivisions of 40 acres or less, the otherwise applicable park and recreational land dedication or school site land dedication may be combined, where practical as determined by the Board of Trustees, with dedications for the same purposes from adjoining subdivisions or developments to produce usable park or recreational areas or school sites.

9. Topography and Grading. The slope, topography, and geology of a site to be dedicated pursuant to the requirements of this Subsection, as well as its surroundings, shall be suitable for the intended purpose of the site. Grading on dedicated land shall not differ greatly from surrounding land. No removal of existing topsoil shall be permitted.

10. Improved Sites. All sites shall be dedicated in a condition ready for full service of electrical, telecommunications, gas, water, sewer and streets (including curb and gutter and enclosed drainage), as applicable to the location of the site, or acceptable provisions shall be made therefor.

11. Dedication Required as Part of Annexation Agreement. Unless waived by the Board of Trustees in its sole and absolute discretion, the dedication of land, or cash contributions in lieu thereof, required by this Subsection also shall be required as a condition of the annexation of any land to the Village for residential purposes. However, the same shall not be required as condition to an amendment of an annexation agreement unless the Board of Trustees finds from a consideration of the purposes of this Subsection that such dedications or payments should be required because of increased burdens to be placed on schools and the park system over and above those covered by the dedications and cash contributions made or provided for in connection with the original annexation agreement. If the Board of Trustees does so find, then additional dedications or cash contributions shall be required, but only to the extent necessary to cover the shortage resulting from such increased burdens. Dedications of land or cash contributions in lieu thereof as specified in any annexation agree-

ment that substantially comply with the requirements of this Subsection shall be deemed to have fulfilled the dedication requirements of this Subsection.

12. Dedication as Condition of Approval of Final Plat. Approval of any Final Plat of Subdivision shall be conditioned on the dedication of land, or cash donations in lieu thereof, as required by this Subsection. When a Subdivision is to be developed over a period of years, dedication of required land may be made after completion of a portion of the Subdivision provided that an escrow fund satisfactory to the Village has been established to guarantee the conveyance of land after completion of such portion of the Subdivision.

13. Title to Dedicated Park Land and School Sites.

(a) General Requirement. All sites to be dedicated pursuant to this Subsection shall be conveyed to the Village either by warranty or trustees deed, or such form of conveyance as the Village shall require. The Applicant shall be responsible for payment of all real estate taxes to the date of conveyance, including any agricultural roll back taxes that might be extended or levied against such sites. In the discretion of the Village, a commitment for title insurance issued by a company authorized to do business in Illinois may be required as evidence of clear title.

(b) Park Land. Conveyance of park land dedications shall occur only after or simultaneously with the passage of an ordinance or resolution by the Northbrook Park District (or by the Village if the Subdivision is not located within the Northbrook Park District), in which it indicates that the land will be accepted by the Park District or by the Village, as the case may be, for park purposes. If the land is in the Park District, then immediately after the adoption of the Park District resolution or ordinance, the Village shall convey the land to the Park District.

(c) School Sites. Conveyance of school sites shall occur only after or simultaneously with the passage of an ordinance or resolution by the school district in which the Subdivision is located in which the district indicates that the site will be accepted by the district for school purposes. Immediately thereafter, the Village shall convey the site to the district.

14. Remedies.

(a) Intergovernmental Agreement. The Northbrook Park District and the affected school districts shall be required, as a condition of receiving the dedications or donations hereunder, to enter into a binding, written intergovernmental agreement with the Village, acceptable in form and content to the Village Attorney, providing for the indemnification and holding harmless of the Village from any loss, claims and causes of actions of every kind that may be incurred by the Village as a result, either directly or indirectly, of the enactment of this Subsection, or the administration or enforcement thereof, including any loss, claims, or causes of action incurred as a result of a lawsuit brought or threatened by the Northbrook Park District or the affected school district. The intergovernmental agreement shall provide that if the Village is sued by any Applicant, subdivider, or developer as a result, directly or indirectly, of the enactment of this Subsection, the Village may, at its option, undertake the defense, and the Villages costs and expenses related thereto, including attorneys fees, shall be immediately reimbursed by the Northbrook Park District and affected school district, as the case may be.

(b) Improper Use of Funds. Where the Northbrook Park District or a school district improperly uses funds or fails to use funds and does not return same as specified in this Subsection, the Village may sue the Park District or the affected school district, or both, as the case may be, and shall be entitled to recover as a part of the judgment therein, or any settlement thereof, all costs and expenses, including attorneys fees, incurred by the Village.

(c) Implied Conditions. Unless otherwise specifically provided, the provisions of this Subsection shall be an implied condition of every intergovernmental agreement entered into pursuant to this Subsection. *(Note: This Entire* Section *Revised by Ordinance No. 98-67)*

## VI. HAWAII DEVELOPMENT AGREEMENT STATUTE

[§46-121]. Findings and purpose

The legislature finds that with land use laws taking on refinements that make the development of land complex, time consuming, and requiring advance financial commitments, the development approval process involves the expenditure of considerable sums of money. Generally speaking, the larger the project contemplated, the greater the expenses and the more time involved in complying with the conditions precedent to filing for a building permit.

The lack of certainty in the development approval process can result in a waste of resources, escalate the cost of housing and other development to the consumer, and discourage investment in and commitment to comprehensive planning. Predictability would encourage maximum efficient utilization of resources at the least economic cost to the public.

Public benefits derived from development agreements may include, but are not limited to, affordable housing, design standards, and on- and off-site infrastructure and other improvements. Such benefits may be negotiated for in return for the vesting of development rights for a specific period.

Under appropriate circumstances, development agreements could strengthen the public planning process, encourage private and public participation in the comprehensive planning process, reduce the economic cost of development, allow for the orderly planning of public facilities and services and the allocation of cost. As an administrative act, development agreements will provide assurances to the applicant for a particular development project, that upon approval of the project, the applicant may proceed with the project in accordance with all applicable statutes, ordinances, resolutions, rules, and policies in existence at the time the development agreement is executed and that the project will not be restricted or prohibited by the county's subsequent enactment or adoption of laws, ordinances, resolutions, rules, or policies.

Development agreements will encourage the vesting of property rights by protecting such rights from the effect of subsequently enacted county legislation which may conflict with any term or provision of the development agreement or in any way hinder, restrict, or prevent the development of the project. Development agreements are intended to provide a reasonable certainty as to the lawful requirements that must be met in protecting vested property rights, while maintaining the authority and duty of government to enact and enforce laws which promote the public safety, health, and general welfare of the citizens of our State. The purpose of this part is to provide a means by which an individual may be assured at a specific point in time that having met or having agreed to meet all of the terms and conditions of the development agreement, the individual's rights to develop a property in a certain manner shall be vested.

[§46-122]. Definitions

The following terms when used in this chapter shall have the following respective meanings:

"County executive agency" means any department, office, board, or commission of a county.

"County legislative body" means the city council or county council of a county.

"Person" means an individual, group, partnership, firm, association, corporation, trust, governmental agency, governmental official, administrative body, or tribunal or any form of business or legal entity.

"Principal" means a person who has entered into a development agreement pursuant to the procedures specified in this chapter, including a successor in interest.

[§46-123]. General authorization

Any county by ordinance may authorize the executive branch of the county to enter into a development agreement with any person having a legal or equitable interest in real property, for the development of such property in accordance with this part; provided that such an ordinance shall:

(1) Establish procedures and requirements for the consideration of development agreements upon application by or on behalf of persons having a legal or equitable interest in the property, in accordance with this part;

(2) Designate a county executive agency to administer the agreements after such agreements become effective;

(3) Include provisions to require the designated agency to conduct a review of compliance with the terms and conditions of the development agreement, on a periodic basis as established by the development agreement; and

(4) Include provisions establishing reasonable time periods for the review and appeal of modifications of the development agreement.

[§46-124]. Negotiating development agreements

The mayor or the designated agency appointed to administer development agreements may make such arrangements as may be necessary or proper to enter into development agreements, including negotiating and drafting individual development agreements; provided that the county has adopted an ordinance pursuant to section 46-123.

The final draft of each individual development agreement shall be presented to the county legislative body for approval or modification prior to execution. To be binding on the county, a development agreement must be approved by the county legislative body and executed by the mayor on behalf of the county. County legislative approval shall be by resolution adopted by a majority of the membership of the county legislative body.

[§46-125]. Periodic review; termination of agreement

(a) If, as a result of a periodic review, the designated agency finds and determines that the principal has committed a material breach of the terms or conditions of the agreement, the designated agency shall serve notice in writing,

227

within a reasonable time period after the periodic review, upon the principal setting forth with reasonable particularity the nature of the breach and the evidence supporting the finding and determination, and providing the principal a reasonable time period in which to cure such material breach.

(b) If the principal fails to cure the material breach within the time period given, then the county unilaterally may terminate or modify the agreement; provided that the designated agency has first given the principal the opportunity, (1) to rebut the finding and determination; or (2) to consent to amend the agreement to meet the concerns of the designated agency with respect to the finding and determination.

[§46-126]. Development agreement; provisions

(a) A development agreement shall:
(1) Describe the land subject to the development agreement;
(2) Specify the permitted uses of the property, the density or intensity of use, and the maximum height and size of proposed buildings;
(3) Provide, where appropriate, for reservation or dedication of land for public purposes as may be required or permitted pursuant to laws, ordinances, resolutions, rules, or policies in effect at the time of entering into the agreement; and
(4) Provide a termination date; provided that the parties shall not be precluded from extending the termination date by mutual agreement or from entering subsequent development agreements.

(b) The development agreement may provide commencement dates and completion dates; provided that such dates as may be set forth in the agreement may be extended at the discretion of the county at the request of the principal upon good cause shown subject to subsection (a)(4).

(c) The development agreement also may cover any other matter not inconsistent with this chapter, nor prohibited by law.

(d) In addition to the county and principal, any federal, state, or local government agency or body may be included as a party to the development agreement. If more than one government body is made party to an agreement, the agreement shall specify which agency shall be responsible for the overall administration of the agreement.

[§46-127]. Enforceability; applicability

(a) Unless terminated pursuant to section 46-125 or unless canceled pursuant to section 46-130, a development agreement, amended development agreement, or modified development agreement once entered into, shall be enforceable by any party thereto, or their successors in interest, notwithstanding any subsequent change in any applicable law adopted by the county entering into such agreement, which alter or amend the laws, ordinances, resolutions, rules, or policies specified in this part.

(b) All laws, ordinances, resolutions, rules, and policies governing permitted uses of the land that is the subject of the development agreement, including but not limited to uses, density, design, height, size, and building specification of proposed buildings, construction standards and specifications, and water utilization requirements applicable to the development of the property subject to a development agreement, shall be those laws, ordinances, resolutions, rules, regulations, and policies made applicable and in force at the time of execution of the agreement, notwithstanding any subsequent change in any applicable law adopted by the county entering into such agreement, which alter or amend the laws, ordinances, resolutions, rules, or policies specified in this part and such subsequent change shall be void as applied to property subject to such agreement to the extent that it changes any law, ordinance, resolution, rule, or policy which any party to the agreement has agreed to maintain in force as written at the time of execution; provided that a development agreement shall not prevent a government body from requiring the principal from complying with laws, ordinances, resolutions, rules, and policies of general applicability enacted subsequent to the date of the development agreement if they could have been lawfully applied to the property which is the subject of the development agreement at the time of execution of the agreement if the government body finds it necessary to impose the requirements because a failure to do so would place the residents of the subdivision or of the immediate community, or both, in a condition perilous to the residents' health or safety, or both.

[§46-128]. Public hearing

No development agreement shall be entered into unless a public hearing on the application therefor first shall have been held by the county legislative body.

[§46-129]. County general plan and development plans

No development agreement shall be entered into unless the county legislative body finds that the provisions of the proposed development agreement are consistent with the county's general plan and any applicable development plan, effective as of the effective date of the development agreement.

[§46-130]. Amendment or cancellation

A development agreement may be amended or canceled, in whole or in part, by mutual consent of the parties to the agreement, or their successors in interest; provided that if the county determines that a proposed amendment would substantially alter the original development agreement, a public hearing on the amendment shall be held by the county legislative body before it consents to the proposed amendment.

[§46-131]. Administrative act

Each development agreement shall be deemed an administrative act of the government body made party to the agreement.

[§46-132]. Filing or recordation

The designated agency shall be responsible to file or record a copy of the development agreement or an amendment to such agreement in the office of the assistant registrar of the land court of the State of Hawaii or in the bureau of conveyances, or both, whichever is appropriate, within twenty days after the county enters into a development agreement or an amendment to such an agreement. The burdens of the agreement shall be binding upon, and the benefits of the agreement shall inure to, all successors in interest to the parties to the agreement.

# APPENDICES

## VII. CALIFORNIA DEVELOPMENT AGREEMENT STATUTE

65864. The Legislature finds and declares that:

(a) The lack of certainty in the approval of development projects can result in a waste of resources, escalate the cost of housing and other development to the consumer, and discourage investment in and commitment to comprehensive planning which would make maximum efficient utilization of resources at the least economic cost to the public.

(b) Assurance to the applicant for a development project that upon approval of the project, the applicant may proceed with the project in accordance with existing policies, rules and regulations, and subject to conditions of approval, will strengthen the public planning process, encourage private participation in comprehensive planning, and reduce the economic costs of development.

(c) The lack of public facilities, including, but not limited to, streets, sewerage, transportation, drinking water, school, and utility facilities, is a serious impediment to the development of new housing. Whenever possible, applicants and local governments may include provisions in agreements whereby applicants are reimbursed over time for financing public facilities.

65865. (a) Any city, county, or city and county, may enter into a development agreement with any person having a legal or equitable interest in real property for the development of the property as provided in this article.

(b) Any city may enter into a development agreement with any person having a legal or equitable interest in real property in unincorporated territory within that city's sphere of influence for the development of the property as provided in this article. However, the agreement shall not become operative unless annexation proceedings annexing the property to the city are completed within the period of time specified by the agreement. If the annexation is not completed within the time specified in the agreement or any extension of the agreement, the agreement is null and void.

(c) Every city, county, or city and county, shall, upon request of an applicant, by resolution or ordinance, establish procedures and requirements for the consideration of development agreements upon application by, or on behalf of, the property owner or other person having a legal or equitable interest in the property.

(d) A city, county, or city and county may recover from applicants the direct costs associated with adopting a resolution or ordinance to establish procedures and requirements for the consideration of development agreements.

65865.1. Procedures established pursuant to Section 65865 shall include provisions requiring periodic review at least every 12 months, at which time the applicant, or successor in interest thereto, shall be required to demonstrate good faith compliance with the terms of the agreement. If, as a result of such periodic review, the local agency finds and determines, on the basis of substantial evidence, that the applicant or successor in interest thereto has not complied in good faith with terms or conditions of the agreement, the local agency may terminate or modify the agreement.

65865.2. A development agreement shall specify the duration of the agreement, the permitted uses of the property, the density or intensity of use, the maximum height and size of proposed buildings, and provisions for reservation or dedication of land for public purposes. The development agreement may include conditions, terms, restrictions, and requirements for subsequent discretionary actions, provided that such conditions, terms, restrictions, and requirements for subsequent discretionary actions shall not prevent development of the land for the uses and to the density or intensity of development set forth in the agreement. The agreement may provide that construction shall be commenced within a specified time and that the project or any phase thereof be completed within a specified time. The agreement may also include terms and conditions relating to applicant financing of necessary public facilities and subsequent reimbursement over time.

65865.3. (a) Except as otherwise provided in subdivisions (b) and (c), Section 65868, or Section 65869.5, notwithstanding any other law, if a newly incorporated city or newly annexed area comprises territory that was formerly unincorporated, any development agreement entered into by the county prior to the effective date of the incorporation or annexation shall remain valid for the duration of the agreement, or eight years from the effective date of the incorporation or annexation, whichever is earlier. The holder of the development agreement and the city may agree that the development agreement shall remain valid for more than eight years, provided that

the longer period shall not exceed 15 years from the effective date of the incorporation or annexation. The holder of the development agreement and the city shall have the same rights and obligations with respect to each other as if the property had remained in the unincorporated territory of the county.

(b) The city may modify or suspend the provisions of the development agreement if the city determines that the failure of the city to do so would place the residents of the territory subject to

the development agreement, or the residents of the city, or both, in a condition dangerous to their health or safety, or both.

(c) Except as otherwise provided in subdivision (d), this section applies to any development agreement which meets all of the following requirements:

(1) The application for the agreement is submitted to the county prior to the date that the first signature was affixed to the petition for incorporation or annexation pursuant to Section 56704 or

the adoption of the resolution pursuant to Section 56800, whichever occurs first.

(2) The county enters into the agreement with the applicant prior to the date of the election on the question of incorporation or annexation, or, in the case of an annexation without an election pursuant to Section 57075, prior to the date that the conducting authority orders the annexation.

(3) The annexation proposal is initiated by the city. If the annexation proposal is initiated by a petitioner other than the city, the development agreement is valid unless the city adopts written findings that implementation of the devel-

opment agreement would create a condition injurious to the health, safety, or welfare of city residents.

(d) This section does not apply to any territory subject to a development agreement if that territory is incorporated and the effective date of the incorporation is prior to January 1, 1987.

65865.4. Unless amended or canceled pursuant to Section 65868, or modified or suspended pursuant to Section 65869.5, and except as otherwise provided in subdivision (b) of Section 65865.3, a development agreement shall be enforceable by any party thereto notwithstanding any change in any applicable general or specific plan, zoning, subdivision, or building regulation adopted by the city, county, or city and county entering the agreement, which alters or amends the rules, regulations, or policies specified in Section 65866.

65866. Unless otherwise provided by the development agreement, rules, regulations, and official policies governing permitted uses of the land, governing density, and governing design, improvement, and construction standards and specifications, applicable to development of the property subject to a development agreement, shall be those rules, regulations, and official policies in force at the time of execution of the agreement. A development agreement shall not prevent a city, county, or city and county, in subsequent actions applicable to the property, from applying new rules, regulations, and policies which do not conflict with those rules, regulations, and policies applicable to the property as set forth herein, nor shall a development agreement prevent a city, county, or city and county from denying or conditionally approving any subsequent development project application on the basis of such existing or new rules, regulations, and policies.

65867. A public hearing on an application for a development agreement shall be held by the planning agency and by the legislative body. Notice of intention to consider adoption of a development agreement shall be given as provided in Sections 65090 and 65091 in addition to any other notice required by law for other actions to be considered concurrently with the development agreement.

65867.5. (a) A development agreement is a legislative act that shall be approved by ordinance and is subject to referendum.

(b) A development agreement shall not be approved unless the legislative body finds that the provisions of the agreement are consistent with the general plan and any applicable specific plan.

(c) A development agreement that includes a subdivision, as defined in Section 66473.7, shall not be approved unless the agreement provides that any tentative map prepared for the subdivision will comply with the provisions of Section 66473.7.

65868. A development agreement may be amended, or canceled in whole or in part, by mutual consent of the parties to the agreement or their successors in interest. Notice of intention to amend or cancel any portion of the agreement shall be given in the manner provided by Section 65867. An amendment to an agreement shall be subject to the provisions of Section 65867.5.

65868.5. No later than 10 days after a city, county, or city and county enters into a development agreement, the clerk of the legislative body shall record with the county recorder a copy of the agreement, which shall describe the land subject thereto. From and after the time of such recordation, the agreement shall impart such notice thereof to all persons as is afforded by the recording laws of this state. The burdens of the agreement shall be binding upon, and the benefits of the agreement shall inure to, all successors in interest to the parties to the agreement.

65869. A development agreement shall not be applicable to any development project located in an area for which a local coastal program is required to be prepared and certified pursuant to the requirements of Division 20 (commencing with Section 30000) of the Public Resources Code, unless: (1) the required local coastal program has been certified as required by such provisions prior to the date on which the development agreement is entered into, or (2) in the event that the required local coastal program has not been certified, the California Coastal Commission approves such development agreement by formal commission action.

65869.5. In the event that state or federal laws or regulations, enacted after a development agreement has been entered into, prevent or preclude compliance with one or more provisions of the development agreement, such provisions of the agreement shall be modified or suspended as may be necessary to comply with such state or federal laws or regulations.

## VIII. WASHINGTON DEVELOPMENT AGREEMENT STATUTE

### RCW 36.70B.170 Development agreements—Authorized.

(1) A local government may enter into a development agreement with a person having ownership or control of real property within its jurisdiction. A city may enter into a development agreement for real property outside its boundaries as part of a proposed annexation or a service agreement. A development agreement must set forth the development standards and other provisions that shall apply to and govern and vest the development, use, and mitigation of the development of the real property for the duration specified in the agreement. A development agreement shall be consistent with applicable development regulations adopted by a local government planning under chapter 36.70A RCW.

(2) RCW through and section 501, chapter 347, Laws of 1995 do not affect the validity of a contract rezone, concomitant agreement, annexation agreement, or other agreement in existence on July 23, 1995, or adopted under separate authority, that includes some or all of the development standards provided in subsection (3) of this section.

(3) For the purposes of this section, "development standards" includes, but is not limited to:

(a) Project elements such as permitted uses, residential densities, and nonresidential densities and intensities or building sizes;

(b) The amount and payment of impact fees imposed or agreed to in accordance with any applicable provisions of state law, any reimbursement provisions, other financial contributions by the property owner, inspection fees, or dedications;

(c) Mitigation measures, development conditions, and other requirements under chapter 43.21C RCW;

(d) Design standards such as maximum heights, setbacks, drainage and water quality requirements, landscaping, and other development features;

(e) Affordable housing;

(f) Parks and open space preservation;

(g) Phasing;

(h) Review procedures and standards for implementing decisions;

(i) A build-out or vesting period for applicable standards; and

(j) Any other appropriate development requirement or procedure.

(4) The execution of a development agreement is a proper exercise of county and city police power and contract authority. A development agreement may obligate a party to fund or provide services, infrastructure, or other facilities. A development agreement shall reserve authority to impose new or different regulations to the extent required by a serious threat to public health and safety.

### RCW 36.70B.180 Development agreements—Effect.

Unless amended or terminated, a development agreement is enforceable during its term by a party to the agreement. A development agreement and the development standards in the agreement govern during the term of the agreement, or for all or that part of the build-out period specified in the agreement, and may not be subject to an amendment to a zoning ordinance or development standard or regulation or a new zoning ordinance or development standard or regulation adopted after the effective date of the agreement. A permit or approval issued by the county or city after the execution of the development agreement must be consistent with the development agreement.

**RCW 36.70B.190 Development agreements—Recording—Parties and successors bound.**

A development agreement shall be recorded with the real property records of the county in which the property is located. During the term of the development agreement, the agreement is binding on the parties and their successors, including a city that assumes jurisdiction through incorporation or annexation of the area covering the property covered by the development agreement.

**RCW 36.70B.200 Development agreements—Public hearing.**

A county or city shall only approve a development agreement by ordinance or resolution after a public hearing. The county or city legislative body or a planning commission, hearing examiner, or other body designated by the legislative body to conduct the public hearing may conduct the hearing. If the development agreement relates to a project permit application, the provisions of chapter 36.70C RCW shall apply to the appeal of the decision on the development agreement.

**RCW 36.70B.210 Development agreements—Authority to impose fees not extended.**

Nothing in RCW 36.70B.170 through 36.70B.200 and section 501, chapter 347, Laws of 1995 is intended to authorize local governments to impose impact fees, inspection fees, or dedications or to require any other financial contributions or mitigation measures except as expressly authorized by other applicable provisions of state law.

## IX. ARIZONA DEVELOPMENT AGREEMENT STATUTE

9-500.05. Development agreements; public safety; definitions

A. A municipality, by resolution or ordinance, may enter into development agreements relating to property in the municipality and to property located outside the incorporated area of the municipality. If the development agreement relates to property located outside the incorporated area of the municipality, the development agreement does not become operative unless annexation proceedings to annex the property to the municipality are completed within the period of time specified by the development agreement or any extension of such time.

B. A development agreement shall be consistent with the municipality's general plan or specific plan, if any, as defined in section 9-461, applicable to the property on the date the development agreement is executed.

C. A development agreement may be amended, or cancelled in whole or in part, by mutual consent of the parties to the development agreement or by their successors in interest or assigns.

D. No later than ten days after a municipality enters into a development agreement, the municipality shall record a copy of the agreement with the county recorder of the county in which the property subject to the development agreement is located, and the recordation constitutes notice of the development agreement to all persons. The burdens of the development agreement are binding on, and the benefits of the development agreement inure to, the parties to the agreement and to all their successors in interest and assigns.

E. Section 32-2181 does not apply to development agreements under this section.

F. Notwithstanding any other law, a municipality may provide by resolution or ordinance for public safety purposes, and with the written consent of an owner of property that has been granted a development agreement pursuant to this section, an owner of a protected development right pursuant to chapter 11 of this title or the owner of any other residential or commercial development subject to the supervision of a municipality pursuant to this title, for the application and enforcement of speed limits, vehicle weight restrictions or other safety measures on a private road that is located in any development in the municipality and that is open to and used by the public. A municipality may require payment from the property owner of the actual cost of signs for speed limits or other restrictions applicable on the private road, before their installation.

G. In this section, unless the context otherwise requires:

1. "Development agreement" means an agreement between a municipality and a community facilities district pursuant to section 48-709, subsection C, a landowner or any other person having an interest in real property that may specify or otherwise relate to any of the following:

(a) The duration of the development agreement.

(b) The permitted uses of property subject to the development agreement.

(c) The density and intensity of uses and the maximum height and size of proposed buildings within such property.

(d) Provisions for reservation or dedication of land for public purposes and provisions to protect environmentally sensitive lands.

(e) Provisions for preservation and restoration of historic structures.

(f) The phasing or time of construction or development on property subject to the development agreement.

(g) Conditions, terms, restrictions and requirements for public infrastructure and the financing of public infrastructure and subsequent reimbursements over time.

(h) Conditions, terms, restrictions and requirements for annexation of property by the municipality and the phasing or timing of annexation of property by the municipality.

(i) Conditions, terms, restrictions and requirements of deannexation of property from one municipality to another municipality and the phasing or timing of deannexation of property from one municipality to another municipality.

(j) Conditions, terms, restrictions and requirements relating to the governing body's intent to form a special taxing district pursuant to title 48.

(k) Any other matters relating to the development of the property.

2. "Governing body" means the body or board which by law is constituted as the legislative body of the municipality.

3. "Municipality" means an incorporated city or town.

## X. SAMPLE DEVELOPMENT AGREEMENT (CALIFORNIA)[1]

**Development Agreement by and between the City
of _____ and _____ Relative to
the Development Known as _____ .**

THIS DEVELOPMENT AGREEMENT is made and entered into this \_\_\_\_
day of \_\_\_\_\_, 20\_\_, by and between the CITY OF _____ \_\_\_\_,
a political subdivision of the Stare of California ("City"), and
_____ , a California corporation ("Developer"), pursu-
ant to the authority of Article 2.5, Chapter 4, Division 1, Title 7 (Section 65864,
et seq. of the Government Code) relating to Development Agreements.

### RECITALS

1. In order to strengthen the public land use planning process, to encourage
private participation in the process, to reduce the economic risk of development
and to reduce the waste of resources, the Legislature adopted the Development
Agreement Statutes (Section 65864, et seq. of the Government Code).

2. The Development Agreement Law permits cities and counties to contract with private interests for their mutual benefit in a manner not otherwise
available to the contracting parties. Such agreements, as authorized by the
Development Agreement Law, can assure property developers they may proceed with projects assured that approvals granted by public agencies will not
change during the period of development of their projects. Cities and counties
are equally assured that costly infrastructure such as roads, sewers, schools,
fire protection facilities, etc. will be available at the time development projects come on line.

3. The Development Agreement relates to the development known as
_____ , a golf course and residential development of mixed
densities. _____ has been in the planning stages since
June of 1988. The parties have, in good faith, negotiated the terms hereinafter
set forth which carry out the legislative purpose set forth above and will assure
the parties to this Agreement of mutually desirable development of the subject
property.

The completion of the Project, which includes two (2) eighteen-hole golf
courses within the City, will provide a long-term source of recreational and service opportunities for the residents of the City in furtherance of the planning objectives contained in the City General Plan, and will, in conjunction with other
approved development within the _____ , (a) maintain an

---

1    This Sample Development Agreement appeared first in William W.
Abbott, *Exactions and Impact Fees in California* (Solano Press 2001). The
authors would like to thank William W. Abbott and Solano Press for
granting permission to reprint the Sample Development Agreement.

economic and social balance between housing supply and employment opportunities; (b) assure that City revenues will be able to meet expenditures necessary to provide an adequate level of municipal services and (c) establish a balance of land uses that assures the City will be able to provide necessary municipal services.

The means of attaining the aforementioned objectives and the public benefit to be received as a result of development of the Project through this Agreement shall provide for:

a. A mix of single-family residential opportunities;

b. Additional recreational opportunities, with the development of a public and a private golf course; and

c. A solid residential base to support the financing mechanisms that will be needed to implement the _____Facilities Plan.

4. Developer owns in fee that certain real property located in the City of _____ and desires to create thereon residential development.

5. City, in response to Developer's applications, after public hearings and extensive environmental analysis, has granted the following entitlements:

a. By Resolution No. _____, dated _____, amended the City General Plan land use designation for the subject property from the former designations to _____.

b. By Resolution No. _____, effective _____, adopted the _____ Specific Plan and Design Guidelines.

c. By Ordinance No. _____, effective _____, amended the zoning designations for the subject property from _____ classifications to _____ classifications, subject to various conditions.

d. By action, dated _____, approved and adopted a vesting tentative subdivision map subject to conditions, a copy of which map and conditions is attached as Exhibit "B."

e. By Ordinance No. _____, effective _____, authorized the City to enter this Development Agreement with Developer.

6. In support of the various entitlements described in paragraph 5 above, and in accord with the California Environmental Quality Act (CEQA) and State and City guidelines, City has certified as adequate and complete a final Environmental Impact Report denominated "Final Environmental Impact Report (FEIR) for _____."

7. In support of this Development Agreement, City concurs in and ratifies the previously certified FEIR for _____ and finds that no subsequent or supplemental environmental impact report in addition to the previously certified FEIR is necessary. In reaching this determination, City finds that there have been no changes proposed to the project by the adoption of this Development Agreement which relate to new significant environmental impacts not previously considered. No subsequent changes are anticipated to occur with respect to the circumstances under which the project will be undertaken, and no information has become, or is anticipated to become available which will relate to significant effects not previously discussed, nor will any significant effect

previously analyzed in the FEIR become more severe, nor will mitigation measures or alternatives not found to be feasible or not previously considered have any significant effect. Except as potentially required for subsequent discretionary entitlements, no further environmental documentation is anticipated.

8. Development of the subject property pursuant to the terms and conditions of the various entitlements, the _____ Facilities Plan and the FEIR will provide for orderly growth and development consistent with the City's General Plan and other developmental policies and programs.

9. On _____, the City Planning Commission, designated by City as the Planning Agency for purposes of Development Agreement review pursuant to Government Code Section 65867, considered this Agreement.

10. City and Developer have taken all actions mandated by and fulfilled all requirements set forth in the Resolution No. 2370.

11. Having duly considered this Agreement and having held the noticed public hearings, City finds and declares that the provisions of this Development Agreement are consistent with the maps and text of the City's General Plan and the Specific Plan and the conditions of approval of the change in zoning and vesting tentative subdivision map.

NOW, THEREFORE, the parties hereto agree as follows:

### Article 1
### General Provisions

**Section 1.1. The Project.** The Project is the development and use of the Subject Property, consisting of approximately 1739.2 acres in the southeast area of the City, in accordance with the Specific Plan therefor. The Specific Plan describes a mixed-use Project consisting of approximately 4188 residential units, 9.4 acres of community serving retail and service uses, an elementary school, 148.1 acres for a public golf course, and 202.2 acres for a private golf course. The land use characteristics of the above uses are described in more detail in the Specific Plan. The Specific Plan also sets forth detailed Development Standards and an Implementation Program for the development of the Project.

**Section 1.2. Subject Property.** The Project site is _____.
The site is comprised of County Assessor's parcel numbers: _____, comprising approximately 1739.2 acres. The property is more specifically described in Exhibit "A" which is incorporated herein and made part of this Agreement.

**Section 1.3. Definitions.** As used in the Agreement, the following terms, phrases and words shall have the meanings and be interpreted as set forth in this Section.

(a) Adopting Ordinance means Ordinance Number _____ entitled: "_____" dated_____, and effective _____, which approves this Development Agreement as required by Government Code Section 65867.5.

241

(b) Assumption Agreement means an agreement substantially conforming to the model assumption agreement described in Exhibit "E," or other agreement in a form approved by the City Attorney, executed by a Landowner with the City, expressly assuming various obligations relating to the development of the Project, or portion thereof.

(c) Certificate of occupancy means either a certificate issued after inspections by City authorizing a person or persons in possession of property to dwell or otherwise use a specified building or dwelling unit, or the final inspection if a formal certificate is not issued.

(d) CEQA means the California Environmental Quality Act, Sections 21000, et seq., of the Public Resources Code of the State of California.

(e) Council means the duly elected legislative body governing the City of _____.

(f) Design Guidelines means the _____ Design Guidelines, set forth as Appendix A to the Specific Plan.

(g) Developer means _____, Inc., a California corporation, or successor in interest.

(h) Director means the Director of Planning and Community Development for the City of _____.

(i) means the Facilities Plan adopted by the City on a copy of which is attached hereto as Exhibit "D."

(j) Effective Date means the effective date of the Adopting Ordinance.

(k) Existing Land Use Regulations mean the ordinances adopted by the City Council of the City of _____ in effect on the Effective Date, including the adopting ordinances that govern the permitted uses of land, the density and intensity of use, and the design, improvement, construction standards and specifications applicable to the development of the Subject Property, including, but not limited to, the General Plan, the Specific Plan, _____ Facilities Plan and Mitigation Monitoring Plan, and the Zoning Ordinance and all other ordinances, codes, rules and regulations of the City establishing subdivision standards, park regulations, impact or development fees and building and improvement standards (but only to the extent the Zoning Ordinance and ocher such regulations are nor inconsistent with this Development Agreement and the Specific Plan). Existing Land Use Regulation does not include non-land use regulations, which includes taxes.

(l) Final Environmental Impact Report (FEIR) means a detailed statement prepared under CEQA as defined in Section 15362(c) of the State Environmental Guidelines.

(m) General Plan means the General Plan of the City of _____, including the text and maps, as amended in connection with the Project.

(n) Landowner is a party who has acquired any portion of the Subject Property from the Developer who, unless otherwise released as provided in this Agreement, shall be subject to the applicable provisions of this Agreement.

(o) Specific Plan means the Specific Plan, a copy of which has been attached hereto as Exhibit "C."

(p) Project means the anticipated development of the Subject Property as specified in paragraph 1.1 and as provided for in the provisions of this Agreement, including the Specific Plan and all other incorporated exhibits.

(q) Subject Property means the property described in Section 1.2, or the remaining portions thereof after releases from the provisions of this Agreement have been executed as authorized by this Agreement.

**Section 1.4. Exhibits.** Exhibits to this Agreement are as follows:

> Exhibit "A" Subject Property
> Exhibit "B" Approved Vesting Tentative Map, with Conditions
> Exhibit "C" _____ Specific Plan
> Exhibit "D" _____ Facilities Plan
> Exhibit "E" Assumption Agreement
> Exhibit "F" Memorandum of Agreement
> Exhibit "G" Map of Interim Water and Sewer Service Areas
> Exhibit "H" Map of Wetlands Areas

**Section 1.5. Incorporation of Recitals.** Recitals 1 through 11 are incorporated herein, including all Exhibits referred to in said Recitals. In the event of inconsistency between the Recitals and the provisions of Articles 1 through 5, the provisions of Articles 1 through 5 shall prevail.

**Section 1.6. Parties to Agreement.** The parties to this Agreement are:

(a) The City of _____. A political subdivision of the State of California, exercising general governmental functions and power. The principal office of the City is located at _____, _____, California.

(b) _____ Developer is a private enterprise which owns in fee the Subject Property.

(c) Landowner. From time to time, as provided in this Agreement, Developer may sell or otherwise lawfully dispose of a portion of the Subject Property to a Landowner who, unless otherwise released, shall be subject to the applicable provisions of this Agreement related to such portion of the Subject Property.

**Section 1.7. Project Is a Private Undertaking.** It is agreed among the parties that the Project is a private development and that City has no interest therein except as authorized in the exercise of its governmental functions.

**Section 1.8. Term of Agreement.** This Agreement shall commence upon the effective date of the Adopting Ordinance approving this Agreement, and shall continue in force for a period of ten years until unless extended or terminated as provided herein. Following the expiration of the term or extension thereof, or if sooner terminated, this Agreement shall have no force and effect, subject, however, to post- termination obligations of Developer or Landowner.

**Section 1.9. Vested Rights of Developer.** During the term of this Agreement, unless sooner terminated in accordance with the terms hereof, in developing the Subject Property consistent with the Project described herein, Developer is assured, and City agrees, that the development rights, obligations, terms and conditions specified in this Agreement, including without limitation, the terms and conditions thereof set forth in **Exhibits "B", "C" and "D",** attached hereto, are fully vested in the Developer and may not be changed or modified by the City except as may be expressly permitted by, and in accordance with, the terms and conditions of this Agreement, including the Exhibits hereto, or as expressly consented thereto by the Developer to the extent such proposed change or modification is applicable thereto.

**Section 1.10. Consistency with General Plan/Finding of Special Public Benefit.** As set forth in greater detail in the Specific Plan, the City Council expressly found that the approvals of the Specific Plan and all other entitlements related thereto (and described in Recital 5 above, were consistent with the text and maps of the General Plan. City Council further finds that this Development Agreement is also consistent with the text and maps of the General Plan.

**Section 1.11. Assignment and Assumption.** Developer shall have the right to sell, assign, or transfer this Agreement with all their rights, title and interests therein to any person, firm or corporation at any time during the term of this Agreement. The conditions and covenants set forth in this Agreement and incorporated herein by exhibits shall run with the land and the benefits and burdens shall bind and inure to the benefit of the parties. Developer shall provide City with written notice of any intent to sell, assign, or transfer all or a portion of the Subject Property at least thirty (30) days in advance of such action, provided such notice requirement shall not apply to the sale of five (5) or fewer single-family lots or residences to an individual or entity in a single transaction. Express written assumption by such purchaser, assignee or transferee, of the obligations and other terms and conditions of this Agreement with respect to the Subject Property or such portion thereof sold, assigned or transferred, shall relieve the Developer selling, assigning or transferring such interest of such obligations so expressly assumed. The form of the Assumption Agreement, is attached hereto as Exhibit "E" and incorporated herein by this reference.

**Section 1.12. Covenants Running with the Land.** Each and every purchaser, assignee or transferee of an interest in the Subject Property, or any portion thereof, shall be obligated and bound by the terms and conditions of this Agreement, and shall be the beneficiary thereof and a party thereto, but only with respect to the Subject Property, or such portion thereof, sold, assigned or transferred to it. Any such purchaser, assignee or transferee shall observe and fully perform all of the duties and obligations of a Developer contained in this Agreement, as such duties and obligations pertain to the portion of the Subject Property sold, assigned or transferred to it. Provided however, notwithstanding anything to the contrary above, if any such sale, assignment or transfer relates to a completed residential unit or non-residential building which has been approved by the City for occupancy, the automatic termination provisions of Section 5.1 hereof shall apply thereto and the rights and obligations of Developer hereunder shall not run with respect to such portion of the Subject Property sold, assigned or transferred and shall not be binding upon such purchaser, assignee or transferee.

**Section 1.13. Amendment to Agreement (Developer and City).** This Agreement may be amended by mutual consent of the parties in writing, in accordance with the provisions of Government Code Section 65868, provided that: any amendment which relates to the term, permitted uses, density, intensity of use, height and size of proposed buildings, or provisions for reservation and dedication of land shall require a public hearing before the parties may execute an amendment. Unless otherwise provided by law, all other amendments may be approved without a noticed public hearing.

**Section 1.14. Amendment to Agreement (Landowner and City).** This Agreement may also be amended, subject to the provisions of Government Code Section 65868 and Section 1.13 above, between a Landowner who has acquired a portion of the Subject Property from Developer and City as to the portions of the Subject Property then owned by Landowner.

**Section 1.15. Releases.** Developer, and any subsequent Landowner, may free itself from further obligations relating to the sold, assigned, or transferred property, provided that the buyer, assignee, or transferee expressly assumes the obligations under this Agreement pursuant to Section 1.11 contained hereinabove.

**Section 1.16. Notices.** Notices, demands, correspondence, and other communication to City and Developer shall be sufficiently given if dispatched by prepaid first-class mail to the principal offices of the parties as designated in Section 1.6. Notice to the City shall be to the attention of both the City Manager and the Director of Community Development. Notices to subsequent Landowners shall be required to be given by the City only for those Landowners who have given City written notice of their address for such notices. The parties hereto may, from time to time, advise the other of new addresses for such notices, demands or correspondence.

**Section 1.17. Reimbursement for Agreement Expense of City.** Developer agrees to reimburse City for actual expenses incurred over and above fees paid by Developer as an applicant incurred by City directly relating to this Agreement, including recording fees, publishing fees and reasonable staff and consultants costs not otherwise included within application fees. This development agreement shall not take effect until the fees provided for in this section, as well as any other processing fees owed by the applicant to the City for the _____ or _____ project are paid to the City. Upon payment of the payment of all expenses, the Developer may request, and the Developer shall issue, written acknowledgement of payment of all fees. Such reimbursement shall be paid within thirty (30) days of presentation from the City of _____ to Developer of a written statement of charges.

**Section 1.18. Recordation of Memorandum.** The City Clerk of City shall, within ten (10) days after the effective date of this Agreement, record a Memorandum of the Agreement in the form attached hereto as **Exhibit "F"** with the County Recorder, County of Sacramento.

**Section 1.19. Applicable Law and Attorneys' Fees.** This Agreement shall be construed and enforced in accordance with the laws of the State of California.

**Section 1.20. Invalidity of Agreement/Severability.** If this Agreement in its entirety is determined by a court to be invalid or unenforceable, this Agreement shall automatically terminate as of the date of final entry of judgment. If any provision of this Agreement shall be determined by a court to be invalid and unenforceable, or if any provision of this Agreement is rendered invalid or unenforceable according to the terms of any statute of the State of California which became effective after the effective date of the adopting ordinance, and either party in good faith determines such provision or provisions are material to its entering into this Agreement, that party may elect to terminate this Agreement as to all of its obligations remaining unperformed.

**Section 1.21. Third Party Legal Challenge.** In the event any legal action or special proceeding is commenced by any person or entity other than a party or a Landowner, challenging this Agreement or any provision herein, the parties and any Landowner agree to cooperate with each other in good faith to defend said lawsuit, each party and any Landowners to be liable for its own legal expenses and costs. Notwithstanding the foregoing, City may elect to tender the defense of any lawsuit filed by a third person or entity to Developer and/or Landowner(s) (to the extent applicable thereto), and, in such event, Developer and/or such Landowner(s) shall hold the City harmless from and defend the City from all costs and expenses incurred in the defense of such lawsuit, including, but not limited to, attorneys' fees and expenses of litigation awarded to the prevailing party or parties in such litigation. The Developer and/or Landowner shall not settle any lawsuit on grounds which include, but are not limited to non-monetary relief without the consent of the City. The City shall act in good faith, and shall not unreasonably withhold consent to settle.

### Article 2
### Project Development

**Section 2.1. Permitted Uses and Development Standards.** The permitted uses, the density and intensity of use, the maximum height and size of proposed buildings, provisions for reservation and dedication of land or payment of fees in lieu of dedication for public purposes, the construction, installation and extension of public improvements, development guidelines and standards, implementation program for processing of subsequent entitlements and other conditions of development for the Subject Property shall be those set forth in this Agreement and all the exhibits incorporated herein. In the event of any conflict between this Agreement, including the Specific Plan and Design Guidelines, and any other Existing Land Use Regulations, the terms and provisions of this Agreement shall prevail. The parties hereto intend hereby that this Agreement, together with the Specific Plan and all other exhibits attached hereto, serve as the definitive and controlling document for all subsequent actions, discretionary or ministerial, relating to the development of the Project and that only in the rare instances, if any, that a development issue is not expressly or impliedly addressed hereby shall any other Existing Land Use Regulations be applied in the decision thereon.

**Section 2.2. Minor Modification.** Minor modifications from the approved exhibits may be approved in accordance with the provisions of the Specific Plan (Section 8.16.2) and shall not require an amendment to this Agreement.

**Section 2.3. Changes to Existing Land Use Regulations.** Only the following changes to the Existing Land Use Regulations shall apply to the development of the Subject Property:

(a) Land use regulations, ordinances, policies, programs and fees adopted or undertaken by City in order to comply with regional, state or federal laws, plans or regulations, provided that in the event that such regional, state or federal laws, plans or regulations prevent or preclude compliance with one or more provisions of this Agreement, such provision or provisions shall be modified or suspended as may be necessary to comply with the such state or federal laws or regulations.

(b) City land use regulations, ordinances, resolutions or policies adopted after the Effective Date, applicable city-wide, and exclusive of new development fees or impact fees, that are not in conflict with the terms and conditions for development of the Subject Property established by this Agreement or otherwise applicable Existing Land Use Regulations and which do not impose additional burdens on such development.

(c) City land use regulations, ordinances, resolutions or policies adopted after the Effective Date, which are in conflict with the Existing Land Use Regulations, but the application of which to the development of the Subject Property has been consented to in writing by the Developer and/or the applicable Landowner.

**Section 2.4. Further Discretionary Actions.** Developer acknowledges that the Existing Land Use Regulations contemplate the exercise of further discretionary powers by the City. These powers include, but are not limited to, finalization of the financing actions necessary to implement the monitoring and implementation of environmental mitigation measures, and CEQA review of individual phases of the project as it builds out. Nothing in this Article shall be construed to limit the authority or the obligation of the City to hold legally required public hearings, or to limit the discretion of City and any of its officers or officials in complying with or applying Existing Land Use Regulations.

**Section 2.5. Financing of Public Facilities.**

(a) Developer acknowledges and agrees hereby that it shall participate in the _____ for its pro-rata share of the costs of the public improvements to be financed thereby, in accordance with the provisions of this Agreement and the _____, and the City agrees that the terms and provisions of the _____ shall apply to such financing of public improvements.

(b) On the request of Developer, the City shall pursue the use of special assessment districts, Mello Roos Community Facilities District(s), and other similar project-related public financing mechanism for financing the construction, improvement, or acquisition of public infrastructure, facilities, lands and improvements to serve the Subject Property, whether located within or outside the Subject Property. Subject to market conditions and fiscal prudence, the City shall use its best efforts to form such financing district(s) and issue and sell bonds in connection therewith.

To the extent allowed by law and subject to approval of the City Council, City shall include in any such financing district or ocher funding mechanism a provision allowing reimbursement to Developer for all expenses incurred by Developer in developing the _____ Facilities Plan, subject to the reasonable approval by the City of written documentation from Developer substantiating the amount thereof. Such reimburseables shall include, without limitation, the following:

(c) Major Roadway Wetlands Mitigation. As an additional cost for improvements, the Developer agrees to pay its, pro-rata share of costs incurred, for any additional costs encountered as a result of wetland mitigation for major roadway improvements not already addressed by the _____.

**Section 2.6. Application, Processing and Inspection Fees.** Application fees, processing fees, and inspection fees that are revised during the term of this Agreement shall apply to the development pursuant to this Agreement provided that (a) such revised fees apply generally to similar private projects or works within City, (b) the application of such fees to development of the Subject Property is prospective only, unless otherwise agreed to, and (c) the application to development of the Subject Property would not require an amendment of any of the exhibits incorporated herein.

**Section 2.7. Existing Land Use Fees.** Land use fees adopted as of the Effective Date, may be increased and shall be applicable to development pursuant to this Agreement provided that (a) such revised fees apply generally to similar private projects or works within City, and (b) the application to development of the Subject Property would not require an amendment of any of the exhibits incorporated herein.

**Section 2.8. Water Quality, Mitigation Monitoring, Light Rail, TSM Fees, AOR and _____ Financing Plan Fees.** Developer acknowledges that the City is considering the adoption of certain water quality pond/drainage maintenance fees, environmental impact mitigation monitoring fees, light rail fees, transportation system management, area of responsibility, and Financing Plan fees. Notwithstanding anything to the contrary herein, Developer agrees that the Subject Property shall be subject to such fees, adopted by the City subsequent to the Effective Date, provided that (a) such fee(s) is adopted in accordance with the requirements of Sections 66000 *et seq.* of the California Government Code that requires establishment of a reasonable nexus between the fee and the impact of the Project which is intended to be mitigated by the fee, and (b) the application to development of the Subject Property would not require an amendment of any of the exhibits incorporated herein.

Fees shall be collected at the time of issuance of the certificate of occupancy.

**Section 2.9. School Financing.** City and Developer acknowledge that the School District has certain facilities needs related to serving the expected student population to be generated by new development. To the extent legally permissible, the developer shall provide full mitigation for school impacts caused by the project. The applicant shall comply with any ordinance or other mechanism approved by the City to ensure that all necessary funding for the construction of required school facilities is available concurrent with the need for such facilities. Any building permit which is issued after the adoption of a school impact ordinance for other plan approved by the City of _____
shall comply with such requirement. Compliance may take the form of any of the following:

a. Developer's agreement to form or join a community facilities district to finance school construction.

b. Payment of a school construction fee which is in addition to the fees imposed by the school district.

c. Other financing mechanism or binding arrangement which is acceptable to the City.

If a fee is used for meeting this requirement, the fee shall only be the proportional cost of the impact to the service demand by _____.

**Section 2.10. No New Impact or Development Fees.** Except as expressly provided in Sections 2.3, 2.5, 2.6, 2.8 and 2.9, Developer and Landowner, or their successors in interest, shall have no obligation to participate in, pay, contribute, or otherwise provide as a condition or exaction of any subsequent approval by City, any new development or impact fee or fees, however described or defined, imposed by City after the Effective Date. This provision will not preclude authorized and reasonable increases in development or impact fees in existence on the Effective Date of this Agreement.

**Section 2.11. Golf Course Facilities Construction.** The City acknowledges owners of other properties planned for residential development within the _____ will benefit from the development of the municipal golf course within the Subject Property and that certain public improvements will need to be sized for the planned development thereof. City agrees that, through the Community Facilities District(s) described in Section 2.5 above, it shall use its best efforts to require the funding of the fair share of the costs of roads, sewer, water and drainage improvements, or allocable portion thereof, serving the municipal golf course.

**Section 2.12. Interim Water Service.** Developer acknowledges that, pursuant to the General Plan, no final map may be recorded in the until a new source of water to serve such area is acquired by the City. Developer further acknowledges that as of the Effective Date, the City has engaged in good faith efforts to obtain a new source of water. Once such a contractual commitment for additional water to serve the _____ is acquired by the City, the City shall allow interim water connections for the initial phases of the Project shown on **Exhibit "G"** hereto, in advance of the expansion of the existing water treatment plant and installation of a permanent water delivery system, *provided* a financing mechanism for such expansion and installation is then established and the City is satisfied that adequate funding therefor will be available to the City as and when such permanent facilities are required, as reasonably determined by the City. In the event the City fails to obtain a new source of water, the City shall not be liable to Developer.

**Section 2.13. Interim Sewer Service.** The City further agrees to provide interim sewer service through its existing sewer network for development of the initial phases of the Subject Property shown on **Exhibit "G"** hereto, until such time that a new sewer outfall serving the can be constructed. Prior to any such interim sewer connections within the Subject Property, a financing mechanism for the construction of such outfall shall be established and the City shall be satisfied that adequate funding therefor will be available to the City for the construction of the outfall when needed, as reasonably determined by the City.

**Section 2.14. Timing of Development.** The parties acknowledge that the most efficient and economic development of the Subject Property depends upon numerous factors, such as market orientation and demand, interest rates, competition, and similar factors, and that generally it will be most economically beneficial to the ultimate purchasers to have the rate of development determined by Developer. Accordingly, the timing, sequencing, and phasing of the development is solely the responsibility of Developer and, except as expressly set forth herein regarding interim services to initial phases of the Project and as set forth in the Specific Plan, the_____, and the conditions of approval of the vesting tentative subdivision map, the City shall not impose, by ordinance, resolution, initiative or otherwise, any restrictions on such timing, sequencing or phasing of development within the Subject Property. In particular, and without limitation thereof, the City acknowledges that it will not withhold or delay approval of any entitlements for development of the Subject Property or the construction of public improvements required therefor that are consistent with the terms and conditions of this Agreement notwithstanding any delay in the planning for or construction of the _____/Highway 50 interchange.

**Section 2.15. Deposit of Construction Lumber.** The Parties agree that to facilitate timely development, Developer may bring upon, and store lumber on, the Subject Property required for construction of the Project at locations to be determined by the Developer, subject to the approval of such location(s) in writing by the Director, prior to the installation of streets. The Director may impose conditions on any approval as determined by the Director to be in the public health, safety and welfare, including, but not limited to, water for fire protection purposes. Any approval by the Director shall require the Developer to execute an agreement prepared and approved by the City Attorney, to defend, indemnify and hold the City harmless from any and all liability and claims resulting from all activities undertaken pursuant to this section. Developer will provide unrestricted access to the lumber storage areas to appropriate City employees on gravel or other hard surfaces adequate to support City's fire suppression equipment. police patrol car, other City authorized vehicles, and other authorized private and government vehicles.

**Section 2.16. Dedication of Public Lands.** Except as otherwise provided herein, the Developer shall dedicate all required public lands within ninety (90) days from the Effective Date, and the City shall accept such dedications upon completion of the improvements to be installed therein, or when otherwise provided herein, as follows:

(a) **Parks.** With respect to the parks within the Subject Property, each park site (or portion of the community park site, which is to be dedicated in phases) shall be dedicated to the City as the maps for the corresponding subdivisions are recorded, as such subdivisions and the corresponding park sites (or applicable portions of the community park site) are delineated on the map attached hereto as **Exhibit "B."**

Developer shall have no obligation hereunder to improve such park sites and the City shall accept the dedication of each park site at the time of dedication thereof by Developer. In consideration of this obligation to dedicate the park sites shown on **Exhibit "B"** Developer shall receive a partial credit as provided for by the City's Park Land Dedication Ordinance, for all eligible parksites, so dedicated within the Specific Plan that is consistent therewith. The Developer shall not receive a credit for either of the golf courses.

(b) **Municipal Golf Course.** Developer shall deed and improve the portion of the Subject Property planned for the municipal golf course in accordance with the terms and conditions of that certain Golf Course Land Purchase and Option Agreements between the City and Developer. Any breach of Developer's obligations thereunder to dedicate and/or improve the municipal golf course shall also constitute a breach of its obligations under this Agreement, provided however, upon completion of the improvements for the municipal golf course and its opening to the public, any subsequent breach of any obligations of Developer thereunder shall not constitute a breach hereunder.

(c) **Water Quality Ponds/Drainage.** Developer shall dedicate the areas within the Project designated "Water Quality Ponds/Drainage" upon recordation of the subdivision maps that either contain such areas or rely on such areas for the filtration of their drainage. With respect to each dedicated area, upon completion of the water quality/drainage improvements thereto by Developer, the City shall accept such areas for ownership and maintenance. The cost of such maintenance shall be funded by a drainage fee, landscape and lighting district or other such mechanism to be created by the City. Prior to the City's acceptance thereof, Maintenance Standards for the maintenance of such water quality ponds and drainage improvements shall be prepared by Developer and subject to the reasonable approval of the Director.

(d) **Wetlands.** Developer shall irrevocably offer to dedicate to the City all areas delineated as wetlands within the Subject Property, as shown on **Exhibit "H"** attached hereto, upon recordation of the first single-family subdivision map. Upon completion by Developer of all mitigation, restoration and/or enhancement of the wetland areas in accordance with the provisions of the Army Corps of Engineers 404 permit therefor, upon satisfaction by Developer of all maintenance related thereto during the 5-year maintenance period required by the 404 permit and implementation of an ongoing finance mechanism, the City shall accept the dedication of such wetlands for purposes of ownership and maintenance thereof. Such maintenance, after acceptance by the City or other entity thereafter, may be funded by a landscape and lighting district or other such financing mechanism that includes the Subject Property. During the developer's period of ownership, Developer shall post security in an amount and form acceptable to the City to assure performance of the Developer's obligations.

(e) **Rights-of-Way.** Upon 30 days written notice, the Developer agrees to dedicate any or all road rights-of-way without expense to the City.

**Section 2.17. Density Banking and Transfers.** [NOT APPLICABLE]

**Section 2.18. Obligation and Rights of Mortgage Lenders.** The holder of any mortgage, deed of trust or other security arrangement with respect to the Subject Property, or any portion thereof, shall not be obligated under this Agreement to construct or complete improvements or to guarantee such construction for completion, but shall otherwise be bound by all of the terms and conditions of this Agreement which pertain to the Subject Property or such portion thereof in which it holds an interest. Any such holder who comes into possession of the Subject Property, or any portion thereof, pursuant to a foreclosure of a mortgage or a deed of trust, or deed in lieu of such foreclosure, shall take the Subject Property, or such portion thereof, subject to any pro rata claims for payments or charges against the Subject Property, or such portion thereof, which accrue prior and subsequent to the time such holder comes into possession. Nothing in this Agreement shall be deemed or construed to permit or authorize any such holder to devote the Subject Property, or any portion thereof, to any uses, or to construct any improvements thereon, other than those uses and improvements provided for or authorized by this Agreement, subject to all of the terms and conditions of this Agreement.

**Section 2.19. Parkland Improvement Requirements.** The Developer agrees to pay parkland improvement fees, or make improvements as provided for in

**Exhibit "I,"** included by reference herein. Developer covenants for itself, and all successors in interest to not challenge the City's Parkland Improvement Ordinance.

### Article 3
### Entitlement and Permit
### Processing, Inspections

**Section 3.1. Cooperation Between City and Developer.** The City agrees to cooperate with Developer in securing all permits which may be required by City.

**Section 3.2. Inapplicability of Subsequent Legislation.** Should an ordinance or resolution or other measure be enacted. whether by action of the City Council, by initiative, referendum or otherwise which relates to the rate, timing or sequencing of the development of construction of the Subject Property, including, but not limited to, development no-growth or slow-growth moratoria, to the extent any such measure is inconsistent with the spirit, intent or letter of the phasing requirements for development already set forth for the Subject Property by the Specific Plan and the _____, City agrees that such ordinance, resolution or other measure shall not apply to the Subject Property, or any development thereof, or construction related thereto or construction of improvements necessary therefor.

### Article 4
### Default

**Section 4.1. General Provisions.** Subject to extensions of time by mutual consent in writing, failure or delay by either party or Landowner not released from this Agreement to perform any term or provision of this Agreement shall constitute a default. In the event of alleged default or breach of any terms or conditions of this Agreement, the party alleging such default or breach shall give the other party or Landowner not less than thirty (30) days notice in writing specifying the nature of the alleged default and the manner in which said default may be cured. During any such thirty (30) day period, the party or Landowner charged shall not be considered in default for purposes of termination or institution of legal proceedings.

After notice and expiration of the thirty (30) day period, if such default has not been cured or is not being diligently cured in the manner set forth in the notice, the other party or Landowner to this Agreement may, at is option, institute legal proceedings pursuant to this Agreement or give notice of its intent to terminate this Agreement pursuant to California Government Code Section 65868 and any regulations of the City implementing said Government Code Section. Following notice of intent to terminate, or prior to instituting legal proceedings, the matter shall be scheduled for consideration and review in the manner set forth in Government Code Sections 65865, 65867, and 65868 and City regulations implementing said sections by the City within thirty (30) calendar days.

Following consideration of the evidence presented in said review before the City and an additional 30-day period to cure, either party alleging the default by the other party or Landowner may institute legal proceedings or may give written notice of termination of this Agreement to the other party; provided, however, a Landowner may only give such notice with respect to such a portion of the Subject Property which Landowner owns in interest.

Evidence of default may also arise in the course of a regularly scheduled periodic review of this Agreement pursuant to Government Code Section 65865.1. If either party or landowner determines that a party or Landowner is in default following the completion of the normally scheduled periodic review, said party or Landowner may give written notice of termination of this Agreement specifying in said notice the alleged nature of the default, and potential actions to cure said default where appropriate. If the alleged default is not cured in thirty (30) days or within such longer period specified in the notice, or the defaulting party or Landowner waives its right co cure such alleged default, this Agreement may be terminated by City as to the Developer or Landowner and the property in which the Developer or Landowner owns an interest.

**Section 4.2. Annual Review.** City shall, at least every twelve (12) months during the term of this Agreement, review the extent of good faith substantial compliance by Developer and Landowner with the terms of this Agreement. The City may charge fees as necessary to cover the costs of conducting the annual review, Such periodic review shall be limited in scope to compliance with the terms of this Agreement pursuant to California Government Code Section 65865.1. Said review shall be diligently completed. Notice of such annual review shall include the statement that any review may result in amendment or termination of this Agreement. A finding by City of good faith compliance by Developer and Landowner with the terms of the Agreement shall conclusively determine said issue up to and including the date of said review.

The City shall deposit in the mail or fax to Developer and/or Landowner a copy of all staff reports and, to the extent practical, related exhibits concerning contract performance at least seven (7) calendar days prior to such periodic review. Developer or Landowner shall be permitted an opportunity to be heard orally or in writing regarding its performance under this Agreement before the City Council and, if the matter is referred to a City Planning Commission, before said Commission.

**Section 4.3. Default by Developer/Withholding of Building Permit.** City may, at its discretion, refuse to issue a building permit for any structure within the geographical confines of the Subject Property as the same is defined at the time of said application, if Developer or Landowner thereof has failed and refuses to complete any requirement enumerated therefor in accordance with the terms of this Agreement. No building permit shall be issued or building permit application accepted for the building shell of any structure on the Subject Property if the permit applicant owns or controls any property subject to this Agreement, and if such applicant or any entity or person controlling such applicant is in default of the terms and conditions of this Agreement as determined pursuant to Section 4.1.

**Section 4.4. Developer Default Limited to Property/Entity; Several Obligations of Owners.** Except as specified herein, no default hereunder in performance of a covenant or obligation with respect co a particular portion of the Subject Property shall constitute a default applicable to any other portion of the Subject Property, and any remedy arising by reason of such default shall be applicable solely to the portion of property where the default has occurred. Similarly, the obligations of the Developer and Landowners shall be several and no default hereunder in performance of a covenant or obligation by any one of them shall constitute a default applicable to any ocher owner who is not affiliated with such defaulting owner, and any remedy arising by reason of such default shall be solely applicable to the defaulting owner and the portion of the Subject Property owned thereby.

Notwithstanding the foregoing, a breach of the Golf Course Land Purchase and/or Option Agreements by Developer, shall constitute a default applicable to the Subject Property, regardless of whether or not the property is owned by the Developer, and the City may withhold building permits anywhere within the Subject Property.

**Section 4.5. Default by City.** In the event City does not accept, review, approve or issue necessary development permits or entitlements for use in a timely fashion as defined by this Agreement, or as otherwise agreed to by the parties, or the City otherwise defaults under the terms of this Agreement, City agrees that Developer or Landowner shall not be obligated to proceed with or complete the project or any phase thereof, nor shall resulting delays in Developer performance constitute grounds for termination or cancellation of, this Agreement.

**Section 4.6. Cumulative Remedies of Parties /Waiver of Right to Damages.** In addition to any other rights or remedies, City, Developer and any Landowner may institute legal or equitable proceedings to cure, correct or remedy any default, to specifically enforce any covenant or agreement herein, to enjoin any threatened or attempted violation of the provisions of this Agreement, provided however, the City and the Developer waives any and all rights hereunder to seek damages as a result of any such breach or alleged breach.

**Section 4.7. Enforced Delay, Extension of Times of Performance.** In addition to specific provisions of this Agreement, performance by either party or Landowner hereunder shall not be deemed to be in default where delays or defaults are due to war, insurrection, strikes, walkouts, riots, floods, earthquakes, .fires, casualties, acts of' God, governmental restrictions imposed or mandated by governmental entities other than the City, enactment of conflicting state of federal laws or regulations, new or supplementary environmental regulation enacted by the state or federal government or litigation. Notwithstanding the foregoing sentence, delays incurred in conjunction with the delivery of water or sewer service shall not result in any extensions. An extension of time for such cause shall be granted in writing by City for the period of the enforced delay or longer, as may be mutually agreed upon, but in no case shall the cumulative extensions add more than five years to the effective period of this Agreement.

## Article 5
## Termination

**Section 5.1. Termination upon Completion of Development.** This Agreement shall terminate upon the expiration of the term or when the subject property has been fully developed and all of the Developer's obligations in connection therewith are satisfied as determined by the City. Upon termination of this Agreement, the City shall record a notice of such termination in a form satisfactory to the City Attorney that the Agreement has been terminated. This Agreement shall automatically terminate and be of no further force or effect as to any single-family residence, any other residential dwelling unit(s), or any non-residential building, and the lot or parcel upon which such residence or building is located, when it has been approved by the City for occupancy.

**Section 5.2. Effects upon Termination on Developer Obligations.** Termination of this Agreement as to the Developer of the Subject Property or any portion thereof shall not affect any of the Developer's obligations to comply with the City general plan and the terms and conditions of any applicable zoning, or subdivision map or other land use entitlements approved with respect to the Subject Property, any other covenants of any other development specified in this Agreement to continue after the termination of this Agreement or obligations to pay assessments, liens, fees, or taxes.

**Section 5.3. Effects upon Termination on City.** Upon any termination of this Agreement as to the Developer of the Subject Property, or any portion thereof, the entitlements, conditions of development, limitations on fees and all other terms and conditions of this Agreement shall no longer be vested hereby with respect to the property affected by such termination (provided vesting of such entitlements, conditions or fees may then be established for such property pursuant to then existing planning and zoning law) and the City shall no longer be limited, by this Agreement, to make any changes or modifications to such entitlements, conditions or fees applicable to such property.

**IN WITNESS WHEREOF,** this Agreement was executed by the parties thereto on the dates set forth below.

CITY OF _____,
a political subdivision of the state of California


_____,
a California corporation

By: _____
    Mayor, City of _____

By: _____
Its: _____

By: _____
Its: _____


ATTEST:

_____
City Clerk

APPROVED AS TO FORM:

_____
City Attorney


LIST OF EXHIBITS
Exhibit "A" Subject Property
Exhibit "B" Approved Vesting Tentative Map, with Conditions
Exhibit "C" _____
             Specific Plan
Exhibit "D" _____
             Facilities Plan
Exhibit "E" Assumption Agreement
Exhibit "F" Memorandum of Agreement
Exhibit "G" Map of Interim Water and Sewer Service Areas
Exhibit "H" Map of Wetlands Areas
Exhibit "I" Land Improvement Ordinance
Exhibit "J" Mitigation Monitoring Program

## XI. ILLINOIS ANNEXATION AGREEMENT STATUTE

The annexation agreement in Appendix XIV was drafted pursuant to the annexation agreement statute set out below:

### Illinois Compiled Statutes, Chapter 65, Act 5, Article 11, Division 15.1. Annexation Agreements

### 5/11-15.1-1. Agreements with owners of record

§11-15.1-1. The corporate authorities of any municipality may enter into an annexation agreement with one or more of the owners of record of land in unincorporated territory. That land may be annexed to the municipality in the manner provided in Article 7 at the time the land is or becomes contiguous to the municipality. The agreement shall be valid and binding for a period of not to exceed 20 years from the date of its execution.

Lack of contiguity to the municipality of property that is the subject of an annexation agreement does not affect the validity of the agreement whether approved by the corporate authorities before or after the effective date of this amendatory Act of 1990.

This amendatory Act of 1990 is declarative of existing law and does not change the substantive operation of this Section.

### 5/11-15.1-2. Contents and scope of agreements

§11-15.1-2. Any such agreement may provide for the following as it relates to the land which is the subject of the agreement:

(a) The annexation of such territory to the municipality, subject to the provisions of Article 7.

(b) The continuation in effect, or amendment, or continuation in effect as amended, of any ordinance relating to subdivision controls, zoning, official plan, and building, housing and related restrictions; provided, however, that any public hearing required by law to be held before the adoption of any ordinance amendment provided in such agreement shall be held prior to the execution of the agreement, and all ordinance amendments provided in such agreement shall be enacted according to law.

(c) A limitation upon increases in permit fees required by the municipality.

(d) Contributions of either land or monies, or both, to any municipality and to other units of local government having jurisdiction over all or part of land that is the subject matter of any annexation agreement entered into under the provisions of this Section shall be deemed valid when made and shall survive the expiration date of any such annexation agreement with respect to all or any part of the land that was the subject matter of the annexation agreement.

(e) The granting of utility franchises for such land.

(e-5) The abatement of property taxes.

(f) Any other matter not inconsistent with the provisions of this Code, nor forbidden by law.

Any action taken by the corporate authorities during the period such agreement is in effect, which, if it applied to the land which is the subject of the agreement, would be a breach of such agreement, shall not apply to such land without an amendment of such agreement.

After the effective term of any annexation agreement and unless otherwise provided for within the annexation agreement or an amendment to the annexation agreement, the provisions of any ordinance relating to the zoning of the land that is provided for within the agreement or an amendment to the agreement, shall remain in effect unless modified in accordance with law. This amendatory Act of 1995 is declarative of existing law and shall apply to all annexation agreements.

### 5/11-15.1-2.1. Annexation agreement; municipal jurisdiction

§11-15.1-2.1. Annexation agreement; municipal jurisdiction.

(a) Property that is the subject of an annexation agreement adopted under this Division is subject to the ordinances, control, and jurisdiction of the annexing municipality in all respects the same as property that lies within the annexing municipality's corporate limits.

(b) This Section shall not apply in (i) a county with a population of more than 3,000,000, (ii) a county that borders a county with a population of more than 3,000,000 or (iii) a county with a population of more than 246,000 according to the 1990 federal census and bordered by the Mississippi River, unless the parties to the annexation agreement have, at the time the agreement is signed, ownership or control of all property that would make the property that is the subject of the agreement contiguous to the annexing municipality, in which case the property that is the subject of the annexation agreement is subject to the ordinances, control, and jurisdiction of the municipality in all respects the same as property owned by the municipality that lies within its corporate limits.

### 5/11-15.1-3. Procedure

§11-15.1-3. Any such agreement executed after July 31, 1963 and all amendments of annexation agreements, shall be entered into in the following manner. The corporate authorities shall fix a time for and hold a public hearing upon the proposed annexation agreement or amendment, and shall give notice of the proposed agreement or amendment not more than 30 nor less than 15 days before the date fixed for the hearing. This notice shall be published at least once in one or more newspapers published in the municipality, or, if no newspaper is published therein, then in one or more newspapers with a general circulation within the annexing municipality. After such hearing the agreement or amendment may be modified before execution thereof. The annexation agreement or amendment shall be executed by the mayor or president and attested by the clerk of the municipality only after such hearing and upon the adoption of a resolution or ordinance directing such execution, which resolution or ordinance must be passed by a vote of two-thirds of the corporate authorities then holding office.

### 5/11-15.1-4. Effect of agreement; enforcement; limitation of actions

§11-15.1-4. Any annexation agreement executed pursuant to this Division 15.1, or in conformity with Section 11-15.1-5 hereof, shall be binding upon the successor owners of record of the land which is the subject of the agreement and upon successor municipal authorities of the municipality and successor municipalities. Any party to such agreement may by civil action, mandamus, injunction or other proceeding, enforce and compel performance of the agreement.

A lawsuit to enforce and compel performance of the agreement must be filed within the effective term of the agreement or within 5 years from the date the cause of action accrued, whichever time is later.

### 5/11-15.1-5. Validation of existing agreements—Extension of terms of agreements

§11-15.1-5. Any annexation agreement executed prior to October 1, 1973 which was executed pursuant to a two-thirds vote of the corporate authorities and which contains provisions not inconsistent with Section 11-15.1-2 hereof is hereby declared valid and enforceable as to such provisions for the effective period of such agreement, or for 20 years from the date of execution thereof, whichever is shorter.

The effective term of any Annexation Agreement executed prior to the effective date of this Amendatory Act of 1985 may be extended to a date which is not later than 20 years from the date of execution of the original Annexation Agreement.

# APPENDICES

## XII. NORTH CAROLINA ANNEXATION AGREEMENT STATUTE

### Part 6. Annexation Agreements.

#### §160A-58.21. Purpose.

It is the purpose of this Part to authorize cities to enter into binding agreements concerning future annexation in order to enhance orderly planning by such cities as well as residents and property owners in areas adjacent to such cities

#### §160A-58.22. Definitions.

The words defined in this section shall have the meanings indicated when used in this Part:

(1) "Agreement" means any written agreement authorized by this Part.

(2) "Annexation" means any extension of a city's corporate limits as authorized by this Article, the charter of the city, or any local act applicable to the city, as such statutory authority exists now or is hereafter amended.

(3) "Participating city" means any city which is a party to an agreement. (1989, c. 143.)

#### §160A-58.23. Annexation agreements authorized.

Two or more cities may enter into agreements in order to designate one or more areas which are not subject to annexation by one or more of the participating cities. The agreements shall be of reasonable duration, not to exceed 20 years, and shall be approved by ordinance of the governing board and executed by the mayor of each city and spread upon its minutes. (1989, c. 143.)

#### §160A-58.24. Contents of agreements; procedure.

(a) The agreement shall:

(1) State the duration of the agreement.

(2) Describe clearly the area or areas subject to the agreement. The boundaries of such area or areas may be established at such locations as the participating cities shall agree. Thereafter, any participating city may follow such boundaries in annexing any property, whether or not such boundaries follow roads or natural topographical features.

(3) Specify one or more participating cities which may not annex the area or areas described in the agreement.

(4) State the effective date of the agreement.

(5) Require each participating city which proposes any annexation to give written notice to the other participating city or cities of the annexation at least 60 days before the adoption of any annexation ordinance; provided, however, that the agreement may provide for a waiver of this time period by the notified city.

(6) Include any other necessary or proper matter.

(b) The written notice required by subdivision (a)(5) of this section shall describe the area to be annexed by a legible map, clearly and accurately showing the boundaries of the area to be annexed in relation to: the area or areas described pursuant to subdivision (a)(2) of this section, roads, streams and any other prominent geographical features. Such notice shall not be effective for more than 180 days.

(c) No agreement may be entered into under this Part unless each participating city has held a public hearing on the agreement prior to adopting the ordinance approving the agreement. The governing boards of the participating cities may hold a joint public hearing if desired. Notice of the public hearing or hearings shall be given as provided in G.S. 160A-31(c).

(d) Any agreement entered into under this Part may be modified or terminated by a subsequent agreement entered into by all the participating cities to that agreement. The subsequent agreement shall be approved by ordinance after a public hearing or hearings as provided in subsection (c).

(e) No agreement entered into under this Part shall be binding beyond three miles of the primary corporate limits of a participating city which is permitted to annex the area under the agreement, unless approved by the board of county commissioners with jurisdiction over the area. Provided however, that an area where the agreement is not binding because of failure of the board of county commissioners to approve it, shall become subject to the agreement if subsequent annexation brings it within three miles. The approval of a board of county commissioners shall be evidenced by a resolution adopted after a public hearing as provided in subsection (c).

(f) A participating city may terminate an annexation agreement unilaterally or withdraw itself from the agreement, by repealing the ordinance by which it approved the agreement and providing five years' written notice to the other participating cities. Upon the expiration of the five-year period, an agreement originally involving only two cities shall terminate, and an agreement originally involving more than two cities shall terminate unless each of the other participating cities shall have adopted an ordinance reaffirming the agreement. (1989, c. 143.)

### §160A-58.25. Effect of agreement.

From and after the effective date of an agreement, no participating city may adopt an annexation ordinance as to all or any portion of an area in violation of the agreement. (1989, c. 143.)

### §160A-58.26. Part grants no annexation authority.

Nothing in this Part shall be construed to authorize the annexation of any area which is not otherwise subject to annexation under applicable law. (1989, c. 143.)

### §160A-58.27. Relief.

(a) Each provision of an agreement shall be binding upon the respective parties. Not later than 30 days following the passage of an annexation ordinance concerning territory subject to an agreement, a participating city which believes that another participating city has violated this Part or the agreement may file a petition in the superior court of the county where any of the territory proposed to be annexed is located, seeking review of the action of the city alleged to have violated this Part or the agreement.

(b) Within five days after the petition is filed with the court, the petitioning city shall serve copies of the petition by certified mail, return receipt requested, upon the respondent city.

(c) Within 15 days after receipt of the copy of the petition for review, or within such additional time as the court may allow, the respondent city shall transmit to the reviewing court:

(1) A transcript of the portions of the ordinance or minute book in which the procedure for annexation has been set forth;

(2) A copy of resolutions, ordinances, and any other document received or approved by the respondent city's governing board as part of the annexation proceeding.

(d) The court shall fix the date for review of the petition so that review shall be expeditious and without unnecessary delays. The review shall be conducted by the court without a jury. The court may hear oral arguments and receive written briefs, and may take evidence intended to show either:

(1) That the provisions of this Part were not met; or

(2) That the provisions of the agreement were not met.

(e) At any time before or during the review proceeding, any petitioner may apply to the reviewing court for an order staying the operation of the annexation ordinance pending the outcome of the review. The court may grant or deny the stay in its discretion upon such terms as it deems proper, and it may permit annexation of any part of the area described in the ordinance concerning which no question for review has been raised.

(f) Upon a finding that the respondent city has not violated this Part or the agreement, the court may affirm the action of the respondent city without change. Upon a finding that the respondent city has violated this Part or the agreement, the court may:

(1) Remand to the respondent city's governing board any ordinance adopted pursuant to Parts 2 or 3 of this Article, as the same exists now or is hereafter amended, for amendment of the boundaries, or for such other action as is necessary, to conform to the provisions of this Part and the agreement.

(2) Declare any annexation begun pursuant to any other applicable law to be void. If the respondent city shall fail to take action in accordance with the court's instructions upon remand under subdivision d)(1) of this section within three months from receipt of such instructions, the annexation proceeding shall be void.

(g) Any participating city which is a party to the review proceedings may appeal from the final judgment of the superior court under rules of procedure applicable in other civil cases. The appealing party may apply to superior court for a stay in its final determination, or a stay of the annexation ordinance, whichever shall be appropriate, pending the outcome of the appeal to the appellate division; provided, that the superior court may, with the agreement of the parties, permit annexation to be effective with respect to any part of the area concerning which no appeal is being made and which can be incorporated into the respondent city without regard to any part of the area concerning which an appeal is being made.

(h) If part or all of the area annexed under the terms of a challenged annexation ordinance is the subject of an appeal to the superior court or appellate division on the effective date of the ordinance, then the ordinance shall be deemed amended to make the effective date with respect to such area the date of the final judgment of the superior court or appellate division, whichever is appropriate, or the date the respondent city's governing board completes action to make the ordinance conform to the court's instructions in the event of remand.

(i) A participating city which is prohibited from annexing into an area under a binding agreement may file a petition in the superior court where any of the territory proposed to be annexed is located, or a response in a proceeding initiated by another participating city, seeking permission to annex territory in the area notwithstanding the agreement. If the territory qualifies for annexation by the city seeking to annex it, the court may enter an order allowing the annexation to proceed with respect to all or a portion of the territory upon a finding that there is an imminent threat to public health or safety that can be remedied only by the city seeking annexation. The procedural provisions of this section shall apply to proceedings under this subsection, so far as applicable. (1989, c. 143.)

### §160A-58.28. Effect on prior local acts.

This Part does not affect Chapter 953, Session Laws of 1983, Chapter 847, Session Laws of 1985 (1986 Regular Session), or Chapters 204, 233, or 1009, Session Laws of 1987, authorizing annexation agreements, but any city which is authorized to enter into agreements by one of those acts may enter into future agreements either under such act or this Part. (1989, c. 143, s. 1; 1991 (Reg. Sess., 1992), c. 1030, s. 48.)

# APPENDICES

## XIII. SAMPLE ANNEXATION AGREEMENT
## (LOCAL GOVERNMENT-ORIENTED)

**THIS ANNEXATION, SUBDIVISION, AND DEVELOPMENT AGREEMENT** (*"Agreement"*) is dated as of the ____ day of _____, 200_ (*"Effective Date"*), and is [by and between] [by, between, and among] the **VILLAGE OF** _____, an Illinois municipal corporation (*"Village"*), [and _____, as Trustee (*"Trustee"*) under Trust Agreement dated _____, and known as Trust No. _____ (*"Trust No. ___"*),] and _____[, the sole beneficiary of Trust No. ___ (*"___"*) (Trust No. ___ and _____ being jointly and severally referred to as *"Owner"* in this Agreement)] [(*"Owner"*)].

**IN CONSIDERATION OF** the recitals and the mutual covenants and agreements set forth in this Agreement, [and pursuant to the Village's home rule powers,] the parties agree as follows:

**Section 1. Recitals.**[1]

A. [The Owner is, as of the Effective Date, the owner of record of the Property] [Trustee and _____ are, as of the Effective Date, the record and beneficial owners of the Property].

B. The Property is contiguous to the corporate limits of the Village and is not within the corporate limits of any municipality.

C. The Owner has filed the Annexation Petition and Annexation Plat with the Village Clerk.

D. [There are no electors residing within the Property] [At least 51% of the electors residing within the Property join in the Annexation Petition].

E. The Owner desires and proposes to have the Property annexed to the Village pursuant to and in accordance with Section 7-1-8 of the Illinois Municipal Code, 65 ILCS 5/7-1-8, and this Agreement.

F. The Owner desires and proposes to have the Property subdivided into [include description of proposal].

G. The Owner desires and proposes to develop [include description of proposal].

H. The Owner has filed with the Village, and the Plan Commission has recommended approval of, the Preliminary Subdivision Plat.

I. The Village and the Owner desire that the Property be developed and used only in compliance with this Agreement.

J. Pursuant to Section 11-15.1-1 *et seq.* of the Illinois Municipal Code, 65 ILCS 5/11-15.1-1 *et seq.*, a proposed annexation agreement, in substantially the

---

[1]     All defined terms initially appear in bold and italics and thereafter as capitalized words and phrases throughout this Agreement. They shall have the meanings set forth in the preamble, in Section 2, and elsewhere in this Agreement.

same form and substance as this Agreement, was submitted to the Corporate Authorities and, pursuant to notice published in the _____ on _____, as provided by statute, the Corporate Authorities held a public hearing on _____[, and continued to [insert dates]].

K. Pursuant to notice published in the _____ on _____, as provided by statute and the Zoning Code, the Plan Commission held a public hearing on _____[, and continued to [insert dates]], and the Plan Commission recommended approval of the requested zoning and subdivision of the Property on _____[, describe form of document if applicable].

L. The Corporate Authorities, after due and careful consideration, have concluded that the annexation, zoning, subdivision, development, and use of the Property pursuant to and in accordance with this Agreement would further enable the Village to control the development of the area and would serve the best interests of the Village.

M. The Corporate Authorities have reviewed and considered the proposed development of the Property, and the zoning and subdivision approvals requested to allow for its implementation, and have found them to be consistent with the character of, and existing development patterns in, the Village.

### Section 2. Definitions; Rules of Construction.

A. Definitions. Whenever used in this Agreement, the following terms shall have the following meanings unless a different meaning is required by the context:

"*Annexation Notice*": The notice, contemplated in Section 3.B of this Agreement, triggering, after its delivery, the effectiveness of the Annexation Ordinance and the Zoning Map Amendment Ordinance

"*Annexation Petition*": The petition, executed by the Owner as the owner of the Property[ and by at least 51% of the electors residing within the territory of the Property], and dated as of _____, seeking annexation of the Property to the Village. The original is on file with the Village Clerk.

"*Annexation Plat*": The annexation plat prepared by _____, consisting of ___ sheets, with latest revision date of _____, a copy of which is attached to this Agreement as **Exhibit** __.

"*Building Code*": Chapter __, entitled "_____," of the _____ Municipal Code, as it has been and may in the future be amended.

"*Common Areas*": Outlots _____ within the Property, as depicted on the Site Plan, together with any and all improvements thereon, including without limitation the pond and detention areas.

"*Corporate Authorities*": The President and Board of Trustees of the Village.

"*Final Engineering Plan*": The engineering plan that receives the approval of the [Village Engineer] pursuant to Section 5.B of this Agreement and in accordance with the Requirements of Law. After that approval, the Final Engineering Plan shall, automatically and without further action by the Corporate Authorities, be deemed to be incorporated in, and made a part of, this Agreement and shall, for all purposes in this Agreement, supersede the Preliminary Engineering Plan. [IF FINAL PLAN AVAILABLE AT TIME

OF EXECUTION, MODIFY PREAMBLE AND SECTIONS 2, 3, AND 5 ACCORDINGLY]

*"Final Landscaping Plan"*: The landscaping plan that receives the approval of the [Village Engineer] pursuant to Section 5.B of this Agreement and in accordance with the Requirements of Law. After that approval, the Final Landscaping Plan shall, automatically and without further action by the Corporate Authorities, be deemed to be incorporated in, and made a part of, this Agreement and shall, for all purposes in this Agreement, supersede the Preliminary Landscaping Plan. [IF FINAL PLAN AVAILABLE AT TIME OF EXECUTION, MODIFY PREAMBLE AND SECTIONS 2, 3, AND 5 ACCORDINGLY]

*"Final Subdivision Plat"*: The subdivision plat that receives the approval of the Corporate Authorities pursuant to Section 5.C of this Agreement and in accordance with the Requirements of Law. After that approval, the Final Subdivision Plat shall, automatically and without further action by the Corporate Authorities, be deemed to be incorporated in, and made a part of, this Agreement and shall, for all purposes in this Agreement, supersede the Preliminary Subdivision Plat. [IF FINAL PLAT AVAILABLE AT TIME OF EXECUTION, MODIFY PREAMBLE AND SECTIONS 2, 3, AND 5 ACCORDINGLY]

*"Force Majeure"*: Strikes, lockouts, acts of God, or other factors beyond a party's reasonable control and reasonable ability to remedy; provided, however, that Force Majeure shall not include delays caused by weather conditions, unless those conditions are unusually severe or abnormal considering the time of year and the particular location of the Property.

**"Improvements"**: All of the public and private improvements and facilities necessary to serve the Property, including without limitation the improvements shown on the Preliminary Subdivision Plat or the Final Subdivision Plat and the Preliminary Engineering Plan or the Final Engineering Plan, the improvements set forth on the list attached to this Agreement as **Exhibit** __, all other storm water detention and retention facilities, water mains, storm sewers, sanitary sewers, streets, lighting, sidewalks, parkways, rough and final grading, trees, sod, seeding, and other landscaping, and all other improvements required pursuant to this Agreement, the Preliminary Subdivision Plat or the Final Subdivision Plat, the Preliminary Engineering Plan or the Final Engineering Plan, the Preliminary Landscaping Plan or the Final Landscaping Plan, and the Requirements of Law[ other than the building(s) and accessory structures].

*"Person"*: Any corporation, partnership, individual, joint venture, trust, estate, association, business, enterprise, proprietorship, or other legal entity of any kind, either public or private, and any legal successor, agent, representative, or authorized assign of the above.

*"Preliminary Engineering Plan"*: The preliminary engineering plan prepared by _____, consisting of _____ sheets, with latest revision date of _____, for public and private improvements necessary to serve the Property, which plan has been approved by the [Village Engineer], a copy of which is attached to this Agreement as **Exhibit** __. [IF FINAL PLAN AVAILABLE AT TIME OF EXECUTION, MODIFY PREAMBLE AND SECTIONS 2, 3, AND 5 ACCORDINGLY]

*"Preliminary Landscaping Plan"*: The preliminary landscaping plan prepared by _____, consisting of _____ sheets, with latest revision date of _____, a copy of which is attached to this Agreement as **Exhibit** __. [IF FINAL PLAN AVAILABLE AT TIME OF EXECUTION, MODIFY PREAMBLE AND SECTIONS 2, 3, AND 5 ACCORDINGLY]

*"Preliminary Subdivision Plat"*: The preliminary subdivision plat prepared by _____, consisting of _____ sheets, with latest revision date of _____, a copy of which is attached to this Agreement as **Exhibit** __. [IF FINAL PLAT AVAILABLE AT TIME OF EXECUTION, MODIFY PREAMBLE AND SECTIONS 2, 3, AND 5 ACCORDINGLY]

*"Property"*: The tract of land consisting of approximately ___ acres of territory, generally located at the _____ corner of _____ in unincorporated _____County, and legally described in **Exhibit** __ to this Agreement.

*"Public Improvements Standards Manual"*: Village Standards and Specifications for Public and Private Improvements, dated _____, as it has been and may in the future be amended.

*"Requirements of Law"*: All applicable federal, state, and local laws, statutes, codes, ordinances, resolutions, orders, rules, and regulations.

*"Site Plan"*: The site plan of the Property prepared by _____, consisting of _____ sheets, with latest revision date of _____, a copy of which is attached to this Agreement as **Exhibit** __.

*"Subdivision Code"*: The Village of _____ Subdivision and Development Code (___), as it has been and may in the future be amended.

*"Zoning Code"*: The _____ Zoning Code (___), as it has been and may in the future be amended.

B. Rules of Construction.

1. Grammatical Usage and Construction. In construing this Agreement, pronouns include all genders, and the plural includes the singular and vice versa.

2. Headings. The headings, titles, and captions in this Agreement have been inserted only for convenience and in no way define, limit, extend, or describe the scope or intent of this Agreement.

3. Calendar Days. Unless otherwise provided in this Agreement, any reference in this Agreement to "day" or "days" shall mean calendar days and not business days. If the date for giving of any notice required to be given, or the performance of any obligation, under this Agreement falls on a Saturday, Sunday, or federal holiday, then the notice or obligation may be given or performed on the next business day after that Saturday, Sunday, or federal holiday.

4. Other Defined Terms. Capitalized terms not defined in this Agreement shall have the meanings set forth in the _____[add reference to applicable Code or other document].

## Section 3. Annexation of the Property.

*ALTERNATIVE I: Delayed Annexation*

A. Annexation Ordinance. Immediately after the approval and execution of this Agreement, the Village shall adopt an ordinance, substantially in the form attached to this Agreement as **Exhibit __** ("*Annexation Ordinance*"), annexing the Property (and any contiguous rights-of-way) to the Village pursuant to Section 7-1-8 of the Illinois Municipal Code, 65 ILCS 5/7-1-8. The Annexation Ordinance shall not be effective until the following conditions are satisfied:

1. The Owner has delivered to the Village Clerk the Annexation Notice in the form attached to this Agreement as **Exhibit __**, executed by the Owner.

2. The Plan Commission has recommended approval of a final subdivision plat for the Property in conformance with the Preliminary Subdivision Plat.

3. The Village Engineer has approved the Final Engineering Plan and the Final Landscaping Plan.

4. The Owner has paid to the Village the amounts due pursuant to Section 11 of this Agreement.

5. The Owner has paid to the Village an amount sufficient to cover the cost of recording this Agreement, all necessary plats, the affidavit of service of notice as required by Section 7-1-1 of the Illinois Municipal Code, 65 ILCS 5/7-1-1, and the Annexation Ordinance.

After the Annexation Ordinance becomes effective, the Village shall promptly cause the Annexation Ordinance to be recorded in the office of the Recorder of _____ County. The annexation of the Property (and any contiguous rights-of-way) shall occur on, but not before, the date of recordation of the Annexation Ordinance, all necessary plats, and the affidavit of service of notice as required by Section 7-1-1 of the Illinois Municipal Code, 65 ILCS 5/7-1-1.

B. Expiration. In the event that all conditions precedent to the effectiveness of the Annexation Ordinance are not satisfied on or before 12:00 noon on _____, this Agreement shall automatically, and without any further action, become null and void and of no force or effect.

*ALTERNATIVE II: Immediate Annexation*

A. Adoption of Annexation Ordinance. Immediately after the execution of this Agreement, the Corporate Authorities shall pass and approve an ordinance ("*Annexation Ordinance*") in substantially the form of **Exhibit __** attached to this Agreement annexing the Property (and any contiguous rights-of-way) to the Village pursuant to Section 7-1-8 of the Illinois Municipal Code, 65 ILCS 5/7-1-8; provided, however, that the Annexation Ordinance shall not be effective unless the following conditions are satisfied:

1. The Owner has paid to the Village the amounts due pursuant to Section 11 of this Agreement.

2. The Owner has paid to the Village an amount sufficient to cover the cost of recording this Agreement, all necessary plats, the affidavit of service of notice as required by Section 7-1-1 of the Illinois Municipal Code, 65 ILCS 5/7-1-1, and the Annexation Ordinance.

After the Annexation Ordinance becomes effective, the Village shall promptly cause the Annexation Ordinance to be recorded in the office of the Recorder of _____ County.

B. Effective Date of Annexation. The annexation of the Property (and any contiguous rights-of-way) shall occur on, but not before, the date of recordation of the Annexation Ordinance, all necessary plats, and the affidavit of service of notice as required by Section 7-1-1 of the Illinois Municipal Code, 65 ILCS 5/7-1-1.

**Section 4. Zoning of the Property**. Immediately after the adoption of the Annexation Ordinance, the Village shall adopt an ordinance, substantially in the form of **Exhibit __** to this Agreement (*"Zoning Map Amendment Ordinance"*), amending the Village's zoning map to classify the Property into the following zoning districts as generally depicted on the Site Plan. The Zoning Map Amendment Ordinance shall not be effective until the recordation of the Annexation Ordinance in accordance with Section 3.A of this Agreement.

**Section 5. Approval of Subdivision, Engineering, and Landscaping Plans and Plats**.

A. Approval of Preliminary Subdivision Plat. Immediately after the adoption of the Zoning Map Amendment Ordinance, the Village shall adopt a resolution, substantially in the form attached to this Agreement as **Exhibit __**, approving the Preliminary Subdivision Plat and the Preliminary Landscaping Plan (*"Preliminary Subdivision Plat Resolution"*). The Owner acknowledges and agrees that no construction, improvement, or development of any kind shall be permitted on any portion of the Property until the Final Engineering Plan, the Final Landscaping Plan, and the Final Subdivision Plat are approved by the Village in accordance with the Subdivision Code and Sections 5.B and 5.C of this Agreement. The Owner agrees to initiate the approval process for the final engineering plan, final landscaping plan, and final subdivision plat promptly after the Effective Date of this Agreement by submitting proper and complete applications for those approvals.

B. Final Engineering and Landscaping Approvals. The Owner agrees to cooperate with the Village Engineer to produce (i) a final engineering plan for the Property that is in conformance with the Preliminary Engineering Plan and (ii) a final landscaping plan for the Property that is in conformance with the Preliminary Landscaping Plan, both of which shall be satisfactory to the Village Engineer, in the Village Engineer's sole and absolute discretion.

C. Approval of Final Subdivision Plat. The Village shall adopt a resolution, in the form attached to this Agreement as **Exhibit __**, approving the Final Subdivision Plat, provided that the plat has been prepared and reviewed in accordance with this Agreement, the Preliminary Subdivision Plat, and the Requirements of Law. After the effective date of the resolution approving the Final Subdivision Plat, the Village shall promptly cause the Final Subdivision Plat to be recorded in the office of the Recorder of _____ County.

**Section 6. Development of the Property**.

A. General Restrictions. Subject to the particular terms for development set forth in Section 6.C of this Agreement, and the restrictive covenants set forth in Section 6.D of this Agreement, development of the Property, except for minor alterations due to final engineering and site work approved by the Village Engineer or the Director of Development, as appropriate, shall be pursuant to and in accordance with the following:

# APPENDICES

1. This Agreement.
2. The Site Plan.
3. The Final Subdivision Plat.
4. The Final Engineering Plan.
5. The Final Landscaping Plan.
6. The Zoning Code.
7. The Subdivision Code.
8. The Building Code.
9. The Public Improvements Standards Manual.
10. The other Requirements of Law.

Unless otherwise provided in this Agreement, in the event of a conflict between or among any of the above plans or documents, the plan or document that provides the greatest control and protection for the Village, as determined by the Village Manager, shall control. All of the above plans and documents shall be interpreted so that the duties and requirements imposed by any one of them are cumulative among all of them, unless otherwise provided in this Agreement.

B. Easements. Utility and enforcement easements shall be granted to the Village and other governmental bodies and utility services over, on, and across the Property, including without limitation the Common Areas, for the purposes of enforcing applicable laws, making repairs, installing and servicing utilities, and providing public and emergency services.

C. Particular Terms for Development. Notwithstanding any use or development right that may be applicable or available to the Property pursuant to the Zoning Code or any other Requirement of Law, the Property shall be used and developed only as follows: [add special restrictions].

D. Restrictive Covenants. All development of and on the Property shall be subject to the following restrictions: [add list of applicable site specific restrictions, if any]

E. Damage to Public Property. The Owner shall maintain the Property and all streets, sidewalks, and other public property in and adjacent to the Property in a good and clean condition at all times during development of the Property and construction of the Improvements. Further, the Owner shall promptly clean all mud, dirt, or debris deposited on any street, sidewalk, or other public property in or adjacent to the Property by the Owner or any agent of or contractor hired by, or on behalf of, the Owner, and shall repair any damage that may be caused by the activities of the Owner or any agent of or contractor hired by, or on behalf of, the Owner. If, within one hour after the Village gives the Owner notice to clean all mud, dirt, or debris deposited on any street, sidewalk, or other public property in or adjacent to the Property by the Owner or any agent of or contractor hired by, or on behalf of, the Owner, the Owner neglects to clean, or undertake with due diligence to clean, the affected public property, then the Village shall be entitled to clean, either with its own forces or with contract forces, the affected public property and to recover from the Owner a [insert dollar amount] per hour charge multiplied by the number of personnel reasonably required to perform the cleaning.

F. Changes in the Final Engineering Plan and the Final Landscaping Plan during Development.

271

1. Minor Adjustments. During the construction and development of the Property, the Village Manager may authorize minor adjustments to any of the Final Engineering Plan and the Final Landscaping Plan when the adjustments are necessary in light of technical or engineering considerations.

2. Major Adjustments. Any major adjustment to any of the Final Engineering Plan and the Final Landscaping Plan not specifically listed in, or approved pursuant to this Agreement shall be considered to be a major adjustment and shall be granted only after application to, and approval by, the Corporate Authorities, by resolution duly adopted. The Corporate Authorities may, but shall have no obligation to, require that the application for a major adjustment be considered at a public hearing before the Corporate Authorities or other board or commission as the Corporate Authorities shall require.

*ALTERNATIVE FOR ANNEXATION AGREEMENTS IN ILLINOIS ONLY: FREEZING OF CODES AND FEES THROUGHOUT TERM OF AGREEMENT*

G. Applicability of Laws.

1. Zoning and Subdivision Codes and Fees. No amendment to the Zoning Code or the Subdivision Code that is adopted after the Effective Date shall apply to the Property during the term of this Agreement except the following:

a. Amendments expressly required by this Agreement; and

b. Amendments to which the Owner has expressly consented; and

c. Amendments that increase fees chargeable pursuant to the Zoning Code or the Subdivision Code, but only to the extent directly necessary to offset the exact amount of any increase over the levels of costs or fees in effect on the Effective Date as imposed by any federal, state, or local governmental entity having jurisdiction or by any other Person to which the Village submits plans and documents for review. Notwithstanding any other provision of this Section 6.G, at no time during the term of this Agreement shall the Village impose on the development of the Property any increase in the fees chargeable pursuant to the Zoning Code or the Subdivision Code that has the effect of being applicable solely to the Property or that is not made generally applicable to similar construction or uses throughout the Village.

2. Construction Codes and Fees. All amendments to the ordinances and administrative orders listed on **Exhibit __** to this Agreement ("***Construction Codes***"), and all increases in the fees chargeable pursuant to the Construction Codes, shall apply to [specify portion of development] on the Property. However, unless the Owner has expressly consented, no amendments or increases after the Effective Date shall be applicable to [specify remainder of development] until the first to occur of the date that is five years after the Effective Date or the date on which [add specific provision]. Notwithstanding any other provision of this Section 6.G.2, at no time during the term of this Agreement shall the Village impose on the Property any amendment or any increase that has the effect of being applicable solely to the Property or that is not made generally applicable to similar construction or uses throughout the Village.

# APPENDICES

**Section 7. Improvements.**

A. Owner Duty to Construct Improvements. The Owner shall, at its sole cost and expense, construct and install all of the Improvements on the Property, including without limitation the following: [add only special items not already included in broad definition of "Improvements"].

B. Standards Applicable to Improvements.

1. General Standards. All Improvements shall be designed and constructed pursuant to, and in accordance with, the Final Engineering Plan, the Final Landscaping Plan, and the Public Improvements Standards Manual, and to the satisfaction of the Village Engineer. All work performed on the Improvements shall be conducted in a good and workmanlike manner and in accordance with the schedule established in Section 7.C of this Agreement. All materials used for construction of the Improvements shall be new and of first-rate quality.

2. Special Standards. [add only any standards not included in improved documents].

3. Contract Terms; Prosecution of the Work. The Owner and all of its contractors shall prosecute the work diligently, continuously, in full compliance with, and as required by or pursuant to, this Agreement, until the work is properly completed. Each Owner's contract with a contractor shall provide that the Owner may take over and prosecute the work if the contractor fails to do so in a timely and proper manner.

4. Engineering Services. The Owner shall provide, at its sole cost and expense, all engineering services for the design and construction of the Improvements, including without limitation full inspection services of a professional engineer responsible for overseeing the construction of the Improvements. The Owner shall promptly provide the Village with the name of the resident engineer and a telephone number or numbers at which the engineer can be reached at all times.

5. Village Inspections and Approvals. Village representatives shall have the full, right, permission, and authority to inspect and approve all work on the Improvements at all times.

6. Other Approvals. If the construction and installation of any Improvement require the consent, permission, or approval of any Person, then the Owner shall take all steps required to obtain the required consent, permission, or approval. No work requiring the consent, permission, or approval of any Person shall commence without that prior consent, permission, or approval.

C. Schedule for Completion of Improvements. All Improvements shall be completed and made ready for inspection, approval, and any required acceptance by the Village pursuant to the construction schedule approved by the Village Engineer as part of the Final Engineering Plan. The Owner shall be allowed extensions of time beyond the completion dates set forth in the construction schedule only for delay caused by Force Majeure. The Owner shall, within two days after any unavoidable delay commences and again within two days after the delay terminates, give notice to the Village for its review and approval of the delay, the cause for the delay, the period or anticipated period of the delay, and the steps taken by the Owner to mitigate the effects of the delay. Any failure

273

of the Owner to give the required notice shall be deemed a waiver of any right to an extension of time for any the delay.

*ALTERNATIVE: specific schedule attached to Agreement*

C. Schedule for Completion of Improvements. The Improvement work and the Improvements shall be completed by the Owner and made ready for inspection, approval, and any required acceptance by the Village, in accordance with the schedule attached to this Agreement as **Exhibit** __ (*"Construction Schedule"*). The Owner shall be allowed extensions of time beyond the completion dates required by the Construction Schedule only for delay caused by Force Majeure. The Owner shall, within two days after any unavoidable delay commences and again within two days after the delay terminates, give notice to the Village for its review and approval of the delay, the cause for the delay, the period or anticipated period of the delay, and the steps taken by the Owner to mitigate the effects of the delay. Any failure of the Owner to give the required notice shall be deemed a waiver of any right to an extension of time for any the delay.

D. Final Inspections and Approvals. When the Owner determines that an Improvement has been properly completed, the Owner shall request final inspection, approval, and, as appropriate, acceptance of the Improvement by the Village. The notice and request shall comply with all requirements of Section ____ of the Subdivision Code and shall be given sufficiently in advance to allow the Village time to inspect the Improvement and to prepare a punch list of items requiring repair or correction and to allow the Owner time to make all required repairs and corrections prior to the scheduled completion date. The Owner shall promptly make all necessary repairs and corrections as specified on the punch list. The Village shall not be required to approve or accept any Improvement until all of the Improvements, including without limitation all punch list items, have been fully and properly completed.

E. Dedication and Acceptance of Specified Improvements. The Owner shall dedicate to the Village the Improvements set forth in the schedule attached to this Agreement as **Exhibit** __. Nothing whatsoever shall constitute an acceptance by the Village of any Improvement except only express acceptance by the Village in compliance with the requirements of the Subdivision Code. Prior to acceptance of the Improvements to be accepted by the Village, the Owner shall execute, or cause to be executed, all documents that the Village shall request to transfer ownership of the Improvements to, and to evidence ownership of the Improvements by, the Village, free and clear of all liens, claims, encumbrances, and restrictions unless otherwise approved by the Village. The documents transferring ownership of the Improvements to, and to evidence ownership of the Improvements by, the Village shall be [substantially in the form attached to this Agreement as **Exhibit** __] [acceptable in form and substance to the Village Attorney]. Owner shall, simultaneously, grant, or cause to be granted, to the Village all insured easements or other property rights as the Village may require to install, operate, maintain, service, repair, and replace the Improvements that have not previously been granted to the Village, free and clear of all liens, claims, encumbrances, and restrictions, unless otherwise approved by the Village.

F. Owner's Guaranty and Maintenance of Improvements. The Owner hereby guarantees the prompt and satisfactory correction of all defects and deficiencies in the Improvements that occur or become evident within two years after approval and any required acceptance of the Improvements by the Village pursuant to this Agreement. If any defect or deficiency occurs or becomes evident during the two-year period, then the Owner shall, after 10 days' prior written notice from the Village (subject to Force Majeure), correct it or cause it to be corrected. In the event any Improvement is repaired or replaced pursuant to the demand of the Village, the Guaranty provided by this Section 7.F shall be extended, as to the repair or replacement, for two full years from the date of the repair or replacement. If an owners' association is required to be created pursuant to a declaration meeting the requirements of Section 9 of this Agreement, then, unless the owners' association has assumed all responsibility for maintenance, and, in all events, for a period of at least two years after Village approval, the Owner shall, at its sole cost and expense, maintain, without any modification, except as specifically approved by the Village Engineer, in a first-rate condition, at all times, the Improvements. In the event the Village Engineer determines, in the Village Engineer's sole and absolute discretion, that the Owner is not adequately maintaining, or has not adequately maintained, any Improvement, the Village may, after 10 days' prior written notice to the Owner, enter on any or all of the Property for the purpose of performing maintenance work on and to any affected Improvement. In the event that the Village shall cause to be performed any work pursuant to this Section 7.F the Village shall have the right to draw from the performance securities deposited pursuant to Section 12 of this Agreement, or the right to demand immediate payment directly from the Owner, based on costs actually incurred or on the Village's reasonable estimates of costs to be incurred, an amount of money sufficient to defray the entire costs of the work, including without limitation legal fees and administrative expenses. The Owner shall, after demand by the Village, pay the required amount to the Village.

G. Issuance of Building and Occupancy Permits. The Village shall have the absolute right to withhold any building permit or certificate of occupancy at any time the Owner is in violation of, or is not in full compliance with, any term of this Agreement.

H. Completion of Construction. If the Owner fails to diligently pursue all construction, as required in, or permitted by, Sections 6 and 7 of this Agreement, to completion within the time period prescribed in the building permit or permits issued by the Village for the construction, and if the building permit or permits are not renewed within three months after expiration, the Owner shall, within 60 days after notice from the Village, remove any partially constructed or partially completed buildings, structures, or improvements from the Property. If the Owner fails or refuses to remove the buildings, structures, and improvements as required, then the Village shall have, and is hereby granted, in addition to all other rights afforded to the Village in this Agreement and by law, the right, at its option, to demolish and/or remove any of the buildings, structures, and improvements, and the Village shall have the right to charge the

Owner an amount sufficient to defray the entire cost of the work, including without limitation legal and administrative costs.

**Section 8. Construction Traffic and Parking; Streets.**
A. Designated Traffic Routes. The Village may designate routes of access to the Property for construction traffic to protect pedestrians and to minimize disruption of traffic and damage to paved street surfaces; provided, however, that the designated routes shall not unduly hinder or obstruct direct and efficient access to the Property for construction traffic. The Owner shall keep all routes used for construction traffic free and clear of mud, dirt, debris, obstructions, and hazards and shall repair all damage caused by the construction traffic. The Village also may designate from time to time temporary construction haul roads on and to the Property that shall be located and constructed in a manner acceptable to the Village Engineer.
B. Parking. All construction vehicles, including passenger vehicles, and construction equipment shall be parked within the Property or in areas designated by the Village.
C. Streets.
1. Owner Requirement. All streets designated to be dedicated to the Village shall be constructed and dedicated to the Village in accordance with this Agreement.
2. Protection of Final Surface Course. Except with the prior express consent of the Village, no construction traffic shall be permitted to utilize any street to be dedicated to the Village after installation of the final surface course of that street. If the Owner uses the street for construction traffic, the Owner shall keep the street free and clear of mud, dirt, debris, obstructions, and hazards and shall, after the use is no longer necessary, restore and repair that street to the standards established in the Public Improvements Standards Manual.
3. Dedication and Acceptance. No street shall be deemed to be accepted by the Village, and the Village shall have no obligation or liability in respect of the street, until the street has been completed, approved, and accepted by the Village in accordance with Section 7.E of this Agreement. The Owner acknowledges and agrees that (a) the Village shall not be obligated to accept any street until all construction traffic on the street has ceased and the street has been completed and, if necessary, restored and repaired as required by this Agreement and (b) the Village shall not be obligated to keep any street cleared, plowed, or otherwise maintained until the street has been completed, approved, and accepted by the Village in accordance with this Agreement, or until other arrangements satisfactory to the Village Engineer, in the Village Engineer's sole and absolute discretion, shall have been made.

**Section 9. Declaration of Covenants.** Concurrent with the recordation of the Final Subdivision Plat, a declaration of covenants, acceptable in form and substance to the Village Attorney, shall be recorded against the Property. The declaration must be approved by the Corporate Authorities prior to becoming effective.

## Section 10. Recaptures.

A. Recapture Fees. The Owner shall pay all costs, including interest if any, due from the Owner as a benefited property owner pursuant to the recapture agreements and ordinances described in the schedule attached to this Agreement as **Exhibit** ____ and pursuant to all other recapture agreements and ordinances previously entered into or adopted by the Village pursuant to Section 9-5-1 of the Illinois Municipal Code. In addition, if the Village at any time in the future enters into a recapture agreement or adopts a recapture ordinance pursuant to Section 9-5-1 in which the Owner is determined to be a benefited property owner, then the Owner does hereby unconditionally agree to pay its proportionate share of the costs, including interest if any, set forth in that agreement or ordinance.

B. Right to Recapture Costs of Oversized Improvements. The Village hereby finds and agrees that, as a result of the construction of _____ by the Owner as required by this Agreement (*"Recapture Improvement[s]"*), substantial benefit will be provided to the properties listed on the schedule attached to this Agreement as **Exhibit** ____ (*"Benefited Properties"*) that lie outside the Property. The Village further finds that the Property and the Benefited Properties will be benefited by the Recapture Improvement[s] in proportion to their respective [total areas] [frontages along _____] [projected water demands] [projected sewage flows]. Within 60 days following completion and acceptance of the Recapture Improvement[s] pursuant to Sections 7.D and 7.E of this Agreement, the Village shall adopt an ordinance substantially in the form attached to this Agreement as **Exhibit** ____ to establish such charges as are necessary to allow the Owner to recover from each Benefited Property its proportionate share of the actual cost of construction of the Recapture Improvement[s] (*"Recapture Ordinance"*), calculated, for each Benefited Property, on the basis of [square feet of area] [lineal feet of frontage] [projected average daily water demand] [projected average daily sewage flow] (*"Recapture Fee"*). The Owner shall, not later than the time it gives the notice of completion and request for acceptance required pursuant to Section 7.D of this Agreement, submit to the Village documentation of the actual cost of construction of the Recapture Improvement[s] for review and approval by the Village and for the Village's use in preparation of the Recapture Ordinance. The Village shall pay to the Owner, within 30 days after collection, the amount of any Recapture Fee collected. The adoption of the Recapture Ordinance and the payment to the Owner of any Recapture Fees collected by Village shall be the sole responsibilities of the Village with respect to the collection or payment of any Recapture Fee, and the Village shall have no other or further obligation to the Owner with respect to the collection or payment of any Recapture Fee. The Village shall, at the Owner's expense, cause a copy of this Agreement to be recorded in the office of the Recorder of _____ County as notice to the owners of the Benefited Properties and required by Section 9-5-2 of the Illinois Municipal Code.

## Section 11. Fees, Dedications, Donations, and Contributions.

A. Annexation Fee. The Owner shall pay to the Village, in addition to all other specific sums required to be paid pursuant to this Agreement or the Re-

quirements of Law, the total sum of _____ Dollars ($_____)
[($_____ per dwelling unit)] to be used at the sole and absolute discretion of the Village for the general purposes of the Village.

B. Negotiation and Review Fees. In addition to all other costs, payments, fees, charges, contributions, or dedications required by this Agreement or by the Requirements of Law, the Owner shall pay to the Village, immediately after presentation of a written demand or demands for payment, all legal, engineering, and other consulting or administrative fees, costs, and expenses incurred or accrued in connection with the review and processing of plans for the development of the Property and in connection with the negotiation, preparation, consideration, and review of this Agreement. Payment of all fees, costs, and expenses for which demand has been made, but payment has not been received, by the Village prior to execution of this Agreement, shall be made by a certified or cashier's check contemporaneous with the execution of this Agreement by the Village. Further, the Owner agrees that it will continue to be liable for and to pay, immediately after presentation of a written demand or demands for payment, the fees, costs and expenses incurred in connection with any applications, documents, or proposals, whether formal or informal, of whatever kind submitted by the Owner during the term of this Agreement in connection with the use and development of the Property. Further, the Owner agrees that it shall be liable for and will pay after demand all fees, costs, and expenses incurred by the Village for publications and recordings required in connection with the above matters.

C. Recapture Fees. The Owner shall pay to the Village the amounts due pursuant to Section 10.A of this Agreement.

D. Other Village Fees. In addition to all other costs, payments, fees, charges, contributions, or dedications required by this Agreement, the Owner shall pay to the Village all application, inspection, and permit fees, all water and sewer general and special connection fees, tap-on fees, charges, and contributions, and all other fees, charges, and contributions pursuant to the Requirements of Law.

E. Dedications, Donations, and Contributions to the Village. The Owner shall dedicate sites, easements, and rights-of-way as required by this Agreement, including without limitation [add description of any dedication, donation, or contribution not otherwise required by this Agreement].

F. Dedications, Donations, and Contributions to Others.

1. School District. The Village and the Owner do hereby acknowledge and agree that the Owner has entered into binding agreements with the School District in satisfaction of all applicable dedications, donations, and contributions to the School District with respect to the Property.

2. Park District. The Village and the Owner do hereby acknowledge and agree that the Owner has entered into binding agreements with the Park District in satisfaction of all applicable dedications, donations, and contributions to the Park District with respect to the Property.

3. [Other Governmental Entity]. [add description of any dedication, donation, or contribution]

## Section 12. Performance Security.

A. Cash Deposit and Performance and Payment Letter of Credit. As security to the Village for the performance by the Owner of the Owner's obligations (1) to construct and complete the Improvements pursuant to and in accordance with this Agreement, (2) to pay all Village costs, fees, and charges due from the Owner pursuant to this Agreement, (3) to maintain and repair streets, sidewalks, and other public property pursuant to this Agreement, and (4) to otherwise faithfully perform its undertakings pursuant to this Agreement, the Owner shall, prior to the recordation of the Final Subdivision Plat, deposit with the Village Administrator cash (*"Cash Deposit"*) and a letter of credit (*"Performance and Payment Letter of Credit"*), in a total amount equal to either 125% of the Approved Cost Estimate or, in cases where executed contracts for construction and installation of an Improvement have been filed with the Village Clerk pursuant to this Agreement, 110% of the amount of the contracts. The Cash Deposit shall, at all times until released as provided below, be maintained at not less than 10% of the total deposit required by this Section 12.A. The Cash Deposit and the Performance and Payment Letter of Credit shall be maintained and renewed by the Owner, and shall be held in escrow by the Village, until any required acceptance of the Improvements by the Village pursuant to this Agreement and the posting of the Guaranty Letter of Credit as required by Section 12.B of this Agreement. After any required acceptance of the Improvements and posting of the Guaranty Letter of Credit, the Village shall release the Performance and Payment Letter of Credit and any amounts remaining in the Cash Deposit.

B. Guaranty Letter of Credit. Immediately after any required acceptance by the Village of the Improvements pursuant to this Agreement, the Owner shall post a new letter of credit in the amount of five percent of the actual total cost of the Improvements as security for the performance of the Owner's obligations under this Agreement (*"Guaranty Letter of Credit"*). The Guaranty Letter of Credit shall be held by the Village in escrow until the last to occur of (i) the date that is the end of the two-year guaranty period set forth in this Agreement or (ii) the date that is two years after the proper correction of any defect or deficiency in the Improvements pursuant to this Agreement and payment of the cost of correction. If the Village is required to draw on the Guaranty Letter of Credit by reason of the Owner's failure to fulfill its obligations under this Agreement, then the Owner shall within 10 days thereafter cause the Guaranty Letter of Credit to be increased to its full original amount.

C. Interest and Costs. The Owner shall not be entitled to interest on the Cash Deposit. The Owner shall bear the full cost of securing and maintaining the Performance and Payment Letter of Credit and the Guaranty Letter of Credit.

D. Form of Letters of Credit. The Performance and Payment Letter of Credit and the Guaranty Letter of Credit each shall be in a form satisfactory to the Village Attorney and each shall be from a bank (i) acceptable to the Village, (ii) having capital resources of at least Fifty Million Dollars ($50,000,000), (iii) with an office located in the Chicago Metropolitan Area, and (iv) insured by the Federal Deposit Insurance Corporation. Each letter of credit shall, at a minimum, provide that (1) it shall not be canceled without the prior consent of the

Village; (2) it shall not require the consent of the Owner prior to any draw on it by the Village; and (3) if at any time it will expire within 45 or any lesser number of days, and if it has not been renewed, and if any applicable obligation of the Owner for which it is security remains uncompleted or unsatisfactory, then the Village may, without notice and without being required to take any further action of any nature whatsoever, call and draw down the letter of credit and thereafter either hold all proceeds as security for the satisfactory completion of the obligations or employ the proceeds to complete the obligations and reimburse the Village for any and all costs and expenses, including without limitation legal fees and administrative costs, incurred by the Village, as the Village shall determine. The Performance and Payment Letter of Credit may provide that the aggregate amount of the letter of credit may be reduced, but only after joint direction by the Owner and the Village, either to reflect a reduction in the total amount of the deposit required pursuant to Section 12.A of this Agreement from 125% of the Approved Cost Estimate to 110% of the amount of an executed contract or to reimburse the Owner for payment of Improvement work satisfactorily completed. No reduction for payment of Improvement work satisfactorily completed shall be allowed except after presentation by the Owner of proper contractors' sworn statements, partial or final waivers of lien, as may be appropriate, and any additional documentation that the Village may reasonably request to demonstrate satisfactory completion of the Improvement in question and full payment of all contractors, subcontractors, and material suppliers. The Guaranty Letter of Credit shall not be reduced by reason of any cost incurred by the Owner to satisfy its obligations under this Agreement.

E. Replenishment of Cash Deposit and Letters of Credit. If at any time the Village determines that the funds remaining in the Cash Deposit and the Performance and Payment Letter of Credit are not, or may not be, sufficient to pay in full the remaining unpaid cost of all Improvements and all unpaid Village fees, or that the funds remaining in the Guaranty Letter of Credit are not, or may not be, sufficient to pay all unpaid costs of correcting any and all defects and deficiencies in the Improvements, then, within 10 days after a demand by the Village, the Owner shall increase the amount of the Cash Deposit and/or the appropriate letter of credit to an amount determined by the Village to be sufficient to pay the unpaid costs and fees. Failure to so increase the amount of the security shall be grounds for the Village to retain any remaining balance of the Cash Deposit and to draw down the entire remaining balance of the letters of credit.

F. Replacement of Letters of Credit. If at any time the Village determines that the bank issuing either the Performance and Payment Letter of Credit or the Guaranty Letter of Credit is without capital resources of at least Fifty Million Dollars ($50,000,000), is unable to meet any federal or state requirement for reserves, is insolvent, is in danger of becoming any of the foregoing, or is otherwise in danger of being unable to honor the appropriate letter of credit at any time during its term, or if the Village otherwise reasonably deems itself to be insecure, then the Village shall have the right to demand that the Owner provide a replacement letter of credit from a bank satisfactory to the Village. The replacement letter of credit shall be deposited with the Village not later than 10 days after the demand. After deposit of the replacement letter of credit, the Village shall surrender the original letter of credit to the Owner.

G. Use of Funds in the Event of Breach of Agreement. If the Owner fails or refuses to complete the Improvements in accordance with this Agreement, or fails or refuses to correct any defect or deficiency in the Improvements as required by Section 7.F of this Agreement, or fails or refuses to restore property in accordance with a demand made pursuant to Section 7.H of this Agreement, or in any other manner fails or refuses to meet fully any of its obligations under this Agreement, then the Village may, in its sole and absolute discretion, retain all or any part of the Cash Deposit and may draw on and retain all or any of the funds remaining in either the Performance and Payment Letter of Credit or the Guaranty Letter of Credit. The Village thereafter shall have the right to exercise its rights under Sections 7.F and 7.H of this Agreement, to take any other action it deems reasonable and appropriate to mitigate the effects of the failure or refusal, and to reimburse itself from the proceeds of the Cash Deposit and letters of credit for all of its costs and expenses, including without limitation legal fees and administrative expenses, resulting from or incurred as a result of the Owner's failure or refusal to fully meet its obligations under this Agreement. If the funds remaining in the Cash Deposit and the letters of credit are insufficient to repay fully the Village for all its costs and expenses, and to maintain a cash reserve equal to the required Guaranty Letter of Credit during the entire time the Guaranty Letter of Credit should have been maintained by the Owner, then the Owner shall, after demand of the Village, immediately deposit with the Village additional funds as the Village determines are necessary to fully repay the Village's costs and expenses and to establish the required cash reserve.

H. Village Lien Rights. If any money, property, or other consideration due from the Owner to the Village pursuant to this Agreement is not either recovered from the performance security deposits required in this Section 12 or paid or conveyed to the Village by the Owner within 10 days after a demand for payment or conveyance, then the money, or the Village's reasonable estimate of the value of the property or other consideration, together with interest at the maximum rate permitted by law and costs of collection, including without limitation legal fees and administrative expenses, shall become a lien on the Property, and the Village shall have the right to collect the amount or value, with applicable interest and costs, including without limitation legal fees and administrative expenses, and the right to enforce the lien in the manner provided by law for mortgage foreclosure proceedings. The lien shall be subordinate to the lien of any first mortgage now or hereafter placed on the Property; provided, however, that the lien subordination shall apply only to charges that have become due and payable prior to a sale or transfer of the Property pursuant to a decree of foreclosure, or any other proceeding in lieu of foreclosure, but the sale or transfer shall not relieve the Property from liability for any charges thereafter becoming due, nor from the lien of any subsequent charge.

### Section 13. Liability and Indemnity of Village.

A. Village Review. The Owner acknowledges and agrees that the Village is not, and shall not be, in any way liable for any damages or injuries that may be sustained as the result of the Village's review and approval of any plans for the Property or the Improvements, or the issuance of any approvals, permits, certificates, or acceptances for the development or use of the Property or the Improvements, and that the Village's review and approval of those plans and the Improvements and issuance of those approvals, permits, certificates, or acceptances does not, and shall not, in any way, be deemed to insure the Owner, or any of its heirs, successors, assigns, tenants, and licensees, or any other Person, against damage or injury of any kind at any time.

B. Village Procedure. The Owner acknowledges and agrees that notices, meetings, and hearings have been properly given and held by the Village with respect to the approval of this Agreement and agrees not to challenge the Village's approval on the grounds of any procedural infirmity or of any denial of any procedural right.

C. Indemnity. The Owner agrees to, and does hereby, hold harmless and indemnify the Village, the Corporate Authorities, the Plan Commission, and all Village elected or appointed officials, officers, employees, agents, representatives, engineers, and attorneys, from any and all claims that may be asserted at any time against any of them in connection with (i) the Village's review and approval of any plans for the Property or the Improvements; (ii) the issuance of any approval, permit, certificate, or acceptance for the Property or the Improvements; and (iii) the development, construction, maintenance, or use of any portion of the Property or the Improvements.

D. Defense Expense. The Owner shall, and does hereby agree to, pay all expenses, including without limitation legal fees and administrative expenses, incurred by the Village in defending itself with regard to any and all of the claims referenced in Section 13.C of this Agreement.

**Section 14. Nature, Survival, and Transfer of Obligations**. All obligations assumed by the Owner under this Agreement shall be binding on the Owner personally, on any and all of the Owner's heirs, successors, and assigns, and on any and all of the respective successor legal or beneficial owners of all or any portion of the Property. To assure that the Owner's heirs, successors, and assigns, and successor owners of all or any portion of the Property have notice of this Agreement and the obligations created by it, the Owner shall:

1. Deposit with the Village Clerk, contemporaneously with the Village's approval of this Agreement, any consents or other documents necessary to authorize the Village to record this Agreement in the office of the Recorder of _____ County; and

2. Notify the Village in writing at least 30 days prior to any date after which the Owner transfers a legal or beneficial interest in any portion of the Property to any Person not a party to this Agreement; and

3. Incorporate, by reference, this Agreement into any and all real estate sales contracts entered into for the sale of all or any portion of the Property to any Person not a party to this Agreement; and

4. Require, prior to the transfer of all or any portion of the Property, or any legal or equitable interest in the Property to any Person not a party to this Agreement, the transferee to execute an enforceable written agreement, in substan-

tially the form attached to this Agreement as **Exhibit** __, agreeing to be bound by this Agreement ("*Transferee Assumption Agreement*"), and to provide the Village, after request, with reasonable assurance of the financial ability of the transferee to meet those obligations as the Village may require;

provided, however, that the requirements stated in the three preceding clauses shall not apply to any contract for, or transfer of, an individual lot or group of lots for which all Improvements have been completed and approved and, if required, accepted pursuant to Section 7.E of this Agreement. The Village agrees that after a successor becoming bound to the personal obligation created in the manner provided in this Agreement and providing the financial assurances required in this Section 14, the personal liability of the Owner shall be released to the extent of the transferee's assumption of liability. The failure of the Owner to provide the Village with a fully executed copy of a Transferee Assumption Agreement required above by the transferee to be bound by this Agreement and, if requested by the Village, with the transferee's proposed assurances of financial capability before completing the transfer shall result in the Owner remaining fully liable for all of the Owner's obligations under this Agreement but shall not relieve the transferee of its liability for those obligations as a successor to the Owner.

**Section 15. Term.** This Agreement shall be in full force and effect from and after the Effective Date for 20 years, or for the longest term allowed under Section 11-15.1-5 of the Illinois Municipal Code, 65 ILCS 11-15.1-5, or its successor statute; provided, however, that this Agreement shall be of no force or effect until the Owner shall have first paid in full the amounts due to the Village as a condition precedent to the execution of this Agreement by the Village, pursuant to Section 11 of this Agreement, but no delay in payment shall serve to extend the date of termination of this Agreement.

**Section 16. Enforcement.** The parties to this Agreement may, in law or in equity, by suit, action, mandamus, or any other proceeding, including without limitation specific performance, enforce or compel the performance of this Agreement; provided, however, that the Owner agrees that it will not seek, and does not have the right to seek, to recover a judgment for monetary damages against the Village, or any of its elected or appointed officials, officers, employees, agents, representatives, engineers, or attorneys, on account of the negotiation, execution, or breach of this Agreement. In addition to every other remedy permitted by law for the enforcement of the terms of this Agreement, the Village shall be entitled to withhold the issuance of building permits or certificates of occupancy for any and all buildings and structures within the Property at any time when the Owner has failed or refused to meet fully any of its obligations under this Agreement. In the event of a judicial proceeding brought by one party to this Agreement against the other party to this Agreement pursuant to this Section 16, the prevailing party shall be entitled to reimbursement from the unsuccessful party of all costs and expenses, including without limitation reasonable attorneys' fees, incurred in connection with the judicial proceeding.

**Section 17. General Provisions.**

A. Notice. Any notice or communication required or permitted to be given under this Agreement shall be in writing and shall be delivered (i) personally, (ii) by a reputable overnight courier, (iii) by certified mail, return receipt requested, and deposited in the U.S. Mail, postage prepaid, (iv) by facsimile, or (v) by electronic internet mail ("*e-mail*"). Facsimile notices shall be deemed valid only to the extent that they are (a) actually received by the individual to whom addressed and (b) followed by delivery of actual notice in the manner described in either (i), (ii), or (iii) above within three business days thereafter at the appropriate address set forth below. E-mail notices shall be deemed valid only to the extent that they are (a) opened by the recipient on a business day at the address set forth below, and (b) followed by delivery of actual notice in the manner described in either (i), (ii), or (iii) above within three business days thereafter at the appropriate address set forth below. Unless otherwise provided in this Agreement, notices shall be deemed received after the first to occur of (a) the date of actual receipt; or (b) the date that is one (1) business day after deposit with an overnight courier as evidenced by a receipt of deposit; or (b) the date that is three (3) business days after deposit in the U.S. mail, as evidenced by a return receipt. By notice complying with the requirements of this Section 17.A, each party to this Agreement shall have the right to change the address or the addressee, or both, for all future notices and communications to them, but no notice of a change of addressee or address shall be effective until actually received.

Notices and communications to the Village shall be addressed to, and delivered at, the following address:

 

Notices and communications to the Owner shall be addressed to, and delivered at, the following address:

 

B. Time of the Essence. Time is of the essence in the performance of this Agreement.

C. Rights Cumulative. Unless expressly provided to the contrary in this Agreement, each and every one of the rights, remedies, and benefits provided by this Agreement shall be cumulative and shall not be exclusive of any other rights, remedies, and benefits allowed by law.

D. Non-Waiver. The Village shall be under no obligation to exercise any of the rights granted to it in this Agreement. The failure of the Village to exercise at any time any right granted to the Village shall not be deemed or construed to

284

be a waiver of that right, nor shall the failure void or affect the Village's right to enforce that right or any other right.

E. Consents. Unless otherwise provided in this Agreement, whenever the consent, permission, authorization, approval, acknowledgement, or similar indication of assent of any party to this Agreement, or of any duly authorized officer, employee, agent, or representative of any party to this Agreement, is required in this Agreement, the consent, permission, authorization, approval, acknowledgement, or similar indication of assent shall be in writing.

F. Governing Law. This Agreement shall be governed by, and enforced in accordance with, the internal laws, but not the conflicts of laws rules, of the State of Illinois.

G. Severability. It is hereby expressed to be the intent of the parties to this Agreement that should any provision, covenant, agreement, or portion of this Agreement or its application to any Person or property be held invalid by a court of competent jurisdiction, the remaining provisions of this Agreement and the validity, enforceability, and application to any Person or property shall not be impaired thereby, but the remaining provisions shall be interpreted, applied, and enforced so as to achieve, as near as may be, the purpose and intent of this Agreement to the greatest extent permitted by applicable law.

*ALTERNATIVE: Non-Severability*

G. Non-Severability. If any term, covenant, condition, or provision of this Agreement is held by a court of competent jurisdiction to be invalid, void, or unenforceable, the entire remainder of this Agreement shall, thereafter, be null and void and of no further force and effect, it being the intent of the parties that all of the provisions of this Agreement be treated as an individual whole.

H. Entire Agreement. This Agreement constitutes the entire agreement between the parties and supercedes any and all prior agreements and negotiations between the parties, whether written or oral, relating to the subject matter of this Agreement.

I. Interpretation. This Agreement shall be construed without regard to the identity of the party who drafted the various provisions of this Agreement. Moreover, each and every provision of this Agreement shall be construed as though all parties to this Agreement participated equally in the drafting of this Agreement. As a result of the foregoing, any rule or construction that a document is to be construed against the drafting party shall not be applicable to this Agreement.

J. Exhibits. Exhibits __ through __ attached to this Agreement are, by this reference, incorporated in, and made a part of this Agreement. In the event of a conflict between an exhibit and the text of this Agreement, the text of this Agreement shall control.

K. Amendments and Modifications. No amendment or modification to this Agreement shall be effective until it is reduced to writing and approved and executed by all parties to this Agreement in accordance with all applicable statutory procedures.

L. Changes in Laws. Unless otherwise provided in this Agreement, any reference to the Requirements of Law shall be deemed to include any modifications of, or amendments to, the Requirements of Law that may occur in the future.

M. Authority to Execute. The Village hereby warrants and represents to the Owner that the Persons executing this Agreement on its behalf have been properly authorized to do so by the Corporate Authorities. The Owner hereby warrants and represents to the Village (i) that it is the record and beneficial owner of fee simple title to the Property, (ii) that no other Person has any legal, beneficial, contractual, or security interest in the Property, (iii) that it has the full and complete right, power, and authority to enter into this Agreement and to agree to the terms, provisions, and conditions set forth in this Agreement and to bind the Property as set forth in this Agreement, (iv) that all legal actions needed to authorize the execution, delivery, and performance of this Agreement have been taken, and (v) that neither the execution of this Agreement nor the performance of the obligations assumed by the Owner will (a) result in a breach or default under any agreement to which the Owner is a party or to which it or the Property is bound or (b) violate any statute, law, restriction, court order, or agreement to which the Owner or the Property are subject.

N. No Third Party Beneficiaries. No claim as a third party beneficiary under this Agreement by any Person shall be made, or be valid, against the Village or the Owner.

O. Recording. After the Owner has paid to the Village the amounts due pursuant to Section 11 of this Agreement and the Owner has paid to the Village an amount sufficient to cover the cost of recording this Agreement, all necessary plats, the affidavit of service of notice as required by Section 7-1-1 of the Illinois Municipal Code, 65 ILCS 5/7-1-1, and the Annexation Ordinance, the Village shall promptly cause this Agreement to be recorded in the office of the Recorder of _____ County.

## SIGNATURE BLOCKS

# APPENDICES

## XIV. SAMPLE ANNEXATION AGREEMENT
## (DEVELOPER-ORIENTED)

**THIS AGREEMENT** is made and entered into as of the __ day of _____,
_____, and is by and between the **TOWN OF** _____, an Illinois home
rule unit of local government and municipal corporation, _____ County, Illinois (the "*Town*") and _____ ("*Owner*").

### RECITALS:

A. Owner is the owner of record of certain real property consisting of approximately _____ acres, which property is generally depicted on *Exhibit A* attached hereto, and is legally described on *Exhibit B* attached hereto (the "*Property*").

B. The Property is currently located in unincorporated _____ County and is occupied, in part, with Owner's tire manufacturing plant buildings and related ancillary structures and facilities, including, without limitation, indoor and outdoor storage, utilities, and parking areas (the "*Existing Facilities*").

C. Pursuant to the provisions of Section 7-1-8 of the Illinois Municipal Code, 65 ILCS 5/7-1-8, Owner has filed with the Town Clerk a voluntary petition for annexation of the Property executed by the owner of record of the Property, conditioned upon the execution of a mutually acceptable annexation agreement.

D. The Corporate Authorities, after due and careful consideration, have concluded that the annexation of the Property to the Town, on the terms and conditions hereinafter set forth, will further the orderly growth of the Town, increase its tax assessable values, and be in the best interests of the Town.

E. Pursuant to the provisions of Sections 11-15.1-1 *et seq.*, of the Illinois Municipal Code, 65 ILCS 5/11-15.1-1 *et seq.*, and pursuant to the other powers and authorities of the Town, a proposed agreement, the same in form and substance as this Agreement, was submitted to the Town Authorities and a public hearing was held thereon pursuant to notice as provided by statute and ordinance.

F. Pursuant to notice as required by statute and ordinance, a public hearing has been held by the Town's Planning Commission with regard to the zoning map amendments described in Section II of this Agreement, and with regard to all other matters herein requiring Planning Commission consideration, and the Planning Commission has submitted its recommendation for approval to the Corporate Authorities.

G. Each township highway commissioner, township trustee, fire protection district, library district, and other entity or person entitled to notice prior to the actions contemplated herein has been given notice thereof by the Town as required by law.

H. This Agreement is made pursuant to and in accordance with the provisions of Sections 11-15.1-1, *et seq.*, of the Illinois Municipal Code, 65 ILCS 5/11-15.1-1 *et seq.*, the Town's home rule powers, and pursuant to such other powers as may be accorded to the Town under the ordinances, laws, codes, regulations, and requirements of the Town (the "*Town Codes*") and the laws, statutes, and constitutions of the State of Illinois and the United States of America.

**NOW, THEREFORE,** in consideration of the aforesaid premises, which shall be deemed to be a part of this Agreement, and of the mutual covenants and agreements hereinafter set forth, the Town and Owner hereby enter into the following:

## I. ANNEXATION

**A. Filing of the Annexation Petition.** Owner has filed with the Town Clerk a petition for annexation (the *"Annexation Petition"*) of the Property to the Town conditioned upon Owner and the Town executing a mutually agreeable annexation agreement. The Annexation Petition was prepared, executed and filed in accordance with Section 7-1-8 of the Illinois Municipal Code, 65 ILCS 5/7-1-8, and the Town Codes.

**B. Filing of Plat of Annexation.** Owner has filed with the Town Clerk a plat of annexation (the *"Plat of Annexation"*) that contains an accurate map of the Property and the contiguous right-of-way to be annexed.

**C. Annexation of the Property.**

1. Adoption of Annexation Ordinance. Immediately after the execution of this Agreement, the Corporate Authorities shall pass and approve an ordinance (the *"Annexation Ordinance"*), in substantially the form of *Exhibit C* attached hereto annexing the Property (and contiguous right-of-way, as depicted in the Plat of Annexation) to the Town, provided, however, that the effective date of the Annexation Ordinance shall be as provided in Section I.C.2 below.

2. Effective Date of Annexation. The annexation of the Property, and the effective date of the Annexation Ordinance, shall occur on, but not before, the date (the *"Annexation Effective Date"*) that is the earlier to occur of (i) the date on which Owner delivers to the Town Clerk a fully executed notice of annexation in substantially the form of *Exhibit D* attached hereto (the *"Notice of Annexation"*); or (ii) the date that is nine years after the date of execution of this Agreement.

**D. Recording of Annexation Documents.** Immediately after, but not before, the Annexation Effective Date, Owner shall, with the cooperation of the Town, cause the recording of all documents necessary to accomplish the annexation of the Property to the Town in the manner provided by law. Owner shall pay the entire cost of such recording.

## II. ZONING.

Immediately after passage and approval of the Annexation Ordinance, the Corporate Authorities shall pass and approve two ordinances (the *"Zoning Map Amendment Ordinances"*), amending the Town's zoning map to add the Property to the zoning map and classify the Property into two zoning districts: (1) the M-2 Manufacturing District; and (2) the B-1 Commercial District, in the manner described on *Exhibit E*, attached hereto. The effective date of the Zoning Map Amendment Ordinance shall not occur until the effective date of the Annexation Ordinance.

## III. DEVELOPMENT OF THE PROPERTY.

**A. Development Approvals**. Owner and the Town acknowledge and agree that, upon and after the Annexation Effective Date, the Property shall be developed and used in accordance with the terms and provisions of (i) this Agreement and (ii) the Town Codes and Town ordinances, as the same have been modified by this Agreement. Owner and the Town further acknowledge and agree that, prior to the Annexation Effective Date, Section 11-15.1-2.1 of the Illinois Municipal Code, 65 ILCS 5/11-15.1-2.1, shall have no application, force, or effect on or with respect to this Agreement or the Property. Accordingly, except as expressly provided otherwise in this Agreement, the Town Codes, and the Town's jurisdiction and control shall not be applicable to the Property at any time prior to the Annexation Effective Date. By its approval of this Agreement and its adoption and approval of the Annexation Ordinance and the Zoning Map Amendment Ordinance, the Town shall be deemed to have approved and granted all amendments, variations, and waivers of the Town Codes necessary to permit the development and use of the Property in accordance with the provisions of this Agreement, it being acknowledged and agreed that all public hearings, if any, that are necessary to enable the Town to grant such amendments, variations, and waivers have been conducted upon proper legal notice.

**B. Use Regulations**. Subject to the provisions of this Agreement, the Property may be developed with any one or more of the permitted and accessory uses listed in the applicable zoning district regulations of the Town Zoning Code.

**C. Permit Requests**. The Town shall employ its "one-step" permit process to allow for an expeditious review of all building and construction permit requests relating to the Property.

## IV. SUBDIVISION.

**A. Subdivision Approval**. Immediately after execution of this Agreement, the Corporate Authorities shall, pursuant to the expedited review and approval process set forth in Section 16.2-5F of the Town Subdivision Code, pass and approve an ordinance subdividing the Property into three lots, as depicted on the Subdivision Plat attached hereto as *Exhibit F.*

**B. Minor Changes**. The Town Council shall approve minor line changes to the subdivision parcel boundaries pursuant to the expedited review and approval process in said Section 16.2-5F of the Town Subdivision Code.

## V. PUBLIC IMPROVEMENTS.

**A. Water Service**.

1. Owner's Option. Notwithstanding any provision of the Town Code to the contrary, Owner shall have the option of (i) connecting to the Town's water system prior to, or at any time after, the Annexation Effective Date; or (ii) remaining connected to the _____ water system indefinitely.

2. Rates. In the event Owner exercises its option to connect to the Town's water system prior to the Annexation Effective Date, Owner shall pay for water consumption at a rate that is one and a half times the usual and customary rate for water. Upon and after the Annexation Effective Date, Owner shall pay for

water consumption at a rate that is equal to the Town's usual and customary rate for similarly situated users thereof.

3. Fee. The Town shall and does hereby agree to waive any and all fees that are or may otherwise be applicable for connection to the Town's water system.

4. Applicability of Town Codes. Upon connection to the Town water system, the Property shall be subject to all Town Codes governing such system only, irrespective of whether the Annexation Effective Date has occurred.

**B. Sanitary Sewer Service.**

1. Sanitary Wastewater.

a. Continued Connection. Owner shall be allowed to continue its current connection to, and use of, the Town's sanitary sewer system for the discharge of sanitary wastewater prior to and after the Annexation Effective Date.

b. Rates. Prior to the Annexation Effective Date, Owner shall pay for usage of the sanitary sewer system for sanitary wastewater discharge at a rate that is one and a half times the Town's usual and customary rate for sanitary sewer usage. Upon and after the Annexation Effective Date, Owner shall pay for usage of the sanitary sewer system for sanitary wastewater discharge at a rate that is equal to the Town's usual and customary rate for similarly situated users thereof.

2. Process Wastewater.

a. Additional Connection. Upon execution of this Agreement, and irrespective of whether the Annexation Effective Date has occurred, the Town shall, and does hereby agree to, allow Owner to establish an additional connection to the Town's sanitary sewer system to enable Owner to discharge process wastewater into the Bloomington/Normal Water Reclamation District. Further, the Town agrees to expeditiously process and issue all necessary and required permit applications to enable such connection.

b. Additional Connection Fee. Owner shall pay to the Town a sanitary sewer connection/tap-in fee for such additional connection in the total amount of $18,000, payable in two installments as follows:

1. $9,000 shall be paid at the time that the connection permit is issued by the _____ Water Reclamation District.

2. $9,000 shall be paid on the Annexation Effective Date.

c. Rates. Prior to the Annexation Effective Date, Owner shall pay for usage of the sanitary sewer system for process wastewater discharge at a rate this is one and one half times the Town's usual and customary rate for sanitary sewer usage. Upon and after the Annexation Effective Date, Owner shall pay for usage of, the sanitary sewer system for process wastewater discharge at a rate that is equal to the Town's usual and customary rate for similarly situated users thereof.

d. Termination. In the event that Owner's April 1998 petition for annexation to, or 1998 application for a permit to connect to, the _____ Water Reclamation District for purposes of discharging process wastewater from the property, is either (i) denied or rejected by said District, or (ii) approved by said District with conditions that are unacceptable to Owner, Owner shall have the right to terminate this Agreement by delivering a termination notice to the Town Clerk (the "*Termination Notice*"); provided, however, that:

    1. Owner shall have no right to terminate after December 31, 1998;

    2. The delivery of the Termination Notice shall not relieve Owner of its obligation to dedicate the easement and right-of-way described in Section V.D. of this Agreement; and

    3. Owner shall not be entitled to reimbursement of any of the application or other fees that it had paid to the Town prior to its delivery of the Termination Notice.

    3. Applicability of Town Codes. So long as the Property is connected to the Town's sanitary sewer system, the Property shall be subject to all Town Codes governing such system only, irrespective of whether the Annexation Effective Date has occurred.

**C. Storm Water Detention.**

    1. Existing Facilities. No storm water detention or fee shall be required for any of the Existing Facilities on the Property.

    2. New Construction. In the event of any new construction on the Property, Owner shall, with respect only to such new construction, either (i) pay a fee in lieu of storm water detention, or (ii) provide detention on-site, at the discretion and direction of the Corporate Authorities by resolution duly adopted.

**D. Easements and Rights of Way.**

    1. Right-of-Way Dedication. Following the execution of this Agreement, Owner shall dedicate to the Illinois Department of Transportation a portion of land consisting of approximately 0.323 acres for expansion of the _____ right-of-way, as depicted on *Exhibit G*, attached hereto.

    2. Sewer Easement. Upon execution of this Agreement, Owner shall grant a sewer easement to the Town at the location depicted on the Subdivision Plat. Owner shall have the right to construct a building or other improvements over such easement, provided that, in such event, Owner shall cause the sewer to be encased to the satisfaction of the Town Engineer, at Owner's sole cost and expense.

## VI. TOWN CODES.

The Town has conducted a complete inspection of the Existing Facilities prior to the execution of this Agreement to ascertain compliance thereof with the applicable provisions of the Town Code. In consideration of Owner's agreement to annex the Property to the Town, and as an essential condition of this Agreement, the Town and Owner shall, and do hereby acknowledge and agree that: Notwithstanding any provisions of the Town Codes to the contrary, no Code improvements, modifications, enhancements, or upgrades shall be required for any portion of the Existing Facilities on the Property, except as follows:

    1. Lighting. Within five years after the date of execution of this Agreement and irrespective of whether the Annexation Effective Date has occurred, Owner shall cause the emergency and exit lighting in the existing plant building on the Property to be in compliance with the specifications delineated on *Exhibit H*, attached hereto.

    2. Sprinkler System. Within five years after the date of execution of this Agreement and irrespective of whether the Annexation Effective Date has oc-

curred, Owner shall cause the sprinkler system in the existing plant building on the Property to cover the following interior areas that are not presently covered: interior offices, the raw rubber storage racks and the mezzanine offices, all in the manner provided in the Town Code.

3. Grounding System. Within five years after the date of execution of this Agreement and irrespective of whether the Annexation Effective Date has occurred, Owner shall contract with an electrical contractor or engineer acceptable to the Town Electrical Inspector to evaluate the grounding system in the existing plant building on the Property and, in the event the grounding system is deficient, cause such grounding system to be in compliance with the Town Code. Such evaluation shall be in a form that is acceptable to the Town Electrical Inspector.

4. Fire Protection. Due to the unique nature of tire manufacturing, and the requirement that all assembly lines associated therewith be completely contiguous, the Town shall, in the event of any desired construction of any expansion or addition to the existing plant building on the Property at any time after the Annexation Effective Date, permit, in lieu of Code required fire separation walls, alternative fire protection systems that afford an equal or greater level of protection, including, without limitation, an "ESFR" type fire suppression system properly designed and calculated, including all signaling, indicating, and alarming devices related to that system.

## VII. TOWN FEES.

A. Annexation Fee. The Town does hereby acknowledge that Owner has previously paid to the Town, at the time of submission of the Annexation Petition and Plat of Annexation, an all-inclusive annexation fee of $500.

B. No Additional Fees. Except as expressly provided in this Agreement, Owner shall not be required to pay any additional application, annexation, tap-in, connection, usage, or other fee of any kind in connection with the annexation of the Property to the Town.

## VIII. ANNEXATION TO _____ AIRPORT AUTHORITY AND WATER RECLAMATION DISTRICT

A. Annexation to _____ Airport Authority. Owner shall, concurrent with, but not before, the Annexation Effective Date, take all action reasonably required and necessary to cause the Property to be annexed to the _____ Airport Authority; provided, however, that such annexation shall be at no cost to Owner.

B. Annexation to _____ Water Reclamation District. Owner shall, if and when requested in writing to do so by the _____ Water Reclamation District, take all action reasonably required and necessary to cause the Property to be annexed to such district; provided, however, that such annexation shall be at no cost to Owner.

## IX. GENERAL PROVISIONS

A. Term of Agreement. Pursuant to the home rule powers of the Town, this Agreement shall be effective from its effective date for 20 years, or for the longest term allowed under Section 11-15.1-5 of the Illinois Municipal Code, 65 ILCS 11-15.1-5, or its successor statute (the *"Term"*).

**B. Notice.** Any notice or other communication required or permitted to be given under this Agreement shall be in writing and shall be (i) personally delivered, or (ii) delivered by a reputable overnight courier, or (iii) delivered by certified mail, return receipt requested, and deposited in the U.S. Mail, postage prepaid. Telecopy notices shall be deemed valid only to the extent they are (a) actually received by the individual to whom addressed and (b) followed by delivery of actual notice in the manner described in either (i), (ii) or (iii) above within three (3) business days thereafter. Unless otherwise expressly provided in this Agreement, notices shall be deemed received upon the earlier of (x) actual receipt; or (y) one (1) business day after deposit with an overnight courier as evidenced by a receipt of deposit; or (z) three (3) business days following deposit in the U.S. mail, as evidenced by a return receipt.

Notices and communications to Owner shall be addressed to, and delivered at, the following address:

[Owner's Name and Address]

Notices and communications to the Town shall be addressed to, and delivered at, the following address:

[Town's Name and Address]

By notice complying with the requirements of this Section, each party shall have the right to change the address or the addressee, or both, for all future notices and communications to such party, but no notice of a change of addressee or address shall be effective until actually received.

**C. Agreement to be Recorded.** Within 30 days after the execution hereof, this Agreement (or a suitable memorandum thereof) shall be recorded at the sole cost and expense of Owner in the Office of the Recorder of Deeds of McLean County, Illinois.

**D. Covenants and Agreements Binding.** This Agreement and the agreements, covenants, and promises set forth herein shall run with the land and inure to the benefit of the grantees, heirs, successors, and assigns of Owner, the Town, the Corporate Authorities and their successors in office, provided that Owner shall have no right to assign this Agreement except in connection with conveyances of all or any portion of the Property. Nothing in this Agreement shall in any way be deemed to prevent the alienation, encumbrance or sale of the Property or any portion thereof and any new owner or owners shall be both benefited and bound by the conditions and restrictions herein expressed. Upon the conveyance by Owner of all or any portion of the Property, Owner shall, automatically and without further action by any party, be released of all liability under this Agreement with respect to that portion of the Property that is so conveyed.

**E. Breach and Enforcement.** Upon a breach of this Agreement, either of the parties to this Agreement, in any court of competent jurisdiction, by an appropriate suit, action, mandamus or other proceeding at law or in equity, may secure specific performance of the covenants and agreements herein contained, may be awarded damages for failure of performance or both, may obtain rescission and disconnection for repudiation or material failure of performance, and may have such other relief as is, by law or in equity, available to them. Before any failure of any party to this Agreement to perform its obligations under this Agreement shall be deemed to be a breach of this Agreement, the party claiming such failure shall notify, in writing, the party alleged to have failed to perform of the alleged failure and demand performance. No breach of this Agreement may be found to have occurred if performance has been commenced within 21 days after the receipt of such notice.

**F. Time of the Essence.** It is understood by the parties hereto that time is of the essence of this Agreement, and that all parties will make every reasonable effort, including the calling of special meetings, to expedite the subject matters herein.

**G. Consents.** Whenever the consent or approval of any party hereto is required in this Agreement such consent or approval shall be in writing and shall not be unreasonably withheld or delayed, and, in all matters contained herein, all parties shall have an implied obligation of reasonableness, except as may be expressly set forth otherwise.

**H. Governing Law.** This Agreement shall be governed by, construed, and enforced in accordance with the internal laws, but not the conflicts of laws rules, of the State of Illinois.

**I. Severability.** It is hereby expressed to be the intent of the parties hereto that should any provision, covenant, agreement, or portion of this Agreement or its application to any person, entity, or property be held invalid by a court of competent jurisdiction, the remaining provisions of this Agreement and the validity, enforceability, and application to any person, entity, or property shall not be impaired thereby, but such remaining provisions shall be interpreted, applied, and enforced so as to achieve, as near as may be, the purpose and intent of this Agreement to the greatest extent permitted by applicable law.

**J. Entire Agreement.** This Agreement shall constitute the entire agreement of the parties to this Agreement; all prior agreements between the parties, whether written or oral, are merged in this Agreement and shall be of no force and effect.

**K. Grammatical Usage and Construction.** In construing this Agreement, feminine or neuter pronouns shall be substituted for those masculine in form and vice versa, and plural terms shall be substituted for singular and singular for plural, in any place in which the context so requires.

**L. Interpretation.** This Agreement shall be construed without regard to the identity of the party who drafted the various provisions of this Agreement. Moreover, each and every provision of this Agreement shall be construed as though all parties to this Agreement participated equally in the drafting of this Agreement. As a result of the foregoing, any rule or construction that a document is to be construed against the drafting party shall not be applicable to this Agreement.

**M. Headings.** The headings, titles, and captions in this Agreement have been inserted only for convenience and in no way define, limit, extend, or describe the scope or intent of this Agreement.

**N. Exhibits.** Exhibits A through I attached hereto are, by this reference, incorporated in and made a part of this Agreement. In the event of a conflict between an exhibit and the text of this Agreement, the text of this Agreement shall control.

**O. Amendments and Modifications.** No modification, addition, deletion, revision, alteration, or other change to this Agreement shall be effective unless and until such change is reduced to writing and executed by the Town and all owners of record of the Property at the time such modification is intended to be effective, pursuant to all applicable statutory procedures.

**P. Calendar Days and Time.** Any reference herein to "day" or "days" shall mean calendar and not business days. If the date for giving of any notice required to be given hereunder or the performance of any obligation hereunder falls on a Saturday, Sunday or Federal holiday, then said notice or obligation may be given or performed on the next business day after such Saturday, Sunday or Federal holiday.

**Q. No Third Party Beneficiaries.** No claim as a third party beneficiary under this Agreement by any person, firm or corporation shall be made, or be valid, against the Town or the Owners.

**R. Counterparts.** This Agreement may be executed in any number of counterparts each of which shall be deemed an original, but all of which shall constitute one and the same instrument.

**IN WITNESS WHEREOF**, the parties hereto have caused this Agreement to be executed as of the day and year first above written.

ATTEST:

**TOWN OF** _____, a municipal corporation, _____ County State of Illinois

By:
    Name:
    Title:

ATTEST:

**[OWNER]**

By:
    Name:
    Title:

## XV. CHECKLIST FOR DRAFTING ANNEXATION AND
## DEVELOPMENT AGREEMENTS

Whether a development agreement will provide the security and control which both parties seek will depend in part upon how well the approved draft of the agreement expresses the interests, intentions, and expectations of both parties. The following checklist describes the basic issues that a development agreement should address. The checklist should be read and used in conjunction with relevant state and local government enabling laws and the sample development agreements provided *infra*.

### 1. Definitions
All technical terms to be used in the development agreement should be precisely defined in a "table" of definitions. Terms which have been defined in any applicable statute or ordinance should be defined the same way in the agreement.

### 2. Parties
All parties to the agreement should be named and their capacities to enter into the agreement clearly stated. In the case of developer/owners, their equitable or legal interests in the property should be stated. In the case of government entities, their authority to enter into development agreements should be recited.

### 3. Relationship of the Parties
The relationship between the parties to the agreement should be stated clearly. Typically, the statement will specify that the relationship is contractual and that the owner/developer is an independent contractor, and not an agent of the local government.

### 4. Property
The property to be subject to the agreement should be clearly and thoroughly identified. An attachment, preferably with a map, specifically describing the property should be provided and incorporated into the agreement by reference.

### 5. Authorization
The state and local government legislation under which the parties are enabled and authorized to enter into the agreement should be cited. This is particularly important in the event a state agency is a party. The ordinance or resolution by which the agreement has been approved by the local government legislative body should be cited.

### 6. Intent of the Parties
The intent of the parties to be bound by the terms of the agreement should be clearly stated.

### 7. Recitation of Benefits and Burdens
The parties should recite the benefits each expects to gain from entering into the agreement, as well as the burdens each agrees to bear. Because the agreement will be treated as a contract, the consideration each party is to receive from the other should be stated clearly in order to ensure enforceability. It is especially crucial that the benefits to the local government and community be expressed in terms which exhibit the agreement as consistent with (or as an exer-

296

cise of) the police power. Stressing such benefits may help protect the agreement against a bargaining-away-the-police-power challenge.

### 8. Notice and Hearings

The date upon which the statutorily required public hearing was held should be noted, as well as all relevant findings resulting from such hearing. All other pertinent notice and hearing requirements should be recited.

### 9. Consistency with Plans

The findings of the local legislative body that the agreement is consistent with the local government's plans (if applicable) should be stated.

### 10. Administrative Act/Legislative Act

The agreement should state that it is deemed to be an administrative act or legislative act of the government body made party to the agreement. The relevant section of the enabling statute should be cited. While this does not guarantee a court will so treat it, it raises the inference that it will.

### 11. Applicable Land Use Regulations

The agreement should contain a precise statement of all land use regulations to which the development project will be subject. The agreement should specify precisely which regulations will apply to the project regardless of future changes, or otherwise be affected by the agreement. The statement should make it clear that regulations not specifically so identified will not be affected by the terms of the agreement, and will be subject to enforcement and change under the same criteria that would apply if no agreement were in effect.

### 12. Status of Applicable Land Use Regulations and Plans

The agreement should contain a statement that no applicable land use regulations or plans are currently under review or reconsideration, and that there are no legal challenges to the validity of such regulations or plans pending.

### 13. Approval and Permit Requirements

As far as possible at the time the agreement is written, the parties should specify all discretionary approvals and permits which will have to be obtained before the development can proceed beyond its various stages. Permits and approvals obtained prior to execution of the agreement should be specified. Any and all conditions precedent to the obtaining of permits and approvals should be listed.

### 14. Permitted Uses Under the Agreement

The agreement should specifically identify elements of development required by statutes. For example, under Hawaii's Development Agreement Statute, the agreement *must* specify:

    (1) the permitted uses of the property;

    (2) the density or intensity of use; and

    (3) the maximum height and size of proposed buildings.

### 15. Uses Prohibited by the Agreement

The parties to the agreement are free to set limits to permissible uses beyond those specified by the applicable zoning classification. All additional limits and requirements should be clearly stated.

### 16. Dedications and Reservations

The agreement should provide, where appropriate, a statement of all reservations or , or policies in effect at the time of entering into the agreement. The agreement should also state all reservations or dedications which are permitted under existing laws at the time the agreement is entered, and to which the parties have agreed.

## 17. Utility Connections

All water and sewer service, either to be provided by the developer or by the local government, should be described in detail, together with schedules of construction completion (if not existing), cost allocation (between or among developers and government and later developers), and hookup or connection schedules.

## 18. Duration of the Agreement

The agreement should state a termination date. It should also specify project commencement and completion dates, either for the project on the whole, or for its various phases. The agreement should specify that the termination date can be extended by mutual agreement, and that commencement and completion dates may also be extended.

## 19. Amendments, Cancellation, or Termination

The agreement should recite the statutory conditions under which the agreement can be amended, canceled, or otherwise terminated.

## 20. Periodic Review

The agreement should provide for periodic reviews of the project in order to determine compliance with the terms of the agreement, as required by statute and ordinance, if appropriate. The agency responsible for performing such reviews should be identified, and specific times for such reviews should be stated. Procedure should be developed and specified for dealing with situations in which minor and major noncompliance is discovered.

## 21. Progress Reports

If the parties agree, the agreement should specify that progress reports should be made available to the local government agency involved by the developer at specified intervals, or upon completion of specified phases of the project, or at whatever time periods the parties choose.

## 22. Remedies

Remedies for breach on the part of either party should be provided. Specific remedies for specific breaches should be stated, if possible. The agreement should include a statement clarifying whether the remedies stated in the agreement are to be exclusive, or whether other statutory or common law remedies will also be available.

## 23. Enforcement

The agreement should specify that the agreement shall be enforceable, unless lawfully terminated or canceled, by any party to the agreement or any party's successor in interest, notwithstanding any subsequent changes in any applicable law adopted by the county entering into the agreement which alters or amends the laws, ordinances, resolutions, rules, or policies frozen by the agreement.

## 24. Hold Harmless Clause

If the parties so agree, the agreement should contain a clause whereby the developer/property owner holds the local government and its agents harmless from liability for damages, injury, or death which may arise from the direct or indirect operations of the owner, developer, contractors, and subcontractors, which relate to the project.

### 25. Insurance, Bonds

Any insurance coverage required and/or secured by either party to the agreement, and affecting any aspect of the development project, should be specified. Existing performance bonds should be listed in detail, as well as bonds not yet obtained but required as conditions precedent for final approval of the subdivision plan. Applicable ordinances relating to bond requirements should be cited.

### 26. Severability Clause

The agreement should include a clause specifying that the provisions of the agreement are severable, if the parties so agree. Any limitations upon the severability of any particular clause or clauses should be clearly stated.

### 27. Merger Clause

A merger clause or other statement should be provided specifying that the terms of the agreement as stated in the written document are both a final and complete expression of the parties' intentions.

### 28. Statements of Incorporation by Reference

All documents related to the agreement or otherwise attached or appended thereto should be expressly stated to be incorporated into the agreement by reference. These might include lists of conditions, schedules of completion for public facilities, imposition of dedications, impact fees, and development plans and specifications.

### 29. Cooperation

The agreement should include a statement of the extent to which the local government will cooperate with the owner in his efforts to secure required permits from nonparty government agencies.

### 30. Subsidiary or Collateral Agreements

If the owner has obtained additional agreements relating to the development project from any nonparty agencies or persons, such agreements and the parties thereto should be specified.

### 31. Conflict of Laws

Procedures should be specified for dealing with situations in which changes in laws promulgated by nonparty government bodies (state or federal) might preempt or otherwise affect county laws frozen by the agreement.